Palgrave Studies in Latin American Heterodox Economics

Series Editor
Juan Eduardo Santarcángelo
National Research Council of Science and Technology (CONICET)
Buenos Aires, Buenos Aires, Argentina

Universidad Nacional de Quilmes (UNQ) Bernal, Argentina

The aim of the series is to analyze the economic, social, and political evolution of countries in Latin America. The authors in the series are serious heterodox economics scholars who want to shine light on Latin America's economic profile. Each book in the series takes on a single topic (crisis, growth, income distribution, the manufacturing sector, etc.), either from the point of view of a single country or a group of them. This analysis then in turn adds to our understanding of Latin America's regional economic character and development challenges and capabilities. In this way, this series makes an unusual contribution to economics by studying a region as a whole without losing sight of the particularities of each country as a part.

More information about this series at
http://www.palgrave.com/gp/series/14614

Victoria Basualdo
Hartmut Berghoff • Marcelo Bucheli
Editors

Big Business and Dictatorships in Latin America

A Transnational History of Profits and Repression

palgrave
macmillan

Editors
Victoria Basualdo
Area of Economics and Technology
Facultad Latinoamericana de Ciencias
Sociales-CONICET
Buenos Aires, Argentina

Hartmut Berghoff
Institute for Economic &
Social History
University of Göttingen
Göttingen, Germany

Marcelo Bucheli
Gies College of Business
University of Illinois at
Urbana-Champaign
Champaign, IL, USA

ISSN 2662-3943 ISSN 2662-3951 (electronic)
Palgrave Studies in Latin American Heterodox Economics
ISBN 978-3-030-43924-8 ISBN 978-3-030-43925-5 (eBook)
https://doi.org/10.1007/978-3-030-43925-5

This Palgrave Macmillan imprint is published by the registered company Springer Nature Switzerland AG.
The registered company address is: Gewerbestrasse 11, 6330 Cham, Switzerland

Praise for *Big Business and Dictatorships in Latin America*

"This volume combines a refreshingly interdisciplinary approach with the very best new Latin American scholarship to provide compelling insights on the vexed relationship between big business and dictators in Latin America. By shifting the focus away from the notorious behavior of some US corporations, the authors provide a more nuanced account, which is enlightened by comparisons made with other contexts, including the story of business and the Nazi regime in Germany."

—Geoffrey Jones, *Isidor Straus Professor of Business History, Harvard Business School*

"This book spans Latin America, from Central America to Patagonia, with illuminating macro analyses and case studies of South America's regional powers: Argentina, Brazil and Chile. It reveals how big business collaborated with their civil-military dictatorships and the dictatorships promoted their business interests. This book is required reading for scholars and students of Latin America's recent past, Cold War and human rights struggles."

—Peter Winn, *Professor of History, Tufts University*

"This *tour de force* exposes the political economy roots of the violent repressive civil-military dictatorships in Latin America during the 1960s-1980s. It presents evidence confirming 'big capital's' role in shaping, legitimizing, and strengthening those regimes. It echoes the call for 'never again' in presenting the dire consequences of the development model: the torture, death, and disappearance of workers and their human rights allies."

—Leigh A. Payne, *Professor of Sociology and Latin America, University of Oxford*

Contents

Notes on Contributors

Eduardo Basualdo is Coordinator of the Area of Economics and Technology and the Director of the Masters Program in Political Economy at FLACSO Argentina, and he retired as a senior researcher at the National Council of Scientific and Technological Research (CONICET). He authored and co-authored several books on Argentine and Latin American economic history, including *Fundamentos de Economía Política: Los patrones de acumulación, de los clásicos al neoliberalismo del siglo XXI* (2019), *Endeudar y fugar. Un análisis de la historia económica argentina de Martínez de Hoz a Macri* (2017), *El Banco de la Nación Argentina y la dictadura: El impacto de las transformaciones económicas y financieras en la política crediticia (1976–1983)* (2016), and *Estudios de Historia Económica Argentina: Desde mediados del siglo XX hasta la actualidad* (2006), among many others.

Victoria Basualdo is a researcher at the Argentine National Scientific Council (CONICET) and at the Area of Economics and Technology of Facultad Latinoamericana de Ciencias Sociales (FLACSO), and Professor in the Political Economy Master's Degree Program at FLACSO, Argentina. She specializes in contemporary economic and labor history, with special focus on structural changes and the transformations of trade-union organizations in Argentina and Latin America. She authored several chapters and articles on the issue of corporate responsibility in human rights violations and was one of the coordinators of the book *Responsabilidad empresarial en delitos de lesa humanidad. Represión a trabajadores durante el* *terrorismo de estado* (Infojus, 2015), by AEyT FLACSO, CELS, PVJ and SDH. She holds a PhD in History from Columbia University (New York).

Hartmut Berghoff is director of the Institute for Economic & Social History at the University of Göttingen, Germany. He was the director of the German Historical Institute in Washington DC (2008–2015) and held various visiting positions at the Center of Advanced Study, Harvard Business School, the Maison des Sciences de l'Homme and the Henley Business School. He has worked on the history of consumption, business history, immigration history and the history of modern Germany.

Juan A. Bogliaccini is Professor of Political Science at Universidad Católica del Uruguay. His work focuses on the political economy of redistribution and inequality. He has published in *Economics & Politics, Latin American Research Review, CEPAL Review, Revista de Ciencia Política, Revista Reforma y Democracia*, and edited collections including the *Oxford Handbook of the Welfare State* (2012). He holds a PhD in Political Science from the University of North Carolina at Chapel Hill.

Juan Pablo Bohoslavsky is coordinator of the postgraduate course on "Public policies and human rights in Covid-19 times," Universidad Nacional de Río Negro, Argentina. He was the United Nations Independent Expert on Debt and Human Rights during 2014–2020. He has worked at the United Nations Conference on Trade and Development (UNCTAD) and as a consultant for the Argentine state and the United Nations Economic Commission for Latin America and the Caribbean (ECLAC). He co-edited *Pinochet's Economic Accomplices: An Unequal Country by Force* (2020) with K. Fernández and S. Smart, and *Sovereign Debt Crises: What have we Learned?* (2017) with K. Raffer. He holds a PhD in law from Universidad de Salamanca.

Marcelo Bucheli is Associate Professor of Business Administration at the Gies College of Business, University of Illinois at Urbana-Champaign, USA. His research focuses on the political economy of multinational corporations in Latin America, theoretical and methodological approaches to the study of the relationship between firms and states in a historical perspective, and business groups.

Juan Geymonat is a master's student in Economic and Social History at the Universidad de la República, Uruguay. His research focuses on the evolution of business groups in Uruguay since the 1980s.

Carlos Huneeus is Professor of Law at Universidad de Chile. He has published extensively on the political economy of the Pinochet regime in Chile including *La Unión de Centro Democrático y la Transición a la Democracia en España* (1985), *The Pinochet Regime* (2007), *La guerra fría chilena. Gabriel González Videla y la ley maldita* (2009), and *La democracia semisoberana. Chile después de Pinochet* (2014). He also co-edited the volumes *Eduardo Frei Montalva: Un gobierno reformista* (2016) with Javier Couso and *El sistema político chileno* (2018) with Octavio Avendaño. He was Chile's ambassador to Germany (1990–1994) and has been a recipient of major fellowships from different institutions including the British Council and the Adenauer, Humboldt, and Guggenheim foundations. He was a fellow at the Rockefeller Center in 2011. He holds a PhD in Political Science from the University of Heidelberg, a master's degree from the University of Essex, and an undergraduate degree in Law from Universidad de Chile.

Christopher Kopper is Professor of Economic and Social History at the Universität Bielefeld, Germany. He was DAAD Professor of German Studies at the University of Minnesota and the University of Pittsburgh (1998–2003) and Assistant Professor at the Universität Göttingen (1992–1998). His major fields of research are history of finance, transport, and mobility. He holds a PhD in Modern History from Universität Bochum (1992) and his Habilitation from Universität Bielefeld (2005).

Martín Monsalve Zanatti is Professor and Head of the Humanities Department at Universidad del Pacífico, Peru. His research focuses on the evolution of family firms and business groups in Peru in the nineteenth and twentieth centuries. He is the editor of *Historia Económica del Sur Peruano (BCRP-IEP 2019)* and author of a dozen of journal articles and chapters in edited collections on Latin American and Peruvian economic and business history. He holds a PhD in History from the State University of New York at Stony Brook.

Martín Opertti is Lecturer in the Department of Social Sciences at the Universidad Católica del Uruguay. He holds a BA degree in Sociology from the Universidad Católica del Uruguay. His research focuses on the political conditioning of economic perceptions.

Pedro Henrique Pedreira Campos is Professor of History and International Relations at the Universidade Federal Rural do Rio de

Janeiro and the Universidade Federal do Rio de Janeiro, Brazil. His research focuses on the socioeconomic history and the Brazilian civil-military dictatorship. He is the author of *Estranhas Catedrais: As empreiteiras brasileiras e a ditadura civil-militar, 1964–1988* (2014) and *Nos Caminhos da Acumulação: Negócios e poder no abastecimento de carnes verdes para cidade do Rio de Janeiro, 1808–1835* (2010). He co-edited *Política Econômica nos Anos de Chumbo* (2018), *Os Donos do Capital: a trajetória das principais famílias empresariais do capitalismo brasileiro* (2017), and *Ensaios de História econômico-social: Séculos XIX e XX* (2012). He holds a PhD from Universidade Federal Fluminense.

Abel Puerta Alarcón is Student in Music Production and Engineering at Berklee College of Music, USA. He holds a bachelor's degree in Economics from Universidad del Pacífico. He worked as a research assistant at the Centro de Investigación de la Universidad del Pacífico from 2013 to 2018, where he focused in Peruvian business history from different perspectives, like social network analysis, sociology, and economic history.

Frederik Schulze is Assistant Professor of Latin American history at Westfälische Wilhelms-Universität Münster, Germany. He is the author of *Auswanderung als nationalistisches Projekt: "Deutschtum" und Kolonialdiskurse im südlichen Brasilien (1824–1941)* (2016) and co-editor of *Brasilien in der Welt: Region, Nation und Globalisierung 1870–1945* (2013). His research focuses on the history of large dams in Latin America, history of knowledge, development and infrastructure, migration history, and global history. He has published articles in journals including *German History, Geschichte und Gesellschaft, Bulletin of Latin American Research, Itinerario*, and several edited collections. He holds a PhD from Freie Universität Berlin.

Meta Stephan is a PhD candidate at Humboldt University, Berlin. Her research focuses on the German-Argentine relationships and on the foreign policy of the Federal Republic of Germany. She holds a bachelor's degree in Cultural Studies from the European University Viadrina and master's degree in History from Humboldt University. She was a fellow of the Berlin Funding for Graduates (Elsa Neumann) and a visiting scholar at Humboldt University.

Joel Stillerman is Professor of Sociology and Faculty-in-Residence in the Honors College at Grand Valley State University, USA. He is the author of *The Sociology of Consumption: A Global Approach* (2015) and co-editor of *What does Work Mean Today?: Continuity and Change in a Global Society* (2012). His qualitative, multi-method research on labor, cities, consumer culture, and social stratification in Chile and Latin America appears in *Journal of Consumer Culture, Journal of Contemporary Ethnography, Poetics, Latin American Politics and Society, Political Power and Social Theory, City & Community, Qualitative Sociology, Mobilization, Social Science History, International Labor and Working-class History, EURE, Revista de Estudios Avanzados, Política, Alamedas*, and several edited volumes.

Stefano Tijerina is Lecturer in Management at the University of Maine, USA. He is also the inaugural recipient of the Canadian Business History Association's Chris Kobrak Research Fellowship. He has published on the political economy and history of the operations of Canadian and American multinationals in Latin America. He is the author of *Filling in the Gaps in the Americas: Canada and Colombia, 1767–1968* (2020), and has published articles in the *Journal of Canadian Studies, American Review of Canadian Studies, Ensayos Sobre Política Económica, Desafíos*, and *Perspectivas Colombo Canadienses.* He has contributed chapters in several edited volumes including *The History of Canada-U.S. Trade Negotiations* (2019), *"A Samaritan State" Revised: Historical Perspectives on Canadian Foreign Aid, 1950–2016* (2019), and *Working for Oil: Comparative Social Histories of Labor in Petroleum* (2018). He holds a PhD from the University of Maine.

Tomás Undurraga is Associate Professor of Sociology at Universidad Alberto Hurtado, Chile. He is also an honorary fellow of the Science and Technology Studies Department at the University College of London. His research focuses on comparative sociology of economic and intellectual elites in Argentina, Brazil, and Chile and the role of the media in the creation of a public sphere. He holds a PhD in Sociology from the University of Cambridge and was postdoctoral researcher in history and philosophy of science at Cambridge and the University College of London. He has an undergraduate degree in Sociology from Universidad Católica de Chile.

List of Figures

List of Tables

CHAPTER 1

Crime and (No) Punishment: Business Corporations and Dictatorships

Victoria Basualdo, Hartmut Berghoff, and Marcelo Bucheli

This volume studies the relationship between big business and the Latin American dictatorial regimes during the Cold War. Between the 1950s and 1970s, many civilian governments in Latin America fell in quick succession and were replaced by military regimes often supported by the US government. These regimes were considered a bulwark against the advance of communism, which was viewed as a credible threat both by Latin American elites and by the United States, particularly after the triumph of

V. Basualdo
Area of Economics and Technology, Facultad Latinoamericana de Ciencias, Sociales-CONICET, Buenos Aires, Argentina

H. Berghoff
Institute for Economic & Social History, University of Göttingen, Göttingen, Germany
e-mail: berghoff@uni-goettingen.de

M. Bucheli (✉)
Gies College of Business, University of Illinois at Urbana-Champaign, Champaign, IL, USA
e-mail: mbucheli@illinois.edu

V. Basualdo et al. (eds.), *Big Business and Dictatorships in Latin America*, Palgrave Studies in Latin American Heterodox Economics, https://doi.org/10.1007/978-3-030-43925-5_1

the Cuban Revolution and its subsequent popularity among significant segments of the Latin American working and middle classes. Contemporary studies viewed big business (both foreign multinationals and domestic firms) as the natural allies of the right-wing military regimes: segments of the military, which were concerned about "foreign infiltration" from international communism through labor activism, were able to find common ground with managers frustrated by union-led disruptions of their business operations and frightened by the growth of anti-business and obstructionist political organizations, not to mention violent ones (as well as the obvious potentially negative effect on their bottom line).[1] During that period, many analysts and casual observers found clear and unequivocal evidence of such business-military collusion in events such as the 1954 overthrow of Guatemala's President Jacobo Arbenz following his conflict with the United Fruit Company, or the 1973 coup against Chile's President Salvador Allende following clashes with foreign firms like the International Telegraph and Telephone Company (ITT) and the Chilean elite.[2] Further evidence of this collusion was also located in the subsequent adoption by the military regimes of Chile in the 1970s and Argentina in the 1980s of open-market policies that overwhelmingly benefited big business and foreign investors.

Despite the perceived importance of the role of the Latin American Cold War dictatorships in creating a business-friendly environment during the 1980s and 1990s, no single volume provides readers with a view of the relationship between big business and the authoritarian regimes on a continental scale. Country-focused studies published by some of this collection's authors have made important contributions. This volume seeks to enrich this debate by bringing together case studies on Argentina, Brazil, Chile, Colombia, Peru, and Central America, plus chapters on particular industries, including infrastructure, defense, finance, and automobile manufacturing. The chapters of this volume go beyond the traditional view, which focuses on US corporations and the global agenda of the United States. To date, the literature has honed in overwhelmingly on

[1] Peter Evans, *Dependent Development: The Alliance of Multinational, State, and Local Capital in Brazil* (Princeton University Press: Princeton, 1979); Guillermo O'Donnell, *El Estado Burocrático Autoritario: 1966–1973* (Buenos Aires: Belgrano, 1982).

[2] Stephen Schlesinger and Stephen Kinzer, *Bitter Fruit: The Story of the American Coup in Guatemala* (Cambridge: Harvard University Press, 2005); Lubna Qureshi, *Nixon, Kissinger, and Allende: U.S. Involvement in the 1973 Coup in Chile* (New York: Rowman & Littlefield, 2009).

firms originating in the United States. In addition to examining US foreign investment and foreign policy in the region, the volume makes an unprecedented contribution by considering firms from Germany, France, Italy, and Canada, with a particular emphasis on the relationship between German foreign policy and the cooperation of German firms with the military dictatorships. In addition to analyzing the operations of multinational corporations, the volume also studies the role of the banking sector in financing authoritarian regimes and the local elites' accommodation of the military governments.

Big Businesses and Dictatorships in Latin America engages in dialogues with recent studies on these types of relationships in other parts of the world. Some recent studies, for example, have shown the complexity and variety of relationships between big business and the Nazi regime. After decades of attempting to silence, deny, and muffle this history, most large German corporations began to open their archives in the 1990s in response to high pressure from a critical public and often from international clients threatening to boycott these firms. Many, but not all, major German corporations have commissioned independent historians to analyze their history during the Nazi dictatorship, yielding an impressive array of high-quality scholarship that illuminates important and often disturbing aspects of this history.[3] None of this has happened in Latin America, where the general attitude of companies is still silence, denial, and closed archives. However, scholars now benefit from the large quantity of evidence and sources, some of which were generated during legal actions against firms involved in repression carried out during the dictatorships. The time that has elapsed since the fall of the Latin American military regimes, the freedom Latin American scholars have managed to achieve since then, and the opening and discovery of new archival sources provide optimal conditions for revisiting, through a variety of lenses, the complex ties between Latin

[3] Gerald D. Feldman, *Allianz and the German Insurance Business, 1933–1945* (Cambridge: Cambridge Univ. Press, 2001); Harold James, *The Deutsche Bank and the Nazi Economic War against the Jews: The Expropriation of Jewish-Owned Property* (Cambridge: Cambridge Univ. Press, 2001); Peter Hayes, *From Cooperation to Complicity: Degussa in the Third Reich* (Cambridge: Cambridge Univ. Press, 2006). See also the chapters in Harold James and Jakob Tanner, eds., *Enterprise in the Period of Fascism in Europe* (Aldershot: Routledge, 2002); Francis R Nicosia and Jonathan Huener, eds., *Business and Industry in Nazi Germany* (New York: Berghahn, 2004); and Hartmut Berghoff, Jürgen Kocka, and Dieter Ziegler, eds., *Business in the Age of Extremes: Essays in Modern German and Austrian Economic History* (Cambridge: Cambridge University Press, 2013).

American military governments and different types of businesses ranging from large domestic firms, family firms, foreign multinationals, and state-owned enterprises.

This project began with a workshop at the University of Göttingen in September 2016 about "Corporations and Authoritarian Regimes in Latin America," where preliminary versions of some of the chapters were presented. It became clear at that academic event that the topic was as relevant as it was complex, with highly contentious dimensions and aspects. Therefore, this book is a product of a conscious attempt to make progress in this field by bringing together contributions from specialists in economic history, business history, labor history, and human rights and Transitional Justice, which are often completely separate realms or in disagreement with one another. To welcome contributions from different theoretical perspectives, scholarly traditions, and research trajectories developed in various geographical and institutional frameworks was a considerable challenge that took time and energy. We hope this collective effort, which is necessarily diverse and multifaceted, will help foster knowledge and debate about issues of relevance not only to global and regional history but also to current economic and social relations.

This volume dialogues with several scholarly communities. First, we reflect on the debates generated by studies on the relationship between the Nazi regime in Germany and the corporate sector and connect them to an important area of the world that was dominated by right-wing dictators (many of them more or less openly inspired by European fascism) in the 1970s and 1980s. Although history never exactly repeats itself and comparisons across different times and continents should be treated with great caution, there are some stunning parallels between the experience of Germany and Latin America as far as the relationship between the business community and right-wing dictatorships is concerned. In all cases, the dictatorships emerged in unstable democracies that were particularly unpopular with the corporate world.

In Germany, most businessmen perceived the Weimar Republic (1918–1933) as the poisoned fruit of World War I. The military defeat and the Treaty of Versailles were generally seen as unfair and humiliating, burdening the republic with a painful legacy. The establishment of the Weimar Republic generated features that were diametrically opposed to business interests. These included an unprecedented rise of the labor movement and the temporary participation of the Social Democrats in government. German business was forced, for the first time in history, to accept labor unions as legitimate representatives of their workers. In 1920, the principle of codetermination was introduced. All companies with more than 20 employees had to set up elected works councils whose task was to advocate for employees' interests vis-à-vis the management. Workers in Germany gained such rights for the first time; never before had there been so many strikes and lockouts. A second business-undermining feature of the Weimar Republic was that, in stark contrast to the German Empire of 1870–1918, it was characterized by economic instability and social unrest. The experience of hyperinflation, recurrent political turmoil, the emergence of an expansive welfare state, and higher levels of corporate and personal taxation added to the business class's disenchantment with democracy, which, in general, was a new historical experience for all Germans that seemed frail by itself. Thus, it comes as no surprise that for the middle classes, in general, and most members of the business community, in particular, the authoritarian monarchy of the German Empire looked like a land of milk and honey in retrospect.[4]

As a result, there was little loyalty to the republic but rather a great deal of disapproval and hostility toward it. However, this negative attitude did not translate into support for the NSDAP (National Socialist German Workers' Party, commonly referred to in English as the Nazi Party), which remained a chaotic splinter party on the lunatic fringe for a long time. Even after it had increased the number of seats it held in parliament from 12 (1928) to 107 (1930), the party disturbed most businessmen with its anti-capitalist manifesto. After all, it was a "National Socialist Party." Most businessmen wanted an authoritarian alternative to the republic that would put labor back on a short leash and ensure law and order as they understood it. The view that big business backed Hitler[5] has proved to be

[4] Eric D. Weitz, *Weimar Germany: Promise and Tragedy* (Princeton: Princeton Univ. Press, 2007) 129–168; Richard J. Evans, *The Coming of the Third Reich* (London: Penguin, 2003), 78–138.

[5] This view has been popular in the left political spectrum. It had become canonized at the 7th World Congress of the Communist Third International in 1935, when Georgi Dimitrov called fascism "the open, terrorist dictatorship of the most reactionary, most chauvinistic, and most imperialist elements of finance capital." Georgi Dimitrov, "The Fascist Offensive and the Tasks of the Communist International," Main Report delivered at the Seventh World Congress of the Communist International—"The class character of fascism"; collected in *VII Congress of the Communist International: Abridged Stenographic Report of Proceedings* (Moscow: Foreign Languages Publishing House, 1939). This thesis proved to be very influential until the 1980s. For Hitler, finance capital was "Jewish" and had to be destroyed. So the majority capitalists had no cause to support him. Ian Kershaw, *The Nazi Dictatorship:*

erroneous. Rather, in addition to the general crisis of the economy and the state, the support of large landowners and parts of the military was decisive. They were under the illusion they could instrumentalize Hitler to make up for lost ground, that is, to secure government subsidies for crisis-ridden agriculture and to restore the army, which had been drastically downsized by the Treaty of Versailles, to its former size and glory. The business community was primarily responsible for having weakened the republic, not for having given direct support to Hitler prior to 1933, although there was a minority of businesspeople who backed Hitler early on and saw Germany's savior in him.[6]

After Hitler became chancellor and acquired dictatorial powers, the business community eagerly looked for ways to come to terms with the new rulers and take advantage of the dictatorship. They joined the NSDAP in large numbers, and some prominent businessmen took up top positions in the new state. Kurt Schmitt from Allianz Insurance became the Reich Minister of Economics in 1933 but was already released from his duties in 1934. His successor became the internationally renowned banker Hjalmar Schacht, who also served the regime as the president of the central bank until 1938, when he was dropped like a hot potato because he insisted on a reasonably sound financial policy, which the regime regarded as dispensable since it intended for the subjugated countries to foot the bill.[7]

Overall, tactically motivated, opportunistic cooperation between regime and the entrepreneurial class prevailed. There was a convergence

Problems and Perspectives of Interpretation, 4th ed. (London: Arnold, 2000). The classic view of East German communists was that the NSDAP had been controlled by big business. See Eberhard Czichon, *Wer verhalf Hitler zur Macht? Zum Anteil der Deutschen Industrie an der Zerstörung der Weimarer Republik* (Cologne: Pahl-Rugenstein, 1967). For a recent summary of the debates and further literature, see Jörg Osterloh, "Die Monopole und ihre Herren. Marxistische Interpretationen," in *Unternehmen im Nationalsozialismus. Zur Historisierung einer Forschungskonjunktur*, edited by Norbert Frei and Tim Schanetzky, 36–47 (Göttingen: Wallstein, 2010).

[6] Henry Ashby Turner, "Big Business and the Rise of Hitler," *American Historical Review* 75, no. 1 (1969): 56–70; idem, *German Big Business and the Rise of Hitler* (Oxford: Oxford Univ. Press, 1987); Reinhard Vogelsang, *Der Freundeskreis Himmler* (Göttingen: Muster-Schmidt Verlag, 1972). For a biographical case study, see Hartmut Berghoff and Cornelia Rauh, *The Respectable Career of Fritz K: The Making and Remaking of a Provincial Nazi Leader* (Oxford: Berghahn Books, 2015).

[7] Adam J. Tooze, *The Wages of Destruction: The Making and Breaking of the Nazi Economy* (London: Penguin, 2006), 99–134 and 285–325; and Richard J. Evans, *The Third Reich in Power 1933–1939* (London: Penguin, 2005) 351–377.

but no identity of interests. Businessmen who were directly involved in the rearmament drive were closer to the regime and benefited more from it than those in the consumer-goods industry. For the most part, they frowned upon severing international connections and implementing capital controls or import quotas. The rearmament boom, however, gave many companies lucrative orders. Full employment and rising profits were highly welcomed. Nevertheless, they saw corporations bow to the primacy of politics and sometimes helplessly watched as state-owned or party-affiliated companies took precedence even over the most powerful private businesses. The most famous cases are Volkswagen and the steel and weapons conglomerate Reichswerke Hermann Göring. Volkswagen was founded with capital that had been stolen from the trade unions because private industry refused to build a car that Hitler wanted them to sell below production costs.[8] The state-owned Reichswerke used taxpayers' money to hasten the exploitation of poor domestic iron ore, which private companies did not want to touch because this raw material was too expensive to process and sell at a profit. There was almost an open confrontation between the steel barons of the Ruhr and the government, but the regime needed both private corporations run by traditional elites preoccupied with profits and state-owned enterprises run by political fanatics without any regard for commercial considerations.[9] Volkswagen and Reichswerke were notorious for their exploitation of forced laborers.[10]

Parts of the private corporate sector also became highly complicit with the regime when it came to "Aryanization," that is, the robbery of Jewish property, or the exploitation of occupied territories, but in these instances, too, the party typically had greater leverage than individual companies when conflicts arose. Complete agreement with Hitler's ideological goals was rare but not absent. Overall, the cooperation of the old elites with the NSDAP never became a happy alliance.

[8] Hans Mommsen and Manfred Grieger, *Das Volkswagenwerk und seine Arbeiter im Dritten Reich* (Düsseldorf: Econ, 1996).

[9] Gerhard Thomas Mollin, *Montankonzerne und "Drittes Reich": Der Gegensatz zwischen Monopolindustrie und Befehlswirtschaft in der deutschen Rüstung und Expansion 1936–1944* (Göttingen: Vandenhoeck & Ruprecht, 1988); and Richard J. Overy, *War and Economy in the Third Reich* (Oxford: Oxford Univ. Press, 1995), 93–174.

[10] Manfred Grieger, "Extermination and Work under the Nazi System of Forced Labor," in *Forced Labor: The Germans, the Forced Laborers, and the War*, edited by Volkhard Knigge, Rikola-Gunnar Lüttgenau, and Jens-Christian Wagner (Weimar: Stiftung Gedenkstätten Buchenwald und Mittelbau-Dora, 2010), 208–220.

Another important difference between the Nazi dictatorship and Latin American ones in the 1970s and 1980s was the role of the military. The *Reichswehr*, the German armed forces, set great hopes on Hitler and welcomed the stripping away of the restrictions of the Treaty of Versailles but never managed to get into the driver's seat. The regime initially left the military forces under the illusion that they could have a say in strategic political issues, but by 1938 Hitler made it clear that the army was to be a subordinate institution. Several conservative generals were either murdered or fired.[11] National Socialists did not want to serve anyone—not the military or the business class. Above all, they pursued their own ideological, racial, and kleptocratic agenda regardless of the consequences.

To add another divergence, it must be stressed that Hitler's seizure of power was an internal German affair, in which neither foreign secret services nor foreign governments or companies played any role. In contrast to Latin America, the United States was not actively involved in the overthrow of the republic. The United States had direct interests in the repayment of Germany's outstanding debts, and it was obvious that any Nazi-led government would refuse to honor these obligations. And the United States wanted to preserve free trade, which the Nazis promised to abandon. Thus, Washington had no reason to support a regime change in Germany.

Foreign capital also played no role in Hitler's seizure of power, in contrast to the Latin American dictatorships. As a rule, foreign companies in Germany were disadvantaged and intimidated, above all by capital controls and threats of confiscation. However, like German companies, they did develop structures of complicity in the interest of profits and the defense of property. Between 1933 and 1939, several hundred US companies made significant portions of their sales in Germany, some of them even until 1941. Around 1935, 26 of the largest American corporations had close business relations with the German dictatorship.[12] Although this was not illegal in the United States, in view of Hitler's treatment of Jews and political opponents and his blatant violations of international law, it was highly distressing and therefore kept a secret.

[11] Rolf-Dieter Müller, *Hitler's Wehrmacht, 1935–1945* (Lexington: University Press of Kentucky, 2016); and Evans, *Power*, 642–645.

[12] Research Services of the German Parliament, *Report on the Alleged Cooperation of US-Corporation with the NS-Regime* (WD 1 – 134/07) (Berlin, 2007) (in German), 3.

There were prominent cases of companies that would later also cooperate with Latin American dictators. The largest car manufacturer in Germany was General Motors through its Opel subsidiary. Opel built the hardy three-ton truck "Blitz," which became the mainstay of the German army. Opel almost doubled its staff in Germany in the 1930s and increased its sales to the Nazi state, which became its most important customer. Opel and GM managers had close contacts with leading Nazi functionaries. James D. Mooney, the president of GM overseas operations and a supporter of the isolationist and racist anti-New-Deal American Liberty League, met with Hitler several times, even after the invasion of Poland, and was treated as the Führer's special guest. In 1938 Mooney was awarded the Grand Cross of the German Eagle Order, the highest party order for foreigners, for his service to the "Third Reich." The first recipient of this new medal had been Mussolini in 1937. Twenty-two American citizens received the award between 1937 and 1940, among them also Thomas Watson, the chief executive of IBM, and Henry Ford. GM obscured Opel's American ownership and control as the rank-and-file Nazis "condemned anything foreign-owned or foreign-made."[13] Prominent German figures and Nazi functionaries were appointed to Opel's board. During the war, Opel also produced essential components for warplanes with the help of forced laborers. At the same time, Opel's American personnel were replaced by Germans handpicked by and loyal to GM.

Ford had opened a factory in Cologne in 1931 but never reached the same importance in Germany as GM did. Still, Ford became an important supplier for the army, providing it with about one-third of its trucks. In 1939, when Hitler's preparations for war were escalating and more than obvious, Ford did not shy away from importing essential truck components from Dearborn to Cologne to meet the rising demands of the German army. Allied forces in the war made the bewildering discovery that they were driving the same brands of trucks as their enemy. Henry Ford, an outspoken anti-Semite, who was admired by Hitler, received the

[13] Edwin Black, "Hitler's Carmaker: The Inside Story of How General Motors Helped Mobilize the Third Reich," *Global Research*, Oct. 1 (2018). This article is one-sided in many ways. A more thorough but partly apologetic account is Henry Ashby Turner, *General Motors and the Nazis: The Struggle for Control of Opel, Europe's Biggest Carmaker* (New Haven: Yale Univ. Press, 2005).

Eagle Order in 1938 on the occasion of his 75th birthday. The certificate was personally signed by Hitler.[14]

During the war, more and more forced laborers were dispatched to the Cologne factory. They accounted for about half of the staff in 1943. Toward the end of the war, Ford requested concentration camp inmates from the SS to keep production going. In 1944 the first inmates from the Buchenwald camp arrived in Cologne. Opel also used forced labor but refused to employ concentration camp inmates. In other words, there was a choice. After the war the parent companies in the United States claimed not to have made any profits from the German war economy and to have lost control of their subsidiaries between late 1941 and 1945, when the United States was at war with Germany. Ford had reduced its share in the German subsidiary to 52 percent in 1941 but kept the majority ever after. In May 1942, the Nazi regime put Ford Werke in "trusteeship" but did not nationalize it. It remained American property.[15]

Human rights violations were endemic at Ford, just as they were in large parts of German industry during the war. In the Ford factory worker-inmates toiled for twelve hours a day. They were given 200 grams of bread and coffee for breakfast, no lunch, and a dinner of spinach and three potatoes or soup made of turnip leaves. In late summer 1944, about eight million workers—that is, roughly a quarter of the workforce in Germany—were foreigners; the majority of these were forced laborers, who were compelled to work in Germany mostly under pitiful conditions.[16] In some cases companies set up production facilities close to concentration camps. Representatives of these companies were often directly involved in the

[14] Stephan Link, "Rethinking the Ford-Nazi Connection," *Bulletin of the German Historical Institute* 49, no. 2 (2011): 135–50.

[15] Ken Silverstein. "Ford and the Führer," *The Nation,* January 6 (2000); and Simon Reich, *The Fruits of Fascism: Postwar Prosperity in Historical Perspective* (Ithaca: Cornell Univ. Press, 1990), 107–145.

[16] Ulrich Herbert, *Hitler's Foreign Workers: Enforced Foreign Labor in Germany under the Third Reich* (Cambridge: Cambridge Univ. Press, 2006); Mark Mazower, *Hitler's Empire: How the Nazis Ruled Europe* (New York: Penguin Press, 2010), 294–318; Mark Spoerer, "Forced Labour in Nazi-Occupied Europe, 1939–1945," in *Economies under Occupation: The Hegemony of Nazi Germany and Imperial Japan in World War II,* edited by Marcel Boldforf and Tetsuji Okazaki, 73–85 (London: Routledge, 2015); idem, *Zwangsarbeit unter dem Hakenkreuz. Ausländische Zivilarbeiter, Kriegsgefangene und Häftlinge im Deutschen Reich und im besetzten Europa 1939–1945* (Stuttgart: DVA, 2001).

selection of workers; people deemed fit to work were thus allowed to live for the time being, while everyone else was sent to certain death.[17]

After the war, the majority of the implicated businessmen were not punished, or only relatively mildly.[18] Quite a few Nazi criminals fled to Latin America via the so-called ratlines where they found safe havens. In the Federal Republic, the economic elites experienced lenience as they were needed for the reconstruction and the integration of the Federal Republic into the Western camp against the backdrop of the emerging Cold War. A broad discussion of the role of the elites and National Socialism only began with the student movement in 1968. It peaked in the 1980s and 1990s when numerous large companies decided to open their archives to investigate their role in the dictatorship. This was often triggered by pressure from the public and international customers, some of whom threatened to boycott these firms. Another key factor was the fact that the generation change had now progressed so far that the companies could easily distance themselves from those responsible at the time. No one who had been complicit was in office anymore, and even the next generation that had been trained and supported by former perpetrators and collaborators found themselves retired. In most cases, discovering the dark period of the dictatorship no longer had immediate personal consequences. Most forced laborers received significant compensation from the companies only in the 1990s and 2000s, after decades of refusal. Class action suits in the United States and public opinion made them change their minds.

This historical review has touched on the key issues also crucial to the Latin American dictatorships, which hold this volume together. How did entrepreneurs stand in relation to democratic governments? Were they involved in regime changes, directly or indirectly? What was the role of foreign powers and capital? To what extent and why did businessmen form alliances with dictators? Were there shared interests or antagonisms? Did

[17] Hermann Kaienburg, ed., *Konzentrationslager und Deutsche Wirtschaft 1939–1945* (Opladen: Leske & Budrich, 1996).

[18] Norbert Frei, *Adenauer's Germany and the Nazi Past: The Politics of Amnesty and Integration* (New York: Columbia Univ. Press, 2002): Hartmut Berghoff, "Zwischen Verdrängung und Aufarbeitung. Die bundesdeutsche Gesellschaft und ihre nationalsozialistische Vergangenheit in den Fünfziger Jahren," *Geschichte in Wissenschaft und Unterricht* 49, no. 2 (1998): 96–114. A more general account with examples from other countries is Manfred Berg and Bernd Schäfer, eds, *Historical Justice in International Perspective: How Societies Are Trying to Right the Wrongs of the Past* (Cambridge: Cambridge Univ. Press, 2009).

businessmen serve in dictatorial governments? Were their expectations fulfilled? Can we observe personal ties? To what extent did industrial relations change? What happened to labor unions? Did human rights violations occur and were companies directly or indirectly involved? Did the dictatorship allow for extra profits? How, after the return to democracy, did the Latin American countries deal with the former representatives of the dictatorships, the economic elites and their companies, as well as the victims?

These questions lead us to explore how the studies in this volume contribute to our understanding of Latin American history. Scholars interested in the business, economic, and political history of the continent have long focused on the relationship between big capital and political elites. When Marxist and neo-Marxist scholarship came to dominate Latin American studies between the 1960s and 1980s, this interest was the norm.[19] Scholars informed by this intellectual tradition paid more attention to the role of foreign capital than their colleagues studying Western powers, which made sense because, between the 1870s and 1950s, the main actors capable of investing large sums in the region were foreign corporations. Roughly (and at the risk of oversimplifying a large body of scholarship), these authors maintained that Latin American nations were inserted into the global division of labor as providers of raw materials to the industrial Western powers starting in the late nineteenth century. This insertion, they maintained, was not just the spontaneous result of market forces driving each country to specialize in their comparative advantages but rather an imposed specialization by industrial nations in need of cheap inputs. The result of this specialization, their argument continued, was gradually increasing dependence on international markets, unfavorable terms of trade by which Latin America sold cheap raw materials in exchange for ever more expensive industrial goods, and, in general, the perpetuation of poverty and archaic institutions. This status quo survived, they posited, because a local *comprador* elite benefited from this configuration. In order to keep this system working despite the impoverishment of the local population, this elite needed to establish non-democratic repressive institutions. As a result, these scholars claimed that dictatorships were an inevitable by-product of the role Latin America played in the global

[19] For a detailed account of how neo-Marxist interpretations became the norm in Latin American studies in the United States and Latin America, see Robert Packenham, *The Dependency Movement: Scholarship and Politics in Development Studies* (Cambridge: Harvard University Press, 1992).

economy. Consequently, foreign and domestic corporations were actors that supported and benefited from repressive regimes.[20]

The neo-Marxist and Marxist scholars also found the process of industrialization, which took place in several Latin American countries between the 1930s and 1970s, consistent with their interpretation. Import substitution industrialization, they maintained, did not break the dependency status of the continent but simply changed it and in some ways reinforced it. Their rationale was as follows: when trying to industrialize their nations, Latin American leaders could not count on domestic firms to possess the technological capabilities or capital for a serious industrialization process, so the governments invited foreign manufacturing multinationals. These multinationals, these scholars posited, made the domestic economies dependent on the Western world because they kept control over patents and technology.[21] Undergoing the process of industrialization, these countries developed what the influential work by Peter Evans called the "Triple Alliance" against organized labor between foreign multinationals, domestic large businesses, and the state. For Evans, certain transitional processes that heavy industrialization required were bound to provoke the opposition of labor unions due to potential layoffs. In order to overcome this obstacle, foreign and domestic capital allied itself with authoritarian regimes.[22] Guillermo O'Donnell followed a similar logic to explain the rise of the Argentine authoritarian regimes and their alliance with big capital.[23]

The fact that there was a generally accepted consensus in academia and among the general public on the close relationship between authoritarian regimes and big business in Latin America during the 1960s–1980s period

[20] The list of studies that follow this approach is too long to summarize in a single footnote. Good general reviews include Susanne Bodenheimer, "Dependency and Imperialism: The Roots of Latin American Underdevelopment," *Politics and Society* 1, no. 3 (1971): 327–357; Theotonio Dos Santos, "The Structure of Development," *American Economic Review* 60, no. 2 (1970): 231–236; Fernando H. Cardoso and Enzo Faletto, *Dependency and Development in Latin America* (Berkeley: University of California Press, 1979); Tulio Halperín-Donghi, "'Dependency Theory' and Latin American Historiography," *Latin American Research Review* 17, no. 1 (1982): 115–130.

[21] Good representative examples of this approach are Theotonio Dos Santos, *Imperialismo y Dependencia* (Mexico City: Era, 1978); Gary Gereffi and Peter Evans, "Transnational Corporations, Dependent Development, and State Policy in the Semiperiphery: A Comparison of Brazil and Mexico," *Latin American Research Review* 16, no. 3 (1981): 31–64; Evans, *Dependent Development*.

[22] Evans, *Dependent Development*.

[23] O'Donnell, *El estado*.

did not mean there were no dissenting voices. Focusing on British investments in the late nineteenth and early twentieth centuries, D. C. M. Platt maintained that foreign investors were too weak to influence domestic politics in the region and that most of Latin America was too poor for it to be worth investors' effort to build alliances with those dictators.[24] Rory Miller added that the British government did very little to help British corporations on a continent irrelevant to its imperial agenda.[25] Even for paradigmatic cases such as General Juan Vicente Gómez's regime in Venezuela, Brian McBeth found a more nuanced relationship between this dictator and foreign American and British investors than the general consensus would imply.[26] While traditional interpretations cast Gómez as a sell-out who was just an instrument of the oil multinationals, McBeth showed how he managed to make them compete against each other in a way that allowed Venezuela to maximize income from oil exports.[27] Paul Garner found similar results in the case of Mexico's authoritarian regime under Porfirio Díaz, which was traditionally portrayed as a staunch ally of foreign interests. In Garner's study, the British oilman Weetman Pearson was regarded as Díaz's partner in development rather than a puppeteer. Additionally, Garner described Díaz as a shrewd negotiator with foreign investors,[28] as was the case with Gómez.

[24] D. C. M. Platt, *Business Imperialism, 1840–1930: An Inquiry Based on British Experience in Latin America* (Oxford: Clarendon, 1977).

[25] Rory Miller, *Britain in Latin America in the Nineteenth and Twentieth Centuries* (New York: Routledge, 1993).

[26] Brian McBeth, *La política petrolera venezolana: una perspectiva histórica* (Caracas: Universidad Metropolitana, 2015); idem, *Dictatorship and Politics: Intrigue, Betrayal, and Survival in Venezuela, 1908–1935* (South Bend: University of Notre Dame Press, 2008); idem, *Juan Vicente Gómez and the Oil Companies in Venezuela, 1908–1935* (Cambridge: Cambridge University Press, 2002).

[27] Examples of the traditional studies showing Gómez as a puppet of foreign capital include Rómulo Betancourt, *Venezuela: Oil and Politics* (Boston: Houghton Mifflin, 1978); and Gastón Parra Luzardo, *El desafío del cartel petrolero* (Maracaibo: Universidad de Zulia, 1981); Franklin Tugwell, *The Politics of Oil in Venezuela* (Stanford: Stanford University Press, 1975).

[28] Paul Garner, *British Lions and Mexican Eagles: Business, Politics, and Empire in the Career of Weetman Pearson in Mexico, 1889–1919* (Stanford: Stanford University Press, 2011). More detailed and influential criticisms of the neo-Marxist approach include Stephen Haber, "Introduction: Economic Growth and Latin American Economic Historiography," in *How Latin America Fell Behind: Essays on the Economic Histories of Brazil and Mexico, 1800–1914*, ed. Stephen Haber, 1–33 (Stanford: Stanford University Press, 1997); D. C. M. Platt, "Dependency in the Nineteenth Century in Latin America: A Historian

A convergence of several events led to a decrease in the scholarly interest on the relationship between authoritarianism and large corporations. First, the debt crisis of the 1980s opened the door to mass privatizations and foreign capital. Although the process started in some countries with authoritarian regimes (as in the paradigmatic case of Chile), it was deepened by elected officials. Second, the crisis also led to the gradual fall of the different Latin American authoritarian regimes. Unmanageable foreign debt and hyperinflation weakened military regimes, which were also slowly losing the support of the United States. Latin America became the showcase of the "third wave" of democratization (as Samuel Huntington put it), which came together with a wave of economic liberalization and a reorientation of the economic structure toward exports of commodities due to what by then seemed like endless Chinese demand.[29] Third, the changes in the economic and political landscape were accompanied by changes in academic disciplines. In the early 1990s, after years in which Marxist and neo-Marxist approaches dominated, Latin American studies in the United States shifted bit by bit toward subaltern studies that sidelined economic issues.[30] As part of the same process, economic history gradually disappeared from both economics and history departments in the United States, while interest in Latin American institutions continued, albeit with more limited funding and reach. Moreover, those that continued studying Latin American economic history adopted a neo-institutional approach that challenged the previous Marxist paradigm with sophisticated quantitative methods.[31]

The new economic history that emerged in the 1990s analyzed authoritarian regimes around their role in creating certain institutional environments that constrained (or permitted) development. Historians in this field targeted previous approaches that regarded foreign corporations and big capital as tools of imperialism in charge of exploiting the region and

Objects," *Latin American Research Review* 15, no. 1 (1980): 113–130; Stephen Haber, "The Political Economy of Industrialization," in *The Cambridge Economic History of Latin America*, ed. Victor Bulmer-Thomas, John Coatsworth, and Roberto Cortés-Conde 537–584 (Cambridge: Cambridge University Press, 2006); Packenham, *The Dependency Movement*.

[29] Samuel Huntington, *The Third Wave: Democratization in the Late Twentieth Century* (Norman: University of Oklahoma Press, 1991).

[30] Ramón Grosfoguel, "The Epistemic Decolonial Turn: Beyond Political-Economy Paradigms," *Cultural Studies* 2, nos. 2–3 (2007): 211–223.

[31] See, for example, Haber, *How Latin America*.

perpetuating poverty and undemocratic regimes, positing instead that some of those regimes created a system of property rights that kept capital from acting as a development force in those countries. Crony capitalism, inconsistency in the protection of property rights, or bad regulatory systems were what eventually impeded big capital and foreign firms from helping to lead those countries to prosperity, these scholars maintained.[32]

This volume aims to reopen discussions about the relationship between big capital and authoritarian regimes in Latin America by bringing in approaches from academic traditions largely absent in previous debates. One particular area of recent but rapid growth has been Latin American business history. A pioneering business historical study on the relationship of foreign banks and Latin American dictatorships is the one by Carlo Edoardo Altamura, who finds how once those countries started being ruled by dictatorships the relationship with the international banks intensified.[33] This field benefited from the dialogue it had with the previous scholarly works produced in Latin America with the methods and questions of business historians in the United States and Europe.[34] By taking corporate strategy into consideration when analyzing how firms related to governments, business historians provide new interpretations that go

[32] Good examples of this approach are Stephen Haber, Armando Razo, and Noel Maurer, *The Politics of Property Rights: Political Instability, Credible Commitments, and Economic Growth in Mexico, 1876–1929* (Cambridge: Cambridge University Press, 2003); Stephen Haber, ed., *Crony Capitalism and Economic Growth in Latin America: Theory and Evidence* (Stanford: Stanford University Press, 2002); William R. Summerhill, *Inglorious Revolution: Political Institutions, Sovereign Debt, and Financial Underdevelopment in Imperial Brazil* (New Haven: Yale University Press, 2015); Jeffrey Bortz and Stephen Haber, eds., *The Mexican Economy, 1870–1930: Essays on the Economic History of Institutions, Revolution, and Growth* (Stanford: Stanford University Press, 2002); Noel Maurer, *The Power and the Money: The Mexican Financial System, 1876–1932* (Stanford: Stanford University Press, 2002); Yovanna Pineda, *Industrial Development in a Frontier Economy: The Industrialization of Argentina, 1890–1930* (Stanford: Stanford University Press, 2009).

[33] Carlo Edoardo Altamura, "Global Banks and Latin American Dictators," *Business History Review* (2020): 1–32. https://doi.org/10.1017/S0007680519001260

[34] An effort to build a bridge between historians and management scholars studying corporate strategy can be found in Marcelo Bucheli and R. Daniel Wadhwani, eds., *Organizations in Time: History, Theory, Methods* (Oxford: Oxford University Press, 2014). An essay in that volume proposes a lens for developing business historical studies that take issues of political economy into consideration (see Marcelo Bucheli and Jin Uk Kim, "The State as a Historical Construct in Organization Studies," in *Organizations in Time: History, Theory, Methods*, ed. Marcelo Bucheli and R. Daniel Wadhwani 241–262 (Oxford: Oxford University Press, 2014)).

beyond, complement, or can potentially challenge the neo-Marxist or new economic history ones.[35] Chapters in this volume that contribute to existing debates and challenge extant views on the relationship between authoritarian regimes and big capital include those by Juan Bogliaccini, Juan Geymonat, and Martín Opertti, who show how Uruguay's corporate elite developed strategies to avoid economic liberalization, as had been the case in Pinochet's Chile, using a novel network analysis. Frederik Schulze's chapter, too, explores the limits the Brazilian government had in managing repressive policies in state-owned enterprises. Also, far from analyzing this period in isolation, many of the chapters offer new insight about the long-lasting impact of the relationship some firms had with the Cold War dictatorships. Victoria Basualdo, Joel Stillerman, and Pedro Campos show how this history is key to explaining the success of some present-day firms in Argentina, Chile, and Brazil. For the case of Argentina, Basualdo considers the steel industry an example of the increasing economic concentration and industrial restructuring that persisted and deepened during the democratic period, while the state oil company Yacimientos Petrolíferos Fiscales (YPF) demonstrates the expansion of "peripheral privatization" benefiting a few construction companies that dominated this economic activity for decades. For the case of Chile, Stillerman finds that the close

[35] The production of scholarly publications on Latin American business history increased significantly after the 1990s. A few examples of these that are relevant to the understanding of the relationship between big capital and government include Norma S. Lanciotti, "Foreign Investments in Electric Utilities: A Comparative Analysis of Belgian and American Companies in Argentina, 1890–1960," *Business History Review* 82, no. 3 (2008): 503–528; Norma S. Lanciotti, "From a Guaranteeing State to an Entrepreneurial State: The Relationship Between Argentina's State and Urban Utility Companies, 1880–1955," in *The Impact of Globalization on Argentina and Chile: Business Enterprises and Entrepreneurship*, ed. Geoffrey Jones and Andrea Lluch (Cheltenham: Edward Elgar, 2015); Norma S. Lanciotti and Andrea Lluch, *Las empresas extranjeras en la Argentina: Del siglo XIX al siglo XXI* (Buenos Aires: Imago Mundi, 2018); Marcelo Bucheli, *Bananas and Business: The United Fruit Company in Colombia, 1899–2000* (New York: New York University Press, 2005); Marcelo Bucheli, "Multinational Corporations, Totalitarian Regimes, and Economic Nationalism: United Fruit Company in Central America, 1899–1975," *Business History* 50, no. 4 (2008): 433–454; Marcelo Bucheli, "Multinational Corporations, Business Groups, and Economic Nationalism: Standard Oil (New Jersey), Royal Dutch-Shell, and Energy Politics in Chile, 1913–2005," *Enterprise and Society* 11, no. 2 (2010): 350–399; Marcelo Bucheli and Erica Salvaj, "Reputation and Political Legitimacy: ITT in Chile, 1927–1972," *Business History Review* 87, no. 4 (2013): 729–756; Marcelo Bucheli and Erica Salvaj, "Political Connections, the Liability of Foreignness, and Legitimacy: A Business Historical Analysis of Multinationals' Strategies in Chile," *Global Strategy Journal* 8, no. 3 (2018): 399–420.

relationship between the copper industry and Augusto Pinochet's dictatorship to repress labor unionism sowed the seeds for one of Chile's largest business groups. Similarly, Campos finds how some of the construction firms the Brazilian military regime needed for its ambitious infrastructure projects eventually became the largest multinational corporations. Carlos Huneeus and Tomás Undurraga also make it clear that, at a larger level, some of the largest business groups in Chile today owe their power to their close relationship to Pinochet. The case of the military government of Juan Velasco Alvarado in Peru (the only left-leaning one in this volume) presents rather different characteristics. Utilizing network analysis, Martín Monsalve and Abel Puerta disclose how the private sector accommodated the perceived hostility of the military government by reshaping the networks they already had with each other and building new ones with government officials. The military government seemed hostile because it promoted a nationalist popular reform that included progressive income distribution policies. In the long-term, these new and reshaped networks opened the door to the creation of some of Peru's most important business groups. Finally, Juan Pablo Bohoslavsky reminds us that in order to stay in power, the dictators required capital to finance the basic operations of the state as well as some of their ambitious plans. In his chapter, he shows the crucial role international financial institutions played in keeping the right-wing dictatorships in power.

Access to new archival sources also permits us to open new windows to our understanding of the relationship between Latin American authoritarian regimes and big capital. For instance, in their chapters Meta Stephan and Christopher Kopper bring German capital into the equation by showing how German investors actively participated in repression efforts in Argentina and Brazil. In her chapter, Stephan uses the case of German investors in Argentina to develop a typology of the relationships between big business and authoritarian regimes. Kopper, on the other hand, uncovers the benefits Volkswagen gained from the coming of the Brazilian dictatorship and the indifference the West German government had for what it perceived as the country's internal affairs. This chapter also highlights how Volkswagen—under political pressure and union power in Germany—eventually changed its attitude. This case is under the spotlight internationally due to the settlement agreement signed in September 2020 by the company with the Federal Attorney's Office in São Paulo, the Public Prosecutor's Office of São Paulo State and the Labor Attorney in São Bernardo do Campo, in compensation over its collaboration with Brazil's dictatorship. Similarly, Eduardo and Victoria Basualdo analyze Ford during the 1976–1983 dictatorship in Argentina, an extreme case both in terms of the company's involvement in human rights violations and in terms of the extraordinary economic benefits it derived from this. Tijerina explores how Canadian investors benefited from the repressive policies of the short dictatorship of General Gustavo Rojas Pinilla in Colombia. Canada has traditionally been perceived as a "neutral" country in Latin America, so unearthing its role in the Cold War in Latin America fills in an important gap in our understanding of the region's authoritarianism.[36] Marcelo Bucheli, in analyzing the evolving relationship between foreign investors and authoritarian regimes in Central America, argues that the main determinants of this alliance were foreign investors' ability to provide the dictators with resources to ensure their political survival and the steady income from exports guaranteeing some economic stability. These factors changed in significant ways in the 1960s and 1970s.

In sum, these articles go beyond analyzing the close cooperation or alliances between big capital and authoritarian governments, offering provocative findings with new nuances and complexities. Many of them also build bridges between the fields of economic, business, and labor history, which are frequently studied separately, despite the significance their potential dialogue and connections could have. Both the national overviews and case studies emphasize how crucial it is to analyze the role of labor struggle and trade union organizations to account for the

[36] Canadian corporations also operated in Latin America as subsidiaries of American capital, which often confused politicians or scholars, prompting them to analyze them as US firms. Such is the case of Imperial Oil Limited, which was partially owned by the American multinational Standard Oil Company of New Jersey and operated in South America through its subsidiary International Petroleum Corporation (Marcelo Bucheli, "Canadian Multinational Corporations and Economic Nationalism: The Case of Imperial Oil Limited in Alberta (Canada) and Colombia, 1899–1938," *Entreprises et Histoire*, no. 54 (2009): 67–85; Marcelo Bucheli and Gonzalo Romero Sommer, "Multinational Corporations, Property Rights, and Legitimization Strategies: US Investors in the Argentine and Peruvian Oil Industries," *Australian Economic History Review* 54, no. 2 (2014): 146–164; Marcelo Bucheli, "National Oil Companies and Political Coalitions: Venezuela and Colombia, 1910–76," in *The Political Economy of Resource Regulation: An International and Comparative History, 1850–2015*, ed. Andreas Sanders, Pal Sandvik, and Espen Storli, 96–117 (Vancouver: University of British Columbia Press, 2019)). Historical studies on Canadian investments in Latin America are still scant, although there are notable classics such as Duncan McDowall, *The Light: Brazilian Traction, Light, and Power Company Limited, 1899–1945* (Toronto: University of Toronto Press, 1988); and Christopher Armstrong and W. V. Nelles, *Southern Exposure: Canadian Promoters in Latin America and the Caribbean, 1896–1930* (Toronto: University of Toronto Press, 1988). The image of Canadian capital in Latin America as more "neutral" than US capital has been challenged in Todd Gordon and Jeffery Webber, *Blood of Extraction: Canadian Imperialism in Latin America* (Black Point: Fernwood, 2016); and Todd Gordon, *Imperialist Canada* (Winnipeg: Arbeiter Ring, 2010).

convergence of business sectors and the armed forces, as previous valuable contributions had underlined.[37] In this sense, this book builds on previous scholarship that has stressed the importance of avoiding purely political explanations of the Cold War dictatorships in Latin America, to foster instead a more complex understanding of their connections with economic, social, and labor-related dimensions of this history.[38]

Following this path, recent scholarship in Latin America has specifically focused on business "complicity" or "responsibility" in human rights violations during the dictatorships. During the last decade, in the context of academic networks throughout the region becoming consolidated and having links to the processes of memory, truth, and justice, a number of books, research reports, articles, and chapters analyzed the role of economic actors in the Cold War dictatorships in Argentina, Brazil, Chile, and Uruguay, while other contributions investigated the part business played in other processes of repression, such as those that took place in Colombia.[39]

[37] Manuel Barrera and Gonzalo Fallabella (eds.), *Sindicatos bajo regímenes militares. Argentina, Brasil, Chile* (Santiago de Chile: CES-Naciones Unidas, 1990); Paul W. Drake, *Labor Movements and Dictatorships: The Southern Cone in Comparative Perspective* (Baltimore: Johns Hopkins University Press, 1996); Gerardo Munck, *Authoritarianism and Democratization: Soldiers and Workers in Argentina, 1976–1983* (University Park: Pennsylvania State University Press, 1998); and Peter Winn (ed.), *Victims of the Chilean Miracle: Workers and Neoliberalism in the Pinochet Era, 1973–2002* (Durham: Duke University Press, 2004), among many others.

[38] See, for example, Tanya Harmer, "The Cold War in Latin America" in Kalinovsky, Artemy and Daigle, Craig, eds., *The Routledge Handbook of the Cold War* (Abingdon, UK; Routledge, 2014); Victoria Basualdo, "The Argentine Dictatorship and Labor (1976–1983): A Historiographical Essay," *International Labor and Working Class History Journal* 93 (Spring 2018): 8–26; Paulo Fontes, Larissa R. Corrêa, "Labor and Dictatorship in Brazil: A Historiographical Review," *International Labor and Working Class History Journal* 93 (Spring 2018): 27–51; Ángela Vergara, "Writing about Workers, Reflecting on Dictatorship and Neoliberalism: Chilean Labor History and the Pinochet Dictatorship," *International Labor and Working Class History Journal* 93 (Spring 2018): 52–73; Paulo Fontes, Alejandra Esteves, Jean Sales, Larissa Rosa Corrêa, Mundos do Trabalho e Ditaduras no Cone Sul (1964–1990) (Rio de Janeiro, Brasil: Multifoco, 2018).

[39] Horacio Verbitsky and Juan Pablo Bohoslavsky, eds., *The Economic Accomplices of the Argentine Dictatorship: Outstanding Debts* (Cambridge: Cambridge University Press, 2015); AEyT FLACSO, CELS, PVJ and SDH, coord., *Responsabilidad empresarial en delitos de lesa humanidad: Represión de trabajadores durante el terrorismo de estado* (Buenos Aires: Infojus-Ministerio de Justicia, 2015); Juan Pablo Bohoslavsky, ed., *El negocio del terrorismo de estado: Los cómplices económicos de la dictadura uruguaya* (Buenos Aires: Debate, 2016); Nelson Sánchez, Leigh Payne, Gabriel Pereira, Laura Bernal, Daniel Marín, and Miguel Barboza, *Cuentas claras: el papel de la comisión de la verdad en la develación de la responsabilidad de*

The case of Argentina emerges as the most extreme according to the evidence presented in these books, which refer to over 25 cases of large companies actively participating in repression by providing logistical support, funding, vehicles, and key information, while business officials were found to be implicated in kidnappings and even torture; in five of the analyzed cases there were clandestine detention facilities within the factories. Even so, the more scattered and fragmentary evidence on other countries reveals that labor repression was a major feature the dictatorships had in common, and that connections between economic actors and the military forces, while different in each of the cases, were strong.

This line of research is closely related to the evolution of the field of studies on Transitional Justice (TJ), which focuses on responses to mass atrocities and systematic abuses that have devastated societies and left a legacy of fragile political and legal institutions. Such abuses often severely damage the confidence citizens may have had in their state to guarantee their rights and safety.[40] While TJ studies have traditionally focused mainly on the role of the state, scholars now increasingly explore the economic dimensions.[41] This is because, as many of the processes studied show, repression tends in many cases to be a response to demands for greater social justice, or to disaffected groups that feel excluded, with little left to lose. Therefore, patterns of economic inequality and exclusion, and disputes regarding economic, social, and cultural rights, lie behind many conflicts. This is also closely linked to the fact that, once a government has embarked on massive and/or systematic rights violations, it is often armed, financed, informed, or otherwise supported by powerful economic actors.[42] For scholars to take these aspects into account, they must pay

empresas en el conflicto armado colombiano (Bogotá: De Justicia, 2018); Karinna Fernández, Juan Pablo Bohoslavsky and Sebastián Smart, eds., Complicidad económica con la dictadura chilena. Un país desigual a la fuerza (Santiago de Chile: LOM, 2019).

[40] Clara Sandoval, Leonardo Filippini, and Roberto Vidal, "Linking Transitional Justice and Corporate Accountability" in *Corporate Accountability in the Context of Transitional Justice*, ed. Sabine Michalowski (New York: Routledge, 2013).

[41] Leigh A. Payne, Gabriel Pereira, and Laura Bernal-Bermúdez, eds., *Transitional Justice and Corporate Accountability from Below. Deploying Archimedes' Lever* (Cambridge: Cambridge University Press, 2020).

[42] Naomi Roht-Arriaza, "Why Was the Economic Dimension Missing for So Long in Transitional Justice? An Exploratory Essay," in *The Economic Accomplices of the Argentine Dictatorship: Outstanding Debt*, ed. Horacio Verbitsky and Juan Pablo Bohoslavsky, 19–28 (Cambridge: Cambridge University Press, 2015). See also Wolfgang Kaleck, "International Criminal Law and Transnational Businesses: Cases from Argentina and Colombia," in

greater attention to the role of economic actors who were complicit in the violence, or even bore greater responsibility for it. Including corporate complicity in TJ thus implies that we recognize businesses were involved in the systematic and widespread human rights violations carried out by states and quasi-states under dictatorships and during severe civil conflicts.

Recent studies show that mechanisms traditionally associated with TJ—trials and truth commissions—have been used around the world to address corporate complicity, while new kinds of civil trials have been added to the tool kit as a kind of "alternative accountability" instrument. However, it is important not to exaggerate the claims about how far TJ has gone in including corporate complicity globally. A preliminary study of TJ and corporate complicity in 116 countries that transitioned from civil conflict or authoritarian rule since 1970 reveals that only seventeen have addressed corporate complicity.[43] These seventeen countries represent all of the regions of the world, suggesting that these innovations may be spreading. Moreover, it is interesting to note that non-judicial mechanisms, particularly truth commissions, have been used in several countries, while judicial mechanisms have also expanded. The use of trials as a TJ mechanism has tended to involve criminal prosecutions. In the case of corporate complicity, however, civil trials have outnumbered criminal trials, and the use of this nontraditional TJ mechanism is observed in both transnational and domestic litigation. The most common use has been in foreign civil trials against businesses. Of these, nearly all (thirty-three of thirty-nine cases) were advanced under the Alien Tort Statute (ATS), which allows foreign citizens to seek justice in US courts for violations committed outside the United States. This is currently under pressure for reform in many states seeking to limit it. Indeed, more than half of all criminal and civil trials studied in this database (54 percent) are involved the ATS.[44]

Corporate Accountability in the Context of Transitional Justice, ed. Sabine Michalowski (New York: Routledge, 2013); and Leigh A. Payne and Gabriel Pereira, "Corporate Complicity in International Human Rights Violations," *Annual Review of Law and Social Science* 12 (October 2016): 63–84.

[43] Leigh A. Payne and Gabriel Pereira, "Accountability for Corporate Complicity in Human Rights Violations: Argentina's Transitional Justice Innovation?" in *The Economic Accomplices of the Argentine Dictatorship: Outstanding Debts*, ed. Horacio Verbitsky and Juan Pablo Bohoslavsky, 29–45 (Cambridge: Cambridge University Press, 2015).

[44] Payne and Pereira, "Accountability for Corporate Complicity," 32–33. The first case brought under the ATS for human rights abuses was Filartiga v. Peña-Irala. In 1976, the father of a young man who had been tortured and killed in Paraguay while in police custody witnessed one of his son's torturers walking the streets of Manhattan. The father called the

The Latin American region has played a most relevant role, particularly in the judicial cases heard in domestic courts, which comprised 36 percent of the total. Argentina, particularly in addressing the human rights violations perpetrated during the 1976–1983 dictatorship, has been the leader in this; the case of Ford, analyzed in chapter 8, is one example. According to these studies, Argentina has gone farther than any other country in its innovations concerning Transitional Justice. Thus, it should not be surprising that Argentina's TJ tool kit includes corporate complicity, particularly considering the extreme cases academics and legal practitioners have documented. In Payne and Pereira's preliminary investigation of corporate complicity cases around the world, 64 percent of all criminal cases and nearly a third of all criminal and civil cases (31 percent) are from Argentina, where the law is being used creatively to hold businesses accountable for their complicity in human rights abuses during the dictatorial period.[45]

These developments in Transitional Justice are, in turn, also connected to the growing international discussion regarding business and human rights violations. In the context of increasing globalization and economic concentration, and the expansion of outsourcing to countries with limited labor rights and unionization, companies have wielded increasing power over economic, social, and political events within national territories and globally. There have been many responses aiming to adapt to this burgeoning influence, including the adoption of codes of business conduct (some of which were already in place in the Cold War context), numerous business and human rights guidelines issued by the United Nations (UN), reports by non-governmental organizations, an expanding body of academic research, and a series of court actions at the national level.[46] A rather

INS, who arrested the former Paraguayan officer for overstaying his visitor's visa. The father and sister then brought an ATS case against the officer, and in 1980, a US federal court in New York upheld their claims, opening the door for future claims under the Alien Tort Statute. Beginning in the mid-1990s, a new class of ATS suits emerged that aimed to hold multinational corporations accountable for complicity in human rights abuses. Although certain sectors of the business community criticized this use of the ATS, attempts to repeal the statute have not succeeded. As of 2009, two corporate accountability cases—*Doe v. Unocal* and *Wiwa v. Shell*—have resulted in settlements with reparations to the survivors and their communities playing an important role. To date, however, no contested corporate ATS case has resulted in a jury verdict in favor of the plaintiffs.

[45] Payne and Pereira, "Accountability for Corporate Complicity," 35–36.

[46] See, for example, United Nations, Declaration on the Establishment of a New International Economic Order, G.A. Res. 3201, UN GAOR, sixth special session, Supp. (No. 1), at 527/8, UN Doc. A/9559 (1974); E.S.C. Res. 1913, UN ESCOR, 57th session,

significant step in this direction was the 2008 publication of a report by the International Commission of Jurists, which contained the conclusions of a panel composed of eight expert jurists on Corporate Complicity in International Crimes.[47] This report, published in three volumes, highlights the responsibility companies bear in providing support for gross human rights violations by enabling, facilitating, or exacerbating the commission of such crimes. With a long-term historical perspective, it recalls the role of the senior company officials convicted of actively helping the Nazi regime to commit some of the worst crimes imaginable, juxtaposing them with more recent reports of business participation in gross human rights abuses across the world. The panel members state that, according to reports based on a wide range of sources, companies knowingly assisted governments, armed rebel groups, or para-military groups to commit gross human rights abuses. Oil and mining companies that seek concessions and security were accused of giving money, weapons, vehicles, and air support that government military forces or rebel groups used to attack, kill, and make civilians "disappear." Private air service operators were reportedly an essential part of government programs of extraordinary and illegal renditions of terrorist suspects across frontiers. Private security companies were accused of colluding with government security agencies to inflict torture in detention centers they jointly operated. Companies reportedly gave information that enabled governments to detain and torture trade unionists or other perceived political opponents. Companies allegedly sold both tailor-made computer equipment so that governments could track and discriminate against minorities and earth-moving equipment used to demolish houses in violation of international law. Others were accused of propping up rebel groups that committed gross human rights abuses by buying conflict diamonds, while some allegedly encouraged child labor and sweatshop conditions by demanding that suppliers deliver goods at ever cheaper prices. In this way, the report's careful work of conceptualization and legal analysis draws on historical processes and

Supp. (No. 1), UN Doc. 5570/Add 1 (1975). For an extensive list of cases in Latin America, Canada, and the United States, see Christopher Hutto and Anjela Jenkins, "Report on Corporate Complicity Litigation in the Americas: Leading Doctrines, Relevant Cases, and Analysis of Trends," in *Human Rights Clinic* (Austin: University of Texas, 2010).

[47] International Commission of Jurists, *Corporate Complicity and Legal Accountability: Report of the International Commission of Jurists Expert Legal Panel on Corporate Complicity in International Crimes*, Vols. 1, 2, and 3 (Geneva: ICJ, 2008).

case studies to produce a useful typology for classifying, describing, and prosecuting the different kinds of business involvement.

Turning now to the present collection, we recognize that it has its limitations, but we view these as research opportunities. First, we focus on the Cold War period, but it is clear that there were several authoritarian regimes for the pre-World War II era that are worth studying. Second, some regimes that held regular elections can barely be classified as "democracies"; this was the case in Mexico under the seventy-year uninterrupted rule of the Partido Revolucionario Institucional (PRI), or what Peruvian novelist Mario Vargas Llosa called "the perfect dictatorship."[48] That the Paraguayan dictatorship of Alfredo Stroessner is not included is clearly a great gap in this volume, as is the long regime of Rafael Leonidas Trujillo in the Dominican Republic, the Duvalier dynasty in Haiti, the Marcos Pérez Jiménez dictatorship in Venezuela, and the several short-lived military regimes in Bolivia. Third, in using the phrase "big capital," we refer only to "legal" capital. However, we cannot deny the enormous and increasing level of political influence of illegal cocaine export groups in the whole continent, particularly after the 1990s. Not only have these groups seen their power grow, but they have also undermined democratic institutions. All these processes and cases clearly deserve attention, and we hope future contributions will expand our knowledge.

Since the beginning of this journey in Göttingen, we have accumulated a number of debts of gratitude. We want to thank Uwe Spiekermann and Jan Logemann for their comments. This volume also benefited from discussions with and comments expressed during the 2016 conference by Antoine Acker, Edward Brudney, Janaina Ferreira dos Santos, Christine Hatzky, Christian Helm, Claudia Müller-Hoff, and Eyal Weinberg. Our special thanks go to Manfred Grieger, who was Volkswagen's chief historian until 2016 when he was ousted by Volkswagen shortly after the conference in November 2016.[49] We are grateful for his enthusiasm in

[48] "Vargas Llosa: México es la dictadura perfecta," *El País*, September 1 (1990). Online edition: URL: https://elpais.com/diario/1990/09/01/cultura/652140001_850215.html (accessed February 26, 2020).

[49] Manfred Grieger had built up Volkswagen's corporate archives and pioneered an exemplary and much-lauded style of corporate history. On the end of his tenure at Volkswagen, see Alison Smale and Jack Ewing, "Volkswagen Parts Ways With the Historian Who Chronicled Its Nazi Past," *New York Times*, Nov. 2, 2016. His departure from Volkswagen was accompanied by a signature list signed in protest by a large number of historians. For their names, see https://www.hsozkult.de/text/id/texte-3936 (accessed March 9, 2020).

organizing the conference that put this volume into motion, as well as for his constructive comments and generous support of this project. We are thankful for the support Palgrave editors Juan Santarcángelo and Elizabeth Graber gave to this project and editorial assistant Sophia Siegler. We also wish to thank Casey Sutcliffe for her meticulous editorial work and assistants Daniella Sánchez Russo and Sebastián Figueroa.

References

AEyT FLACSO, CELS, PVJ, and SDH, eds. *Responsabilidad empresarial en delitos de lesa humanidad: Represión de trabajadores durante el terrorismo de estado.* Buenos Aires: Infojus-Ministerio de Justicia, 2015.

Altamura, Carlo E. "Global Banks and Latin American Dictators." *Business History Review* (2020): 1–32. https://doi.org/10.1017/S0007680519001260

Armstrong, Christopher, and W. V. Nelles. *Southern Exposure: Canadian Promoters in Latin America and the Caribbean, 1896–1930.* Toronto: University of Toronto Press, 1988.

Barrera, Manuel, and Gonzalo Fallabella, eds. *Sindicatos bajo regímenes militares. Argentina, Brasil, Chile.* Santiago de Chile: CES-Naciones Unidas, 1990.

Basualdo, Victoria. "The Argentine Dictatorship and Labor (1976–1983): A Historiographical Essay." *International Labor and Working Class History Journal* 93 (Spring 2018): 8–26.

Berg, Manfred, and Bernd Schäfer, eds. *Historical Justice in International Perspective: How Societies Are Trying to Right the Wrongs of the Past.* Cambridge: Cambridge University Press, 2009.

Berghoff, Hartmut. "Zwischen Verdrängung und Aufarbeitung. Die bundesdeutsche Gesellschaft und ihre nationalsozialistische Vergangenheit in den Fünfziger Jahren." *Geschichte in Wissenschaft und Unterricht* 49, no. 2 (1998): 96–114.

Berghoff, Hartmut, and Cornelia Rauh. *The Respectable Career of Fritz K: The Making and Remaking of a Provincial Nazi Leader.* Oxford: Berghahn Books, 2015.

Berghoff, Hartmut, Jürgen Kocka, and Dieter Ziegler, eds. *Business in the Age of Extremes: Essays in Modern German and Austrian Economic History.* Cambridge: Cambridge University Press, 2013.

Betancourt, Rómulo. *Venezuela: Oil and Politics.* Boston: Houghton Mifflin, 1978.

Bodenheimer, Susanne. "Dependency and Imperialism: The Roots of Latin American Underdevelopment." *Politics and Society* 1, no. 3 (1971): 327–357.

Bohoslavsky, Juan Pablo, ed. *El negocio del terrorismo de estado: Los cómplices económicos de la dictadura uruguaya.* Buenos Aires: Debate, 2016.

Bortz, Jeffrey, and Stephen Haber, eds. *The Mexican Economy, 1870–1930: Essays on the Economic History of Institutions, Revolution, and Growth.* Stanford: Stanford University Press, 2002.

Bucheli, Marcelo. "Canadian Multinational Corporations and Economic Nationalism: The Case of Imperial Oil Limited in Alberta (Canada) and Colombia, 1899–1938." *Entreprises et Histoire* 54 (2009): 67–85.

Bucheli, Marcelo. "Multinational Corporations, Business Groups, and Economic Nationalism: Standard Oil (New Jersey), Royal Dutch-Shell, and Energy Politics in Chile, 1913–2005." *Enterprise and Society* 11, no. 2 (2010): 350–399.

Bucheli, Marcelo. "Multinational Corporations, Totalitarian Regimes, and Economic Nationalism: United Fruit Company in Central America, 1899–1975." *Business History* 50, no. 4 (2008): 433–454.

Bucheli, Marcelo. "National Oil Companies and Political Coalitions: Venezuela and Colombia, 1910–76." In *The Political Economy of Resource Regulation: An International and Comparative History, 1850–2015*, edited by Andreas Sanders, Pal Sandvik, and Espen Storli, 96–117. Vancouver: University of British Columbia Press, 2019.

Bucheli, Marcelo. *Bananas and Business: The United Fruit Company in Colombia, 1899–2000.* New York: New York University Press, 2005.

Bucheli, Marcelo, and Erica Salvaj. "Political Connections, the Liability of Foreignness, and Legitimacy: A Business Historical Analysis of Multinationals' Strategies in Chile." *Global Strategy Journal* 8, no. 3 (2018): 399–420.

Bucheli, Marcelo, and Erica Salvaj. "Reputation and Political Legitimacy: ITT in Chile, 1927–1972." *Business History Review* 87, no. 4 (2013): 729–756.

Bucheli, Marcelo, and Gonzalo Romero Sommer. "Multinational Corporations, Property Rights, and Legitimization Strategies: US Investors in the Argentine and Peruvian Oil Industries." *Australian Economic History Review* 54, no. 2 (2014): 146–164.

Bucheli, Marcelo, and Jin Uk Kim. "The State as a Historical Construct in Organization Studies." In *Organizations in Time: History, Theory, Methods*, edited by Marcelo Bucheli and R. Daniel Wadhwani 241–262. Oxford: Oxford University Press, 2014.

Bucheli, Marcelo, and R. Daniel Wadhwani, eds. *Organizations in Time: History, Theory, Methods.* Oxford: Oxford University Press, 2014.

Cardoso, Fernando H., and Enzo Faletto. *Dependency and Development in Latin America.* Berkeley: University of California Press, 1979.

Dimitrov, Georgi. "The Fascist Offensive and the Tasks of the Communist International," (Main Report delivered at the Seventh World Congress of the Communist International). In The United Front. The Struggle Against Fascism and War, edited by Georgi Dimitrov, 1–72. London: Lawrence and Wishart, 1938.

Dos Santos, Theotonio. "The Structure of Development." *American Economic Review* 60, no. 2 (1970): 231–236.

Dos Santos, Theotonio. *Imperialismo y Dependencia*. Mexico City: Era, 1978.

Drake, Paul W. *Labor Movements and Dictatorships: The Southern Cone in Comparative Perspective*. Baltimore: Johns Hopkins University Press, 1996.

Eberhard Czichon. *Wer verhalf Hitler zur Macht? Zum Anteil der Deutschen Industrie an der Zerstörung der Weimarer Republik*. Cologne: Pahl-Rugenstein, 1967.

Edwin, Black. "Hitler's Carmaker: The Inside Story of How General Motors Helped Mobilize the Third Reich," *Global Research*, Oct. 1 (2018). https://www.globalresearch.ca/hitler-s-carmaker-the-inside-story-of-how-general-motors-helped-mobilize-the-third-reich/5571 Accessed May 11 2020.

Evans, Peter. *Dependent Development: The Alliance of Multinational, State, and Local Capital in Brazil*. Princeton: Princeton University Press, 1979.

Evans, Richard J. *The Coming of the Third Reich*, 78–138. London: Penguin, 2003.

Evans, Richard J. *The Third Reich in Power 1933–1939*. London: Penguin, 2005.

Feldman, Gerald D. *Allianz and the German Insurance Business, 1933–1945*. Cambridge: Cambridge University Press, 2001.

Fernández, Karinna, Juan Pablo Bohoslavsky, and Sebastián Smart, eds. *Complicidad económica con la dictadura chilena. Un país desigual a la fuerza*. Santiago de Chile: LOM, 2019.

Fontes, Paulo, Alejandra Esteves, Jean Sales, and Larissa Rosa Corrêa. *Mundos do Trabalho e Ditaduras no Cone Sul (1964–1990)*. Rio de Janeiro, Brasil: Multifoco, 2018.

Fontes, Paulo, Larissa R. Corrêa. "Labor and Dictatorship in Brazil: A Historiographical Review." *International Labor and Working Class History Journal* 93 (Spring 2018): 27–51.

Frei, Norbert. *Adenauer's Germany and the Nazi Past: The Politics of Amnesty and Integration*. New York: Columbia University Press, 2002.

Garner, Paul. *British Lions and Mexican Eagles: Business, Politics, and Empire in the Career of Weetman Pearson in Mexico, 1889–1919*. Stanford: Stanford University Press, 2011.

Gereffi, Gary, and Peter Evans. "Transnational Corporations, Dependent Development, and State Policy in the Semiperiphery: A Comparison of Brazil and Mexico." *Latin American Research Review* 16, no. 3 (1981): 31–64.

Gordon, Todd. *Imperialist Canada*. Winnipeg: Arbeiter Ring, 2010.

Gordon, Todd, and Jeffery Webber. *Blood of Extraction: Canadian Imperialism in Latin America*. Black Point: Fernwood, 2016.

Grieger, Manfred. "Extermination and Work under the Nazi System of Forced Labor." In *Forced Labor: The Germans, the Forced Laborers, and the War*, edited by Volkhard Knigge, Rikola-Gunnar Lüttgenau, and Jens-Christian Wagner,

208–220. Weimar: Stiftung Gedenkstätten Buchenwald und Mittelbau-Dora, 2010.

Grosfoguel, Ramón. "The Epistemic Decolonial Turn: Beyond Political-Economy Paradigms." *Cultural Studies* 2, nos. 2–3 (2007): 211–223.

Haber, Stephen. "Introduction: Economic Growth and Latin American Economic Historiography." In *How Latin America Fell Behind: Essays on the Economic Histories of Brazil and Mexico, 1800–1914*, edited by Stephen Haber, 1–33. Stanford: Stanford University Press, 1997.

Haber, Stephen. "The Political Economy of Industrialization." In *The Cambridge Economic History of Latin America*, edited by Victor Bulmer-Thomas, John Coatsworth and Roberto Cortés-Conde, 537–584. Cambridge: Cambridge University Press, 2006.

Haber, Stephen, Armando Razo, and Noel Maurer. *The Politics of Property Rights: Political Instability, Credible Commitments, and Economic Growth in Mexico, 1876–1929.* Cambridge: Cambridge University Press, 2003.

Haber, Stephen, ed. *Crony Capitalism and Economic Growth in Latin America: Theory and Evidence.* Stanford: Stanford University Press, 2002.

Halperín-Donghi, Tulio. "Dependency Theory' and Latin American Historiography." *Latin American Research Review* 17, no. 1 (1982): 115–130.

Harmer, Tanya. "The Cold War in Latin America." In *The Routledge Handbook of the Cold War*, edited by Artemy Kalinovsky and Craig Daigle. Abingdon, UK; Routledge, 2014.

Hayes, Peter. *From Cooperation to Complicity: Degussa in the Third Reich.* Cambridge: Cambridge University Press, 2006.

Herbert, Ulrich. *Hitler's Foreign Workers: Enforced Foreign Labor in Germany under the Third Reich.* Cambridge: Cambridge University Press, 2006.

Huntington, Samuel. *The Third Wave: Democratization in the Late Twentieth Century.* Norman: University of Oklahoma Press, 1991.

Hutto, Christopher, and Anjela Jenkins. "Report on Corporate Complicity Litigation in the Americas: Leading Doctrines, Relevant Cases, and Analysis of Trends." In *Human Rights Clinic*, edited by, Christopher Hutto and Anjela Jenkins, 1–49. Austin: University of Texas, 2010.

International Commission of Jurists. *Corporate Complicity and Legal Accountability: Report of the International Commission of Jurists Expert Legal Panel on Corporate Complicity in International Crimes*, Vols. 1, 2, and 3. Geneva: ICJ, 2008.

James, Harold, and Jakob Tanner, eds. *Enterprise in the Period of Fascism in Europe.* Aldershot: Routledge, 2002.

James, Harold. *The Deutsche Bank and the Nazi Economic War against the Jews: The Expropriation of Jewish-Owned Property.* Cambridge: Cambridge University Press, 2001.

Kaienburg, Hermann, ed. *Konzentrationslager und Deutsche Wirtschaft 1939–1945*. Opladen: Leske & Budrich, 1996.

Kaleck, Wolfgang. "International Criminal Law and Transnational Businesses: Cases from Argentina and Colombia." In *Corporate Accountability in the Context of Transitional Justice*, edited by Sabine Michalowski, 174–188. New York: Routledge, 2013.

Kershaw, Ian. *The Nazi Dictatorship: Problems and Perspectives of Interpretation*. 4th ed. London: Arnold, 2000.

Lanciotti, Norma S., and Andrea Lluch. *Las empresas extranjeras en la Argentina: Del siglo XIX al siglo XXI*. Buenos Aires: Imago Mundi, 2018.

Lanciotti, Norma S. "Foreign Investments in Electric Utilities: A Comparative Analysis of Belgian and American Companies in Argentina, 1890–1960." *Business History Review* 82, no. 3 (2008): 503–528.

Lanciotti, Norma S. "From a Guaranteeing State to an Entrepreneurial State: The Relationship Between Argentina's State and Urban Utility Companies, 1880–1955." In *The Impact of Globalization on Argentina and Chile: Business Enterprises and Entrepreneurship*, edited by Geoffrey Jones and Andrea Lluch, 182–214. Cheltenham: Edward Elgar, 2015.

Link, Stephan. "Rethinking the Ford-Nazi Connection." *Bulletin of the German Historical Institute* 49, no. 2 (2011): 135–50.

Maurer, Noel. *The Power and the Money: The Mexican Financial System, 1876–1932*. Stanford: Stanford University Press, 2002.

Mazower, Mark. *Hitler's Empire: How the Nazis Ruled Europe*, 294–318. New York: Penguin Press, 2010.

McBeth, Brian. *La política petrolera venezolana: una perspectiva histórica*. Caracas: Universidad Metropolitana, 2015.

McDowall, Duncan. *The Light: Brazilian Traction, Light, and Power Company Limited, 1899–1945*. Toronto: University of Toronto Press, 1988.

Miller, Rory. *Britain in Latin America in the Nineteenth and Twentieth Centuries*. New York: Routledge, 1993.

Miller, Rory. *Dictatorship and Politics: Intrigue, Betrayal, and Survival in Venezuela, 1908–1935*. South Bend: University of Notre Dame Press, 2008.

Miller, Rory. *Juan Vicente Gómez and the Oil Companies in Venezuela, 1908–1935*. Cambridge: Cambridge University Press, 2002.

Mollin, Gerhard Thomas. *Montankonzerne und "Drittes Reich": Der Gegensatz zwischen Monopolindustrie und Befehlswirtschaft in der deutschen Rüstung und Expansion 1936 – 1944*. Göttingen: Vandenhoeck & Ruprecht, 1988.

Mommsen, Hans, and Manfred Grieger. *Das Volkswagenwerk und seine Arbeiter im Dritten Reich*. Düsseldorf: Econ, 1996.

Müller, Rolf-Dieter. *Hitler's Wehrmacht, 1935–1945*. Lexington: University Press of Kentucky, 2016.

Munck, Gerardo. *Authoritarianism and Democratization: Soldiers and Workers in Argentina, 1976–1983.* University Park: Pennsylvania State University Press, 1998.

Nicosia, Francis R., and Jonathan Huener, eds. *Business and Industry in Nazi Germany.* New York: Berghahn, 2004.

O'Donnell, Guillermo. *El Estado Burocrático Autoritario: 1966–1973.* Buenos Aires: Belgrano, 1982.

Osterloh, Jörg. "Die Monopole und ihre Herren. Marxistische Interpretationen." In *Unternehmen im Nationalsozialismus. Zur Historisierung einer Forschungskonjunktur*, edited by Norbert Frei and Tim Schanetzky, 36–47. Göttingen: Wallstein, 2010.

Overy, Richard J. *War and Economy in the Third Reich,* 93–174. Oxford: Oxford University Press, 1995.

Packenham, Robert. *The Dependency Movement: Scholarship and Politics in Development Studies.* Cambridge: Harvard University Press, 1992.

Parra Luzardo, Gastón. *El desafío del cartel petrolero.* Maracaibo: Universidad de Zulia, 1981.

Payne, Leigh A., and Gabriel Pereira. "Accountability for Corporate Complicity in Human Rights Violations: Argentina's Transitional Justice Innovation?" In *The Economic Accomplices of the Argentine Dictatorship: Outstanding Debts*, edited by Horacio Verbitsky and Juan Pablo Bohoslavsky, 29–45. Cambridge: Cambridge University Press, 2015.

Payne,Leigh A., Gabriel Pereira, and Laura Bernal-Bermúdez, eds., Transitional Justice and Corporate Accountability from Below. Deploying Archimedes' Lever. Cambridge: Cambridge University Press, 2020.

Payne, Leigh A., and Gabriel Pereira. "Corporate Complicity in International Human Rights Violations." *Annual Review of Law and Social Science* 12 (October 2016): 63–84.

Pineda, Yovanna. *Industrial Development in a Frontier Economy: The Industrialization of Argentina, 1890–1930.* Stanford: Stanford University Press, 2009.

Platt, D. C. M. "Dependency in the Nineteenth Century in Latin America: A Historian Objects." *Latin American Research Review* 15, no. 1 (1980): 113–130.

Platt, D. C. M. *Business Imperialism, 1840–1930: An Inquiry Based on British Experience in Latin America.* Oxford: Clarendon, 1977.

Qureshi, Lubna. *Nixon, Kissinger, and Allende: U.S. Involvement in the 1973 Coup in Chile.* New York: Rowman & Littlefield, 2009.

Research Services of the German Parliament. *Report on the Alleged Cooperation of US-Corporation with the NS-Regime* (WD 1 – 134/07). Berlin, 2007.

Roht-Arriaza, Naomi. "Why Was the Economic Dimension Missing for So Long in Transitional Justice? An Exploratory Essay." In *The Economic Accomplices of the Argentine Dictatorship: Outstanding Debt*, edited by Horacio Verbitsky and Juan Pablo Bohoslavsky, 19–28. Cambridge: Cambridge University Press, 2015.

Sánchez, Nelson, Leigh Payne, Gabriel Pereira, Laura Bernal, Daniel Marín, and Miguel Barboza. *Cuentas claras: el papel de la comisión de la verdad en la develación de la responsabilidad de empresas en el conflicto armado colombiano.* Bogotá: De Justicia, 2018.

Sandoval, Clara, Leonardo Filippini, and Roberto Vidal. "Linking Transitional Justice and Corporate Accountability." In *Corporate Accountability in the Context of Transitional Justice*, edited by Sabine Michalowski, 9–26. New York: Routledge, 2013.

Schlesinger, Stephen, and Stephen Kinzer. *Bitter Fruit: The Story of the American Coup in Guatemala.* Cambridge: Harvard University Press, 2005.

Silverstein, Ken. "Ford, and the Führer." *The Nation,* January 6, 2000.

Simon Reich. *The Fruits of Fascism: Postwar Prosperity in Historical Perspective,* 107–145. Ithaca: Cornell Univ. Press, 1990.

Smale, Alison, and Jack Ewing. "Volkswagen Parts Ways With the Historian Who Chronicled Its Nazi Past." *New York Times,* November 2, 2016.

Spoerer, Mark. "Forced Labour in Nazi-Occupied Europe, 1939–1945." In *Economies under Occupation: The Hegemony of Nazi Germany and Imperial Japan in World War II,* edited by Marcel Boldforf and Tetsuji Okazaki, 73–85. London: Routledge, 2015.

Spoerer, Mark. *Zwangsarbeit unter dem Hakenkreuz. Ausländische Zivilarbeiter, Kriegsgefangene und Häftlinge im Deutschen Reich und im besetzten Europa 1939–1945.* Stuttgart: DVA, 2001.

Summerhill, William R. *Inglorious Revolution: Political Institutions, Sovereign Debt, and Financial Underdevelopment in Imperial Brazil.* New Haven: Yale University Press, 2015.

Tooze, Adam J. *The Wages of Destruction: The Making and Breaking of the Nazi Economy.* London: Penguin, 2006.

Tugwell, Franklin. *The Politics of Oil in Venezuela.* Stanford: Stanford University Press, 1975.

Turner, Henry Ashby. "Big Business and the Rise of Hitler." *American Historical Review* 75, no. 1 (1969): 56–70.

Turner, Henry Ashby. *General Motors and the Nazis: The Struggle for Control of Opel, Europe's Biggest Carmaker.* New Haven: Yale Univ. Press, 2005.

Turner, Henry Ashby. *German Big Business and the Rise of Hitler.* Oxford: Oxford Univ. Press, 1987.

United Nations. Declaration on the Establishment of a New International Economic Order. G.A. Res. 3201, UN GAOR, sixth special session, Supp. (No. 1), at 527/8, UN Doc. A/9559 (1974); E.S.C. Res. 1913, UN ESCOR, 57th session, Supp. (No. 1), UN Doc. 5570/Add 1 (1975). https://digitallibrary.un.org/record/218450?ln=en

"Vargas Llosa: México es la dictadura perfecta." *El País,* September 1 (1990). Accessed February 26, 2020. https://elpais.com/diario/1990/09/01/cultura/652140001_850215.html

Verbitsky, Horacio, and Juan Pablo Bohoslavsky, eds. *The Economic Accomplices of the Argentine Dictatorship: Outstanding Debts.* Cambridge: Cambridge University Press, 2015.

Vergara, Ángela. "Writing about Workers, Reflecting on Dictatorship and Neoliberalism: Chilean Labor History and the Pinochet Dictatorship." *International Labor and Working Class History Journal* 93 (Spring 2018): 52–73.

Vogelsang, Reinhard. *Der Freundeskreis Himmler.* Göttingen: Muster-Schmidt Verlag, 1972.

Weitz, Eric D. *Weimar Germany: Promise and Tragedy,* 129–168. Princeton: Princeton University Press, 2007.

Winn, Peter, ed. *Victims of the Chilean Miracle: Workers and Neoliberalism in the Pinochet Era, 1973–2002.* Durham: Duke University Press, 2004.

CHAPTER 2

Business and the Military in the Argentine Dictatorship (1976–1983): Institutional, Economic, and Repressive Relations

Victoria Basualdo

The military coup on March 24, 1976, marked the beginning of the most repressive period in the history of Argentina and consolidated the country's transition from having an economic model in which the industrial sector played a leading role to having a model of financial valorization, growth of external debt, and profound industrial restructuring. This transition transformed not only the economic but also the social structure of the country. This chapter analyzes relationships between sectors of the business community and the military in Argentina from 1976 to 1983 within the crucial framework of the structural economic and social transformations implemented from the mid-1970s onward. It highlights the intellectual and institutional relations between the military and big business, including their economic and financial relations, as important companies and economic groups obtained benefits by means of various

V. Basualdo (✉)
Area of Economics and Technology, Facultad Latinoamericana de Ciencias, Sociales-CONICET, Buenos Aires, Argentina

V. Basualdo et al. (eds.), *Big Business and Dictatorships in Latin America*, Palgrave Studies in Latin American Heterodox Economics, https://doi.org/10.1007/978-3-030-43925-5_2

forms of state funding and their common involvement in repressive policies, particularly against workers and trade unionists.

The 1976–1983 Dictatorship in Argentina

Ever since the coup, the 1976–1983 dictatorship was headed by a military junta composed of General Jorge Rafael Videla, Admiral Emilio Massera, and Brigadier Orlando Ramón Agosti. This coup was one in a series of military coups that had taken place in Argentina beginning in 1930. Since the military coup that overthrew Juan Domingo Perón in 1955, the political system had been particularly unstable because even democratically elected governments operated in a system that banned the Justicialist Party, whose leader, Perón, had been forced to leave the country. However, the 1976–1983 dictatorship, while undoubtedly part of a longer process of the expansion of the National Security Doctrine in Latin America, is considered a watershed in Argentine history. The military junta established a terrorist state with a dramatic record of violence and human rights violations: nearly 30,000 people disappeared and thousands were imprisoned for political reasons, while many others were tortured, murdered, or exiled; their personal property seized; and, in hundreds of cases, the children of those who disappeared were kidnapped. These extreme human rights violations were investigated after a democratic government was elected by the CONADEP (National Commission on the Disappeared) in 1984, and then began to be prosecuted in the so-called Juntas Trial in 1985. This trial determined which crimes some military leaders were responsible for and convicted them.[1] In 1986–1987, new laws in Argentina restricted the scope and timing of the criminal trials concerning these human rights violations (called "Full Stop" and "Due Obedience" laws), and in 1989–1990 President Carlos Menem issued executive pardons in an attempt to promote "reconciliation" at the expense of justice. It was only in 2005 that the Supreme Court ruled the 1986–1987 laws unconstitutional and reopened the criminal trials to prosecute the crimes against humanity without time limits or restrictions on scope. These trials continue to this day.

The historiography about this dictatorship is vast and rich, shedding light on many of its significant features. Increasingly, historians have begun to reveal the tensions and contradictions within factions of the armed forces and to debate the role different sectors of civil society played during

[1] Emilio Crenzel, *The Memory of the Argentina Disappearances: The Political History of Nunca Más* (New York: Routledge, 2017).

the period. This chapter, due to space limitations, will only focus on summarizing some of the most recent findings related to the role of big business during the dictatorship. From an economic perspective, it could be argued that the 1976 coup ended a phase of ever greater conflict between rival projects of economic, political, and social organizations that had been in discussion since 1955. Labor historians have emphasized that in the late 1960s and early 1970s, Argentina had one of the strongest and most powerful union movements in Latin America, with the industrial working class, which had grown constantly since the 1930s, at its core. Workers in the most dynamic industrial activities, such as the steel, automobile, and chemical industries, together with those from other labor organizations, such as the Light and Power Union, increasingly agitated for political representation and a just income distribution. In this Latin American context, the Cuban Revolution, the process of decolonization, and the wave of urban protests in the late 1960s were influential to the labor movement. This became clear in social upheavals such as the "Cordobazo," which labor organizations and students in the industrial city of Córdoba led against the dictatorship headed by General Juan Carlos Onganía in 1966.[2] This marked a peak in a series of mass mobilizations in different cities across the country. It was followed by the so-called Viborazo in Córdoba in 1971, among many others. This process prompted the call for presidential elections in 1973, and while the military prohibited Perón himself from running, the Peronist candidate Héctor Cámpora was elected president. Once in office, he called for new elections without proscriptions, and Juan Domingo Perón was elected president with nearly 62 percent of the votes. When he died on July 1, 1974, his wife and vice-president María Estela Martínez de Perón succeeded him at a turbulent time of political upheaval and social confrontation. The armed forces also got increasingly involved in different operations throughout the country, the most extreme of which was the "Independence Operation," a military campaign in the province of Tucumán against guerrilla organizations but also political and labor activism. This campaign anticipated the brutal repressive practices

[2] James Brennan, *The Labor Wars in Cordoba, 1955–1976: Ideology, Work, and Labor Politics in an Argentine Industrial Society* (Boston: Harvard University Press, 1998); Daniel James, *Resistance and Integration: Peronism and the Argentine Working Class, 1946–1976* (Cambridge: Cambridge University Press, 1988); Alejandro Schneider, *Los compañeros. Trabajadores, izquierda y peronismo, 1955–1973* (Buenos Aires: Imago Mundi, 2007).

that would be extended to the whole national territory from March 24, 1976, onward.

The Argentine regime combined this policy of repression with strong economic and labor policies in the context of significant international changes related to the oil crisis and the transition from Fordism to post-Fordism. More and more, this transition fostered the end of import substitution industrialization in Latin America. Meanwhile, the Argentine dictatorship promoted increasing commercial openness and financial liberalization from 1976, reducing the industrial sector's participation in the economy and encouraging the establishment of a new economic model, with financial activity playing a dominant role. The state imposed these economic transformations utilizing terror and control, significantly restricting or eliminating labor rights. Labor, economic, and repressive policies were closely interrelated and influenced each other, drastically transforming the situation of workers and unions.[3] The armed forces deployed military personnel to control the General Confederation of Labor (Confederación General del Trabajo, CGT) and many significant trade-union organizations. Wage bargaining, the right to strike, and all other labor actions were suspended indefinitely; trade-union privileges were eliminated; dismissal without cause was authorized for state employees; military supervisors were appointed to control the leading trade-union organizations; the Ministry of Education was authorized to suspend the application of the Teachers' Statute; and the Residence Act was reintroduced, enabling anyone suspected of anti-national security activities to be expelled from the country.[4] The methods for disciplining industrial workers, who formed the dynamic core of the working class, were particularly brutal. Not only were they repressed and denied their most basic social rights, but their livelihoods were directly affected by the systematic downsizing of employment in manufacturing. Industrial employment dropped steadily over twenty-seven consecutive quarters (from the second quarter

[3] For a recent appraisal of the expansion of this field of studies in Argentina, see Victoria Basualdo, "The Argentine Dictatorship and Labor (1976–1983): A Historiographical Essay," *International Labor and Working Class History Journal* 93 (Spring 2018): 8–26.

[4] Victoria Basualdo, Ivonne Barragán, and Florencia Rodríguez, *La clase trabajadora durante la última dictadura militar argentina (1976–1983). Apuntes para una discusión de la "resistencia" obrera* (La Plata: Comisión Provincial por la Memoria, 2010); Héctor Recalde, "Suppression of Workers Rights," in *The Economic Accomplices to the Argentine Dictatorship: Outstanding Debts*, ed. Horacio Verbitsky and Juan Pablo Bohoslavsky (Cambridge: Cambridge University Press, 2016).

of 1976 to the fourth quarter of 1982), even as an increase in labor intensity significantly raised productivity.

Despite the severe implications these policies had for the industrial working class and the trade-union movement, different social and political actors and sectors of the labor movement protested them.[5] During the first years of the dictatorship, all forms of mass organization and protest were harshly repressed, yet even in these conditions both underground activities and strikes and protests developed in the factories. From 1979 onward, a relative slowdown in repression coincided with more visible opposition, with the national day of protest in April of that year being one salient example. This was the first mass demonstration of national importance, after which several labor leaders were arrested, with international repercussions.[6] Another way laborers opposed the dictatorship was by appealing to international solidarity, not only by participating in the transnational human rights organizations and networks but also by getting involved in labor networks. The international campaign against the dictatorship, developed mainly by exiles in different countries in Europe and the Americas with the support of militants in Argentina, put pressure on the military junta and drummed up concern about the country's image abroad.[7]

International relations scholars emphasize that the Gerald Ford administration initially gave the Argentine dictatorship a green light, which was of crucial importance. The United States formally recognized the new government two days after the coup, and the International Monetary Fund granted it a previously approved loan of US $127 million.[8] Despite serious reports of human rights abuses perpetrated by members of the security forces, the U.S. Secretary of State Henry Kissinger met with Argentina's Minister of Foreign Affairs César Augusto Guzzetti to discuss

[5] See, among others, Pablo Pozzi, *Oposición obrera a la dictadura, 1976–1982* (Buenos Aires: Contrapunto, 1988); Pablo Pozzi, "Argentina 1976–1982: Labour Leadership and Military Government," *Journal of Latin American Studies* 20, no. 1 (1988): 111–138; Pablo Pozzi and Alejandro Schneider, *Los setentistas. Izquierda y clase obrera (1969–1976)* (Buenos Aires: Editorial de la Universidad de Buenos Aires, 2000).

[6] Basualdo, Barragán, and Rodríguez, *La clase trabajadora*.

[7] Victoria Basualdo, "La participación de trabajadores y sindicalistas en la campaña internacional contra la última dictadura militar argentina," in *Revista Sociedad*, no. 25, Facultad de Ciencias Sociales de la Universidad de Buenos Aires (Spring 2006).

[8] Jorge Taiana, "Foreign Powers, Economic Support, and Geopolitics," in *The Economic Accomplices to the Argentine Dictatorship: Outstanding Debts*, ed. Horacio Verbitsky and Juan Pablo Bohoslavsky, 61–71 (Cambridge University Press, 2016).

bilateral relations during an Organization of American States (OAS) conference in Santiago de Chile in June 1976. Kissinger made it clear that reports of human rights abuses had no chance of interfering with the U.S. support for Argentina, and Guzzetti was also received by Vice-President Nelson Rockefeller. Meanwhile, the junta strengthened foreign investments in the country and increased Argentina's participation in international commerce. The military developed a strategy to clean its public image, whereby its good relations with the U.S. business community and conservative politicians were of great help. This activity was carried out in coordination with the Council for the Americas, an association founded by David Rockefeller, who also was its president at that time. It brought leading U.S. companies together with Latin American interests.

At the beginning of the Carter administration in 1977, the U.S. Department of State created the Bureau of Democracy, Human Rights, and Labor under the coordination of Patricia Derian, which counted on the collaboration of Tex Harris at the U.S. Embassy in Buenos Aires. Along with members of the U.S. Congress and human rights organizations based in Washington, DC, this office received information from peers in Argentina and from exile groups and played a key role in documenting and reporting the human rights violations perpetrated in the country. This process determined a change in the U.S. policy toward the dictatorship. The U.S. government implemented an economic system of rewards and penalties, such as reducing military aid from US $48 million to US $15 million and withholding over US $1 billion in nonmilitary imports, including bank transactions until the regime improved its human rights record.[9] In fact, the United States made the approval of credits for Argentina to purchase hydroelectric turbines contingent on the Argentine government accepting a mission headed by the Inter-American Commission on Human Rights into the country, which finally took place in 1979. After the Soviet Union invaded Afghanistan and the United States imposed an embargo on grain exports to that country, a paradoxical shift occurred in Argentina-U.S. relations when Argentina decided to sell a considerable volume of grain to the USSR. Nonetheless, diplomatic ties between Argentina and the United States strengthened again when Ronald Reagan was elected president in 1980.

[9] Taiana, "Foreign Powers," 69.

Intellectual and Institutional Relations Between the Military and Big Business

One central feature of the 1976–1983 dictatorship was the intellectual and institutional alliance between the military and sectors of the business community and intellectuals who were economically liberal and politically conservative. The key figure in this sense was José Alfredo Martínez de Hoz, Minister of Economy from 1976 to 1981, who had been the CEO of Acindar, a steel company deeply implicated in labor repression from 1975 onward. This firm became a symbol of the alliance between economic power and the military during the period.

Recent valuable studies in the history of ideas and institutions show that during the decades when Argentina was undergoing import substitution industrialization, from the 1930s to the early 1970s, key exponents of the liberal and pro-business ideology, such as Martínez de Hoz, Roberto Alemann, and Álvaro Alsogaray, occupied different positions in government. Nevertheless, their idea of reducing the size of the state structure met with the intransigence of their military partners in government at that time. It was only in the mid-1970s that such advocates of liberalization could openly question what they considered an "interventionist" state. By the mid-1970s, some political and military sectors, accompanied by a group of intellectuals and journalists, as well as an active core of the business community, felt that the problem was not only in guerrilla groups, which they regarded as weakened, but mainly in the way society had been organized in Argentina since the 1940s. In particular, they held that trade unions had too much power and the state took on an overly active role in economic and social affairs.[10]

In this context, figures such as Alberto Benegas Lynch, Jaime Perriaux, and Ricardo Zinn argued that the key goals society needed to achieve to secure order were reducing public intervention and breaking labor power. They posited that respect for property rights and free enterprise were the only means for achieving prosperity.[11] The global revitalization of liberalism; the founding and expansion of the Mont Pèlerin Society; and works

[10] Mariana Heredia, "Economic Ideas and Power during the Dictatorship," in *Economic Accomplices to the Argentine Dictatorship*, ed. Verbitsky and Bohoslavsky, 47–59.

[11] Ibid., 56–57; and Sergio Morresi, "Neoliberales antes del neoliberalismo. Consideraciones acerca del análisis del neoliberalismo desde un ángulo ético-político," in *Política y variaciones de escalas en el análisis de la Argentina*, comp. Sabina Frederic and Germán Soprano, 321–350 (Buenos Aires: Prometeo-UNGS, 2009).

by Ludwig von Mises, Friedrich von Hayek, Milton Friedman, and Gary Becker were already inspiring these Argentine liberals. But these circles did not limit their involvement to instigating actions through thinking and writing. Some intellectuals and a sector of the business community formed informal organizations like the so-called Azcuénaga Group, which then facilitated the coup by organizing business lockouts and media campaigns during the crucial year of 1975.[12] Once the government had been overthrown, group members participated in the new government, some through appointments to government positions and many others through outside advising positions.

The dictatorship's economic team had close ties with liberal think tanks that resulted from the convergence of the economists training in the United States and domestic business leaders seeking to strengthen their representation and influence in the state. The first think tank was the Foundation for Latin American Economic Research (Fundación de Investigaciones Económicas Latinoamericanas, FIEL), established in 1964.[13] The initial financial support for this center came from the Ford Foundation, and when these funds dried up, some of Argentina's largest private corporations continued its funding; key officials in the dictatorship came from FIEL. Two other organizations created during the dictatorship were of crucial importance: the Institute for Economic Studies on Argentine and Latin American Reality of the Mediterranean Foundation (Instituto de Estudios Económicos de la Realidad Argentina y Latinoamericana de la Fundación Mediterránea, IEERAL-FM) and the Center for Macroeconomic Studies of Argentina (CEMA). Both organizations received support from business operators to finance their activities and included economist members, including Domingo Cavallo, Pedro Pou, Carlos Rodríguez, and Roque Fernández, who had just completed their graduate studies in the United States.[14] Their involvement in the dictatorship was less organic but equally decisive. To cite an example of this involvement, in the early 1980s, after Martínez de Hoz was replaced

[12] Alfredo Pucciarelli (coord.), *Empresarios, Tecnócratas y Militares. La Trama Corporativa de la Última Dictadura* (Buenos Aires: Siglo Veintiuno, 2004); Martín Vicente, "Los intelectuales liberal-conservadores argentinos y la última dictadura. El caso del Grupo Azcuénaga," *KAIROS. Revista de Temas Sociales* 29, Year 16 (2012): 1–17.

[13] Hernán Ramírez, *Corporaciones en el poder. Institutos económicos y acción política en Brasil y Argentina: IPÊS, FIEL y Fundación Mediterránea* (Buenos Aires: Lenguaje Claro Editora, 2007).

[14] Heredia, "Economic ideas," 56–57.

and the currency was devalued, the state implemented a number of mechanisms that led to the nationalization of private debts contracted by important firms, a policy that economist Domingo Cavallo enforced after he was appointed president of the Central Bank.

Former officials of the most significant economically diversified economic groups in Argentina were prominent in every state office of economic or institutional importance. The following list is not meant to be exhaustive but gives a sense of the extensive ties between economic and state actors: the Minister of Economy had connections with the groups Acindar, Roberts, and Bracht; Francisco P. Soldati, the director of the Central Bank, was a salient figure of the Soldati economic group; and Guillermo Walter Klein, the secretary of economic planning, had a long-term connection with the groups Shaw and Renault. Further, Raymundo Podestá, the undersecretary of industrial development, had ties with the Firpo economic group; Eugenio Ianella, the president of Banade (National Development Bank), was related to the group Banco Federal Argentino; and Daniel Brunella, Secretary of Energy, was connected to the groups Renault and Ericsson. At the same time, Pablo J. Terán Nougués, the vice-president of the Central Bank, and Alejandro M. de Achával, the director of Banco Nación, were prominent officials of the economic group Garovaglio y Zorraquín; Eduardo Oxenford, the director of YPF (Yacimientos Petrolíferos Fiscales, a state-owned oil company), and Javier Gamboa, the vice-president of Banade (Banco Nacional de Desarrollo, National Development Bank), were connected with the Roberts economic group; Gabriel Meoli, the manager of Gas del Estado (a gas utility company), and Alberto Plunkett, the CEO of Gas del Estado, belonged to the group Astra; Fernando Puca Prota, Secretary of Mining, responded to the group National Lead-St. Joseph Lead (Mina El Aguilar); Martín Braun Lasala, the undersecretary of institutional matters, was connected with the group Braun Menéndez; Juan A. Nicholson, the undersecretary of planning, was related to the Ledesma group; and Carlos Etcheverrigaray, the vice-president of Banco Nación, was related to the Camea group.[15] This preliminary list clearly shows that representatives of the economic groups

[15] Martín Schorr, "Industrial Economic Power as Promoter and Beneficiary of Argentina's Refounding Project (1976–1983)," in *The Economic Accomplices to the Argentine Dictatorship: Outstanding Debts*, ed. Horacio Verbitsky and Juan Pablo Bohoslavsky (Cambridge: Cambridge University Press, 2016), 240, citing information from Daniel Azpiazu, Eduardo Basualdo, Miguel Khavisse, *El nuevo poder económico en la Argentina de los años 80* (Buenos Aires: Editorial Siglo Veintiuno, 2003). See also Ana Castellani, *Estado, empresas y empresa-*

played a leading role in critical economic and institutional positions within the dictatorship.

Economic and Financial Relations Between the Military and Big Business

Key contributions from the field of economic history have emphasized that Argentina's "Proceso de Reorganización Nacional" implemented economic policies that drastically affected the country's import substitution industrialization and put financial valorization at the center of the economic structure and macro- and microeconomic behavior. At the same time, these policies drastically redistributed income to the detriment of workers. This combination of processes delineated a new pattern of accumulation that can be considered a homegrown variant of the neoliberal model. The foreign industrial business sector that had been so significant during the period of industrialization was fractured, and some transnational companies aligned themselves with the new power bloc while others repatriated their capital. At the same time, there were profound changes in the financial sector, which included a transformation of the role of key public institutions such as the National Bank, which not only funded the armed forces but also promoted the expansion of key business sectors during this period.[16] Therefore, according to these studies, the dictatorship was based on an alliance between local economic groups and international financial capital, which included private banks and international bodies as the political representatives of financial capital.[17]

These economic sectors benefited from regressive income redistribution on an unprecedented scale. Between 1976 and 1977, real wages fell by more than 40 percent, so that wage earners' share in the national income dropped sharply from 45 to 25 percent; it then remained far below the level of 1969, the worst year in the second stage of import

rios. La construcción de ámbitos privilegiados de acumulación entre 1966 y 1989 (Buenos Aires: Prometeo, 2009).

[16] See Eduardo Basualdo, Juan Santarcángelo, Andrés Wainer, Cintia Russo and Guido Perrone, *El Banco de la Nación Argentina y la Dictadura: El Impacto de las Transformaciones Económicas y Financieras en la política crediticia (1976–1983)* (Buenos Aires: Siglo Veintiuno, 2016.

[17] Eduardo Basualdo, *Estudios de Historia Económica Argentina. Desde mediados del siglo XX a la actualidad* (Buenos Aires: Siglo Veintiuno, 2006).

substitution, throughout the dictatorship.[18] This took place when industry was displaced as the driving force of the economy while oligopolistic capital expanded its role. From then on, wages were no longer considered a determining factor for the level of aggregate demand and profits and came to be seen as a production cost that needed to be minimized to guarantee greater returns for business.

In this context, the dictatorship passed Law 21,526, which consolidated financial reform by decentralizing deposits, in February 1977. This qualitatively changed the economic and social structure because it entailed the state yielding control over the intersectoral transfer of resources to the dominant power bloc.[19] After this reform, there was a succession of attempts to lower inflation: an orthodox monetary policy from June 1977 to April 1978, based on contracting the monetary base; a policy aimed at decreasing inflationary expectations applied from May to December 1978; and a monetary approach to the balance of payments, implemented from January 1979 to February 1981, in which the financial reform converged with external openness in the product and capital markets.[20]

After the first two attempts failed, the monetary approach to the balance of payments finally brought about lasting structural changes. It set the exchange rate in accordance with a devaluation of the currency that decreased over time, combining this with import liberalization, lowered tariffs, and liberalized capital outflows, which benefited some and seriously damaged others.[21] The free movement of capital was crucial, determining the nature of the economic and social restructuring that accompanied the new economic policy. In addition, the policy entailed a domestic interest rate that systematically exceeded the cost of external debt and accelerated capital flight. As of 1979, the dictatorship found the policy key it needed to achieve the restructuring it sought: driving out significant sectors of the

[18] Basualdo, "The Legacy of the Dictatorship: The New Pattern of Capital Accumulation, Deindustrialization, and the Decline of the Working Class," in *The Economic Accomplices to the Argentine Dictatorship: Outstanding Debts*, ed. Horacio Verbitsky and Juan Pablo Bohoslavsky, 75–89 (Cambridge: Cambridge University Press, 2016).

[19] Basualdo, *Estudios de Historia Económica Argentina*.

[20] Adolfo Canitrot, "La Disciplina Como Objetivo de La Política Económica. Un Ensayo Sobre El Programa Económico Del Gobierno Argentino Desde 1976," *Desarrollo Económico* 19, no. 76 (1980): 453–475; and "Teoría y Práctica Del Liberalismo. Política Anti-inflacionaria y Apertura Económica En La Argentina, 1976–1981," *Desarrollo Económico* 21, no. 82 (1981): 131–89.

[21] Basualdo, "The Legacy of the Dictatorship," 75–89; and Jorge Schvarzer, *La política económica de Martínez de Hoz* (Buenos Aires: Hyspamérica, 1986).

business community while simultaneously expanding the dominant capital factions that formed its economic and social base.

Against this backdrop, strong players were able to rise and consolidate their power. A clear example of this is the steel industry. While workers endured one of the most severe processes of repression in their history, right before and during the dictatorship, the steel company Acindar enjoyed a time of expansion.[22] As industry contracted and internal demand declined, the company rapidly expanded, increasing production from 401,001 tons in 1977 to nearly one million tons in 1981.[23] The company introduced technological changes to accompany this transformation between 1978 and 1982, in particular, inaugurating the Integral Production Plant Arturo Acevedo (PIIA).[24] Moreover, during this period Acindar, together with Siderca, the steel company owned by the economic group Techint, played a fundamental role in the concentration of the steel industry. In 1981, Acindar bought the companies belonging to Gurmendi group, its main competitor.[25] These changes prompted extensive rationalization and the dismissal of many workers. Of the eight original plants belonging to both economic groups, five were partially or totally closed. Simultaneously, Acindar closed its original plant located in Rosario, which had employed nearly 1000 workers, concentrating all of its production in Villa Constitución. Therefore, by 1982 only two plants were still involved in production: Villa Constitución (an integral plant that also produced common steel) and La Matanza (formerly Santa Rosa, dedicated to the production of special steel). In 1983, Acindar bought Marathon, a factory that produced special steels, located next to Acindar Villa Constitución, and integrated it to the factory complex. All these changes entailed a decrease in fixed costs, extremely high participation in the market of non-flat steels, and a considerable increase in the scale of production for the

[22] See Victorio Paulón, "Acindar and Techint: Extreme Militarization of Labor Relations," in *The Economic Accomplices to the Argentine Dictatorship. Outstanding Debts*, ed. Horacio Verbitsky and Juan Pablo Bohoslavsky, 174–185 (Cambridge: Cambridge University Press, 2015).

[23] Marcela Jabbaz, *Modernización social o flexibilidad salarial. Impacto selectivo de un cambio organizacional en una empresa siderúrgica argentina* (Buenos Aires: CEAL, 1996), 25.

[24] Victoria Basualdo, "Labor and Structural Change: Shop-floor Organization and Militancy in Argentine Industrial Factories (1943–1983)" (PhD diss., Columbia University, 2010); *Modernización social*, 30.

[25] Jabbaz, *Modernización social*, 26; Eduardo Basualdo, Miguel Angel Fuks and Claudio Lozano, *El conflicto de Villa Constitución. Ajuste y flexibilidad sobre los trabajadores. El caso Acindar* (Buenos Aires: IDEP-CTA, 1991), 19.

company.[26] In addition to the expansion, Acindar received other benefits: there were transfers from the National Treasury, which amounted to US $81.1 million in 1976 and US $67.4 million in 1978[27]; a significant amount of its external debt was transferred to the state (the estimated transfer amount was US $897 million); it took out US $113 million in loans from financial entities, such as the BANADE, that it never repaid; and it enrolled in the "industrial promotion" program that the military dictatorship implemented, which ensuing democratic governments continued.[28]

In the same way that a combination of tariff reform and the revaluation of the peso brought about industrial restructuring, the expansion of the dominant factions resulted from fixed capital transfers and closures of companies in the real economy, and particularly from the appropriation of financial returns. These returns, for their part, derived from the difference between domestic and international interest rates that enabled these factions to receive most of the income generated from wage earners' and weaker business sectors' reduced participation (Table 2.1).

Foreign debt played a central role during this period as it ceased to be an instrument for financing productive investments or working capital to become a means for obtaining financial returns; the flip side of this indebtedness was capital flight.[29] Large local economic groups and foreign capital took on external debt, using these funds to purchase financial assets (such as securities, bonds, and deposits) in the domestic market, and then took advantage of the difference between the domestic interest rate and the foreign interest rate to send their profits abroad. The state also played a very relevant role in the three main steps of this process. First, the state was the largest borrower in the domestic financial market and grew increasingly indebted. The interest rate in the domestic financial market was sys-

[26] Jabbaz, *Modernización social*, 26; Basualdo, Lozano, Fuks, *El conflicto de Villa Constitución*, 19.

[27] Basualdo, Lozano, Fuks, *El conflicto de Villa Constitución*, 28.

[28] Regarding the impact of the policies of "industrial promotion" in economic and labor terms, see Eduardo Basualdo and Daniel Azpiazu, *Cara y contracara de los grupos económicos. Estado y promoción industrial en la Argentina* (Buenos Aires: Cántaro Editores, 1989). For a recent discussion see Juan Grigera, "Economic Policy and Global Change: *The Puzzle of Industrial Policy Under the Proceso" in The Argentinian Dictatorship and its Legacy Rethinking the Proceso*,ed. Juan Grigera and Luciana Zorzoli (London: Palgrave Macmillan, 2019).

[29] Mario Damill, "La economía y la política económica: del viejo al nuevo endeudamiento," in *Dictadura y Democracia (1976–2001)*, coordinated by Juan Suriano, 155–224 (Buenos Aires: Editorial Sudamericana, 2005).

Table 2.1 Argentina. Participation of business fractions in total sales within the to 200 selling firms in 1976 and 1983 (in percentages)

Business fraction	*1976*	*1983*	*Firms*
Diversified oligarchic economic groups	62.0%	60.7%	Acindar, Bunge y Born, Alpargatas, Garovaglio y Zorraquín, Celulosa Argentina, Astra, Pérez Companc, Bagley, Bridas, Ingenio Ledesma, Loma Negra, Tabacal, Terrabusi, Ferrum, Corcemar, Bemberg, Nougués
National companies	19.6%	18.8%	Fate/Aluar, Arcor, Agea/Clarín, Massuh, Aceros Bragado, Canale, Roggio, Laboratorios Bagó, Schcolnik, Astilleros Alianza, Noel, Werthein, BGH, H. Zupan, Grafex, Inta
Foreign conglomerates	18.4%	19.5%	Techint, Macri, Soldati
Associations		1%	Atanor
Total	100	100	

Source: Eduardo Basualdo, ***Estudios de Historia Económica Argentina. Desde mediados del siglo XX a la actualidad*** (Buenos Aires: Siglo Veintiuno, 2006), 160, based on information from the publications *Mercado*, *Prensa Económica*, and the database of the Area of Economics and Technology of FLACSO Argentina

tematically higher than international interest rates, so that the cost of indebtedness there was greater. Second, the state also took on external debt, using it to supply the diversified economic groups whose members held key public offices with the foreign currency they needed to take local capital outside the country. Third, the state absorbed the private external debt through the various exchange rate insurance regimes implemented in 1981. In 1983, the external debt was 6.6 times greater than in 1975 (rising from US $7.7 billion to US $45.9 billion in that time). Local capital flight in 1983 was almost seven times that of 1975 (increasing from US $5.4 billion to US $37.1 billion), and the interest paid to foreign creditors was 5.4 times that of 1975 (growing from US $2.5 billion to US $13.5 billion).

Each of these variables grew exponentially in a critical economic context, and, at the same time, capital flight increased significantly, gaining importance with respect to external debt. From this empirical evidence, one can infer that at the start of the period analyzed, when capital flight amounted to US $5.4 billion, US $70.10 left the country for every US $100 of debt. In 1983, with external debt of US $37.1 billion, the country lost US $81.70 for every US $100 of debt to capital flight.[30] This confirms that the process of financial valorization consolidated during the dictatorship, coinciding with the state taking the monetary approach toward to the balance of payments (Table 2.2).

Table 2.2 Argentina. Ranking of external debt of private companies, 1983 (in thousands of US dollars and percentages)

Ranking positions	*Amount of external debt*	*% of the total private external debt*	*% of accumulated debt*	*Average debt*	*Firms*
1–10	5,799,306	34.9	34.9	579,931	Cogasco, Autopistas Urbanas, Celulosa Argentina, Acindar, Banco Río, Alto Paraná, Banco de Italia, Banco de Galicia, Bridas, Alpargatas
11–20	1,764,805	10.6	45.5	176,481	Cía Naviera Pérez Companc, Citibank, Dálmine, Banco Francés, Papel del Tucumán, Juan Minetti, Aluar, Celulosa, P. Piray, Banco Ganadero Argentino, Banco de Crédito Argentino
21–30	1,264,308	7.6	53.1	126,431	Banco Mercantil Argentino, Banco de Londres, Banco Comercial del Norte, Banco Tornquist, Sade, Sevel, Banco de Quilmes, Parque Interama, Cía de Perforaciones, Río Colorado, Swift, Armour
31–40	948,846	5.7	58.8	94,885	IBM, Banco Sudameris, Astra-A. Evangelista, Astilleros Alianza, Mercedes-Benz, Banco Español, Bank Boston, IMPSA, Banco Roberts, Banco General de Negocios

(*continued*)

[30] Basualdo, "The Legacy of the Dictatorship," 86–87.

Table 2.2 (continued)

Ranking positions	*Amount of external debt*	*% of the total private external debt*	*% of accumulated debt*	*Average debt*	*Firms*
41–50	756,781	4.6	63.4	75,678	Banco de Crédito Rural, Alianza Naviera Argentina, Ford, Massuh, Continental National Bank, Banco Shaw, Deere y Co, Cementos NOA, Alimentaria San Luis
Over 50	6,093,025	36.6	100	15,909	Banco Supervielle, Loma Negra, Selva Oil, Macrosa, Sideco, Chase Manhattan Bank, Bank of America, Astra, Corcemar, Deminex, etc.
Total	16,627,071	100	–	38,400	–

Source: Eduardo Basualdo, ***Estudios de Historia Económica Argentina. Desde mediados del siglo XX a la actualidad*** (Buenos Aires: Siglo Veintiuno, 2006), 168, based on information of the Central Bank of Argentina

Another major step the dictatorship took to further the economic dominance of these business sectors was to nationalize a significant portion of the private external debt. When the monetary approach to the balance of payments had been exhausted, Martínez de Hoz resigned as Minister of Economy and Roberto Viola replaced Jorge Rafael Videla as dictator in early 1981. The resulting shortage of foreign currency triggered a cycle of devaluations. Under these circumstances, the economic team recommended that the state absorb the private external debt that companies had taken on. It was not that the economic groups, as the leading private external debtors, were trying to resolve a critical financial situation via economic policy. On the contrary, they intended to further increase their assets by transferring their debt to the state while the resources they had transferred abroad remained untouched. The transfer of private external debt to the state took place by means of a system of exchange rate insurances: these were contracts between private debtors and the Central Bank of Argentina that guaranteed the debtor a fixed exchange rate and repayment of the debt in pesos at the end of the contract, provided they extended the maturity date with the creditor bank. According to World Bank estimates, the subsidy that the indebted companies received from the state via these transfers up to 1983 amounted to US $8.243 billion, the equivalent of 58 percent of the total private external debt and 67 percent of the private external debt with exchange rate insurance. The effect of these debt transfers was even greater given that the exchange insurances were valid until 1985 and 1986, when the first external debt capitalization regime was implemented with that insurance.

Another central characteristic of Argentina's economic policy during this period was that state-owned companies were restructured to serve the interests of local economic groups. This "peripheral privatization" did not transfer the ownership of state companies but only their profitable operations through contracts. Consequently, some companies were able to seize a significant portion of the income of state-owned companies. At the time, Yacimientos Petrolíferos Fiscales (YPF), an oil and gas concern, was the country's largest company. Between 1977 and 1980, the state awarded private contracts for twenty-one areas of oil extraction, paying contractors an oil price that far exceeded the original costs of the state-owned company.[31] Under these contracts, various local economic groups took over production in those areas with the participation of foreign companies, which made this strategy viable within the dominant sectors. Among the economic groups that most benefited were Pérez Companc, Bridas, Astra, Soldati, and Macri (SOCMA). State companies, including YPF, were also forced to take out debt abroad to supply the foreign currency that would enable capital flight. This had a deeply negative impact on them during the post-dictatorship constitutional government. According to available data, YPF's US $375 million in debt at the end of 1975 expanded to US $6 billion toward the end of the dictatorship, so that the company's external debt had become equal to its total assets.[32]

[31] Eduardo M. Basualdo and Mariano A. Barrera, "Las Privatizaciones Periféricas en la Dictadura Cívico-Militar: el Caso de YPF en La Producción de Petróleo," *Desarrollo Económico* 55, N° 216 (setiembre-diciembre 2015): 279–304.

[32] Basualdo, "The Legacy of the Dictatorship," 86–87.

Business Leadership Participation in Repressive Policies

Both academic contributions to Argentine history and the judicial proceedings that have occurred since the end of the regime have proven that there were connections between the military and a sector of the business leadership. These ties were not only intellectual, institutional, and economic but also included forms of business participation in repressive policies that the military carried out during the dictatorship. The historiography on repression in Argentina is extensive, complex, and diverse, and illuminates the continuities the dictatorship had with—as well as changes it made—from the CONINTES (Conmoción Interna del Estado, State of National Emergency) plan applied in the 1950s, the National Security Doctrine, and repressive policies in the 1960s to the 1970s. Recent scholarship also illuminated the connections with other dictatorships in South America, analyzing particularly the Plan Cóndor, in the mid-1970s, which could be considered the highest point of articulation of repressive policies among the Southern Cone countries.[33] Labor repression has attracted increasing attention within this field, with recent studies identifying different types of repression that business sectors and leaders were involved in. One important research project that analyzed such repression was developed between 2014 and 2015; the Area of Economics and Technology of FLACSO, the Center of Legal and Social Studies (CELS, a human rights organization), the Program of Truth and Justice, and the Secretary of Human Rights within the Minister of Justice and Human Rights of Argentina put a team together to conduct the study.[34]

These organizations published the final report in two volumes totaling over 1000 pages. It summarized the research on twenty-five companies in various economic sectors based in different regions of the country. Utilizing a wide range of sources (including oral interviews, judicial documents, archival documents, and media sources), the report systematically

[33] See, among many others, Gabriela Águila, Santiago Garaño and Pablo Scatizza, *Represión estatal y violencia paraestatal en la historia reciente argentina: nuevos abordajes a 40 años del golpe de estado* (La Plata: FAHCE-UNLP, 2016); Paulo Fontes, Alejandra Esteves, Jean Sales, Larissa Rosa Corrêa, *Mundos do Trabalho e Ditaduras no Cone Sul (1964–1990)* (Rio de Janeiro, Brasil: Multifoco, 2018).

[34] AEyT de FLACSO, CELS, PVJ and SDH, *Responsabilidad empresarial en delitos de lesa humanidad: Represión a Trabajadores durante el Terrorismo de Estado*, 2 vols. (Buenos Aires: Infojus, 2015).

Table 2.3 Argentina. Cases of corporate responsibility in human rights violations during the dictatorship analyzed for each region during research project (2014–2015)

Region	*Case studies*
Northwestern region (provinces of Jujuy, Tucumán, Salta)	Ledesma (sugar mill), Mina "El Aguilar" (mining company), La Veloz del Norte (transportation company), La Fronterita y Concepción (sugar mills)
Southern industrial belt and La Plata, Berisso, and Ensenada (CABA and province of Buenos Aires)	Alpargatas (textile and shoe industry), Molinos Río de la Plata (food industry), Swift (meatpacking industry), Propulsora Siderúrgica (steel mill), Astillero Río Santiago (navy shipyard) and Petroquímica Sudamericana (petrochemical)
Northern industrial belt (North of CABA and province of Buenos Aires, and south of Santa Fe)	Grafa (textile industry), Ford (automobile industry), Mercedes-Benz (automobile industry), Lozadur and Cattaneo (ceramic industry), Astarsa and Mestrina (shipyards), Dálmine Siderca and Acindar (steel mills)
Central region (Córdoba)	Fiat (automobile industry)
Northeastern region (Corrientes)	Las Marías (yerba mate production)
Center of province of Buenos Aires	Loma Negra (cement industry) and La Nueva Provincia (media company, graphic industry)

Source: AEyT de FLACSO, CELS, PVJ and SDH, Responsabilidad empresarial en delitos de lesa humanidad: Represión a Trabajadores durante el Terrorismo de Estado, 2 vols. (Buenos Aires: Infojus, 2015)

drew upon the archives of public institutions, particularly the Archivo Nacional de la Memoria, Archivo General de la Nación, and the Archivo de la Dirección de Inteligencia de la Policía de la Provincia de Buenos Aires, among many others. While the report focused overall on workplaces, the individual chapters analyzed dimensions related to the business trajectories, the history of labor organization, the process of repression, and, finally, the forms of business involvement in repression (Table 2.3).

The analysis of these cases clearly demonstrated that there was a pattern of business involvement in human rights violations during the dictatorship (1976–1983). In 88 percent of the case studies, workers and shop-floor delegates were kidnapped from their work stations at the factories, while in 76 percent the companies provided private and sensitive information about the persecuted workers to the military. In 72 percent of the cases, the military had a presence within the private property of the firms, and military personnel were in charge of the control and oversight of workers, and in 68 percent, military officers participated in the board of directors or the managerial structure of the firms. Moreover, in 56 percent of the cases, there were major military operations within the factories. Regarding the involvement of top business officials, 52 percent of the cases found top officials present in the process of detention and kidnapping, and in some cases even torture. In nearly 50 percent of the cases, the companies temporarily granted space within their private property for the military to settle, while in 48 percent the firms made financial contributions to the armed forces, and in 40 percent they provided vehicles to the military to use in the repressive action. Finally, at five of the twenty-five companies—Acindar, Astilleros Río Santiago, Ford, Ingenio "La Fronterita," and the transportation company "La Veloz del Norte"—clandestine detention centers were located on site. Workers were kept and tortured for different periods of time, ranging from hours to days, after which they usually disappeared or were imprisoned.[35]

The evidence proving the participation of companies and their top officials in the most extreme repressive policies is striking. Not only did it have historical and political implications but also legal consequences in criminal courts. Historically, business involvement was clearly crucial to carrying out the acts with the nearly 900 victims associated only with these 25 cases. It also increased the impact such repression had on the rest of the working class and the social communities surrounding these major firms that were central in their economic sectors, and thus also relevant regionally and internationally. This research project also verified that this extreme pattern of repression was associated with a process of "militarization" in large factories, as well as with numerous setbacks and losses in labor rights and forms of shop-floor organization. Labor had to relinquish many of the advances it had made in previous years concerning labor conditions, safety and security measures in the production processes, and the right to protest. The expansion of sub-contracting and regressive changes in labor relations also accompanied the repression.

A number of executives from these companies have been investigated, accused, and prosecuted in criminal trials for their alleged participation in human rights violations. Argentine courts were placed at the center of a judicial debate that erupted after the Mauricio Macri administration (2015–2019) actively sought to dismantle pro-human rights policies for four years. The turning point was the case of Ford Motor Argentina, analyzed in depth in Chap. 8 of this book, when a military chief and two top Ford officials were convicted of human rights violations. In 2015, a businessman, Marcos Levín, the owner and president of the transportation company "La Veloz del

[35] AEyT de FLACSO, CELS, PVJ, and SDH, "*Responsabilidad empresarial*," 408–409.

Norte," and his right-hand man, Víctor Hugo Bocos, had been convicted of human rights violations as well, but a higher court of appeals reversed this verdict in 2016, arguing that although the crimes had been proven, they could not be considered crimes against humanity. Another prominent case was that of Ledesma sugar mill in Jujuy. Businessman Carlos Pedro Blaquier, also a member of the Azcuénaga group and close friend of Martínez de Hoz, and his right-hand man Alberto Lemos were indicted for their participation in human rights violations, particularly for providing the trucks used in kidnapping workers. However, a court decided in 2015 that the case lacked merit, again based on technicalities that did not call the facts into question. Also, two top officials of the steel mill Acindar have been indicted in criminal proceedings in Rosario for their involvement in human rights violations, while two top managers of Mercedes-Benz are being investigated for direct human rights violations for having provided key information and a blacklist of workers who were subsequently kidnapped. In the region of La Plata, Berisso, and Ensenada, in the province of Buenos Aires, the verdict regarding the criminal trial prosecuting human rights crimes perpetrated by the Navy Task Force 5 indicated that business responsibility had to be analyzed. As a result, new criminal trials have begun concerning the companies Propulsora Siderúrgica (Techint group), Petroquímica Sudamericana, Astilleros Río Santiago, SIAP, Swift, and Molinos Río de la Plata, among others. In Tucumán, as well, judges in the case of Independence Operation recommended that Ingenio "La Fronterita" be investigated for possible corporate involvement in human rights violations, and so a new case was launched.

Cases related to business responsibility in human rights violations have also been brought to civil or labor courts, charging companies with failing to protect their workers' safety. The case of Enrique Roberto Ingegnieros, who worked at Dálmine Siderca of the Techint group until his disappearance, is one example. His daughter requested financial compensation for her father's disappearance during the civil-military dictatorship. She claimed that Techint SA, having been complicit in the crime on the company's grounds, should pay compensation. The Supreme Court rejected that claim in 2019, declaring that the statute of limitations applied to compensation claims linked to crimes against humanity. In 2007, another case regarding Dálmine Siderca was brought by Ana María Cebrymsky, the wife of Oscar Orlando Bordisso, who disappeared shortly after he left work in 1977. In 1995, his wife demanded compensation from Siderca under

Argentine labor law, specifically arguing that the country's work safety law obliged the company to protect her husband on entering and exiting the work site. The company rejected the claim and argued against legal action owing to the statute of limitations. The court of first instance accepted the claim against the company, and the provincial Supreme Court upheld the decision, ordering compensation for Bordisso's widow.[36]

Business corporations and top officials also became involved in human rights violations against other businessmen during the dictatorship. In 2010, Alejandro Vanoli, who was president of the National Securities Commission (Comisión Nacional de Valores, CNV) at the time, received requests from different courts for reports on the CNV officials' involvement in the kidnapping and dispossession of entrepreneurs and financiers during the dictatorship. One official the courts sought information about was Juan Alfredo Etchebarne, who had assumed the presidency of the CNV on June 10, 1976, when it had been placed under the control of the Ministry of Economy. Etchebarne was a lawyer, a member of the Azcuénaga Group, and closely related to José Alfredo Martínez de Hoz, who was then the Minister of the Economy. The CNV had been created as the regulating body of the capital market in 1968 by the dictatorship headed by Juan Carlos Onganía. Some of the victims testified that Etchebarne had been present at interrogations conducted in clandestine detention centers, and as the number of denunciations against CNV officials mounted and the commission's files began to be examined, a much broader universe of involvement emerged. Consequently, the CNV formalized an agreement with the National Secretariat of Human Rights and established a research team to study documentation from 1976 to 1983. The team worked for ten months, examining more than 500 board-meeting minutes and resolutions and interviewing direct victims to interpret the data gathered. On March 25, 2013, the team issued a report with preliminary findings that, under Etchebarne, the CNV functioned as an "intelligence agency," similar to spaces within the armed forces that operated as "information gathering places."[37] The report analyzed the administrative machinery that applied a double standard, favoring or stimulating the growth of certain

[36] Leigh A. Payne and Gabriel Pereira, "Accountability for Corporate Complicity in Human Rights Violations: Argentina's Transitional Justice Innovation?," in *The Economic Accomplices to the Argentine Dictatorship: Outstanding Debts*, ed. Horacio Verbitsky and Juan Pablo Bohoslavsky, 29–45 (Cambridge: Cambridge University Press, 2016).

[37] Walter Bosisio, Bruno Napoli and Celeste Perosino, "Economía, política y sistema financiero. La última dictadura cívico-militar en la Comisión Nacional de Valores (CNV)," 2013.

sectors while undermining others, including specific entrepreneurs, financiers, and stockbrokers. It confirmed that this agency functioned as an operational tool to persecute a number of entrepreneurs and financiers accused of "economic subversion" in the framework of the dictatorship's fight against "armed organizations."[38] According to prosecutor Federico Delgado, the aim of "combating subversion," a public policy, was invoked to conduct private business operations.[39] The Economic Subversion Act, a national security law passed in September 1974 and amended during the dictatorship, was designed to punish actions that went against the constitutional program. It characterized different political and economic actions as criminal offenses and gave military courts jurisdiction to hear cases brought for these offenses during the dictatorship—a framework intended to persecute businessmen. The report on the CNV includes the names of 143 businessmen accused of "economic subversion" who were kidnapped or dispossessed during the dictatorship, eleven of whom disappeared and were never seen again.

The impact of this study and others has been not only academic and political but also legal, as Argentine courts have begun to investigate companies' involvement in illegal business transactions. "Papel Prensa" is an important case in this context. At the end of 2012, files related to the case were discovered along with other military regime files at air force headquarters.[40] The case revolves around events that followed the death of David Graiver, the owner of "Papel Prensa" newsprint company, in a suspicious airplane crash in 1976. Graiver was considered to have links to the left-wing urban guerrilla Montonero movement that opposed the dictatorship. After his death, the company's heirs—Graiver's wife, Lidia Papaleo, and his brother, Isidoro Graiver—were allegedly threatened and pressured into selling the company to FAPEL (Fábrica Argentina de Papel). FAPEL subsequently sold the company to the three biggest

[38] Alejandra Dandan, "The National Securities Commission and the Assault on 'Economic Subversion'," in *The Economic Accomplices to the Argentine Dictatorship: Outstanding Debts*, ed. Horacio Verbitsky and Juan Pablo Bohoslavsky, 277–291 (Cambridge: Cambridge University Press, 2016).

[39] Federico Delgado, "Organized Pillaging," in *The Economic Accomplices to the Argentine Dictatorship: Outstanding Debts*, ed. Horacio Verbitsky and Juan Pablo Bohoslavsky, 269–276 (Cambridge: Cambridge University Press, 2016).

[40] Andrea Gualde, "The Papel Prensa Case: Notes for a Study," in *The Economic Accomplices to the Argentine Dictatorship: Outstanding Debts*, ed. Horacio Verbitsky and Juan Pablo Bohoslavsky, 292–305 (Cambridge: Cambridge University Press, 2016).

Argentine newspapers loyal to the military regime (*La Nación, Clarín*, and *La Razón*), securing their monopoly over news production in the country during the dictatorship.

Finally, some other cases have been brought pertaining to human rights violations committed by companies, their top officials, and the military that need to be mentioned in this context. In the "Vildoza" case, several military officers and civilians stand accused of illegally procuring property from detained individuals and selling real estate to private individuals and companies connected to the military. A public prosecutor with private partners initiated the case; later, the Financial Information Unit (Unidad de Información Financiera), the state agency in charge of investigating money laundering activities, also got involved.[41] Courts have also investigated cases in which businesses collaborated financially with the dictatorship's repressive apparatus in illegal economic activity, such as the Ibañez case, started in 2009 in a civil court, and the Garragone case, filed by Martin Garragone in 2010 against Citibank and the Bank of America. Garragone, whose father disappeared during the dictatorship, argued that Citibank and the Bank of America's loans to the dictatorship helped to enable its human rights abuses, and he demanded the right to know the truth about the links between the companies and his father's disappearance.

Conclusion

This article briefly summarizes some of the main research findings regarding the relationships between important sectors of business leadership and the armed forces during the 1976–1983 dictatorship. The analysis of the intellectual, institutional, economic, and repressive relationships confirms that a purely political interpretation of the dictatorship's history that focuses on the armed forces and the guerrilla organizations cannot fully explain the profound transformations that took place during this period, which significantly marked and conditioned the transition to democracy in 1983, when Raúl Alfonsín was elected president. The focus on the role of business corporations and their leadership in this process illuminates some of the significant economic, social, and labor transformations that occurred, as well as business links with the severe repression that the

[41] Payne and Pereira, "Accountability for Corporate Complicity in Human Rights Violations."

country endured, during this period. It shows that sectors of the business leadership consolidated an alliance with the military, strongly benefited from economic policies, and participated actively in the repression of labor leaders, workers, and political militants, and also even of businessmen in some other sectors, all of whom were targeted by the dictatorship and became victims of state terrorism. Historians should continue to analyze the economic and social dimensions of this history. Doing so will improve not only our understanding of the past but also the scrutiny of historical and legal responsibilities in the present, and the debates surrounding them.

References

Archival Sources

Argentina, Ministerio de Justicia y Derechos Humanos. Secretaría de Derechos Humanos de la Nación. Archivo Nacional de la Memoria.

Bibliography

AEyT de FLACSO, CELS, PVJ, and SDH. *Responsabilidad empresarial en delitos de lesa humanidad: Represión a Trabajadores durante el Terrorismo de Estado*, 2 vols. Buenos Aires: Infojus, 2015.

Águila, Gabriela, Santiago Garaño, and Pablo Scatizza. *Represión estatal y violencia paraestatal en la historia reciente argentina: nuevos abordajes a 40 años del golpe de estado*. La Plata: FAHCE-UNLP, 2016.

Azpiazu, Daniel, Eduardo Basualdo, and Miguel Khavisse. *El nuevo poder económico en la Argentina de los años 80*. Buenos Aires: Editorial Siglo Veintiuno, 2003.

Basualdo, Eduardo. "The Legacy of the Dictatorship: The New Pattern of Capital Accumulation, Deindustrialization, and the Decline of the Working Class." In *The Economic Accomplices to the Argentine Dictatorship: Outstanding Debts*, edited by Horacio Verbitsky and Juan Pablo Bohoslavsky, 75–89. Cambridge: Cambridge University Press, 2016.

Basualdo, Eduardo. *Estudios de Historia Económica Argentina. Desde mediados del siglo XX a la actualidad*. Buenos Aires: Siglo Veintiuno, 2006.

Basualdo, Eduardo M., and Mariano A. Barrera. "Las Privatizaciones Periféricas en la Dictadura Cívico-Militar: el Caso de YPF en La Producción de Petróleo." *Desarrollo Económico* 55, no. 216 (setiembre-diciembre 2015): 279–304.

Basualdo, Eduardo, Juan Santarcángelo, Andrés Wainer, Cintia Russo, and Guido Perrone. *El Banco de la Nación Argentina y la Dictadura: El Impacto de las Transformaciones Económicas y Financieras en la política crediticia (1976–1983)*. Buenos Aires: Siglo Veintiuno, 2016.

Basualdo, Eduardo, Miguel Angel Fuks, and Claudio Lozano. *El conflicto de Villa Constitución. Ajuste y flexibilidad sobre los trabajadores. El caso Acindar*. Buenos Aires: IDEP-CTA, 1991.

Basualdo, Victoria, Ivonne Barragán, and Florencia Rodríguez. *La clase trabajadora durante la última dictadura militar argentina (1976–1983). Apuntes para una discusión de la "resistencia" obrera"*. La Plata: Comisión Provincial por la Memoria, 2010.

Basualdo, Victoria. "La participación de trabajadores y sindicalistas en la campaña internacional contra la última dictadura militar argentina." *Revista Sociedad* 25 (Spring 2006): 197–221.

Basualdo, Victoria. "Labor and Structural Change: Shop-floor Organization and Militancy in Argentine Industrial Factories (1943–1983)." PhD diss., Columbia University, 2010.

Basualdo, Victoria. "The Argentine Dictatorship and Labor (1976–1983): A Historiographical Essay." *International Labor and Working Class History Journal* 93 (Spring 2018): 8–26.

Bosisio, Walter, Bruno Napoli, and Celeste Perosino. *Economía, política y sistema financiero. La última dictadura cívico-militar en la Comisión Nacional de Valores (CNV)*. Buenos Aires: Comisión Nacional de Valores, 2013.

Brennan, James. *The Labor Wars in Cordoba, 1955–1976: Ideology, Work, and Labor Politics in an Argentine Industrial Society*. Boston: Harvard University Press, 1998.

Canitrot, Adolfo, "La Disciplina Como Objetivo de La Política Económica. Un Ensayo Sobre El Programa Económico Del Gobierno Argentino Desde 1976." *Desarrollo Económico* 19, no. 76 (1980): 453–475.

Canitrot, Adolfo. "Teoría y Práctica Del Liberalismo. Política Anti-inflacionaria y Apertura Económica En La Argentina, 1976–1981." *Desarrollo Económico* 21, no. 82 (1981): 131–89.

Castellani, Ana. *Estado, empresas y empresarios. La construcción de ámbitos privilegiados de acumulación entre 1966 y 1989*. Buenos Aires: Prometeo, 2009.

Crenzel, Emilio. *The Memory of the Argentina Disappearances: The Political History of Nunca Más*. New York: Routledge, 2017.

Damill, Mario. "La economía y la política económica: del viejo al nuevo endeudamiento." In *Dictadura y Democracia (1976–2001)*, coordinated by Juan Suriano, 155–224. Buenos Aires: Editorial Sudamericana, 2005.

Dandan, Alejandra. "The National Securities Commission and the Assault on 'Economic Subversion." In *The Economic Accomplices to the Argentine Dictatorship: Outstanding Debts*, edited by Horacio Verbitsky and Juan Pablo Bohoslavsky, 277–291. Cambridge: Cambridge University Press, 2016.

Daniel James. *Resistance and Integration: Peronism and the Argentine Working Class, 1946–1976*. Cambridge: Cambridge University Press, 1988.

Delgado, Federico. "Organized Pillaging." In *The Economic Accomplices to the Argentine Dictatorship: Outstanding Debts*, edited by Horacio Verbitsky and Juan Pablo Bohoslavsky, 269–276. Cambridge: Cambridge University Press, 2016.

Fontes, Paulo, Alejandra Esteves, Jean Sales, and Larissa Rosa Corrêa. *Mundos do Trabalho e Ditaduras no Cone Sul (1964–1990)*. Rio de Janeiro, Brasil: Multifoco, 2018.

Gualde, Andrea. "The Papel Prensa Case: Notes for a Study." In *The Economic Accomplices to the Argentine Dictatorship: Outstanding Debts*, edited by Horacio Verbitsky and Juan Pablo Bohoslavsky, 292–305. Cambridge: Cambridge University Press, 2016.

Heredia, Mariana. "Economic Ideas and Power during the Dictatorship." In *The Economic Accomplices to the Argentine Dictatorship*, edited by Horacio Verbitsky and Juan Pablo Bohoslavsky, 47–59. Cambridge: Cambridge University Press, 2016.

Jabbaz, Marcela. *Modernización social o flexibilidad salarial. Impacto selectivo de un cambio organizacional en una empresa siderúrgica argentina*. Buenos Aires: CEAL, 1996.

Morresi, Sergio. "Neoliberales antes del neoliberalismo. Consideraciones acerca del análisis del neoliberalismo desde un ángulo ético-político." In *Política y variaciones de escalas en el análisis de la Argentina*, compiled by Sabina Frederic and Germán Soprano, 321–350. Buenos Aires: Prometeo-UNGS, 2009.

Payne, Leigh A., and Gabriel Pereira. "Accountability for Corporate Complicity in Human Rights Violations: Argentina's Transitional Justice Innovation?" In *The Economic Accomplices to the Argentine Dictatorship: Outstanding Debts*, edited by Horacio Verbitsky and Juan Pablo Bohoslavsky, 29–45. Cambridge: Cambridge University Press, 2016.

Pozzi, Pablo. "Argentina 1976–1982: Labour Leadership and Military Government." *Journal of Latin American Studies* 20, no. 1 (1988): 111–138.

Pozzi, Pablo. *Oposición obrera a la dictadura, 1976–1982*. Buenos Aires: Contrapunto, 1988.

Pozzi, Pablo, and Alejandro Schneider. *Los setentistas. Izquierda y clase obrera (1969–1976)*. Buenos Aires: Editorial de la Universidad de Buenos Aires, 2000.

Pucciarelli, Alfredo, coord. *Empresarios, Tecnócratas y Militares. La Trama Corporativa de la Última Dictadura*. Buenos Aires: Siglo Veintiuno, 2004.

Ramírez, Hernán. *Corporaciones en el poder. Institutos económicos y acción política en Brasil y Argentina: IPÊS, FIEL y Fundación Mediterránea*. Buenos Aires: Lenguaje Claro Editora, 2007.

Recalde, Héctor. "Suppression of Workers Rights." In *The Economic Accomplices to the Argentine Dictatorship: Outstanding Debts*, edited by Horacio Verbitsky and Juan Pablo Bohoslavsky. Cambridge: Cambridge University Press, 2016.

Schneider, Alejandro. *Los compañeros. Trabajadores, izquierda y peronismo, 1955–1973*. Buenos Aires: Imago Mundi, 2007.

Schorr, Martín. "Industrial Economic Power as Promoter and Beneficiary of Argentina's Refounding Project (1976–1983)." In *The Economic Accomplices to the Argentine Dictatorship: Outstanding Debts*, edited by Horacio Verbitsky and Juan Pablo Bohoslavsky, 235–251 Cambridge: Cambridge University Press, 2016.

Schvarzer, Jorge. *La política económica de Martínez de Hoz*. Buenos Aires: Hyspamérica, 1986.

Taiana, Jorge. "Foreign Powers, Economic Support, and Geopolitics." In *The Economic Accomplices to the Argentine Dictatorship: Outstanding Debts*, edited by Horacio Verbitsky and Juan Pablo Bohoslavsky, 61–71. Cambridge University Press, 2016.

Vicente, Martín. "Los intelectuales liberal-conservadores argentinos y la última dictadura. El caso del Grupo Azcuénaga." *KAIROS. Revista de Temas Sociales* 29, Year 16 (2012): 1–17.

CHAPTER 3

Building the Dictatorship: Construction Companies and Industrialization in Brazil

Pedro Henrique Pedreira Campos

Introduction

Brazilian engineering companies, at the end of the period of the military dictatorship in the 1980s, became some of the largest economic groups in the country. Among these companies, the heavy construction industry represented the largest ones in the sector, responsible for infrastructure construction projects, such as roads, ports, airports, and power plants. During the military dictatorship established in 1964, they performed major road and electrical projects, in particular emblematic construction works such as the Trans-Amazonian Highway, the Angra dos Reis nuclear plant, and the Itaipu hydroelectric dam, the largest in the world at that time. In addition, since the late 1960s, they were also developing various infrastructure projects abroad, being present in the South American, African, and Middle Eastern markets. In the late 1970s, the average equity of the four largest Brazilian contractors—Camargo Corrêa, Andrade

P. H. Pedreira Campos (✉)
Universidade Federal Rural do Rio de Janeiro, Seropédica, Brazil

Universidade Federal do Rio de Janeiro, Rio de Janeiro, Brazil

V. Basualdo et al. (eds.), *Big Business and Dictatorships in Latin America*, Palgrave Studies in Latin American Heterodox Economics, https://doi.org/10.1007/978-3-030-43925-5_3

Gutierrez, Norberto Odebrecht, and Mendes Júnior—was equivalent to roughly 80% of the average equity of the four largest car manufacturers in Brazil, Volkswagen do Brasil, General Motors, Ford, and Fiat, which were the largest industrial corporations in the country.[1] Sebastião Camargo, the owner of the largest Brazilian construction company of that period—Camargo Corrêa—was the first Brazilian to appear in the 1980s on both *Forbes* and *Fortune* magazines' list of billionaires, featured as one of the wealthiest men in the world.[2] His company was, then, listed by the world's leading construction equipment manufacturer, the American Caterpillar, as the company that owned the most equipment of its brand around the globe, therefore appearing as, virtually, the largest, if not one of the largest, construction companies on the planet.[3] At that time, the Brazilian contractor was responsible for the construction of the three largest capacity hydroelectric plants in existence, Itaipu (14,000 megawatts of installed generation capacity), Guri (in Venezuela, 10,000 MW), and Tucuruí, with a capacity of 8000 MW of power.[4]

In this chapter, we seek to understand how Brazilian construction companies in 1980s reached the status of some the most powerful businesses in the country, and as some of the largest engineering companies in the world. With this goal, we will discuss the relationship between the businessmen who led these economic groups and, also, the ties between their organizations and the dictatorial regime implemented in the country by the 1964 military coup. Therefore, the text is divided into two parts. In the first section, we make brief comments on the military coup, the Brazilian dictatorship, the role of the national business community, and the general terms of economic policies implemented during the regime. In the second section, we discuss the role of heavy construction company leaders during the dictatorship, analyzing their origins, their associative entities, their movement in the coup, their inclusion in the state apparatus during the regime, and the way specific policies developed by the state affected companies in the sector.

[1] Galeno Tinoco Ferraz Filho, "A Transnacionalização da Grande Engenharia Brasileira" Master diss. Universidade de Campinas, 1981.

[2] Lúcio Flávio Pinto, *Tucuruí: A barragem da ditadura* (Belém: Edição do autor, 2010).

[3] Wilson Quintella, *Memórias do Brasil Grande: A história das maiores obras do país dos homens que as fizeram* (São Paulo: Saraiva/Vigília, 2008).

[4] Pedro Henrique Pedreira Campos, *"Estranhas Catedrais": As empreiteiras brasileiras e a ditadura civil-militar, 1964–1988* (Niterói: Eduff, 2014).

Dictatorship, Business Community, and Economic Policies in Brazil

The military dictatorship in Brazil was established during the 1964 coup and lasted more than 20 years. By 1985, five generals had served as presidents of the country, and only in 1988 a democratic institutional order was enacted with the approval of the new Constitution. The authoritarian regime in the country had different phases and conjunctures, being peculiar of the Brazilian dictatorship the attempt to maintain the appearance of institutional normality and legal order. Thus, the political regime in the Brazil did not have—as it happened in other countries—a personalist tone or an uninterrupted succession of a dictator in office. There was a succession of presidential and legislative terms, and subnational governments, despite the rearrangements and arbitrary changes in them. The most authoritarian and repressive period of the dictatorship comprises the decade that followed the issuance of the Institutional Act Number 5, between 1968 and 1978, when the president was invested with power to revoke political rights of persons and even the prerogative writ of habeas corpus was partially removed as an individual political right.[5]

The 1964 coup resulted from the combined action of civil, corporate, and military political forces, with outspoken external support. Hence, the action that overthrew the democratic system and turned against the basic reforms proposed by the João Goulart administration had a decisive participation of businessmen, especially of those associated with international capital. René Armand Dreifuss' research shows how the business community was organized at the Institute of Social Research and Studies (Ipes) and at the Brazilian Institute of Democratic Action (Ibad), organizations that worked to destabilize the Goulart government, to formulate public policy projects, and to restructure the Brazilian state, in addition to organizing the action of the civil-military coup. To a large extent, the groups operating in the Ipes-Ibad complex occupied some of the key agencies of the state apparatus after the coup was achieved. Moreover, the policies

[5] Thomas Skidmore, *Brasil: De Castelo a Tancredo (1964–1985)* (Rio de Janeiro: Paz e Terra, 1988); Carlos Fico, *O Grande Irmão: Da Operação Brother Sam aos anos de chumbo; o governo dos Estados Unidos e a ditadura militar brasileira.* (Rio de Janeiro: Civilização Brasileira, 2008); Elio Gaspari, *A Ditadura Envergonhada* (São Paulo: Companhia das Letras, 2002); Elio Gaspari, *A Ditadura Escancarada* (São Paulo: Companhia das Letras, 2002).

implemented during the dictatorship, especially at early stages, corresponded to the guidelines and proposals elaborated under Ipes.[6]

The process of capital accumulation in the Brazilian economy underwent a significant increase during the dictatorship period, based on a widespread repression of workers and discipline imposed on income distribution and establishment of wage rates. In this sense, it seems quite revealing and pertinent the formulation developed by Guido Mantega and Maria Moraes, who wrote this in a book originally published in 1980:

> Over the past two decades, production growth rates have been the object of envy even of the admirers of the Japanese "miracle" as the country has become a true haven for foreign capital. But it was not just the colossal American and German companies that shaped the "new emerging power" of the American continent. Alongside and in the shadows of foreign monopolies were forged national monopolistic groups that, broadly anchored in the generosity of the state, play an important role in shaping Brazilian capitalism.[7]

As the two authors point out, the dictatorship was marked by a process of acceleration of the capitalist accumulation in the Brazilian economy, especially in the 1970s. The new institutional frameworks and the new balance unfavorable to the lower classes allowed the intensification of the expansion of the productive forces and increased profit margins for companies. The greatest beneficiaries of this process, to a certain extent, were the multinational companies, which had industrial and productive bases in Brazil, which were installed, expanded or, consolidated during this period. At the time, Brazil figured as a kind of "paradise" for transnational corporations, which used this space as a platform for exporting their goods, given the facilities afforded by state policies and all the modest costs of the

[6] René Armand Dreifuss, *1964: A conquista do Estado* (Petrópolis: Vozes, 1981). See also Elaine de Almeida Bortone, "A Participação do Instituto de Pesquisas e Estudos Sociais (Ipes) na Reforma Administrativa da Ditadura Civil-Militar." Master diss. Universidade Federal Fluminense, 2013; Martina Spohr, "American Way of Business: o empresariado brasileiro e norte-americano no golpe empresarial-militar de 1964." PhD diss., Universidade Federal do Rio de Janeiro, 2016; Hernan Ramírez, *Corporaciones en el Poder: institutos económicos y acción política en Brasil y Argentina; Ipes, Fiel y Fundación Mediterránea* (San Isidoro: Lenguaje Claro, 2007); Caio Navarro de Toledo, *O Governo Goulart e o Golpe de 64* (São Paulo: Brasiliense, 1982).

[7] Maria Moraes and Guido Mantega, *Acumulação Monopolista e Crises no Brasil* (Rio de Janeiro: Paz e Terra, 1980), 83–84.

labor force and other items of labor production in the country. However, in certain specific economic segments, the dictatorship proved to be protectionist by deciding to strengthen Brazilian state and private companies through market reserve policies, tax incentives, facilitated financing, among other mechanisms of favoritism. This was the case of public works contractors, which achieved great development in this period, reaching a new size of capital and a monopolistic level of accumulation of wealth, as we shall examine in the following section.

Contractors and Dictatorship: Helping Build Authoritarianism

Brazilian engineering companies in the heavy construction sector that were among the largest in the industry during the dictatorship were not usually founded during the regime. Most of the largest companies in the sector were launched in an earlier period, especially in the 1930s, 1940s, and 1950s. They were created during the implementation of the *Vargas* development model, a time when there was a redefinition of the Brazilian state, with the formation of state agencies responsible for contracting services and public works with private companies. These were municipalities and state-owned firms, such as the following: the National Department of Roads (DNER), created in 1937, which is responsible for the implementation, paving, expansion, and improvement of the country's federal highways; Petróleos Brasileiros S. A. (Petrobrás), created in 1953, which has the monopoly of oil exploration, refining, and transport throughout the country; Eletrobrás, formed in 1962, which is accountable for the public policy of the Brazilian electric sector and was also responsible for commissioning works of production, transmission and distribution of energy in the Brazilian territory, in particular from its subsidiaries.[8]

Brazilian contractors were expanding precisely from the appropriation of the public fund.[9] Or rather, they were hired to carry out engineering works and projects mostly demanded by Brazilian state agencies. Originally, these firms had a more markedly local and regional scope. However, since

[8] Júlio Sérgio Gomes de Almeida and Sulamis Dain and Jonas Zoninsein, *Indústria de Construção e Política Econômica Brasileira do Pós-Guerra: relatório de pesquisa* (Rio de Janeiro: IEI/UFRJ, 1982), 1–145; Campos, *Estranhas Catedrais*.

[9] Francisco de Oliveira, *Os Direitos do Antivalor: A economia política da hegemonia imperfeita* (Petrópolis: Vozes, 1998).

the administration of Juscelino Kubitschek (1956–1961), the largest companies in the sector reached a national level, since they were involved in the construction of the new federal capital—Brasília, inaugurated in 1960—and with the completion of the several projects of the Kubitschek government's "Goals Plan," highlighting the more than 12,000 kilometers of highways built in the period. The road system dates to this time as the predominant mode of the cargo and passenger transportation system in the Brazilian territory. In addition, the national electric model was also gaining shape, based predominantly on generation of energy from hydroelectric plants, such as Furnas, which was carried out during this period. The hydraulic matrix gained strength representing the main power source of the Brazilian electric system at that time. The building of these plants and construction of highways came to be a specialty of Brazilian contractors, given that the various hydroelectric dams were built by these companies. In addition to the federal agencies, the municipalities and state-owned companies created a significant demand for engineering ventures for Brazilian construction companies, especially in the most economically dynamic states, particularly the states of São Paulo and Minas Gerais.[10]

These companies were also very organized. Since the Kubitschek administration, they were organized in national associations, such as the Brazilian Chamber of Construction Industry (Cbic, formed in 1957) and the National Heavy Construction Union (Sinicon, founded in Rio de Janeiro in 1959), an association constituted by heavy construction companies from all over the country. These organizations had among their functions collective bargaining with labor unions on rights and wages; the division of work between the partners, with agreements for certain competitions and bidding notoriously in cartelist's practices; the elaboration of projects for works and the attempt to include these enterprises in the state agenda, in an attempt to influence public policies; and, finally, the organization of the businessmen of the sector so that they could develop a collective political action, as occurred in the 1964 coup.[11]

Therefore, on the eve of the 1964 coup, large engineering companies were already established in the country. Infrastructure works carried out in

[10] Maria Victoria Benevides, *O Governo Juscelino Kubitschek: Desenvolvimento econômico e estabilidade política, 1956–61* (Rio de Janeiro: Paz e Terra, 1976); Campos, *Estranhas Catedrais.*

[11] Marilena Chaves, "Indústria da Construção no Brasil: desenvolvimento, estrutura e dinâmica." Master diss. Universidade Federal do Rio de Janeiro, 1985; Campos, *Estranhas Catedrais.*

the Brazilian territory were, by then, largely dominated by national companies in the 1960s. Some of them had actions and projects distributed in various geographic regions of the Brazilian territory and were intensively performing works with government agencies such as DNER, Petrobrás, and Eletrobrás and its subsidiaries.[12]

The contractors had a participation in the 1964 coup; they were listed in Dreifuss' work as companies that contributed to the business-military effort that assisted overthrowing the Goulart government. The president of Ipes, central body in the process of overthrowing the democratic regime, was a public works contractor. Businessman Haroldo Poland was president of *Metropolitana*, one of the largest construction companies in the country at the time. He also led Sinicon from 1960 to 1962 and acted as a kind of contractor leader, guiding other industry entrepreneurs to contribute and collaborate with Ipes. He was an agent close to military officers and multinational corporations, and, according to several reports, he had a significant participation in the 1964 coup, being closely linked to the then army colonel Golbery do Couto e Silva, who was a military officer who had a key role in the coup being responsible for the establishment of the National Information Service, the SNI.[13]

René Armand Dreifuss studied the composition of Ipes and found a significant number of engineering companies that contributed financially and participated in the activities sponsored by the institute, which played an important role in destabilizing and overthrowing the João Goulart government. He identified 27 engineering companies that acted or contributed to Ipes. Besides being a significant number, the intense role of these entrepreneurs in the agency is not expressed only in a quantitative level. These representatives had a relevant role in Ipes, being responsible for working groups at the Institute, such as the one that guided the discussion and preparation of proposals in the area of low-income homes and public housing. On that account, sector entrepreneurs, "technicians," and other agents made a preliminary proposal within Ipes that was later implemented as the National Housing Bank (BNH), the dictatorship agency responsible for establishing policies for building low-income housing.[14]

[12] Júlio Sérgio Gomes de Almeida and Sulamis Dain and Jonas Zoninsein, *Indústria de Construção;* Campos, *Estranhas Catedrais.*

[13] Luiz Maklouf Carvalho, *Cobras Criadas: David Nasser e O Cruzeiro* (São Paulo: EdSENAC-SP, 2001); Dreifuss, 1964.

[14] Dreifuss, 1964.

Table 3.1 Brazil: Some entrepreneurs who held positions in state agencies during the dictatorship

Agent	*Company*	*State agency*
Octávio Marcondes Ferraz	Const. Noreno do Brasil	President of Eletrobrás (1964–1967)
Antonio Carlos Magalhães	Construtora OAS	President of Eletrobrás (1975–1978)
Eduardo Celestino Rodrigues	Construtora Cetenco	Advisor to the Ministry of Mines and Energy (1979–1985)
José de Magalhães Pinto	Banco Nacional	Minister of Foreign Affairs (1967–1969)
Paulo Salim Maluf	Eucatex	Mayor of São Paulo (1969–1971)
José Carlos de Figueiredo Ferraz	Const. Figueiredo Ferraz	Mayor of São Paulo (1971–1973)
Olavo Egidio de Souza Aranha Setúbal	Banco Itaú	Mayor of São Paulo (1975–1979)
Israel Klabin	Grupo Klabin	Mayor of Rio de Janeiro (1979–1980)
Ângelo Calmon de Sá	Odebrecht/ Econômico	Minister of Industry and Commerce (1977–1979)

Source: Campos, *Estranhas Catedrais*

These entrepreneurs not only helped to overthrow the democratic system, but also developed guidelines and state policies for projects that came to be implemented after 1964. Some contractors of public works sector held relevant positions in public office during the authoritarian regime. This can be observed in the summary report shown in Table 3.1.

Table 3.1 provides a non-exhaustive survey of notable entrepreneurs who occupied relevant positions in agencies of the Brazilian state apparatus during the dictatorship. It is possible to identify several agents of the sector responsible for large private groups, occupying leadership positions in key agencies of the Brazilian state. It is remarkable to note that several public works contractors are among the names listed, some of them presiding over the Brazilian state electricity company (Eletrobrás), serving as mayor of the largest city in the country, or as minister of state. The participation of businessmen in state agencies and in the establishment of public policies was not limited to performing leadership functions in municipalities and state enterprises. They also had frequent meetings with ministers and public officials, organized events attended by them, and even participated in organizations such as the National Commission of the Civil

Construction Industry, established in 1975, which comprised of businessmen and leading figures in the state apparatus.[15]

Many members of the business community worked at state agencies during the dictatorship and demonstrated satisfaction with the regime and its policies. In advertising and marketing campaigns, their companies echoed dictatorship slogans and official propaganda. Particularly, construction industry corporations had their image highly associated with dictatorship, as most of these companies had a significant growth during this period, but also because they had their operations, the works produced, acting as emblems and propaganda pieces of the regime. There was a whole nationalistic publicity, loaded with excessive pride of the nation, that used the great engineering works as objects of government promotion.[16] Moreover, another peculiarity of this sector concerns the intense proximity that some of the leaders of companies and businessmen had with the military and senior leaders of the dictatorship. For illustration purposes, the contractor Jadir Gomes de Souza, owner of construction company Sisal, was very close to dictator Artur da Costa e Silva, and used to play cards with him.[17] Similarly, João Machado Fortes, owner of the construction company that bears his name, was a military officer and a close friend of dictator João Baptista Figueiredo, who attended the ceremony where Mr. Fortes took office as president of Cbic in 1980.[18]

Joining the regime also included the support of the state terrorism policy by part of the business community. Consequently, some executives of São Paulo-based companies supported the so-called Operation Bandeirantes, which sought to persecute and arrest members of the armed resistance to the dictatorship using methods such as torture and murder. Companies such as the ultra group, Ultragás, Folha de S. Paulo, the Camargo Corrêa construction company, as well as foreign firms such as Nestlé, General Electric, Mercedes-Benz, Siemens, among others, contributed to the efforts of the campaign. It is reported that the head of Ultragás, the Danish Henning Boilesen, not only contributed financially, but also enjoyed attending torture sessions and may have helped with methods of interrogation. The Brazilian armed left decided to "take the

[15] Campos, *Estranhas Catedrais.*

[16] Carlos Fico, *Reinventando o Otimismo: Ditadura, propaganda e imaginação social no Brasil* (Rio de Janeiro: EdFGV, 1997).

[17] Gaspari, *A Ditadura Envergonhada.*

[18] Campos, *Estranhas Catedrais.*

law with their own hands" on the company's leader and murdered him in 1971. Almost all those responsible for the action of the National Liberating Alliance (ALN) and the Tiradentes Revolutionary Movement (MRT) were later killed by the regime's repression. Businessman Sebastião Camargo, owner of Camargo Corrêa, was one of the targets of the guerrilla movements. Upon learning of an operation to assassinate him, the contractor strengthened his personal security and sent his family to live abroad. He ended up unharmed in the actions of these groups; however, he developed various forms of support and rapprochement with the regime and its repression mechanism.[19]

Despite the efforts of some of these companies to assist with the coup and to support the regime, the Castello Branco's administration (1964–1967) caused dissatisfaction in the industry. This was due to cuts on state spending and investments in public works. During this period, several engineering services were contracted with foreign companies. National companies complained and even organized a campaign "in defense of national engineering."[20] They approached the "authoritarian nationalist" military and succeeded in reversing policies for the sector in the next administration led by General Costa e Silva (1967–1969), which also corresponded to the harsh period of the regime, which became a "full dictatorship" after Institutional Act Number Five.[21]

The escalating process of the authoritarian phase of the dictatorship also favored the contractors. Thus, with AI-5, the National Congress was closed. The following year, the president had the right to legislate by decree. Thus, on April 10, 1969, Decree 64.345 was issued. It imposed a market reserve for engineering works and projects in the country. The terms of the decree were as follows:

[19] Jorge José de Melo, "Boilesen, um Empresário da Ditadura: A questão do apoio do empresariado paulista à Oban/Operação Bandeirantes." Master diss., Universidade Federal Fluminense, 2012; Luiz Alberto Moniz Bandeira, *Cartéis e Desnacionalização: A experiência brasileira, 1964–1974* (Rio de Janeiro: Civilização Brasileira, 1975); Gaspari, *A Ditadura Escancarada*. On this subject, there is also a documentary by Chaim Litewski, *Cidadão Boilesen*. 93 minutes. Brasil: 2009.

[20] Jaime Rotstein, *Em Defesa da Engenharia Brasileira* (Rio de Janeiro: Engenharia, 1966).

[21] Gaspari, *A Ditadura Escancarada*.

Decree N. 64.345 – April 10, 1969

Establishes norms for contracting services, aiming the development of national engineering. The President of the Republic, using the powers conferred upon him by article 88 item II of the Constitution, decrees:

Article 1. The Federal Administration bodies, including the Indirect Administration entities, may only contract the provision of technical consulting and engineering services of foreign companies, in cases where there is no national company reasonably capable and qualified to perform the services to be contracted.

Sole paragraph. For the purposes of this article, national companies are considered to be legal entities that, regularly incorporated in the Country, have their head office and forum here, are under the shareholding control of Brazilians born in the Country, or residents in the Country, and have at least half of their technical staff integrated by native or naturalized Brazilians.[22]

From that action, all orders made by state agencies should necessarily contract Brazilian companies, with headquarters in the country and national capital, unless there were no national firms specialized in the business or service assigned. More than simply a nationalistic measure, the move was in line with a demand from industry entrepreneurs, who did not want foreign competition and wanted to keep their group of companies operating without difficulty. It was a claim formulated at the heart of the campaign "in defense of national engineering." The measure was extremely beneficial to national construction companies, as it would guarantee to them what would become the largest construction works boom in Brazilian history over the 1970s.[23]

At the time, major engineering projects were carried out, based on a model introduced during the president Kubitschek period (1956–1961). The road transport was strengthened, and large projects were carried out such as the Trans-Amazonian Highway, the Northern Perimeter Road, the Cuiabá-Santarém, the Manaus-Porto Velho, the Rio-Santos, among others. The energy production system based on the hydroelectric plants was also encouraged and major works such as the Itaipu and Tucuruí plants were initiated. Other major undertakings of the period were the

[22] BRASIL, Presidência da República, *Atos do Poder Executivo*, Decreto nº 64.345, de 10 de abril de 1969, p. 29. Available in the site of Câmara dos Deputados. Link: http://www2.camara.leg.br/atividade-legislativa/legislacao/republica/Colecao8.html, access in November 21, 2018.

[23] Regina Coeli Moreira Camargos, "Estado e Empreiteiros no Brasil: Uma análise setorial." Master diss., Universidade Estadual de Campinas, 1993.

metropolitan cities of São Paulo and Rio de Janeiro, the Angra dos Reis thermonuclear plant, the Rio-Niterói bridge, among others.[24]

This high set of engineering projects was made possible through the reorientation of budget policies. The Brazilian dictatorship reduced public spending, civil service and other purposes, and increased the share of state spending on investments. As a result, there was great economic growth and a higher of demand for contractor companies. In the midst of the budget, this was at the expense of social spending. During the dictatorship, the law that set a minimum allocation for health and education was revoked. This led to the gradual and proportional fall in the volume of resources controlled by the portfolios for these sectors in the budget. As a result, the funds allocated for education were reduced from 10.6% of the federal budget in 1965 to just 4.3% in 1975, and health spending fell from 4.29% to 0.99% between 1966 and 1974. All that was subtracted from social spending was directed to investments and spending on military portfolios.[25] To illustrate this trend, we present the expenditure in three ministries announced in the 1974 federal budget in Fig. 3.1.

The graph in the figure seems to express well the priorities of the Brazilian dictatorship. Expenditures of the transportation portfolio far

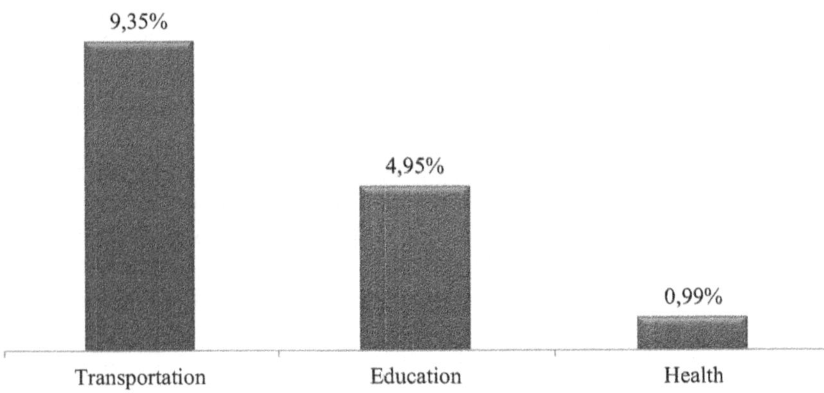

Fig. 3.1 Brazil: Proportion of planned expenditures in the federal budget of three ministries in 1974. (Source: Campos, Estranhas Catedrais)

[24] Campos, *Estranhas Catedrais*.

[25] Wilson Edson Jorge, "A Política Nacional de Saneamento Pós-64." PhD diss., Universidade de São Paulo, 1987.

exceeded the sum of the budgets of the Ministry of Education and Culture (MEC) and the Ministry of Health. Another highly endowed portfolio in the period was the Ministry of Mines and Energy (MME), which is responsible for Brazilian state-owned companies and which commissioned the works of hydroelectric plants, transmission lines, and other construction projects which had a large expansion in the period.[26]

Other forms of benefits granted for public works contractors also occurred through credit lines and subsidized financing. This occurred from the National Housing Bank (BNH), an organization created in 1964 that should finance the construction of low-income houses to meet the country's housing shortage. The agency had as first president in 1964, Sandra Cavalcanti, who was former secretary of the state government of Guanabara and also a shareholder and manager of a real estate developer in Rio de Janeiro, Hosken Engenharia. The bank's initial objective was to ease the social issue and to generate some degree of adherence of the lower classes to the regime by building low-income houses for the most impoverished segments of society. In addition, the agency aimed to activate the construction sector, with a view to growing the economy and boosting an economic sector that employed a significant contingent of labor force.[27]

Despite the initial objective of building houses for the lower classes of society and creating jobs, BNH was reoriented throughout its existence during the dictatorship to finance the construction and purchase of real estate for the higher segments of society and the middle class. In addition, in the 1970s, the bank also inserted resources into infrastructure project design. Consequently, the public works contractors were able to arrogate the large resources available to this institution, as it mobilized the voluntary savings deposits of the Brazilian banking system, in addition to the FGTS (Personal Reserve Savings) accounts created by the dictatorship payroll and which served as a compensation to the end of the right to job security in private companies after ten years of service.[28]

In addition to BNH, the National Bank for Economic Development (BNDE) also maintained credit lines for contractors, mainly for the

[26] Paulo Brandi de Barros Cachapuz, *Panorama do Setor de Energia Elétrica no Brasil* (Rio de Janeiro: Centro de Memória da Eletricidade, 2006); Campos, *Estranhas Catedrais.*

[27] Dreifuss, *1964.*

[28] Virgínia Fontes, "Rupturas e Continuidades na Política Habitacional Brasileira, 1920–79." Master diss., Universidade Federal Fluminense, 1986.

purchase of machinery and equipment used in the construction works.[29] Despite having fixed sources of income, these public banks were contemplated in the period with large loans taken by the Brazilian state, mainly in the form of credit obtained abroad. Thus, dictatorship governments had a practice of borrowing in dollars and other currencies in a period of intense international liquidity. The effect of this, combined with unfavorable financial conditions after 1973 and 1979, was the sharp rise in Brazilian state debt, especially in the form of foreign debt, which went from 15.75% of Brazilian gross domestic product (GDP) in 1964 to 54.09% in 1984.[30]

This priority given to investments, at the expense of personnel and social spending, was also expressed in the gross fixed capital formation indicators. The dictatorship significantly increased the rate of investment in the economy, favoring the state expenditure predominantly on infrastructure projects. This process took place with the severity and increase of the regime's authoritarianism throughout the 1960s, as shown in Fig. 3.2.

In Fig. 3.2, it is possible to verify the increase in the level of investments in the economy as the authoritarianism emerges in the country. With the 1964 coup, the index will begin to grow, and it will get a boost with the regime's authoritarian escalation after Institutional Act 5 of 1968. Therefore, it starts from 15% of its share of GDP in 1964 to the historical mark 24% in 1975—never reached again before or after this period.

All economic incentive policies, particularly in the construction industry segment, led to the Brazilian "miracle" cycle (1968–1973), a remarkably positive time for contractors. The fastest growing sectors of the economy in the period were those related to the automobile industry, infrastructure works, and exports.[31] The annual growth of the construction industry in the period was extremely high, as can be seen from Fig. 3.3.

As one can observe from Fig. 3.3, the annual expansion rates of the construction industry in Brazil were quite high, accumulating a high of 216.6% between 1967 and 1977. Not surprisingly, the 1970s is the most

[29] Campos, *Estranhas Catedrais.*

[30] Juan Pablo Bohoslavsky and Marcelo Dalmás Torelly, "Cumplicidade financeira na ditadura brasileira: implicações atuais," *Revista Anistia Política e Justiça de Transição* 6 (2011): 70–117.

[31] Luiz Carlos Delorme Prado and Fábio Sá Earp, "O 'milagre' brasileiro: crescimento acelerado, integração internacional e concentração de renda (1967–1973)" in *O Brasil Republicano*, ed. Jorge Ferreira and Lucília de Almeida Delgado (Rio de Janeiro: Civilização Brasileira, 2003), 209–41.

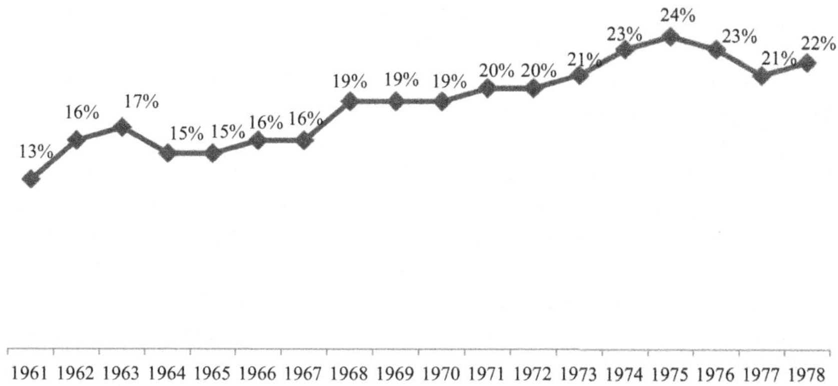

Fig. 3.2 Brazil: Gross fixed capital formation between 1961 and 1978. (Source: Luiz Carlos Delorme Prado and Fábio Sá Earp, "O 'milagre' brasileiro: crescimento acelerado, integração internacional e concentração de renda (1967–1973)" in *O Brasil Republicano*, ed. Jorge Ferreira and Lucília de Almeida Delgado (Rio de Janeiro: Civilização Brasileira, 2003), 209–41)

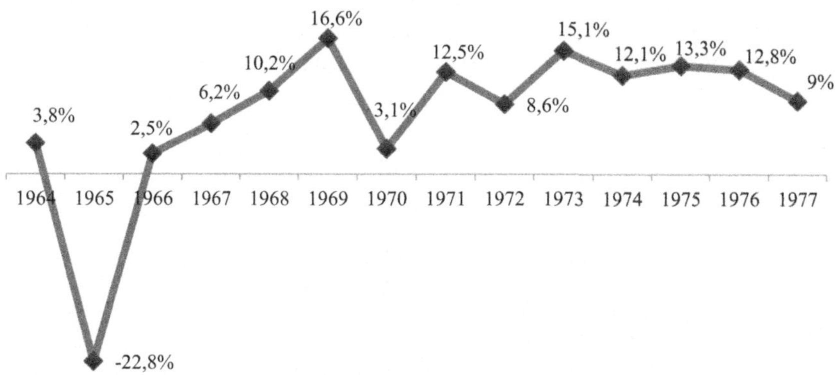

Fig. 3.3 Brazil: Annual variation of the product of the construction industry between 1964 and 1977. (Source: úlio Sérgio Gomes de Almeida and Sulamis Dain and Jonas Zoninsein, *Indústria de Construção e Política Econômica Brasileira do Pós-Guerra: Relatório de pesquisa* (Rio de Janeiro: IEI/UFRJ, 1982), 1–145)

prosperous period of the history of the construction industry in Brazil. From international financing, BNH credit, and investments in public works, companies in the sector saw their revenues grow in the period at rates incomparably high in their trajectory.

A sector that expanded greatly in the period was the generation of electricity. The dictatorship had as its goal to increase the installed capacity of electricity production in the country, favoring the construction of hydroelectric plants. The objective was to generate low-cost power for preferential service for electro-intensive consumers, especially aluminum, steel, petrochemical, and paper plants. The energy was supplied to these customers by state-owned companies, and the energy directed to them was subsidized by the state. The contractors entered these policies as key stakeholders, given that Brazilian construction companies were responsible for the civil works of most of the hydroelectric plants built during this period —Itaipu, Tucuruí, Ilha Solteira, Paulo Afonso, and so on. Figure 3.4 contrasts the growth of gross domestic product during the dictatorship with the annual increase in electricity production capacity in Brazil.

It can be seen from the chart above how the increase in electricity generation capacity in several years surpasses the economic growth, even though it is a period of intense rise in GDP growth rates. The cumulative

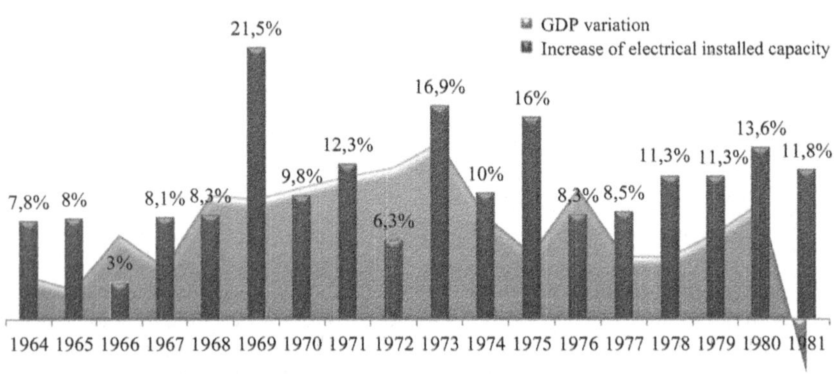

Fig. 3.4 Brazil: Annual increase in installed electricity generation capacity. (Source: Cachapuz, *Panorama do Setor de Energia Elétrica no Brasil*; IPEA. Site of *Instituto de Pesquisa Econômica Aplicada* (Ipea). http://www.ipea.gov.br/ access in August 10, 2018)

expansion of national installed capacity between 1964 and 1981 is 516.5%, against an increase of 243% of GDP in the same period.[32]

Due to the model signed in the period in the Brazilian electricity system, the construction of large dams and the implementation of large hydroelectric plants, with high generation capacity and low cost of electricity, we had a concentration in the public works market in the country. This was largely due to the fact that these works are very complex and require the participation of large companies with high capital, technical, and labor force capacities. Associated with the regressive policies imposed in the period and all the favoring of the largest construction companies in the country, this centralization of capital verified in the contractor segment can be seen in Fig. 3.5.

Figure 3.5, based on data from *O Empreiteiro* (The Contractor) magazine, which annually ranked the largest construction companies in the country, reveals a process of concentration of activities in a few contractors in the heavy construction segment. The five largest Brazilian construction companies (all in the heavy construction business) had 31.2% of the global earnings of the 100 largest contractors in 1978. Six years later, this index soared to 56.9%, following a rise in concentration felt year after year. This indicates that during the period of the political transition, there was a

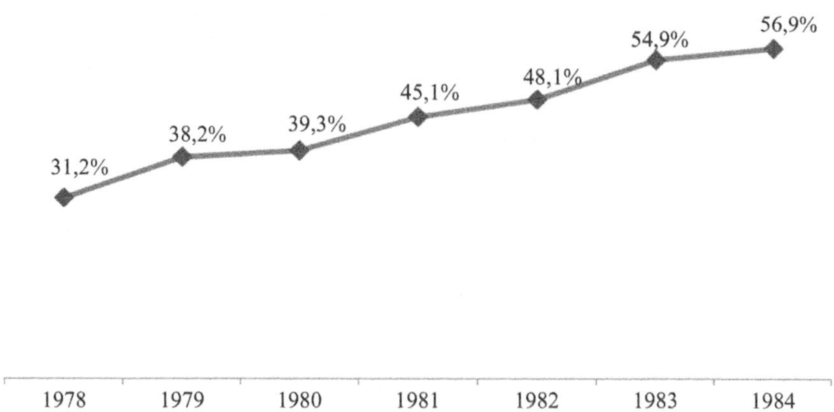

Fig. 3.5 Revenue of the 5 largest Brazilian contractors in relation to the 100 largest ones. (Source: Campos, Estranhas Catedrais)

[32] Cachapuz, *Panorama do Setor de Energia Elétrica no Brasil.*

process of capital centralization in the sector, amid the economic crisis that caused the resources for public works to stagnate. It was an economic scenario in which the largest contractors were able to maintain, in general, their high activity, while the small and medium builders struggled. This process was combined with a wave of mergers and acquisitions that led to a significant concentration of activities in the sector around the four mega-contractors—Camargo Corrêa, Andrade Gutierrez, Norberto Odebrecht, and Mendes Júnior. They were precisely the "dam builders," or, rather, the contractors specialized in carrying out the most expensive and complex works carried out in the period, the large hydroelectric plants. These firms would not only become powerful at the end of the regime in economic terms, but also influential political actors in the country's public scene.

In addition to the favors granted by the dictatorship to Brazilian constructors in the domestic market, several mechanisms were set in place to promote the internationalization of these companies in this same period. Since 1968, the first Brazilian contractors began to work in other countries, such as Bolivia, Paraguay, Algeria, and then Uruguay, Venezuela, Peru, Chile, Mauritania, Iraq, Angola, and others. In the 1970s, the government granted a series of incentives to companies operating abroad, such as low-interest financing from the *Carteira de Comércio Exterior* (Cacex) of the Bank of Brazil, as well as insurance for works by the *Instituto de Resseguros do Brasil* (IRB), being both public institutions. There was also the possibility of deducting the revenues obtained abroad by the company in the collection of the Corporate Income Tax (IRPJ) charged to the contractor. These incentives led to the intensification of the internationalization process of Brazilian companies starting around the 1970s, which continued and expanded further after the dictatorship[33] (Ferraz Filho, 1981). Image 3.1 shows the countries in which Brazilian contractors carried out works until 1988.

It is possible to notice in Image 3.1 a significant process of internationalization of Brazilian construction companies during the dictatorship. It began in 1968, and, 20 years later, national engineering companies had already reached 23 countries. This movement of Brazilian contractors cannot be understood without considering all the protectionism and incentive that was made with these companies in the domestic market. This

[33] Galeno Tinoco Ferraz Filho, "A Transnacionalização da Grande Engenharia Brasileira" Master diss. Universidade de Campinas, 1981.

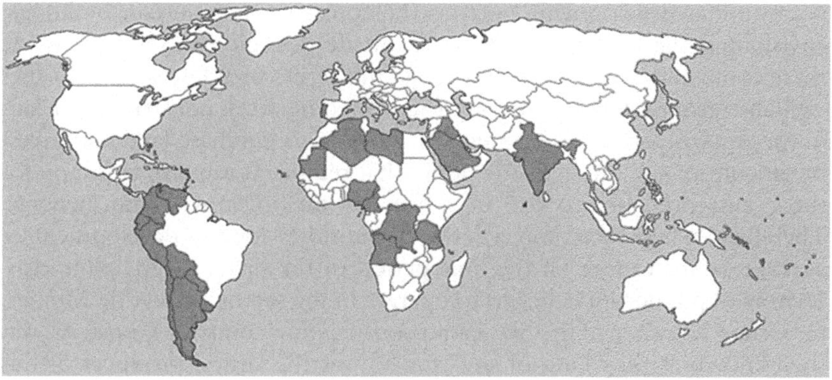

Image 3.1 Countries in which Brazilian construction companies performed works until 1988. (Source: Author's elaboration)

policy allowed them to increase their capital, invest in technical training to empower themselves, and prepare operate abroad. In addition, there was an incentive package for the internationalization of these companies, which made public funds available to enable them to operate abroad. It is noted in the process of international expansion of these companies that they have great success in the peripheral countries, with wide presence in South America and reasonable presence in Africa, Central America, and the Middle East. Brazilian construction companies had more difficulty in reaching markets in dominant countries. However, after the dictatorship, the transnationalization process continued and deepened, and these companies consolidated their positions in Latin America and African countries and reached European markets and the United States.[34]

In parallel to the internationalization process, there was a business branching process by these companies. Thus, the contractors began to develop activities outside the heavy construction sector, which intensified significantly during the dictatorship. With the growth of these companies and the increase in revenues, expansion of personnel and assets, there was also a tendency toward diversification of actions and niches of activity. Thus, several of these companies entered areas located near the public

[34] Galeno Tinoco Ferraz Filho, "A Transnacionalização da Grande Engenharia Brasileira" Master diss. Universidade de Campinas, 1981; Pedro Henrique Pedreira Campos, "O processo de transnacionalização das empreiteiras brasileiras, 1969–2010: Uma abordagem quantitativa," *Tensões Mundiais* 10 (2014): 103–123.

works under development, such as the construction of urban buildings, envisioning the heating of the sector made possible by BNH loans. As these companies were present in geographic areas with few shares of other capitalist groups and considering their ongoing work constructing roads in the Amazon area, for example, they began to purchase land and invest in agriculture and mining activities in that region. It was also common for these entrepreneurs to act in niches of tax incentives and benefits. Therefore, when there was a series of subsidies for the development of agriculture for export, in the final period of the dictatorship, some contractors of public works began to operate in the sector. Olacyr de Moraes, for example, owner of the São Paulo construction company Constran, was then known as the "king of soy" for he was the largest producer of this grain crop in Brazil, owning farms in Mato Grosso. This process was not exhausted during the dictatorship, being intensified after the end of the regime, when these companies participated in the privatization processes of toll roads, steel mills, telecommunications companies, stadiums, airports, and other state assets granted and sold from the 1990s onward.[35]

Thus, we can see in Table 3.2 some trends of the ramification of activities of Brazilian contractors in the period of the civil-military dictatorship.

It is possible to notice in Table 3.2 some patterns of the branches of the Brazilian contractors' activities during the dictatorship. The characteristics of this process can be verified in each of the columns of the table. In the left column, it can be noticed that the areas to which these companies most diversify their activities were, in general, those favored by state policies through exemptions and tax incentives by the state, particularly in the 1970s, 1980s, and, later, 1990s. In the right column, one can notice that this is a typical process of big businesses in the sector. Consequently, the largest builders in the country are intensely present in this movement — Camargo Corrêa, Andrade Gutierrez, Odebrecht, and Mendes Júnior, who diversified their activities to various economic branches during the period.

Also, policies directed at workers were highly beneficial for contractors. Thus, the wage policy was favorable to these entrepreneurs, who employed tens of thousands of workers at some of their construction sites. For being labor-intensive companies, the stagnant wage of the period was very

[35] Aloysio Biondi, *O Brasil Privatizado: Um balanço do desmonte do Estado* (São Paulo: Perseu Abramo, 2003); Campos, *Estranhas Catedrais*.

Table 3.2 Diversification of the activities of Brazilian contractors during the dictatorship

Branch area	*Companies involved*
Farming	Constran, Mendes Júnior, Camargo Corrêa, Queiroz Galvão, Andrade Gutierrez, Odebrecht, Ecisa, Tenenge, and Servienge
Industry in general	Camargo Corrêa, Mendes Júnior, and CR Almeida
Cement	Camargo Corrêa, Servienge, and João Fortes
Materials and equipment	Barbosa Mello, Odebrecht, Lix da Cunha
Engineering projects	Servix, Rabello, Camargo Corrêa, Andrade Gutierrez
Ship building	Mendes Júnior and Odebrecht
Petroleum	Queiroz Galvão, Odebrecht, Andrade Gutierrez, Montreal, and CBPO
Petrochemical	Odebrecht and Camargo Corrêa
Bank and finance	Camargo Corrêa, Constran, and Queiroz Galvão
Commercial centers	Ecisa, CR Almeida, and Alfredo Mathias
Steel industry	Mendes Júnior and Queiroz Galvão
Mining	CR Almeida, Andrade Gutierrez, Camargo Corrêa, Odebrecht, Mendes Júnior, Montreal, and Ecisa
Garbage collection and urban cleaning	Vega-Sopave
Public concessions *	Andrade Gutierrez, Odebrecht, Camargo Corrêa, Queiroz Galvão, OAS, CR Almeida, Serveng-Civilsan, and Carioca

Source: Campos, Estranhas Catedrais

Note: * Process occurs after dictatorship, in the 1990s

beneficial to builders. The dictatorship inhibited the salary increase in private companies and established a policy of containing the minimum wage, a government-determined index that worked as a gravitational pole around which most of the economy's wages were determined, mainly the ones of segments which required low technical qualifications, as were most of the income received in the construction industry. In Fig. 3.6, we can see that there was a significant reduction in the real value of the minimum wage during the first ten years of the dictatorship.

The chart shows what was, then, known as "arrocho salarial." The drop of the real value of wages, which accumulated a loss of 41% in the decade, benefited entrepreneurs once it reduced the costs they had with the labor force, enabling the expansion of investments and profits. This was especially positive for sectors that employed large groups of workers, as it was the case of the construction industry. Similarly, the repression of workers and trade unions also hit the construction industry sector, which had some

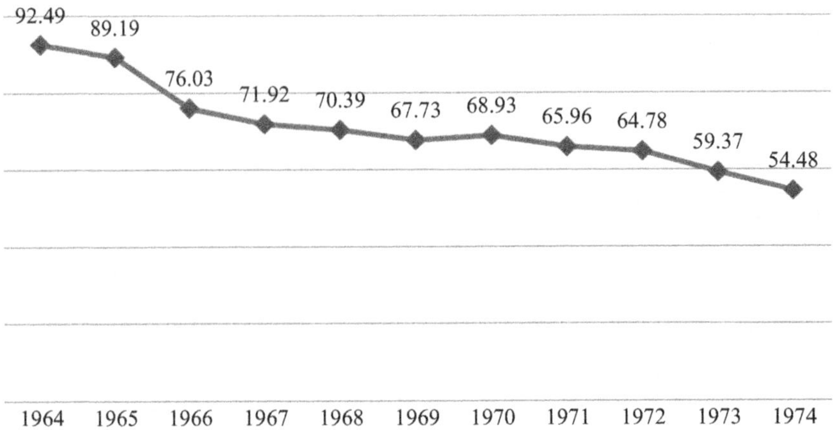

Fig. 3.6 Brazil: Real value of the minimum wage between 1964 and 1974 (in 1940 = 100). (Source: DIEESE (Departamento Intersindical de Estatística e Estudos Socioeconômicos). Dieese site. http://www.dieese.org.br/ access in August 10, 2018)

boards of directors dissolved experiencing an intense control by the government, given that infrastructure projects performed by these companies had a direct interest of the dictatorship.[36]

Finally, a remarkably perverse dimension to the policy addressed to workers during the dictatorship was especially visible in the construction industry. Because of that, the dictatorship had a poorly active and highly flawed policy in relation to the control of safety conditions in the workplace of companies. As a result of this, in sync with the repression on the unions, the entrepreneurs stopped providing protective equipment to workers and took little care of their workers' health and well-being, which was considered as an "uneconomical" cost. Consequently, there was an explosion of work-related injuries, which was especially common in construction companies. Hence, according to the World Health Organization (WHO), in 1972, Brazil had 77 million workers and, out of these, 1.47 million had been injured in that year. It was a quite large number and

[36] Octavio Ianni, *A Ditadura do Grande Capital* (Rio de Janeiro: Civilização Brasileira, 1981); Paul Singer, *A Crise do "Milagre": Interpretação crítica da economia brasileira* (Rio de Janeiro: Paz e Terra, 1977).

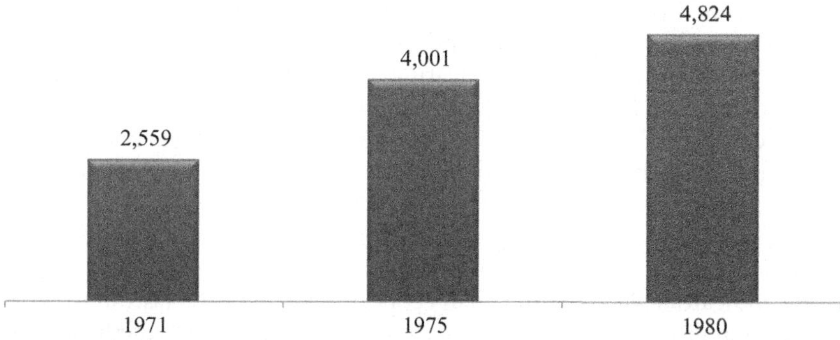

Fig. 3.7 Brazil: Number of deaths in work-related accidents. (Source: Maria Luiza Cristofaro Klausmeyer, O Peão e o Acidente de Trabalho na Construção Civil no Rio de Janeiro)

many of these accidents were lethal[37] (Klausmeyer, 1988). According to the Brazilian newspaper Folha de São Paulo, the number of deaths in work-related accidents had steadily increased during the dictatorship, as shown in Fig. 3.7.

One can observe a growing trend of the number of deaths in work-related accidents in Brazil in the period. Despite the impressive data brought by the newspaper and quoted in Maria Klausmeyer's master's dissertation, other sources presented even higher numbers. Thus, according to the International Labor Organization (ILO), Brazil had 8892 deaths linked to work-related accidents in 1980. The United States, which had more than twice the Brazilian economically active population, had half the deaths of Brazil in the same year, more precisely, 4400. According to the ILO, out of every 100,000 Brazilian workers in 1980, 20 died in accidents. In France, the rate for the same year was 6, and in the United States 4, out of every 100,000.[38]

[37] Maria Luiza Cristofaro Klausmeyer, "O Peão e o Acidente de Trabalho na Construção Civil no Rio de Janeiro: elementos para uma avaliação do papel da educação nas classes trabalhadoras." Master diss., Fundação Getúlio Vargas, 1988.

[38] Miriam Cantelli Rocca, "Uma das Faces do Capitalismo Selvagem no Brasil: A (in)segurança do trabalho na construção civil." Master diss., Pontifícia Universidade Católica de São Paulo, 1991.

At the end of the dictatorship, Brazilian construction companies constituted some of the largest national private groups in the country, with some of the Brazilian contractors appearing in the international rankings as some of the 15 largest contractors in the world (CAMPOS, 2014A). These companies remained highly powerful in the Brazilian economy and in politics amid the process of political transition to the New Republic.

Conclusion

Some indicators place the Brazilian economy as one of the fastest growing in the capitalist world in the twentieth century. This rapid growth, accompanied by intense urbanization, industrialization, and the increase of social inequalities, has led to a high demand for infrastructure equipment. Therefore, many works such as highways, railways, ports, airports, urbanization services, and construction of power plants, among other projects were carried out in the country, especially during the first eight decades of the twentieth century. The period of greatest acceleration in the realization of these works corresponded precisely to the period of dictatorship. However, such thing did not happen by chance. Only an authoritarian government with very little popular participation in the policy-making process and driven by the business interests that supported the regime could set large infrastructure projects with dubious gains for the population as national priorities. Thus, the dictatorship promoted a process of authoritarian and exclusionary capitalist modernization in the country, and the great works performed in the period were not a result of popular decision. On the contrary, they were the result of the decision of a small group of individuals who provided high profit margins for contractors and other entrepreneurs, expanding social inequalities and generating intense impacts on the populations that suffered from the harms of this "progress."

Contractors, organized in governmental chambers and trade unions in civil society, supported the coup, composed state boards during the dictatorship, and benefited from state policies implemented during the regime. These companies reached the 1980s inflated with economic and political power, becoming some of the great examples of the Brazilian monopoly of capital, conducting their business across the country, exploring other economic niches, and developing their activities in other countries. This occurred due to the protection that the dictatorship provided to them, empowering them to remain as important agents of the new government that was inaugurated with the Constitution of 1988.

References

Almeida Bortone, Elaine de. "A Participação do Instituto de Pesquisas e Estudos Sociais (Ipes) na Reforma Administrativa da Ditadura Civil-Militar". Master diss., Universidade Federal Fluminense, 2013.

Barros Cachapuz, Paulo Brandi de. *Panorama do Setor de Energia Elétrica no Brasil.* Rio de Janeiro: Centro de Memória da Eletricidade, 2006.

Benevides, Maria Victoria. O Governo Juscelino Kubitschek: desenvolvimento econômico e estabilidade política, 1956–61. Rio de Janeiro: Paz e Terra, 1976.

Biondi, Aloysio. *O Brasil Privatizado: um balanço do desmonte do Estado.* São Paulo: Perseu Abramo, 2003.

Bohoslavsky, Juan Pablo, and Marcelo Dalmás Torelly. "Cumplicidade financeira na ditadura brasileira: implicações atuais." *Revista Anistia Política e Justiça de Transição* 6 (2011): 70–117.

BRASIL, Presidência da República, *Atos do Poder Executivo*, Decreto nº 64.345, de 10 de abril de 1969, p. 29. Available in the site of Câmara dos Deputados. Link: http://www2.camara.leg.br/atividade-legislativa/legislacao/republica/Colecao8.html access in November 21, 2018.

Cantelli Rocca, Miriam. "Uma das Faces do Capitalismo Selvagem no Brasil: a (in) segurança do trabalho na construção civil." Master diss., Pontifícia Universidade Católica de São Paulo, 1991.

Chaim Litewski. *Cidadão Boilesen.* 93 minutes. Brasil: 2009.

Chaves, Marilena. "Indústria da Construção no Brasil: desenvolvimento, estrutura e dinâmica." Master diss., Universidade Federal do Rio de Janeiro, 1985.

Cristofaro Klausmeyer, Maria Luiza. "O Peão e o Acidente de Trabalho na Construção Civil no Rio de Janeiro: elementos para uma avaliação do papel da educação nas classes trabalhadoras." Master diss., Fundação Getúlio Vargas, 1988.

Melo, Jorge José de. "Boilesen, um Empresário da Ditadura: a questão do apoio do empresariado paulista à Oban/Operação Bandeirantes." Master diss., Universidade Federal Fluminense, 2012.

Delorme Prado, Luiz Carlos, and Fábio Sá Earp. "O 'milagre' brasileiro: crescimento acelerado, integração internacional e concentração de renda (1967–1973)." In *O Brasil Republicano*, edited by Jorge Ferreira and Lucília de Almeida Delgado, 209–41. Rio de Janeiro: Civilização Brasileira, 2003.

Dreifuss, René Armand. *1964: a conquista do Estado.* Petrópolis: Vozes, 1981.

Ferraz Filho, Galeno Tinoco. "A Transnacionalização da Grande Engenharia Brasileira." Master diss., Universidade de Campinas, 1981.

Fico, Carlos. *O Grande Irmão: da Operação Brother Sam aos anos de chumbo; o governo dos Estados Unidos e a ditadura militar brasileira.* Rio de Janeiro: Civilização Brasileira, 2008.

Fico, Carlos. *Reinventando o Otimismo: ditadura, propaganda e imaginação social no Brasil*. Rio de Janeiro: EdFGV, 1997.

Flávio Pinto, Lúcio. *Tucuruí: a barragem da ditadura*. Belém: Edição do autor, 2010.

Fontes, Virgínia. "Rupturas e Continuidades na Política Habitacional Brasileira, 1920–79." Master diss., Universidade Federal Fluminense, 1986.

Gaspari, Elio. *A Ditadura Envergonhada*. São Paulo: Companhia das Letras, 2002.

Gaspari, Elio. *A Ditadura Escancarada*. São Paulo: Companhia das Letras, 2002.

Gomes de Almeida, Júlio Sérgio, Sulamis Dain, and Jonas Zoninsein, *Indústria de Construção e Política Econômica Brasileira do Pós-Guerra: relatório de pesquisa*. Rio de Janeiro: IEI/UFRJ, (1982), 1–145.

Ianni, Octavio. *A Ditadura do Grande Capital*. Rio de Janeiro: Civilização Brasileira, 1981.

Jorge, Wilson Edson. "A Política Nacional de Saneamento Pós-64." PhD diss., Universidade de São Paulo, 1987.

Maklouf Carvalho, Luiz. *Cobras Criadas: David Nasser e O Cruzeiro*. São Paulo: EdSENAC-SP, 2001.

Moniz Bandeira, Luiz Alberto. *Cartéis e Desnacionalização: a experiência brasileira, 1964–1974*. Rio de Janeiro: Civilização Brasileira, 1975.

Moraes, Maria, and Guido Mantega. *Acumulação Monopolista e Crises no Brasil*. Rio de Janeiro: Paz e Terra, 1980.

Moreira Camargos, Regina Coeli. "Estado e Empreiteiros no Brasil: uma análise setorial." Master diss., Universidade Estadual de Campinas, 1993.

Navarro de Toledo, Cai. *O Governo Goulart e o Golpe de 64*. São Paulo: Brasiliense, 1982.

Oliveira, Francisco de. Os Direitos do Antivalor: a economia política da hegemonia imperfeita. Petrópolis: Vozes, 1998.

Pedreira Campos, Pedro Henrique. *"Estranhas Catedrais": as empreiteiras brasileiras e a ditadura civil-militar, 1964–1988*. Niterói: Eduff, 2014.

Pedreira Campos, Pedro Henrique. "O processo de transnacionalização das empreiteiras brasileiras, 1969–2010: uma abordagem quantitativa." *Tensões Mundiais* 10 (2014): 103–123.

Quintella, Wilson. *Memórias do Brasil Grande: a história das maiores obras do país dos homens que as fizeram*. São Paulo: Saraiva/Vigília, 2008.

Ramírez, Hernan. *Corporaciones en el Poder: institutos económicos y acción política en Brasil y Argentina; Ipes, Fiel y Fundación Mediterránea*. San Isidoro: Lenguaje Claro, 2007.

Rotstein, Jaime. *Em Defesa da Engenharia Brasileira*. Rio de Janeiro: Engenharia, 1966.

Singer, Paul. *A Crise do "Milagre": interpretação crítica da economia brasileira*. Rio de Janeiro: Paz e Terra, 1977.

Skidmore, Thomas. *Brasil: de Castelo a Tancredo (1964–1985)*. Rio de Janeiro: Paz e Terra, 1988.

Spohr, Martina. "American Way of Business: o empresariado brasileiro e norte-americano no golpe empresarial-militar de 1964." PhD diss., Universidade Federal do Rio de Janeiro, 2016.

CHAPTER 4

Authoritarian Rule and Economic Groups in Chile: A Case of Winner-Takes-All Politics

Carlos Huneeus and Tomás Undurraga

Introduction

Of all the dictatorships that spread through Latin America beginning in the 1960s, none acted so decisively in favor of big business as that of General Augusto Pinochet (1973–1990). Following a paradigm of radical neoliberalism[1] promoted by the *Chicago boys*, it set in motion a profound economic transformation that reshaped the foundations of the state and

[1] We use the category "radical neoliberalism" to mark a difference with the neoliberal policies implemented by the conservative administrations of Margaret Thatcher (1979–1990) and John Major (1991–1997) in the United Kingdom. See Mariusz Mark Dobek, "Privatization as a Political Priority: The British Experience," *Political Studies*, vol. XLI: 1 (1993): 24–40 y Massimo Florio, *The Great Divestiture. Evaluating the Welfare Impact of the British Privatization 1979–1997* (Cambridge: MIT Press, 2004).

C. Huneeus (✉)
Universidad de Chile, Santiago, Chile
e-mail: chuneeus@derecho.uchile.cl

T. Undurraga
Universidad Alberto Hurtado, Santiago, Chile

V. Basualdo et al. (eds.), *Big Business and Dictatorships in Latin America*, Palgrave Studies in Latin American Heterodox Economics, https://doi.org/10.1007/978-3-030-43925-5_4

society, reversing the "revolution in freedom" reforms[2] of the government of Christian Democratic leader Eduardo Frei Montalva (1964–1970), which had expanded the entrepreneurial state, agrarian reform, and peasant unionization. Pinochet's "capitalist revolution,"[3] also reversed the "Chilean road to socialism" of the Popular Unity government of socialist president Salvador Allende (1970–1973), which had deepened the agrarian reform and sought to eliminate monopolies through nationalization or government control of hundreds of companies.[4]

This economic transformation dismantled the entrepreneurial state and the welfare state through privatizations reaching even to the pension system, and incorporated market mechanisms in education and health. Privatizations were one of the main pillars of the dictatorship's economic policy. They outdistanced comparable experiences elsewhere in their breadth, radical nature, and political objectives rather that the economic ones of raising income to cover the fiscal deficit. Also privatized were the companies taken over by the state or intervened by the Popular Unity government and those that came under state control (known as "the strange area"), due to the economic crisis of 1982 which caused the collapse of the two main groups, Manuel Cruzat and Javier Vial.[5] In each of these three privatizations, the government acted with discretionary power

[2] For studies on the Frei administration, see Sergio Molina Silva, *El proceso de cambio* (Santiago: Editorial Universitaria, 1971); Ricardo Yocelevsky, *La democracia cristiana chilena y el gobierno de Eduardo Frei Montalva (1964–1970)* (México: Universidad Autónoma Metropolitana, Unidad Xochimilco, 1987) y Carlos Huneeus and Javier Couso, eds., *Eduardo Frei Montalva: Un gobierno reformista. A 50 años de la "Revolución en Libertad"* (Santiago: Editorial Universitaria, 2016).

[3] Manuel Gárate Chateau, *La revolución capitalista en Chile (1973–2003)* (Santiago: Ediciones Universidad Alberto Hurtado, 2012).

[4] Allende received 36.6% of the votes and was elected by Parliament with the supporting votes of the Christian Democrats. Within the vast scholarship on Allende, see Dieter Nohlen, *Chile. Das sozialistische Experiment* (Hamburg: Hoffmann & Campe, 1973); Philip O'Brien, ed., *Allende's Chile* (New York: Praeger Publishers, 1976); Joan E. Garcés, *Allende y la experiencia chilena* (Barcelona: Ariel, 1976); Sergio Bitar, *Transición, socialismo y democracia: La experiencia chilena* (México: Siglo XXI, 1979); Federico Gil, Ricardo Lagos, E. and Henry A. Landsberger, eds., *Chile at the Turning Point* (Philadelphia: Institute for the Study of Human Issues, 1979) y Claudio Llanos Reyes, *Cuando el pueblo unido fue vencido. Estudios sobre la vía chilena al socialismo* (Valparaíso: Pontificia Universidad Católica de Valparaíso, 2014).

[5] Ricardo Ffrench-Davis, *Reformas económicas en Chile, 1973–2017* (Santiago: Taurus, 2018); Tomás Undurraga, *Divergencias. Trayectorias del neoliberalismo en Argentina y Chile* (Santiago: Ediciones Universidad Diego Portales, 2014).

and a high degree of patronage, benefiting their top executives, advisors, and supporters of the dictatorship.[6]

The economic transformation included other measures that favored big business, such as labor policy, which weakened work institutionally, together with a severe squeeze on wages.[7] The 1979 labor plan banned unionization of seasonal workers, limited the days of strike, and gave employers full approval to fire workers for "company reasons." It also restricted collective bargaining to the level of the individual enterprise, which helped to implant authoritarianism within companies. The labor force was slowly depoliticized and relations between capital and labor left to the mercy of the market. According to Frank,[8] the ability of entrepreneurs to lower wages while increasing the workload and length of the workday helped Chilean capitalism expand during the 1980s. The working class and unions were the main victims of the "Chilean miracle."[9]

These profound changes in ownership and economic relations were carried out without establishing regulations that are essential after privatization to prevent public monopolies from continuing as private monopolies, to control the quality of services delivered, and to protect consumers.[10]

The economic transformation led to an extreme concentration of ownership in a small number of economic groups. The beneficiaries were groups that originated before 1973 (Angelini, Luksic, and Matte), groups formed during the dictatorship by businessmen with careers before the military coup, and a third group that emerged under the dictatorship's

[6] Mario Marcel, "Privatización y finanzas públicas: El caso de Chile 1985–1988." Estudios CIEPLAN 26 (1989): 5–60; Carlos Huneeus, *The Pinochet Regime* (Boulder: Lynne Rienner Publishers, 2007); Gárate, *La revolución capitalista en Chile (1973–2003)*.

[7] The strategy also included a process of weakening of the state by decreasing it fiscal income. The 1984 tax reform decreased the government tax income in around 40% and the 1988 tax reform decreased tax revenues in nearly 2% of the gross national product. Patricio Meller, *Un siglo de economía política chilena (1890–1990)* (Santiago: Andrés Bello, 1996), 273; Guillermo Campero, *Los gremios empresariales en el período 1970–1983: Comportamiento sociopolítico y orientaciones ideológicas* (Santiago: ILET, 1984); Fernando Dahse, *Mapa de la extrema riqueza* (Santiago: Aconcagua, 1979).

[8] Volker Frank, "Politics without Policy: The Failure of Social Concertation in Democratic Chile, 1990–2000" in *Victims of the Chilean Miracle*, ed. Peter Winn (Durham: Duke University Press, 2004), 73.

[9] Peter Winn, ed., *Victims of the Chilean Miracle: Workers and Neoliberalism in the Pinochet Era, 1973–2002* (Durham: Duke University Press, 2004).

[10] John Francis, *The Politics of Regulation. A Comparative Perspective* (Oxford: Blackwell, 1993); Giandomenico Majone, "The Rise of the Regulatory State in Europe," *West European Politics* 17, no. 3 (July 1994): 77–101.

wing,[11] notably those who gained control of the privatized companies they had previously directed (for example, Julio Ponce Lerou (SQM), Roberto de Andraca (CAP) and José Yuraseck (Chilectra and Endesa).[12]

The economic system inherited from the dictatorship was left unchanged in democracy. The Concertación, a center-left coalition that controlled the government for two decades (1990–2010), with two Christian Democrat[13] and two socialist[14] presidents, chose to maintain the inherited economic system rather than reform it. It continued with the policies of the authoritarian era, such as the privatization of public companies and the strengthening of market mechanisms in education and health, and preserved the low regulatory capacity of the state.

The prevailing informal rules of the financial system—featuring the use of priviledged information and the lack of barriers to separate the public interest from the interests of investors—were not eliminated in democracy. Moreover, an unknown number of the hundreds of companies belonging to the Cruzat and Vial groups that went bankrupt in the 1982 crisis would be used by big business in the dictatorship and in democracy until 2003 to pay less taxes for the high profits of the companies that business leaders controlled. During the first eight years of democracy, the economy grew faster than ever before in Chilean history, at an annual average rate of 6.8%, reaching 2.8% in the four years that followed. Rather than putting an end to neoliberalism, the Concertación sought to "correct it" through social policies,[15] giving it a "human face."[16]

In short, governments in democracy of parties that had opposed the dictatorship deepened its economic transformation, providing it with a

[11] Sebastián Piñera is one of those businessmen and is included among the 11 Chilean billionaires of *Forbes* magazine 2018 list.

[12] Tomás Undurraga and Carlos Huneeus, "Renovación discursiva y continuación de prácticas del empresariado en Chile post-transición (2010–2017)," in *Pensamiento empresarial latinoamericano en el siglo XXI*, ed. Rita Giacalone. (Bogotá: Editorial Universidad Cooperativa de Colombia, 2019).

[13] Patricio Aylwin (1990–1994) and Eduardo Frei Ruiz-Tagle (1994–2000). The latter is the son of former president Eduardo Frei Montalva.

[14] Ricardo Lagos (2000–2006) and Michelle Bachelet (2006–2010). The latter was reelected in 2014 as the candidate of the Nueva Mayoría coalition composed by the Concertación and the Communist Party.

[15] Manuel Antonio Garretón, *Neoliberalismo corregido y progresismo limitado. Los gobiernos de la Concertación en Chile, 1990–2010* (Santiago: Editorial Arcis-CLACSO, 2012).

[16] Fernando Atria, *Veinte años después. Neoliberalismo con rostro humano* (Santiago: Editorial Catalonia, 2013).

certain legitimacy it lacked. They ignored the "original sin" of the economic system—its establishment by force under military rule—as admitted by Arturo Fontaine Talavera (1992), director of the Center for Public Studies (CEP), the think tank formed in 1980 by the Chicago boys to defend the "model." This strategic decision to abandon their criticisms made during the dictatorship, and to follow economic policies that did not clearly differ from the latter's, had negative effects on the electoral support of the Christian Democrat Party and the left.

The main difference in the continuity of the "model" was in the social policies to reduce poverty, moving away from the neoliberal paradigm that considered that this objective would be achieved with growth ("the trickle-down effect").[17] However, these policies were not part of a framework of ideas aimed at establishing another economic paradigm. Nor did they deal with the other face of growth: economic concentration and income inequalities.

In terms of growth, the economic performance of the dictatorship was mediocre and led to a serious economic crisis in 1982, with a fall in production of 14.5%, unemployment at over 30% in the metropolitan region, and social spending cuts to reduce the public debt. In 1988, 40% of the population, five million Chileans, were living in poverty.[18]

The economic transformation of the Pinochet dictatorship, and privatizations in particular, point to the importance of structural factors in the origin and permanence of inequalities and the concentration of wealth in the superrich, the 1% of the population which remained intact through different regimes and governments of different political color. Chile confirms the thesis of "winner-takes-all politics" by Hacker and Pierson and its revision by Hopkin and Shaw in light of the economic transformation in Great Britain driven by Conservative governments from 1979 to 1997.[19]

[17] Dagmar Raczynski and Claudia Serrano, "Las políticas y estrategias de desarrollo social. Aportes de los años 90 y desafíos futuros," in *La paradoja aparente. Equidad y eficiencia: Resolviendo el dilema,* ed. Patricio Meller (Santiago: Taurus, 2005), 225–286; Osvaldo Larrañaga and Dante Contreras, eds., *Las nuevas políticas de protección social en Chile* (Santiago: Uqbar Editores, 2010); Jennifer Pribble, *Welfare and Party Politics in Latin America* (Cambridge: Cambridge University Press, 2013).

[18] Oscar Muñoz Goma, *El Modelo Económico de la Concertación 1990–2005: ¿Reformas o Cambio?* (Santiago: CIEPLAN/FLACSO, 2007).

[19] Jacob S. Hacker and Paul Pierson, *The Winner-Take-All Politics. How Washington Made the Rich Richer and Turned its Back on the Middle Class* (New York: Simon and Schuster, 2010); Jonathan Hopkin and Kate Alexander Shaw, "Organized Combat or Structural

There too, the concentration of wealth in the 1% increased during the Labor governments that followed (1997–2016).

The Chilean economic transformation has been studied from different angles. One of these has been the study of the formation of large conglomerates, including changes in the ownership of companies and "maps of extreme wealth."[20] Other research has investigated changes in the business class as an economic actor and the features of business culture.[21] A third type of study has focused on the ideas that influenced the economic paradigm, the epistemic communities that inspired their actions, and the main policies implemented.[22] Finally, other studies have focused on recent

Advantage? The Politics of Inequality and the Winner-Take-All Economy in the United Kingdom," *Politics and Society* 44, no. 3 (2016): 345–371.

[20] Dahse, *Mapa de la extrema riqueza;* Patricio Rozas and Gustavo Marín, *El "Mapa de la extrema riqueza" 10 años después* (Santiago: Ediciones Chile-América CESOC, 1989); Hugo Fazio, *Mapa actual de la extrema riqueza* (Santiago: LOM-ARCIS, 1997); Hugo Fazio, *La Transnacionalización de la economía chilena. Mapa de la Extrema Riqueza al año 2000* (Santiago: LOM, 2000); Hugo Fazio, *Mapa de la Extrema Riqueza al año 2005* (Santiago: LOM Ediciones, 2005); Hugo Fazio, *Los mecanismos fraudulentos de hacer fortuna. Mapa de la extrema riqueza 2015* (Santiago: LOM, 2015); María Olivia Mönckeberg, *El saqueo de los grupos económicos al Estado chileno* (Santiago: Ediciones B., 2001); María Olivia Mönckeberg, *Los magnates de la prensa* (Santiago: Debate, 2009); María Olivia Mönckeberg, *La máquina para defraudar. Los casos Penta y Soquimich* (Santiago: Debate, 2015).

[21] Claudio Ramos, *La transformación de la empresa chilena: Una modernización desbalanceada.* (Santiago: Universidad Alberto Hurtado, 2009); Tomás Undurraga, "Instrucción, indulgencia y justificación: los circuitos culturales del capitalismo chileno," in *Adaptación. La empresa chilena después de Friedman*, ed. José Ossandón and Eugenio Tironi (Chile: Ediciones UDP, 2013); Tomás Undurraga, "Business, politics and ideology: neoliberalism and capitalist class formation in Argentina and Chile (1990–2014)," *Política/Revista de Ciencia Política* 54, no. 2 (2016): 177–210.

[22] Juan Gabriel Valdés, *Pinochet's Economists: The Chicago School of Economics in Chile* (Cambridge: Cambridge University Press, 1995); Marcus Kurtz, "Chile's Neo-Liberal Revolution: Incremental Decisions and Structural Transformation, 1973–1989," *Journal of Latin American Studies* 31, (May 1999): 399–427; Yves Dezalay and Bryant Garth. *The Internationalization of Palace Wars* (Chicago: University Chicago Press, 2002); Eduardo Silva, *The State and Capital in Chile: Business Elite, Technocrats, and Market Economics.* (Boulder: Westview Press, 1996). Patricio Silva, "Technocrats and politics in Chile: from the Chicago Boys to the CIEPLAN Monks," *Journal of Latin American Studies* 23, no. 2 (1992): 385–410; Patricio Silva, *In the Name of Reason. Technocrats and Politics in Chile*

political and social processes and have studied their impact on the business class.[23]

However, there is no systematic study of the impact of the dictatorship's economic policies on the formation of economic groups and how the authoritarian context influenced economic practices and the business culture shaped under the regime. This is related to the fact that successor governments decided to maintain the inherited economic system and tolerated the continuity of business practices acquired in dictatorship. These found expression not only in the continuity of the institutions, in particular the 1980 Constitution, but also in the practices of patronage, use of discretionary power, and secrecy in decision-making especially in the financial sector,[24] and anti-union, monopolistic, and collusive corporate practices.

The chapter is divided into five sections. The first highlights the singularities of the economic transformation in dictatorship and its consequence for democracy. The second defines the programmatic content of the dictatorship and the political forces that drove it. The third, the main part of the chapter, focuses on privatizations. The fourth analyzes the first democratic government's decision not to modify "the model." The fifth summarizes the conclusions, highlighting how an economic system was consolidated that in its main institutional components was defined by a dictatorship.

(University Park: Pennsylvania State University Press, 2008); Verónica Montecinos, *Economists, Politics, and the State: Chile 1958–1994* (Amsterdam: CEDLA, 1998); Gárate, *La revolución capitalista en Chile (1973–2003)*.

[23] Genaro Arriagada, *Los empresarios y la política* (Santiago: LOM, 2004); Carlos Huneeus, "El comportamiento político de los empresarios en Chile," *Perspectivas* 4, no. 2 (2001): 315–337; Carlos Huneeus, *La democracia semisoberana. Chile después de Pinochet* (Santiago: Taurus, 2014); UNDP – Programa de las Naciónes Unidas para el Desarrollo, *Power: For what and for who* (Santiago: UNDP, 2004); Undurraga, *Divergencias*; Tomás Undurraga, "Neoliberalism in Argentina and Chile: Common antecedents, divergent path," *Revista de Sociologia e Politica* 23, no. 55 (2015): 11–34.

[24] Sergio Jara, *Piñera y los Leones de Sanhattan. Crónica del Auge de la Elite Financiera chilena* (Santiago: Planeta, 2018); Carlos Tromben, *Crónica secreta de la economía chilena* (Santiago: Ediciones B., 2016); Juan Andrés Guzmán and Jorge Rojas, *Empresarios zombies. La mayor elusión tributaria de la élite chilena* (Santiago: Catalonia-UDP Periodismo, 2017).

Economic Modernization in Dictatorship

The extensive literature on the neoliberal policies of the dictatorship has not stressed sufficiently the importance of the context of authoritarian regimes.[25] The political system in which an economic transformation is carried out is not a matter of indifference. It not only determines the institutional scenario in which the action unfolds, but also influences the content of the policies, the transparency and speed of the changes, and who will be their main beneficiaries.

Economic transformations in democracy or dictatorship have distinct profiles and produce very different institutional and policy results.[26] Those carried out in democracy, like those of England in the 1980s and of Argentina in the 1990s, take into account the interests of various actors in the economic system, such as businesspeople, workers, and their corresponding interest organizations. The governments promoting them are scrutinized by citizens and the rule of law ensures equal access to the market and stimulates competition. Privatizations are carried out after regulations have been drawn up to prevent state monopolies from becoming private monopolies, national and foreign investors are invited to participate, and decisions are made transparently. There are norms to separate public and private interests to prevent public decision-makers and state-owned company executives from benefiting from privatizations.

These institutional and political conditions were absent in the privatizations of the Chilean dictatorship. Pinochet's concentration of power—he was simultaneously head of state, head of government, and commander-in-chief of the army[27]—produced a decisive centralization, while the delegation of economic issues to the treasury and the economic team gave

[25] For example, Marion Fourcade-Gourinchas and Sarah Babb, "The Rebirth of the Liberal Creed: Paths to Neoliberalism in Four Countries," *American Journal of Sociology* 108, no. 3 (November 2002): 533–79; Kurtz, "Chile's Neo-Liberal Revolution: Incremental Decisions and Structural Transformation, 1973–1989," 399–427; Silva, "Technocrats and politics in Chile: From the Chicago Boys to the CIEPLAN Monks," 385–410; Silva, *In the Name of Reason*.

[26] We analyze the post-1983 reforms in Argentina in Carlos Huneeus, "Technocrats and Politicians in the Democratic Politics of Argentina (1983–1995)," in *The Politics of Expertise in Latin America*, eds. Miguel A. Centeno and Patricio Silva (London: MacMillan, 1997); Undurraga, *Divergencias*; Undurraga, "Neoliberalism in Argentina and Chile," 11–34; Undurraga, "Business, politics and ideology: Neoliberalism and capitalist class formation in Argentina and Chile (1990–2014)," 177–210.

[27] Huneeus, *The Pinochet Regime*.

them enormous power and discretion, even with respect to the governing Junta and the judiciary. In addition, there was a convergence of ideology and interest between the economic team and the private sector in expediting policy implementation, favoring individuals who were closest to the authorities. Some employees of the economic groups were advisors to the authorities or had personal relationships with their members, giving them access to information on important government decisions before other market players.[28] In the privatizations, the top executives of these groups had power to direct the change of ownership, carrying it out in such a way that it put them in control of public companies when they were transferred into private hands.[29]

The state controlled public companies created since the 1940s through the Chilean Economic Development Agency (CORFO) with private sector participation,[30] leading to the formation of what became known as the "entrepreneurial state."[31] Key investments were in strategic sectors such as telecommunications (National Telecommunications Company, ENTEL), energy (National Electricity Company, ENDESA), the steel industry (Pacific Steel Company, CAP), oil exploitation (National Petroleum Company, ENAP), and air transport (National Airline, LAN). During the Frei Montalva government, they extended to the petrochemical industry (Soquimich, currently SQM), forestry (Arauco Cellulose, Constitution Cellulose), insurance, (the National Insurance Institute, INS), and tourism (National Hotels, Honsa). Chilectra (the Chilean Electricity Company) was nationalized. The state presence in the economy had grown significantly since 1940. By 1970, it controlled 47% of gross domestic product (GDP) and generated 40.6% of employment.[32]

[28] The close relations between the government and the business elite led to the appointment of influential businessmen in high-ranking positions of the government's economic advisors. José Piñera held an executive position at Cruzat–Larraín group when he was appointed as minister of labor in 1978. Rolf Lüders was a high-ranking executive at the Vial Group at the time he was appointed minister of finance in 1982.

[29] Huneeus, *The Pinochet Regime*; Gárate, *La revolución capitalista en Chile.*

[30] Constantine Menges, "Public policy and organized business in Chile," *Journal of International Affairs* 20, no 2 (1966): 343–365.

[31] On the origins of the entrepreneurial state, see Óscar Muñoz and Ana María Arriagada "Orígenes políticos y económicos del Estado empresarial en Chile," *Estudios CIEPLAN 16* (1977); Luis Ortega Martínez et al., *Corporación de Fomento de la Producción. 50 años de realizaciones 1939–1989* (Santiago: Universidad de Santiago de Chile, 1989) and Aníbal Pinto, *Chile, un caso de desarrollo frustrado* (Santiago: Editorial Universitaria, 1958).

[32] Barbara Stallings, *Class Conflict and Economic Development in Chile, 1958–1973* (Stanford: Stanford University Press, 1978), 46 and table 2–3.

The Dictatorship's Economic Transformation: Objectives

We noted above that the structural changes against which the dictatorship acted began with the reformist government of Frei Montalva.[33] Its policies provoked opposition from both the right and the left, each for different reasons. The counterrevolutionary stance of the new rulers of 1973 and their transformative aspirations[34] ran deep: to reverse the changes driven by the Frei and Allende governments and establish a new political and economic system that would hold firm after the military returned to barracks.

Guided by ideas inspired by radical neoliberalism, the new rulers, along with the "Chicago boys,"[35] carried out an ambitious program of change, aiming to build an economic system in which the state would play a limited role in economic activity and business would enjoy broad autonomy, receiving generous financial incentives, without having to interact with powerful workers' organizations, as it had before the military coup. Before long this radical neoliberalism had become a paradigm,[36] a framework of ideas and standards that specifies political goals and indicates the nature of the problems to which they directed, and the type of instruments policymakers may use.[37] Paradigms, Hall adds, are not rigid over time; they have a capacity to face new challenges, introduce changes to the policies they have promoted, and even to the institutions initially established.[38]

The paradigm of radical neoliberalism had a totalizing vision. It was an ideological and cultural project consisting of different, loosely connected

[33] Huneeus and Couso, eds., *Eduardo Frei Montalva.*

[34] Manuel Antonio Garretón, *El proceso político chileno* (Santiago: FLACSO, 1983).

[35] The economic program had been written by a group of economists who opposed the Allende administration. They finished it just a few days before the coup, sharing a copy with members of the Chilean Navy. The document, titled *El Ladrillo*, presented the ideas of economists from Universidad Católica, who later gained masters or doctoral degrees at the University of Chicago. See Arturo Fontaine, *Los economistas y el Presidente Pinochet* (Santiago: Zig-Zag, 1988); Valdés, *Pinochet's Economists*; Gárate, *La revolución capitalista en Chile.*

[36] Peter A. Hall, "Policy Paradigms, Social Learning and the State: The Case of Economic Policymaking in Britain," *Comparative Politics* 25, no.3 (1993): 275–296.

[37] In most countries, economic paradigms tend to last over several administrations. Such was the case of Keynesian economics in Great Britain, or the case of import substitution industrialization in Chile after 1929, until Frei Montalva replaced it with what was known as "structuralism."

[38] Hall, "Policy Paradigms, Social Learning and the State," 278.

discourses, whose central premise was an attempt to disenchant politics by subjecting it to economic logic.[39] It considered politics as subordinate to the economy, particularly to the rules of the market, and conceived the citizen as a consumer who is guided by the appearances of products and material interests. It was applied to all areas of public policy, from purely economic ones, such as openness to foreign trade, to deregulations in other areas, including culture. Thus, it served as the basis for a new higher education policy which included the promotion of private universities at the expense of weakening the state universities. During the democratic governments, the number of students at the former overtook those at public institutions.

Deregulation also extended to interest groups, since professional associations were impugned for monopolizing union representation and were reduced to voluntary guilds, establishing freedom of affiliation and without powers to monitor members' performance. It also held sway in urban planning. The liberalization of land use allowed cities to expand without regulatory plans, with enormous environmental consequences and higher costs for the state in public services, and boosted the growth of a powerful and highly concentrated real estate industry. The state's role was limited to providing security, protecting private property and creating and maintaining markets.

As we have noted, privatizations played an extraordinarily important role in the economic transformation of the dictatorship. The numerous privatized and reprivatized companies, with the massive transfer of property and assignment of state resources to the new controllers, benefited especially long-established economic groups and new groups that had emerged since the 1970s, especially in retail. Firstly, between 1974 and 1979, there was a process of reprivatization of the many companies belonging to the "social property area" ("área de propiedad social," APS) nationalized or already controlled by the Allende government. This change became known as "first wave privatizations." Later, beginning in 1984, there were "second wave privatizations," which included the reprivatization of banks and companies that had come under government control as a result of the economic crisis of 1982 and 1983, the so-called "strange area," and the privatization of almost all public companies. The rescue of collapsed banks, the major ones in the country, included the transfer of

[39] Davies, *The limits of neoliberalism: authority, sovereignty and the logic of competition.*

abundant public resources to their new controllers and provided for repayment over 30 years on very favorable terms for the banks.[40]

Both privatization waves had at least three aspects in common:

(i) They were carried out in the context of serious economic crises, although of different origins: the first was caused by the economic policy of the Allende government; the second, the economic crisis of 1982–1983, was due to the economic opening and deregulation of the financial sector, which allowed the economic groups to become overindebted to international banks, leading to a cessation of payments due to a sharp increase in interest rates introduced in 1981 by the U.S. Federal Reserve.[41]

(ii) In both cases, the government was more concerned with getting rid of the companies than seeking income for the treasury, so they were sold at very low prices. Gárate[42] notes that the public companies were in good shape when they were privatized, which reinforces the idea that privatization responded more to political and ideological interests than technical efficiency criteria, as the regime's promoters argued. The numerous companies privatized in both waves were sold under their book value, including companies that the state had rescued by allocating extensive economic resources for the use of future controllers. The main economic groups of today, with few exceptions, expanded in one of these two stages of privatization.

(iii) Both privatization processes had in common a lack of transparency,[43] with the use of privileged information and discretionary decisions favoring economic groups and entrepreneurs linked to Pinochet's economic team and executives of public or state-controlled companies. In other words, without establishing a separation of public from private interests.

The "second wave" privatizations differed from the first by the participation of new private and for-profit actors, the pension fund

[40] Muñoz, *El Modelo Económico de la Concertación*.

[41] Ffrench-Davis, *Reformas económicas en Chile*.

[42] Gárate, *La revolución capitalista en Chile*.

[43] Marcel, "Privatización y finanzas públicas: El caso de Chile 1985–1988," 5–60; Dominique Hachette and Rolf Lüders, *La privatización en Chile* (Santiago: Centro Internacional para el Desarrollo Económico, CINDE, 1992); Huneeus, *The Pinochet Regime*.

administrators (AFPs), which were created as a result of the privatization in 1980 of the public (co-payment) pension system. Part of the funds accumulated in workers' contributions were invested by the AFPs in acquiring share packages of the state companies that were being privatized. This enabled the AFPs to elect directors at shareholder meetings of companies in which the AFPs held a sizeable part of their capital and thus could influence their corporate governance.

In this way, minority shareholders were able to secure a majority on company boards with the votes of the directors elected by the AFP—the latter being also former dictatorship officials—without needing to have a majority of the capital. In addition, the pension funds were destined for the financial market, thus favoring the banks, which were controlled by the main economic groups or in which big business had considerable power.

"First Wave" Privatizations (1974–1979): Reversing the Nationalizations and Company Interventions by the Allende Government

In this first stage, the state privatized companies that had been legally nationalized by the Allende government and returned them to their controllers; or it reprivatized those that were under its control because they had been intervened or requisitioned by that administration.[44] In total there were about 250 companies. This process was not accident free. The two groups that accrued most economic power were the Cruzat group, led by Manuel Cruzat and Fernando Larraín, and the Vial group, led by Javier Vial.[45] With a heavy external debt and of the banks they would control, these two groups came to control 62 of the 250 largest private companies; respectively, they held 24.72% and 12.61% of the assets of all these companies (Dahse 1979: Table 59). Long-established groups with financial resources also participated in these privatizations, like the Matte

[44] On the privatization process, see Hachette and Lüders, *La privatización en Chile*; Marcel, "Privatización y finanzas públicas: el caso de Chile 1985–1988"; Gárate, *La revolución capitalista en Chile*; Huneeus, *The Pinochet Regime.*

[45] Manuel Cruzat and Fernando Larraín were brothers-in-law. Javier Vial and Ricardo Claro were young entrepreneurs who worked together in the late 1960s when they created a business group popularly known as "las pirañas." The group dissolved when Allende became president (Tromben, *Crónica secreta de la economía chilena*).

group, which secured 8.59% of the assets of the 250 companies, the Angelini group, with 3.74%, and Luksic with 3.67% (Dahse 1979: Table 59). In summary, in 1978 these five economic groups held 53.33% of the assets of those 250 private companies; 13.01% belonged to foreign capitalist groups and the rest (a mere 9.58%) was distributed among smaller groups and 37 individual entrepreneurs.

The deregulation of the financial system and the companies' huge external debt added to changes in the international financial conditions and sparked an economic crisis that led to the bankruptcy in 1982–1983 of the Cruzat and Vial groups and numerous other companies and banks. As damage control, the state ordered the intervention of numerous companies and 13 financial institutions, including the Bank of Santiago (Cruzat) and the Bank of Chile (the Vial group). Important companies came under state control on a scale comparable to the nationalization policy of the Allende government, creating what became known as the "strange area" of the economy ("área rara de la economía").[46]

In July 1984, the Vial group and its associates signed an agreement through which the group surrendered its assets, which included the Bank of Chile, in favor of its creditors. A short time later, the Cruzat group secured a better deal from the government: it signed an agreement with the "Progresa Commission," appointed by the Ministry of Finance, which allowed it to retain 8.5% of its asset while handing over the rest, including the Santiago Bank, to be administered by the commission. Once the companies and the bank had been restored to health, they would be sold in order to pay off the total debts incurred by the group (Rozas and Marín 1989: 58).

The three main historical groups—Matte, Angelini, and Luksic—had followed a conservative debt policy, which enabled them to surmount the 1982–1983 crisis and exploit the opportunities offered by the reprivatization since 1984 of companies and banks in the "strange area." As a result, they grew and dramatically diversified their assets. A decade later, Fazio (1997) highlighted the fact that *Forbes* magazine listed them as billionaires

[46] The "strange area" was composed of 43 firms that belonged to the Vial and Cruzat Larraín groups and included two of the country's main banks (Banco de Chile and Banco de Santiago), and the AFPs Provida and Santa María. It also included the COPEC (Compañía de Petróleos de Chile) holding, Forestal Arauco and Industria Forestal S.A, among others. See Gárate, *La revolución capitalista en Chile*.

with assets almost 20 times greater than they possessed in 1978, according to an estimate made by Dahse (1979).

The Privatization of the Pension System

The AFP system is based on workers contributing 10% of their monthly pay into a personal account in an AFP, to which the employer does not contribute to finance their workers' insurance. The AFPs administer the contributions, for which they charge a large commission.

This important privatization was promoted with unusual skill by the minister of labor, José Piñera, brother of twice-president Sebastián Piñera (2010–2014; 2018–2022). Piñera used political arguments to convince Pinochet and the members of the Junta of the need to eliminate the co-payment system, on grounds of its alleged use by political parties to deliver "favors" to their "electoral clientele."[47] José Piñera resorted to "popular capitalism" arguments to justify the reform, arguing that it would produce a change in workers' values and attitudes; because they owned their own accounts, they would defend the permanence of the new system. In addition, their interest would be vested in the stability of the economic system, and the AFPs in particular, to secure their future pensions.[48]

However, the minister failed to consider the complexities of the new pension system. He invited mainly financial experts to participate in the preparation of the draft law, without considering the views of labor economists able to report on evolutionary trends in the labor market. Nor did he consult demographers for background on the evolution of life expectancy in order to estimate the number of years that AFPs would have to pay future pensions, and the funding implications this might have. To fast track its approval, the draft was not submitted to the Council of State for consideration, as had been the case with other economic reforms. It was discussed only in the governing Junta, in which Pinochet expressed concern that the AFPs were controlled by the dominant economic groups at that moment (1980). With these suspicions in mind, the armed forces stuck to their independent pension system. Today, the pensions they receive are considerably better than those of workers on equivalent salaries who are in the AFP system.

[47] José Piñera, *El cascabel al gato. La batalla por la reforma previsional* (Santiago: Zig-Zag, 1990).

[48] Huneeus, *The Pinochet Regime*.

The AFPs very quickly accumulated enormous financial resources following their inauguration on May 1, 1981, and have been highly profitable ever since. Some of these resources were used to acquire shares of public companies that were privatized starting in 1984. Since the shares were sold at a low price and the companies that were being nationalized had been restructured, there was a big incentive for AFPs to participate in the privatizations and obtain great returns on their investment. According to Hachette and Lüders[49] (1992: 86), 25% of the capital of the privatized public companies sold was acquired by the AFPs, making them "the most important way of financing the privatizations carried out in Chile after 1985."

Moreover, AFP investments in privatized public companies had an important political role. Despite being minority partners, the top executives of the companies that were being privatized controlled their management, due to the support of directors chosen by the AFPs at shareholder meetings of the companies in which they held a share of the capital, thereby obtaining a majority on the company boards. This support was given behind the backs of subscribers, public opinion, and the superintendency of pensions, because the AFPs were not obliged to report how they voted in shareholder meetings to elect directors.[50] This political-economic cooperation would persist over time because most of the directors of privatized companies chosen by the AFP were former military regime officials, reinforcing the revolving door that would characterize relations between the state and senior business executives ever since.[51]

Second Wave Privatizations (1984–1989)

The political context of the "second wave" differed from the first. It was carried out not only in the context of an economic crisis, in 1982, but also in a difficult political scenario for the dictatorship, given the discontent of middle and popular sectors affected by the crisis. Unemployment soared in 1983 with the bankruptcy of numerous companies, topping 30% in the metropolitan region.[52] The crisis triggered mass citizen protests, which the military regime countered with a political liberalization, allowing par-

[49] Hachette and Lüders, *La privatización en Chile*, 86.

[50] This was a result of the 1994 capital markets reform.

[51] Huneeus, *La democracia semisoberana*.

[52] Ffrench-Davis, *Reformas económicas en Chile, 1973–2017*.

ties to function, elections to be held for student federation and professional association leaders, and press censorship was suspended.[53] The opposition emerged forcefully, casting doubt over the regime's expectations of holding onto power after the succession plebiscite of 1988.[54] This uncertainty led the minister of finance, Hernán Büchi, to accelerate privatizations. These continued even after the defeat of Pinochet in the plebiscite of October 5, 1988, now with the purpose of preventing their stoppage or reversal by the democratic government, which evidently would be of the opposition.[55]

To dodge criticism from the military that the previous privatizations had led to a high concentration of companies in the economic groups, Büchi resorted to the "popular capitalism" argument, much in use in those years of privatizations in Britain,[56] promising to "spread property" and make Chile into "a country of owners." There were attempts, too, to attract workers in public companies in order to neutralize the rejection of privatization by union leaders and opposition economists.

Conditions for the purchase of shares were extraordinarily favorable. CORFO granted loans for a ten-year term, without interest or readjustments, with a cash down payment of only 5%. In addition, these shares had huge tax incentives, as private buyers could deduct 20% of their value from their annual taxable income. Essentially, this meant that "popular capitalism" enabled individuals to become shareholders at zero cost.[57]

In practice, privatizations were left to the decisions of the top executives of each company, which allowed them to control the process by which ownership was changed, and to become company controllers. Already in democracy, these new entrepreneurs would expand the size of

[53] Carlos Huneeus, "Political Mass Mobilization Against Authoritarian Rule: Pinochet's Chile, 1983–8," in *Civil Resistance and Power Politics: The Experience of Non-violent Action from Gandhi to the Present*, eds. Adam Roberts and Timothy Garton Ash (New York: Oxford University Press, 2009): 197–212.

[54] Huneeus, "Political Mass Mobilization Against Authoritarian Rule," 197–212.

[55] A small number of major firms was not privatized during this process. One example is Línea Area Nacional (LAN), which was partially privatized under the Pinochet regime and the remaining 24% was privatized under Aylwin. The water and sewage companies were privatized by Frei Ruiz-Tagle's government.

[56] Peter Saunders and Colin Harris, *Privatization and Popular Capitalism* (Buckingham: Open University Press, 1994).

[57] Reinaldo Sapag, "El derecho de propiedad en los bancos con deuda subordinada," in *Páginas periodísticas*, Andrés Aylwin, César Díaz-Muñoz and Reinaldo Sapag (Santiago: Ediciones Copygraph, 1997), 157.

the companies they controlled in the manner explained above. Some of them backed by democratic governments, spread across Latin America, participating in the privatization of companies and increasing their economic power.

An executive who illustrates these individuals' managerial capacity, political ability, and the broad discretion they enjoyed in decision-making was Julio Ponce Lerou, the first executive to start acting this way since the 1970s, who would later become the controller of Soquimich.[58] A forest engineer whose career took off rapidly under the military regime (favored by his being Pinochet's son-in-law), he began holding managerial positions in the Ministry of Agriculture and later moved to CORFO, where he became a business manager, a key position to prepare privatizations. From there he joined the management of Soquimich. When its sale began, he took charge of the privatization, became the company's main controlling partner and was its president for decades. At the same time, he was director of other public companies, such as Enami, Iansa, and Endesa.[59]

The privatization of the 33 public companies between 1984 and 1989 was notable for its speed and scope. According to Marcel,[60] "the flow of tax revenues in just four years represented at least double that implemented in Great Britain over eight years, in terms of their relative weight in GNP, public revenues and stock transactions." The difference was that in this case there was no plan to indicate what criteria would be used, nor were there any international tenders. There were only general guidelines given by a "share sale committee."

The Continuity of the Economic System Imposed by the Dictatorship

As we said above, the Concertación governments did not reverse the economic transformation wrought by the dictatorship; the reforms they introduced were not intended to change the neoliberal paradigm for a different one. They took this decision for political and economic reasons:

[58] Other examples include Roberto de Andraca, who controlled CAP, one of the main metallurgical corporations in Latin America, and José Yuraszeck, who would control Chilectra and Endesa, with which he and his associates created the Enersis conglomerate, which expanded throughout Latin America in the 1990s and was later sold to Spain's Endesa in 1997. See Huneeus, *The Pinochet Regime*.

[59] Mönckeberg, *La máquina para defraudar. Los casos Penta y Soquimich*.

[60] Marcel, "Privatización y finanzas públicas: el caso de Chile 1985–1988," 37.

in the short term, they considered that the military's subordination to the civilian authority and General Pinochet's attitude were crucial to the stability of the fragile democracy[61]; in the medium term, the stability of the political order hinged on good economic management, considering that, as noted above, 40% of the population lived in poverty. The economic program of "growth with equity" followed a strategy based on the concepts of Albert Hirschman, to do "one thing at a time": first ensure growth and afterwards equity.[62] As Hirschman had warned, there was no second stage due to the opposition of the economic interests that had been consolidated in the first.[63]

The option for continuity was expressed mainly in the new authorities' acquiescence to the economic system established by the dictatorship, accepting policies they had previously fiercely criticized. This preference for continuity was reinforced by the policy of consensus on economic policy. Fearful of the structural and instrumental power of business organizations[64] and of the rightist parties, the Concertación rulers froze center-left policies such as strengthening unions, regulations to protect consumers, reinforcement of the regulatory powers of the state, and correction of economic concentration and inequalities. As the years passed, the economic authorities continued to be reactive rather than proactive in the face of corporate malfeasance, influence peddling, collusion, and monopolistic practices.[65]

Only as recently as 2004 was a relatively modern set of institutions established for the defense of free competition, with reinforcement of the office of the National Economic Prosecutor and the creation of a court for the Defense of Free Competition. But even then, in order to maintain political power, the Concertación parties engaged in collusive practices

[61] The 1980 Constitution allowed Pinochet to remain in the position of army commander in chief for eight years after the transition to democracy. In order to avoid hostility with the armed forces, the new democratic regime did not challenge this rule.

[62] Albert O. Hirschman, "The Case against One Thing at the Time," *World Development*, 18 No. 8 (1990), 1119–1122, republished in Albert O. Hirschman, *A Propensity to Self-Subversion* (Harvard: Harvard University Press, 1995), 69–76.

[63] Huneeus, *La democracia semisoberana*.

[64] Undurraga, "Instrucción, indulgencia y justificación: Los circuitos culturales del capitalismo chileno."

[65] To analyze the limitations that the Chilean government had to avoid predatory or corrupt activities by the private sector, see Diego G. Pardow, "La experiencia chilena disuadiendo ilícitos corporativos," *Derecho Público Iberoameriano* 1 (2012): 55–83.

with the political competition,[66] by removing important economic issues from the public agenda that would have given them a policy profile and set them apart from the right-wing collectivities.

The main reasons advanced to justify the continuity of the "model" were economic: to give confidence to entrepreneurs, who were considered indispensable actors in achieving economic growth and reducing poverty.[67] The Concertación rulers, however, did not consider the political components of the economic transformation, nor the institutional features of the economic order imposed by the dictatorship: the weak state, with its limited regulatory capabilities, and the highly politicized entrepreneurs who defended Pinochet's legacy. Nor did they consider the persistence of big business practices developed in dictatorship that were incompatible with democracy, including various unlawful acts that ranged from the use of privileged information, abuses against consumers, and regime officials, and monopolistic practices that hurt small and medium-sized companies and consumers. They neglected, finally, to establish institutional mechanisms to ensure the autonomy of politics from economic power, failing to establish public funding for electoral campaigns until 2003, and for parties until 2015. These conditions facilitated a close relationship between money and politics which helped to create a political agenda favorable to big business and which remains an important source of corruption.

The option in favor of the continuity of the economic order was facilitated by the favorable macroeconomic indicators, with an annual GDP growth rate averaging 5% between 1990 and 2009. During the governments of the Concertación, per capita GDP expanded at an average annual rate of 3.6%, considerably higher than the 1.3% recorded during the military regime. Poverty dropped to 15.1% in 2009.[68] These good results caused a path dependence effect in maintaining the continuity of the economic system. Emphasis would be placed on growth and investment, accentuating the features the system had had since the military regime.[69]

[66] We follow Bartolini's concept on political collusion. Stefano Bartolini, "Electoral and Party Competition: Analytical Dimensions and Empirical Problems," in *Political Parties. Old Concepts and New Challenges,* eds. Richard Gunther, José Ramón Montero and Juan J. Linz (Oxford: Oxford University Press, 2002) 84–110.

[67] Huneeus, *La democracia semisoberana.*

[68] Ffrench-Davis, *Reformas económicas en Chile, 1973–2017.*

[69] Huneeus, *La democracia semisoberana.*

The Weaknesses of the Economic System

The continuity was preserved despite the major weaknesses and flaws revealed by the economic system: (i) It still depends on the exploitation of natural resources, which has high environmental costs. (ii) 80% of employment is produced by small and medium-sized companies providing unstable or precarious work, with low pay, stimulating the informal economy. This limits capacity for individual savings in the private pension system, resulting in very low pensions that are far from the promises of an improvement on the co-payment system. (iii) The economic concentration and inequalities stand out. The five largest groups are present in the main economic areas and owned almost 50% of the assets of publicly traded companies (Molina 2005: 3). The controllers of these groups have enormous economic and political power. According to *Forbes* magazine in 2018, there are 11 Chilean billionaires, with a combined wealth of 15% of GDP, a considerably higher relative weight than in the other OECD countries and Russia, with the exception of Mexico. These billionaires include the families of four historical economic groups (Luksic, Angelini, Matte, and Yarur); the new billionaires who emerged in the dictatorship favored by privatizations (Julio Ponce Lerou) and the reprivatizations of the "strange area" of the economy (Alvaro Saieh); and those who took advantage of its economic policies (Falabella, Horst Paulmann, and President Piñera).

According to the methodology of economists Thomas Piketty and Emmanuel Sáez, with data from 2010, the concentration of income in Chile is higher than other countries of Latin America—the most unequal region in the world[70]—and higher than the countries of the OECD.[71] The richest 1% accounts for 28.7% of income,[72] well above the other countries, in none of which it reaches 20%. According to OECD estimates, this percentage of people in 2005 had 17.4% of national income in the United States, 14% in the United Kingdom, 13.8% in Norway, and less than 10% in the remaining European countries. Economic notables (Dahl 1961) who make up 0.1% of the population hold 13.7% of income, higher than

[70] Goran Therborn, *The killing fields of inequality* (Cambridge: Polity, 2013).

[71] We follow Eduardo Engel, "El uno por ciento: Chile y el mundo," *La Tercera*, October 5, 2013.

[72] In Uruguay, it is 14.1%; Argentina, 16.75%; Colombia, 20.45%; Spain, 8.24%; See http://topincomes.g-mond.parisschoolofeconomics.eu/#Country:*Argentina*, accessed February 19, 2014.

the United States (10.5%) and the double of France. Examining an even smaller percentage of the population (0.01%), about 1700 individuals have 6.2% of the income, well above that of the same percentage in the United States (4.08%).

Upon returning to La Moneda in 2014, Michelle Bachelet carried out program of reforms to change the neoliberal paradigm. She faced opposition from big business and even from the parties of the former Concertación. The controllers and top executives of the main groups entered the political arena, assuming control of the business organizations. Alfredo Moreno, one of the chief executives of the Falabella (retail) group and a former minister of Piñera, was elected president of the Confederation of Production and Commerce (CPC), a meeting point of the different business organizations.[73] Bernardo Larraín Matte, of the Matte group, was elected president of Sofofa, the historical organization of industrialists. Personalities from the main groups, especially Luksic and Angelini, were elected to the Sofofa council, as well as representative personalities of large companies, including three former ministers of the Piñera government.

As we argued above, the authoritarian ethos of the main business groups forged in dictatorship has led to the continuation in democracy of their bad business practices. These include the following: (i) conflicts of interest; (ii) the revolving door; (iii) illegal financing of politics; (iv) collusion; and (v) the use of privileged information in business dealings, (vi) the use of tax evasion practices using companies bankrupted in 1982. Here are some illustrative cases.

Conflicts of Interest

In 1997, José Yuraszeck, accompanied by the five senior executives who accompanied him from Chilectra, negotiated the sale of Enersis to Endesa Spain, the main electricity company of that country, without informing the Enersis board of directors. He privileged the value of the political rights that they had through various companies ("Las Chispas"), which allowed them to control Enersis by electing five of its nine directors, while

[73] Octavio Avendaño and Rodrigo Cuevas Ossandon, "Gremios empresariales y sindicatos," in *The Political System of Chile*, eds. Carlos Huneeus and Avendaño Octavio (Santiago: LOM Ediciones, 2018), 333–377.

having 0.06% of the capital of those companies (they were class B shares).[74] Yuraszeck concealed this operation announcing a "strategic alliance." This was monitored by the Superintendency of Securities and Insurance (SVS), which detected its true nature. The minority shareholders, including the AFPs, who held most of the class A shares, protested that the negotiation had been conducted behind their backs and removed the key operatives, causing a commotion in the market and public opinion that was known as "the scandal of the century."[75] The contracts, which had not yet been executed, were rescinded, and the SVS ordered the six executives to pay a fine of $70 million, the largest in the country's history. The Supreme Court confirmed the SVS's decision in a June 7, 2005, ruling. The penalized executives negotiated with the government the amount of interest, which was reduced to 40% to avoid a trial that would have delayed its collection. In the end, the executives paid $49 million.[76]

The Revolving Door

The Luksic group, to mention one of the biggest names, has made ample use of the revolving door. In 2013, it appointed to the board of Channel 13 TV two important collaborators of President Bachelet in her electoral campaign, Nicolás Eyzaguirre and Alberto Arenas. They would be in the first cabinet of her second government (2014–2018) as ministers of education and finance, respectively. In March 2015, four of Channel 13's ten directors had been ministers of state: three in the Concertación governments and one in Piñera's. At the end of Piñera's first government, his former interior minister, Rodrigo Hinzpeter, was appointed chief lawyer

[74] "Gobiernos Corporativos Chile," Recuperación de información pública sobre casos emblemáticos, las modified March 10, 2010, https://gobiernoscorporativoschile.wordpress.com/2010/03/30/caso-chispas/. Accessed April 7, 2020.

[75] One of the minority shareholders who claimed to have been damaged by that operation was the then senator Sebastián Piñera (RN), who negotiated with Endesa Spain the value of his shares. This allowed him to reach a higher price per share than the one gained by the other shareholders. See Loreto Daza N. and Bernardita Del Solar, *Piñera. Historia de un ascenso* (Santiago: Random House Mondadori, 2010).

[76] The sixth individual who was sanctioned for this operation passed away right before the case was concluded at the Supreme Court. His heirs were not legally obliged to pay the penalty fee. "El caso 'Chispas,'" Cooperativa, accessed October 8, 2019, https://www.cooperativa.cl/noticias/pais/presidente-pinera/el-caso-chispas/2006-01-12/080740.html

of Quiñenco, the parent corporation of the group's companies.[77] Luksic group companies have been involved in tariff and prices collusion: the South American Steam Company (CSV) was sanctioned by the U.S. regulator, and Enex was denounced by the Chilean National Economic Prosecutor for similar conduct. Both companies benefited from a plea bargain to avoid stiffer penalties.

Illegal Financing of Politics

Public financing of electoral campaigns began in 2005, 15 years after the end of the dictatorship. For a quarter of a century, there was no public funding for political parties, which only began to operate in the 2017 elections.[78] This pushed candidates to seek funds from the business sector. The practice was widespread, involving candidates from all parties, with the exception of the Communist Party, who would reach out to the controllers of large companies and economic groups. This would have an enormous political cost for democracy, as it reduced parliamentarians' autonomy and independence from economic power, and was reflected in a cordial agenda with the private sector and gestures in favor of companies, opening the way to corruption.

The Penta group, formed by two former Cruzat group executives, benefited from the reprivatizations of the "strange area," and in particular the privatization of ISE General Insurance and "popular capitalism," to control the Bank of Chile in the 1990s.[79] These businessmen gave millions in contributions to UDI candidates, issuing invoices for services that had never been rendered, a violation of tax laws. The Angelini group, through Corpesca, made contributions to Jaime Orpis, a UDI senator who had lost his parliamentary immunity and was under prosecution, to influence the drafting of a law that would guarantee indefinite fishing quotas only to the seven large existing companies in the area. This bad practice of illegal financing later spread to Concertación politicians. SQM financed politicians of all parties, including the left, laying out a minefield in defense of its interests.

[77] For the revolving door, see PNUD, *Desiguales. Orígenes, cambios y desafíos de la brecha social en Chile* (Santiago: PNUD, 2017).

[78] Ricardo Gamboa and Mauricio Morales, "Chile's 2015 Electoral Reform: Changing the Rules of the Game," *Latin American Politics and Society* 58, no. 4 (2016): 126–144.

[79] Mönckeberg, *La máquina para defraudar.*

Knowledge in 2015 of this illegal practice of political financing due to the action of the attorney general's office impacted public opinion. None of the parliamentarians who received contributions from SQM or other large companies were elected in the senatorial and deputies' race of 2017.

Collusion

Collusion is a capital sin for a business class that defends the private sector's role by glorifying the virtues of free competition and its supposed efficiency. Speeches aside, price collusion practices are widespread in several sectors in Chile: chicken, pharmacies, toilet paper, and diapers are just some of the scandals that have been uncovered.[80] In 2008, the National Economic Prosecutor's Office revealed that the three large pharmaceutical chains that control more than 90% of the market—Cruz Verde, Ahumada, and Salcobrand—had for years concerted price increases as an established practice. The investigation found that the price inflation of 222 remedies vital for patients had been coordinated through a triangulation between pharmacy and laboratory managers. One of the pharmacies, Farmacias Ahumada, admitted the collusion and paid more than a million dollars in fines. In 2011, in addition, the Free Competition Tribunal (TDLC) revealed that the chicken industry had been operating as a cartel for more than 15 years. The three main producers—Agrosuper, Ariztía, and Don Pollo—agreed on the distribution of market shares and carefully set the price so that it was not high enough to lead to competition from imported chickens that would lower prices and harm them. This coordinated price increase generated more than 1.5 billion extra dollars at the expense of Chileans. The Supreme Court confirmed the TDLC fine of over $15 million exacted from these three companies.

In addition, in 2015, CMPC, the main corporation of the Matte Group which controls 75% of the market in the paper industry, was caught in a massive paper collusion scandal. From 2001 to 2013, CMPC, together with SCA Chile—the other monopolistic company in the paper market—assigned market share quotas and set sale prices for its tissue products: toilet paper, napkins, tissues, and paper towels. The scandal meant not

[80] "Pollos, Farmacias, Confort y Pañales: Cuatro mega portonazos al bolsillo de todos los chilenos los últimos 20 años," The Clinic, accessed October 8, 2019, http://www.theclinic.cl/2016/12/20/cuatro-mega-portonazos-al-bolsillo-de-todos-los-chilenos-los-ultimos-20-anos/

only the resignation of the group's patriarch, Eliodoro Matte, from the presidency of CMPC and the CEP, but also a generational renewal of its leadership. Bernardo Larraín Matte—who in 2015 was the general manager of the electricity company Colbún and director of CMPC-Tissue, which was involved in the collusion—became the group's main public figure. In 2017, the National Economic Prosecutor's office fined SCA Chile $18.3 million. CMPC reached an agreement with the National Consumer Service (Sernac) and consumer groups to pay $150 million, that is, 7000 pesos to each Chilean (allow time to collect).[81]

Use of Privileged Information

This is a bad practice that has existed for years among directors and executives of companies and financial investors. As documented by Sergio Jara (2018), this practice pervades social ties and the *modus operandi* of Chilean big business, especially in the financial sector. For example, President Piñera was sanctioned in 2009 by the Superintendency of Securities and Insurance for making use of privileged information to buy shares of the LAN airline in 2006, of which he was one of the controllers.

Use of Tax Evasion Practices Using Companies Bankrupted in 1982

Big businessmen and some economic groups (Luksic, Penta, and Said, among others) resorted to a ruse to reduce their tax payments. It involved "zombie" companies.[82] Their only real existence was on the books of the Internal Revenue Service (SII), to which they had not filed a tax return since that year. Guzmán and Rojas explain how this mechanism worked: "a good part of the Chilean business elite spent a whole decade (during

[81] "Sernac y Conadecus explican por qué la compensación pactada con CMPC es un "buen" acuerdo," Emol, last modified January 27, 2017, https://www.emol.com/noticias/Economia/2017/01/27/842216/Sernac-y-Asociacion-de-Consumidores-defienden-compensacion-pactada-con-CMPC.html; "Histórico triunfo de los consumidores: Cómo y cuándo se pagarán los 7 mil pesos," Conadecus, last modified May 31, 2018, http://www.conadecus.cl/conadecus/?p=17742

[82] Jorge Rojas, "El ardid con el que algunas empresas quisieron 'ahorrar' $24.521.682.331 en impuestos," *The Clinic*, May 28 2012: https://www.theclinic.cl/2012/05/28/el-ardid-con-que-algunas-empresas-quisieron-ahorrar-24-521-682-331-en-impuestos-2/. Accessed April 27, 2020.

which) they bought failed companies with large debts on their balance sheets and brought them back to life with complex legal and accounting maneuvers. Then they allowed the zombies to absorb their most prosperous companies. Voila! Large amounts of profit vanished from the sight of the Internal Revenue Service (SII)."[83]

A true industry of zombie companies for sale emerged, there being no complete list of those that achieved their goal. Only 73 large companies and the same number of bankrupt companies are known to have used this scam. This list comes from a statement issued by the SII in 2007 about the results of its investigation. It does not include the smaller failed companies that were later used for these tax purposes. The state failed to receive a huge amount in lost taxes, equivalent to 1.5% of the GDP in 2007.[84]

For 13 years the SII tolerated this as a "legal" practice, since the conditions for reducing taxes due on company profits were not regulated by law. These were politically incorrect and ethically reprehensible acts in democracy, when the government had to deal with the pressing economic demands of the popular sectors affected by the economic legacies of the dictatorship. This was another incentive for big business, added to the ones already mentioned that were explicitly recognized: not to review the privatizations of the dictatorship and to maintain the continuity of the institutional architecture of the economy and its main policies, such as privatizations.

Among the businessmen who used zombie companies in democracy was Sebastian Piñera, twice president of Chile. He lived through the crisis of 1982 as general manager of Citicorp (which belonged to the Cruzat group), a bank that would participate in the second wave of privatizations, which he would benefit from. He had his own parallel businesses which expanded in the 1980s and already owned a considerable fortune in 1989 when he entered politics. His fortune grew exponentially in democracy, especially in his "golden years" when as a senator (1990–1998) he continued to actively boost his investments. In 2007, he featured in *Forbes* as a Chilean billionaire, and by 2018 his fortune had more than doubled at $2.8 billion, or 0.94% of GDP. For a comparison of his wealth when he returned to the presidency in 2018, Donald Trump's amounted to 0.022% of GDP of the United States at the time.

[83] Juan Andrés Guzmán and Jorge Rojas, *Empresarios zombies. La mayor elusión tributaria de la élite chilena* (Santiago: Catalonia-UDP, 2017), 18.

[84] Guzmán and Rojas, *Emmpresarios zombies,* 19.

As Carlos Tromben has shown, Piñera became one of the controllers of LAN Chile, a state-owned airline that was finally privatized in May 1994, when Corfo tendered 24% of its state-held capital. Piñera obtained it through his historical partner, who appeared as the only interested party. He used his political power to forestall the participation of the AFPs in the tender, because it was a good business for them and for all the workers who were AFP subscribers. The airline's new controllers began a process of expansion and internationalization, and since 2000 it has become one of Latin America's biggest air carriers.[85]

Conclusion

The economic transformation oriented by a radical neoliberal paradigm that the dictatorship imposed laid the institutional and political foundations of Chilean capitalism and its extreme economic concentration. As Hacker and Pierson[86] show for the United States, and Hopkin for Great Britain,[87] it was the political context of authoritarianism that explains the concentration of wealth in Chile, as well as policies favoring traditional groups and the new ones that emerged from under Pinochet's wing. State companies in energy and telecommunications remained private monopolies after privatization, without the establishment of regulatory bodies to protect consumers. The position of strength from which business leaders emerged in democracy[88] is explained, in part, by a series of institutional and political factors that favored the large economic groups: very business-friendly labor legislation that weakened the unions and allowed layoffs "for company reasons"; the rescue of companies with public resources followed by their sale to their controllers at absurdly low prices; conflicts of interest and shady mechanisms for using privileged information to benefit from state or private company decisions; illegal financing of politics, with parliamentarians and parties in debt to their financiers rather than to their voters; and the revolving door between government and company

[85] Carlos Tromben, *Crónica secreta de la economía chilena*. Santiago: Ediciones B, 2016.

[86] Jacob S. Hacker and Paul Pierson, *The Winner-Take-All Politics. How Washington Made the Rich Richer and Turned its Back on the Middle Class* (New York: Simon and Schuster, 2010).

[87] Hopkin and Lynch, "Winner-Take-All-Politics in Europe?"; Hopkin and Shaw, "Organized Combat or Structural Advantage?"

[88] Cecilia Montero, *La revolución empresarial chilena* (Santiago: CIEPLAN-Domen Ediciones, 1997).

management positions that inhibits a culture of transparency between public and private sectors, among other practices.

The dictatorship's policies, and their continuation in democracy, had a huge impact on the consolidation of the dominant economic groups in Chile. The authoritarian context influenced not only the capture of public resources—the restoration of class power that Harvey[89] warns of in neoliberalism—generating broad economic concentration. It also impacted business practices and culture. The patronage culture of the political and economic elites, discretionary practices and cronyism in decision-making, and the subordination of politics to economic decisions,[90] are all dictatorship legacies that were reproduced in democracy. Democratic governments showed no concern about protecting the regulatory functions of the state in defense of consumers and to safeguard competition. The pro-business,[91] "*pure market economy*"[92] capitalism developed in Chile has hindered efforts in the political arena to consolidate democracy. Chile is a paradigmatic case of "*winner-takes-all politics.*" Those who were in positions of power during the dictatorship benefited economically, confirming the importance of political factors in economic inequalities.

Concerned about justifying the capitalist revolution imposed under the dictatorship, businessmen have financed institutions since the 1980s that aim to legitimize the new economic system. They have invested in business associations, think tanks, executive training, economic media, and private universities, aimed at transmitting their ideas and doing business in the process. These "cultural circuits of Chilean capitalism"[93] are characterized by their arguments justifying private sector actions and refuting adverse criticism. The pro-business press, dominated by the Edwards and Sahié groups' duopoly,[94] has been particularly functional to the business sector. Despite the rhetoric of corporate social responsibility and "country loyalty" parroted by businessmen, the sector's bad practices, combined with the vertical ethos that inspires its conception of society, are

[89] David Harvey, *A brief history of neoliberalism* (Oxford University Press: Oxford, 2005).

[90] Davies, *The limits of neoliberalism.*

[91] Undurraga, *Divergencias.*

[92] Juan J. Linz and Alfred Stepan, *Problems of Democratic Transition and Consolidation* (Baltimore: Johns Hopkins University Press, 1996).

[93] Undurraga, "Instrucción, indulgencia y justificación: Los circuitos culturales del capitalismo chileno"; Undurraga, *Divergencias.*

[94] Mönckeberg, *Los magnates de la prensa*; Víctor Herrero, *Agustín Edwards Eastman. Una biografía desclasificada del dueño de El Mercurio* (Santiago: Debate, 2014).

dictatorship legacies that precede tensions, conflicts, and crises. Despite the visibility that these circuits give to businessmen, the multiple scandals in which they have been involved reveal the authoritarian origin of this winner-takes-all politics, with its institutional and cultural roots that are widely spread in society.

Now that inequalities are turning into a new source of conflict,[95] it remains to be seen how much legitimacy the economic system will retain with its institutional weaknesses and authoritarian entrepreneurial ethos. Intolerance of injustices and the demand for transparency make it increasingly difficult to justify predatory practices. This is especially so in an economic system that is growing more slowly than in the past, while the concentration of wealth prevents most Chileans from sharing its benefits.

References

Arriagada, Genaro. *Los empresarios y la política*. Santiago: LOM, 2004.

Atria, Fernando. *Veinte años después. Neoliberalismo con rostro humano*. Santiago: Editorial Catalonia, 2013.

Avendaño, Octavio, and Rodrigo Cuevas Ossandon. "Gremios empresariales y sindicatos." In *El sistema político de Chile*, edited by Carlos Huneeus and Avendaño Octavio, 333–377. Santiago: LOM Ediciones, 2018.

Bartolini, Stefano. "Electoral and Party Competition: Analytical Dimensions and Empirical Problems." In *Political Parties. Old Concepts and New Challenges*, edited by Richard Gunther, José Ramón Montero and Juan J. Linz, 84–110. Oxford: Oxford University Press, 2002.

Bitar, Sergio. *Transición, socialismo y democracia: la experiencia chilena*. México: Siglo XXI, 1979.

Campero, Guillermo. *Los gremios empresariales en el período 1970–1983: comportamiento sociopolítico y orientaciones ideológicas*. Santiago: ILET, 1984.

Dahl, Robert A. *Who governs? Democracy and Power in an American City*. New Haven: Yale University Press, 1961

Dahse, Fernando. *Mapa de la extrema riqueza*. Santiago: Aconcagua, 1979.

Daza N., Loreto, and Bernardita Del Solar. *Piñera. Historia de un ascenso*. Santiago: Random House Mondadori, 2010.

Dezalay, Yves, and Bryant Garth. *The Internationalization of Palace Wars*. Chicago: University Chicago Press, 2002.

Dobek, Mariusz Mark. "Privatization as a Political Priority: the British Experience." *Political Studies* XLI: 1 (1993): 24–40.

[95] Ronald Inglehart, "Inequality and Modernization. Why Equality is Likely to Make a Comeback," *Foreign Affairs* 95 (January 2016): 2–10.

Engel, Eduardo. "El uno por ciento: Chile y el mundo." *La Tercera*, October 5, 2013.

Fazio, Hugo. *La Transnacionalización de la economía chilena. Mapa de la Extrema Riqueza al año 2000.* Santiago: LOM, 2000.

Fazio, Hugo. *Los mecanismos fraudulentos de hacer fortuna. Mapa de la extrema riqueza 2015.* Santiago: LOM, 2015.

Fazio, Hugo. *Mapa actual de la extrema riqueza.* Santiago: LOM-ARCIS, 1997.

Fazio, Hugo. *Mapa de la Extrema Riqueza al año 2005.* Santiago: LOM Ediciones, 2005.

Ffrench-Davis, Ricardo. *Reformas económicas en Chile, 1973–2017.* Santiago: Taurus, 2018.

Florio, Massimo. *The Great Divestiture. Evaluating the Welfare Impact of the British Privatization 1979–1997.* Cambridge: MIT Press, 2004.

Fontaine, Arturo. *Los economistas y el Presidente Pinochet.* Santiago: Zig-Zag, 1988.

Fontaine Talavera, Arturo."El pecado original de la transformación capitalista de Chile", in El desafío neoliberal. El fin derl tercermundismo en América Latina, edited by Barry B. Levine, 93–139. Bogotá: Grupo Editorial Norma, 1992.

Fourcade-Gourinchas, Marion, and Sarah Babb. "The Rebirth of the Liberal Creed: Paths to Neoliberalism in Four Countries," *American Journal of Sociology* 108, no. 3 (November 2002): 533–79.

Francis, John. *The Politics of Regulation. A Comparative Perspective.* Oxford: Blackwell, 1993.

Frank, Volker. "Politics without Policy: The Failure of Social Concertation in Democratic Chile, 1990–2000." In *Victims of the Chilean Miracle*, edited by Peter Winn, 73. Durham: Duke University Press, 2004.

Gamboa, Ricardo and Mauricio Morales. "Chile's 2015 Electoral Reform: Changing the Rules of the Game." *Latin American Politics and Society* 58, no. 4 (2016): 126–144.

Gárate Chateau, Manuel. *La revolución capitalista en Chile (1973–2003).* Santiago: Ediciones Universidad Alberto Hurtado, 2012.

Garcés, Joan E. *Allende y la experiencia chilena.* Barcelona: Ariel, 1976.

Garretón, Manuel Antonio. *El proceso político chileno.* Santiago: FLACSO, 1983.

Garretón, Manuel Antonio. *Neoliberalismo corregido y progresismo limitado. Los gobiernos de la Concertación en Chile, 1990–2010.* Santiago: Editorial Arcis-CLACSO, 2012.

Gil, Federico, Ricardo Lagos, E., and Henry A. Landsberger, eds. *Chile at the Turning Point.* Philadelphia: Institute for the Study of Human Issues, 1979.

"Gobiernos Corporativos Chile." Recuperación de información pública sobre casos emblemáticos. Accessed March 10, 2010. https://gobiernoscorporativo-schile.wordpress.com/2010/03/30/caso-chispas/

Guzmán, Juan Andrés, and Jorge Rojas. *Empresarios zombies. La mayor elusión tributaria de la élite chilena.* Santiago: Catalonia, Periodismo UDP, 2017.

Hacker, Jacob S., and Paul Pierson. *The Winner-Take-All Politics. How Washington Made the Rich Richer and Turned its Back on the Middle Class*. New York: Simon and Schuster, 2010.

Hall, Peter A. "Policy Paradigms, Social Learning and the State: The Case of Economic Policymaking in Britain." *Comparative Politics* 25, no.3 (1993): 275–296.

Harvey, David. *A brief history of neoliberalism*. Oxford University Press: Oxford, 2005.

Herrero, Víctor. *Agustín Edwards Eastman. Una biografía desclasificada del dueño de El Mercurio*. Santiago: Debate, 2014.

"Histórico triunfo de los consumidores: Cómo y cuándo se pagarán los 7 mil pesos." Conadecus. Last modified May 31, 2018. http://www.conadecus.cl/conadecus/?p=17742

Hirschman, Albert O. "The Case against One Thing at the Time." *World Development,* 18 No. 8 (1990), 1119–1122.

Hopkin, Jonathan, and Kate Alexander Shaw. "Organized Combat or Structural Advantage? The Politics of Inequality and the Winner-Take-All Economy in the United Kingdom." *Politics and Society* 44, no. 3 (2016): 345–371.

Huneeus, Carlos. "Technocrats and Politicians in the Democratic Politics of Argentina (1983–1995)." In *The Politics of Expertise in Latin America*, edited by Miguel A. Centeno and Patricio Silva. London: Macmillan, 1997.

Huneeus, Carlos. "El comportamiento político de los empresarios en Chile." *Perspectivas* 4, no. 2 (2001): 315–337.

Huneeus, Carlos. "Political Mass Mobilization Against Authoritarian Rule: Pinochet's Chile, 1983–8." In *Civil Resistance and Power Politics: The Experience of Non-violent Action from Gandhi to the Present,* edited by Adam Roberts and Timothy Garton Ash, 197–212. New York: Oxford University Press, 2009.

Huneeus, Carlos. *La democracia semisoberana. Chile después de Pinochet*. Santiago: Taurus, 2014.

Huneeus, Carlos. *The Pinochet Regime*. Boulder: Lynne Rienner Publishers, 2007.

Huneeus, Carlos, and Javier Couso, eds. *Eduardo Frei Montalva: un gobierno reformista. A 50 años de la "Revolución en Libertad"*. Santiago: Editorial Universitaria, 2016.

Inglehart, Ronald. "Inequality and Modernization. Why Equality is Likely to Make a Comeback." *Foreign Affairs* 95 (January 2016): 2–10.

Jara, Sergio. *Piñera y los Leones de Sanhattan. Crónica del Auge de la Elite Financiera chilena*. Santiago: Planeta, 2018.

Kurtz, Marcus. "Chile's Neo-Liberal Revolution: Incremental Decisions and Structural Transformation, 1973–1989." *Journal of Latin American Studies* 31, (May 1999): 399–427.

Larrañaga, Osvaldo, and Dante Contreras, eds. *Las nuevas políticas de protección social en Chile*. Santiago: Uqbar Editores, 2010.

Linz, Juan J., and Alfred Stepan. *Problems of Democratic Transition and Consolidation*. Baltimore: Johns Hopkins University Press, 1996.

Llanos Reyes, Claudio. *Cuando el pueblo unido fue vencido. Estudios sobre la vía chilena al socialismo*. Valparaíso: Pontificia Universidad Católica de Valparaíso, 2014.

Majone, Giandomenico. "The Rise of the Regulatory State in Europe." *West European Politics* 17, no. 3 (July 1994): 77–101.

Marcel, Mario. "Privatización y finanzas públicas: el caso de Chile 1985–1988." Estudios CIEPLAN 26 (1989): 5–60.

Meller, Patricio. *Un siglo de economía política chilena (1890–1990)*. Santiago: Andrés Bello, 1996.

Menges, Constantine. "Public policy and organized business in Chile." *Journal of International Affairs* 20, no 2 (1966): 343–365.

Molina, Sergio. *Es el tiempo de la equidad*. Santiago: Academia Chilena de Ciencias Sociales, Políticas y Morales, Instituto de Chile y Banco del Desarrollo, 2005.

Molina Silva, Sergio. *El proceso de cambio*. Santiago: Editorial Universitaria, 1971.

Mönckeberg, María Olivia. *El saqueo de los grupos económicos al Estado chileno*. Santiago: Ediciones B., 2001.

Mönckeberg, María Olivia. *La máquina para defraudar. Los casos Penta y Soquimich*. Santiago: Debate, 2015.

Mönckeberg, María Olivia. *Los magnates de la prensa*. Santiago: Debate, 2009.

Montecinos, Verónica. *Economists, Politics, and the State: Chile 1958–1994*. Amsterdam: CEDLA, 1998.

Montero, Cecilia. *La revolución empresarial chilena*. Santiago: CIEPLAN-Domen Ediciones, 1997.

Muñoz Goma, Óscar. *El Modelo Económico de la Concertación 1990–2005: ¿Reformas o Cambio?* Santiago: CIEPLAN/FLACSO, 2007.

Muñoz, Óscar, and Ana María Arriagada. *Orígenes políticos y económicos del Estado empresarial en Chile. Estudios CIEPLAN 16*. Santiago: CIEPLAN, 1977.

Nohlen, Dieter. *Chile. Das sozialistische Experiment*. Hamburg: Hoffmann & Campe, 1973.

O'Brien, Philip, ed. *Allende's Chile*. New York: Praeger Publishers, 1976.

Ortega Martínez, Luis, *Corporación de Fomento de la Producción. 50 años de realizaciones 1939–1989*. Santiago: Universidad de Santiago de Chile, 1989.

Pardow, Diego G. "La experiencia chilena disuadiendo ilícitos corporativos." *Derecho Público Iberoameriano* 1 (2012): 55–83.

Piñera, José. *El cascabel al gato. La batalla por la reforma previsional*. Santiago: Zig-Zag, 1990.

Pinto, Aníbal. *Chile, un caso de desarrollo frustrado*. Santiago: Editorial Universitaria, 1958.

PNUD. *Desiguales. Orígenes, cambios y desafíos de la brecha social en Chile.* Santiago: PNUD, 2017.

"Pollos, Farmacias, Confort y Pañales: Cuatro mega portonazos al bolsillo de todos los chilenos los últimos 20 años." The Clinic. Accessed October 8, 2019. http://www.theclinic.cl/2016/12/20/cuatro-mega-portonazos-al-bolsillo-de-todos-los-chilenos-los-ultimos-20-anos/

Pribble, Jennifer. *Welfare and Party Politics in Latin America.* Cambridge: Cambridge University Press, 2013.

Raczynski, Dagmar, and Claudia Serrano. "Las políticas y estrategias de desarrollo social. Aportes de los años 90 y desafíos futuros." In *La paradoja aparente. Equidad y eficiencia: Resolviendo el dilema,* edited by Patricio Meller, 225–286. Santiago: Taurus, 2005.

Ramos, Claudio. *La transformación de la empresa chilena: una modernización des-balanceada.* Santiago: Universidad Alberto Hurtado, 2009.

Rojas, Jorge. "El ardid con el que algunas empresas quisieron "ahorrar" $24.521.682.331 en impuestos." *The Clinic,* May 28 2012. Accessed April 27, 2020. https://www.theclinic.cl/2012/05/28/el-ardid-con-que-algunas-empresas-quisieron-ahorrar-24-521-682-331-en-impuestos-2/

Rozas, Patricio, and Gustavo Marín. *El "Mapa de la extrema riqueza" 10 años después.* Santiago: Ediciones Chile-América CESOC, 1989.

Sapag, Reinaldo. "El derecho de propiedad en los bancos con deuda subordinada." In *Páginas periodísticas,* Andrés Aylwin, César Díaz-Muñoz and Reinaldo Sapag, 157. Santiago: Ediciones Copygraph, 1997.

Saunders, Peter, and Colin Harris. *Privatization and Popular Capitalism.* Buckingham: Open University Press, 1994.

"Sernac y Conadecus explican por qué la compensación pactada con CMPC es un "buen" acuerdo." Emol. Last modified January 27, 2017. Accessed April 7, 2020. https://www.emol.com/noticias/Economia/2017/01/27/842216/Sernac-y-Asociacion-de-Consumidores-defienden-compensacion-pactada-con-CMPC.html

Silva, Eduardo. *The State and Capital in Chile: Business Elite, Technocrats, and Market Economics.* Boulder: Westview Press, 1996.

Silva, Patricio. "Technocrats and politics in Chile: from the Chicago Boys to the CIEPLAN Monks." *Journal of Latin American Studies* 23, no. 2 (1992): 385–410.

Silva, Patricio. *In the Name of Reason. Technocrats and Politics in Chile.* University Park: Pennsylvania State University Press, 2008.

Stallings, Barbara. *Class Conflict and Economic Development in Chile, 1958–1973.* Stanford: Stanford University Press, 1978.

Therborn, Goran. *The killing fields of inequality.* Cambridge: Polity, 2013.

Tromben, Carlos. *Crónica secreta de la economía chilena.* Santiago: Ediciones B., 2016.

UNDP – Programa de las Naciónes Unidas para el Desarrollo. *Power: for what and for who*. Santiago: UNDP, 2004.

Undurraga, Tomás. "Business, politics and ideology: neoliberalism and capitalist class formation in Argentina and Chile (1990–2014)." *Política/Revista de Ciencia Política* 54, no. 2 (2016): 177–210.

Undurraga, Tomás. "Instrucción, indulgencia y justificación: los circuitos culturales del capitalismo chileno." In *Adaptación. La empresa chilena después de Friedman*, edited by José Ossandón and Eugenio Tironi, 135–166. Chile: Ediciones UDP, 2013.

Undurraga, Tomás. "Neoliberalism in Argentina and Chile: common antecedents, divergent path." *Revista de Sociologia e Politica* 23, no. 55 (2015): 11–34.

Undurraga, Tomás. *Divergencias. Trayectorias del neoliberalismo en Argentina y Chile*. Santiago: Ediciones Universidad Diego Portales, 2014.

Undurraga, Tomás, and Carlos Huneeus. "Renovación discursiva y continuación de prácticas del empresariado en Chile post-transición (2010–2017)." In *Pensamiento empresarial latinoamericano en el siglo XXI*, edited by Rita Giacalone, 211–244. Bogotá: Editorial Universidad Cooperativa de Colombia, 2019.

Valdés, Juan Gabriel. *Pinochet's Economists: The Chicago School of Economics in Chile*. Cambridge: Cambridge University Press, 1995.

Winn, Peter, ed. *Victims of the Chilean Miracle: Workers and neoliberalism in the Pinochet Era, 1973–2002*. Durham: Duke University Press, 2004.

Yocelevsky, Ricardo. *La democracia cristiana chilena y el gobierno de Eduardo Frei Montalva (1964–1970)*. México: Universidad Autónoma Metropolitana, Unidad Xochimilco, 1987.

CHAPTER 5

Big Business and Bureaucratic Authoritarianism in Uruguay: A Network-Based Story of Policy Infiltration for Self-Preservation

Juan A. Bogliaccini, Juan Geymonat, and Martín Opertti

Introduction

Bureaucratic-Authoritarian[1] regimes in Latin America faced the stagnation and beginning of collapse of Import Substitution Industrialization (ISI) in highly dissimilar ways and with different results. Whereas in Chile ISI institutions were displaced early on following the neoliberal recipe, Brazil

Juan A. Bogliaccini acknowledges research for this manuscript was partially funded by the Uruguayan Research and Innovation Agency (ANII), Fondo Clemente Estable (FCE_1_2017_1_135444).

[1] Guillermo O'Donnell's seminal work on authoritarianisms in Latin America, *Modernization and Bureaucratic-Authoritarianism: Studies in South American Politics*

J. A. Bogliaccini (✉) • M. Opertti
Universidad Católica del Uruguay, Montevideo, Uruguay
e-mail: juan.bogliaccini@ucu.edu.uy

V. Basualdo et al. (eds.), *Big Business and Dictatorships in Latin America*, Palgrave Studies in Latin American Heterodox Economics, https://doi.org/10.1007/978-3-030-43925-5_5

gradually adapted a modest but vibrant industrial sector to the requirements of the open-market model. Argentina, in turn, although it attempted radical liberalization, was not able to sustain the process. The military government in Uruguay, by contrast, exhibited an erratic and irresolute trajectory of incomplete liberalization with businesses engaging heavily in capturing resources and taking subsidies.

Uruguay stands alone as an example of how the collapse of the ISI, the erosion and ulterior displacement of political institutions and cadres, and the severe oppression of organized labor set the stage for big business to continue with a rent-seeking orientation inherited from the ISI, although it adapted this to the requirements and opportunities of the new circumstances. There were two main adaptive responses to the threat of liberalization. The first strategy was a direct response to the exhaustion of available instances of institutionalized participation in policy-making resulting from a set of gradual reforms beginning in 1959: businesses increased direct and individualized participation in key government positions. The second strategy was a response to the competitive shock arising from the combination state subsidies being exhausted and businesses gradually being exposed to international competition: businesses engaged in overborrowing to take advantage of the fact that the most important private banks in the country were owned by the same families that presided over big business groups. These adaptive strategies on the part of businesses infiltrated the government, enabling the liberalization process to be compromised. An important merit of our argument compared to previous accounts of the period is that we put the emphasis in the role of agents—in this case, businesses and politicians—to complement the structural hypothesis that is widely used as the basis of analysis.

Our analysis unpacks the links among family-owned groups, between these groups and the banking system, and with the political system during the military period. Thus, it combines a historical case-oriented analysis with a network analysis. The historical analysis serves two purposes. On the one hand, the chapter carefully describes the historical evolution of

(Berkeley: University of California, 1973) during the Cold War classified the military governments in the Southern Cone as Bureaucratic Authoritarianism in order to differentiate them from traditional military coups. In Bureaucratic-Authoritarian regimes, among other important characteristics, the military takes over the government as a corporation after the coup, without handing it back to civilians immediately.

J. Geymonat
Universidad de la República, Montevideo, Uruguay

accounts that forged the context in which business and the military government interacted. Of particular importance is the account of businesses' rent-seeking behavior during the ISI period to clarify why adaptive strategies evolved in the directions they did. On the other hand, case studies of the business groups serve to illustrate the two adaptive strategies. The network analysis, in turn, aims to provide an account of the structure of the big business community circa 1979–1984 as this is essential for understanding how this structure made the two aforementioned adaptive strategies possible.

The chapter is organized as follows. In the first section, we provide the relevant historical background. Then, we characterize big business in Uruguay using network analysis. Third, we provide detailed case studies of how influential and politically connected groups adapted rent-seeking strategies, managing to undermine the liberalization process in surgically precise ways. Finally, we explore the merits of the argument in the conclusion.

From Domestically Oriented Industrialization to Market Liberalization

Like several countries in Latin America, Uruguay began a process of industrialization by import substitution in the 1930s. Between 1930 and 1955, the ratio of industrial product to GDP went from 12% to 22%.[2] This process led the country to achieve historic growth rates, as Fig. 5.1 shows, with annual maximums above 4% in GDP, 3.4% in per capita product from 1944 to 1950, and 7.7% of industrial growth yearly between 1945 and 1955.[3]

Industrialization strongly relied on the import of inputs and capital goods based on foreign exchange. Through deliberate intervention and protection policies, the state diverted part of the income of the primary sector to the secondary sector, offsetting its productivity deficits. In the end, while the ISI failed to boost productivity-oriented strategies on the part of employers, it ended up strengthening a vicious cycle of

[2] Julio Millot, Carlos Silva & Lindor Silva, *El desarrollo industrial del Uruguay; de la crisis de 1929 a la posguerra* (Montevideo: Instituto de Economía-Universidad de la República, 1973).

[3] Henry Finch, *La economía política del Uruguay contemporáneo: 1870–2000* (Montevideo: Ediciones de la Banda Oriental, 2005).

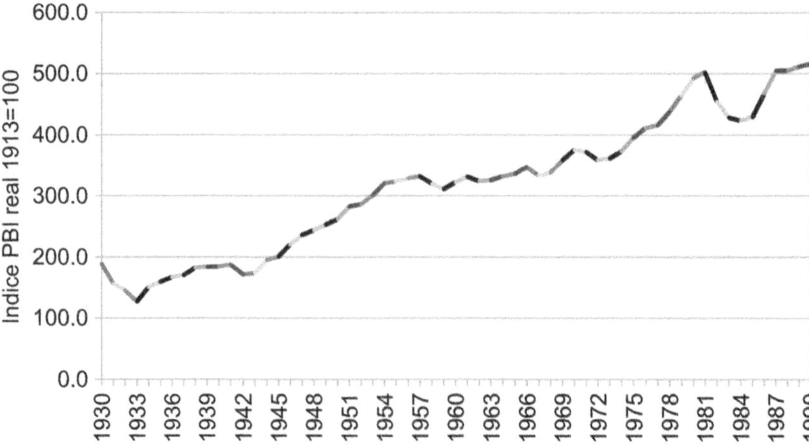

Fig. 5.1 Uruguay: Real GDP index (1930–1990, 1913 = 100). (Source: Banco de datos Facultad de Ciencias Sociales, Área Historia Económica)

never-ending subsidies and rent-seeking strategies. Subsidies and participation in decision-making fueled the proliferation of rent-seeking strategies across the region.

Between 1955 and 1970, the average annual GDP growth was 0.9%, although in per capita terms it was −0.3% (Fig. 5.1). The decrease in the prices of primary goods internationally in the 1950s, paired with the small size of the domestic market, began to reveal the bottleneck of the model and call its sustainability into question.[4] These demand-side conditions met a complex panorama in the Uruguayan agro-exporter sector as price controls had discouraged technological innovation to increase output. The stagnation produced a strong dispute over income, which evolved into a spiral of wages and prices coupled with a high inflationary process.[5] The average rates of annual growth in prices, calculated by 5-year periods, were 23.4% for 1956–1960, 30.4% for 1961–1965, and 66.1% for

[4] Luis Bértola, *La industria manufacturera uruguaya, 1913–1961: un enfoque sectorial de su crecimiento, fluctuaciones y crisis.* (Montevideo: Facultad de Ciencias Sociales- Universidad de la República, 1991).

[5] Instituto de Economía- Facultad de Ciencias Económicas y de Administración. Universidad de la República, *El proceso económico del Uruguay contribución al estudio de su evolución y perspectivas.* (Montevideo: Fundación de Cultura Universitaria, 1969).

1966–1970.[6] This upward spiral of prices and wages happened alongside increased fiscal deficits and domestic debt.

Economic stagnation fueled social conflict and polarization. Democratic institutions rapidly became unstable by the end of the 1960s while the public image of political parties plummeted under the siege of corruption, scandals, and allegations of inefficiency. A left-wing guerrilla movement (*Movimiento de Liberación Nacional*, MLN) also made its appearance in the political arena, fueling radicalization.

In 1973, the democratically elected President Juan M. Bordaberry dissolved the parliament, suppressing political activity to allegedly defeat the MLN and inaugurating an authoritarian regime that lasted until 1985. The military coup displaced traditional political elites, bringing new opportunities for influential business groups that crystallized around tailored exceptions and particularities for different sectors, as we shall explain in the next section.

The economic program of the new authoritarian government, in alignment with most of the region at the time, sought to implement a package of reforms aimed at liberalizing the economy. It was based on the following strategies: to diversify exports by promoting less devolved sectors; drastically reducing the real salary, partly by rendering unions illegal and repressing them; rapidly liberalizing the capital account in order to increase capital flows; and engaging in a process of trade liberalization.[7] It is important to bear in mind that articulated plans to move away from the ISI had been developing since the times of the Economic Development and Investment Commission (CIDE; 1960–1967) because this indicates that the business community had been familiar with the idea of the ISI gradually becoming exhausted and the need for market-oriented reforms to be introduced for at least a decade and a half before the military coup.

Reforms began in late 1974 and advanced more rapidly in the capital market than in the trade market until 1978. While average tariffs were scheduled to drop to an average of 35% by 1985, this was modified in late

[6] Finch, *La economía política del Uruguay contemporáneo*.

[7] Jorge Notaro. *La política económica en el Uruguay, 1968–1984* (Montevideo: Ediciones de la Banda Oriental, 1984); Jorge Notaro, La economía del Uruguay 1998–2014. Caracterización e hipótesis explicativas. https://www.researchgate.net/publication/284174297_La_economia_del_Uruguay_1998_-_2014_Caracterizacion_e_hipotesis_explicativas (accessed February 2017); Danilo Astori. *La política económica de la dictadura*. (Montevideo: Ediciones de la Banda Oriental, 1989); Jaime Yaffé (2010). "Dictadura y neoliberalismo en Uruguay (1973–1985)." *Séptimas Jornadas de Historia Económica*. Asociación Uruguaya de Historia Económica. Montevideo, 2010.

1979 when a stabilization program was implemented, which included additional selective cuts on some 500 items.[8] Export taxes were lowered from 21% of export value in 1973 to 2% in 1976 for traditional exports (Fig. 5.2). However, financial and fiscal subsidies were put in place for non-traditional exports (Fig. 5.2). In those years, subsidies for non-traditional exports escalated from US $15 to 59 million. Tax rebates amounted to about 15% of export values.[9]

Overall, the process of trade liberalization included tailored exceptions and particularities for different sectors. For instance, Rama's[10] analysis of protective measures in the industrial sector for the period 1975–1980 provides evidence that the liberalization process was not as effective as it

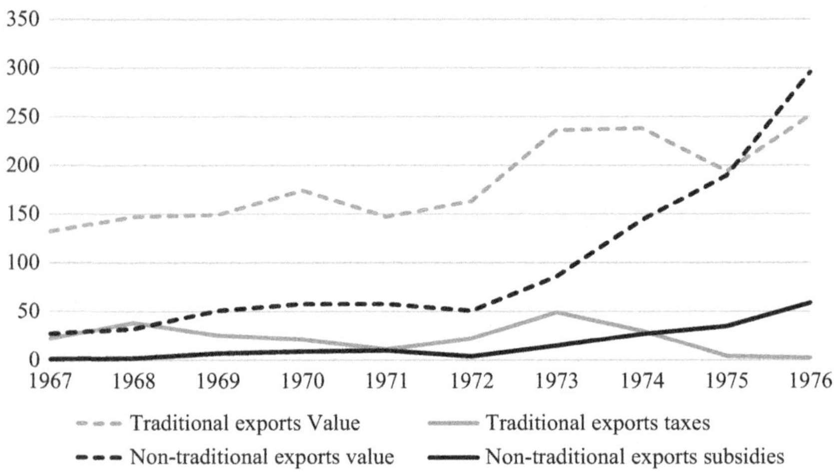

Fig. 5.2 Uruguay: Value and taxes of traditional exports, and value and subsidies of non-traditional exports (millions USD, 1967–1976). (Source: Authors' elaboration based on Bensión & Caumont, "Alternative trade strategies and employment")

[8] James Hanson & Jaime De Melo, "The Uruguayan experience with liberalization and stabilization, 1974–1981." *Journal of Interamerican studies and world affairs*, 25 No. 4 (1983): 477–508.

[9] Alberto Bensión & Jorge Caumont, "Alternative trade strategies and employment." In *Trade and Employment in Developing Countries* (University of Chicago Press Chicago, 1981): 495–528.

[10] Martín Rama, *Protección y crecimiento industrial 1975–1980* (Montevideo: Cinve, 1982).

seemed. The significant reductions on import tariffs, which occurred in 1977, 1978, and 1979, did not necessarily translate into a reduction in industrial protection. Industries such as tobacco, chemical products, and oil derivatives were not subjected to such reductions.[11] Although average formal nominal protection decreased significantly from 1975 to 1980 in this sector, the implied nominal protection was higher in 1980 than in 1975 (Fig. 5.3). Two factors account for this fact: superfluous protection and exchange policy (a fixed exchange rate with scheduled currency devaluations was instituted in 1978).

As in the rest of the region, economic liberalization was paired with restrictions of organized labor. This, along with the previous suppression of collective wage bargaining at the industry level since 1968, produced a steep fall in real wages during the following years (Fig. 5.4). By 1984, the purchasing power of wages had been reduced by 57% in respect to its 1973 level.[12] Both the steep decline in real wages and the dismantling of

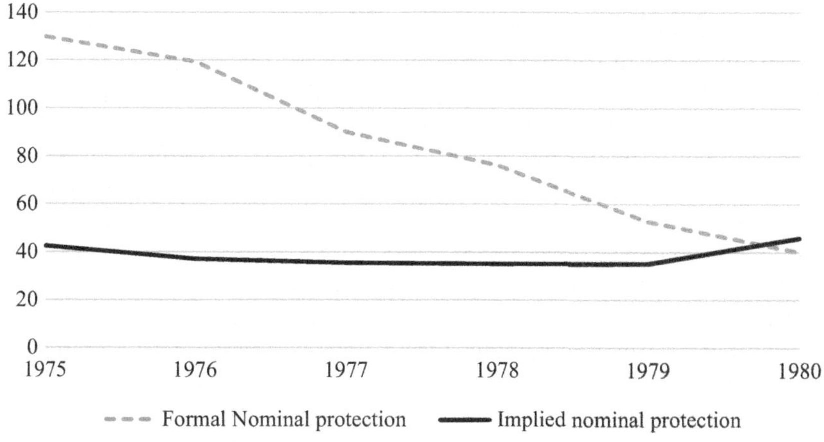

Fig. 5.3 Uruguay: Formal and implied nominal protection of industry (1975–1980). (Source: Authors' elaboration based on Rama's *Protección y crecimiento industrial*)

[11] Rama, *Protección y crecimiento industrial 1975–1980.*

[12] Jaime Yaffé, "La sociedad uruguaya durante la dictadura." In *El negocio del terrorismo de estado,* edited by Juan Pablo Bohoslasvky, 123–143 (Montevideo: Debate, 2016).

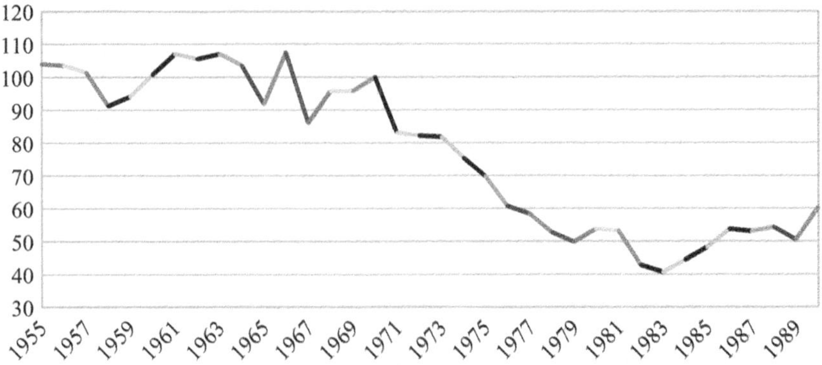

Fig. 5.4 Uruguay: Real wages index (1970 = 100). (Source: Authors' elaboration based on National Accounts 1955–1963 and Central Bank 1963–1990)

trade union movements benefited the business sector.[13] In this context, private consumption contracted and inequality increased rapidly—the Gini Index went from 0.37 before the coup to 0.49 in 1979, earners in the top 10% being the only ones with real income growth between 1973 and 1979. In terms of economic growth, however, the country was able to overcome the stagnation of the previous decades between 1973 and 1981, fueled by private and public investment and a boom in construction.[14] In spite of a few years of economic growth, the situation rapidly deteriorated with the 1982 debt crisis, which gave rise to one of the most important crises in national history and contributed to the already declining legitimacy of the military government.

By the end of the military period, the impulse toward liberalization had created space for a restoration of democratic institutions and a brief return to centralized wage bargaining during the Julio Sanguinetti administration (1985–1989). Not until the second democratically elected administration (1990–1994) began did the liberalization impulse strengthen again in the midst of a sustained period of high inflation.

[13] Juan Pablo Bohoslavsky, *El Negocio del Terrorismo de Estado. Los cómplices económicos de la dictadura uruguaya*. (Montevideo: Debate, 2016). Carlos Demasi, "El apoyo de las cámaras comerciales," in *El negocio del terrorismo de estado*, edited by Juan Pablo Bohoslavsky, 143–161 (Montevideo: Debate, 2016).

[14] Finch, *La economía política del Uruguay*, 291–292.

Big Business and the Mutation of Rent-Seeking Strategies

Historical Evolution of Business Groups and Their Political Influence

At the turn of the twentieth century, large domestic firms began a slow process leading to the formation of economic groups. These groups were organized as a set of legally independent firms, operating in multiple industries and bound together by persistent formal or informal links.[15] They usually had unrelated product portfolios in industry and primary sectors, were family-owned, and were organized as "loose networks."[16] In other words, no single firm exercised pyramid control over the group; the participation of family members on firms' boards of directors was the main top-down control mechanism.

By the time the ISI consolidated, business groups had increased their diversification, although industrial activity remained primary.[17] This was also the case all around Latin America at the time.[18] Groups evolved largely to diversify risk in an unstable region.

Corporate finance was mostly dependent on domestic credit. Banks, which were owned by domestic capital at the time—and often by big business groups themselves—strengthened their position as corporate financiers in this context. Only between 1973, with the onset of the oil crisis, and 2002, with the Argentinean crisis, did the banking sector gradually become more internationalized, clearly diluting the pervasive endogenous web between financiers and investors.

The ISI incentivized governments to deliver special benefits, mostly in the form of subsidies, to individual business sectors and groups because of their organizational strength or strategic importance. Governments at the

[15] Tarun Khanna & Yishay Yafeh, "Business groups in emerging markets: Paragons or parasites?" In *Journal of Economic Literature*. Vol. 45, No. 2 (2007): 331–372.

[16] Geoffrey Jones & Asli Colpan, "Business groups in historical perspectives" in *The Oxford Handbook of Business Groups*, edited by Asli Colpan, Takashi Hikino & James Lincoln, 67–96, (Oxford University Press, 2010).

[17] Finch, *La economía política del Uruguay*. Luis Stolovich, Juan Manuel Rodríguez & Luis Bértola, *El poder económico en el Uruguay actual*. (Montevideo: Centro Uruguay Independiente, 1987). Vivian Trías, *Reforma agraria en el Uruguay* (Montevideo: Ediciones El Sol, 1958).

[18] Ben Ross Schneider, *Business Politics and the State in 20th century Latin America*. (Cambridge: Cambridge University Press 2004).

time also granted some sectors institutionalized participation in decision-making related to business.[19] This, in turn, meant that employers' interests and demands, which became progressively more onerous as the ISI model deteriorated, infiltrated into the state.

Institutionalized sectoral participation in decision-making motivated rent-seeking behavior at the expense of productivity-oriented strategies. A prime instrument for rent-seeking was the exchange rate through the Import and Export Control Commission (CIE: *Contralor de Importaciones y Exportaciones*); its board of directors had 9 members: 4 business representatives and 5 members from the government. This commission operated until 1959 and controlled foreign exchange decisions, the main tool for implementing economic policies that supported the ISI.[20] Sectoral-based business coordination strategies strengthened during the ISI because of this access to institutionalized decision-making bodies.[21] There is consensus in the literature that when multiple exchange rates were abolished in 1959, rent-seeking turned toward higher nominal protection rates. Then, by 1974, in the aftermath of the military coup and at the onset of the liberalization process, rent-seeking efforts focused on increasing the reference price for the calculation of subsidies and taxes.[22]

Rama[23] shows how, in spite of the change in rent-seeking strategies, the number of rent-seeking actions remained stable during the 1960s and 1970s (Table 5.1).[24] The change in rent-seeking strategies was fueled, at least in part, by two important phenomena. On the one hand, institutional

[19] Gerardo Caetano, "El asedio conservador," *Series investigaciones CLAEH, vol. 42 and 43* (1984). Cristina Zurbriggen, *Estado, empresarios y redes rentistas* (Montevideo: Instituto de Ciencias Políticas-Universidad de la República- Ediciones de la Banda Oriental, 2006).

[20] Ulises Garcia-Repetto, "El contralor de exportaciones e importaciones en Uruguay (1941–1959)." *Series de Documentos de trabajo del Instituto de Economía N°13* (Montevideo, 2017): 3–41.

[21] Juan A. Bogliaccini, "Small Latecomers into the Global Market [electronic Resource]: Power Conflict and Institutional Change in Chile and Uruguay" (PhD diss., University of North Carolina, 2012); Juan A Bogliaccini, "The Reconstruction of Business Interests after the ISI Collapse: Unpacking the Effect of Institutional Change in Chile and Uruguay." *Third World Quarterly.* (2019).

[22] Rama, *Protección y crecimiento industrial;* Martín Rama. "Crecimiento y estancamiento económico en Uruguay." In *Trayectorias Divergentes. Comparacion de un siglo de desarrollo economico latinamericano y escandinavo,* edited by Magnus Blomstron, & Patricio Meller. 115–144 (Chile: Cieplan-Hachete, 1990).

[23] Rama, "Crecimiento y estancamiento económico en Uruguay."

[24] Rent-seeking actions are identified as all those actions and decrees enacted on a single product—or type of merchandise—related to tariff rates and reference prices for the reliabil-

Table 5.1 Uruguay: Rent-seeking actions by private businesses

Year	*Rent-seeking actions*
1955	50
1960	78
1965	92
1970	88
1975	251
1980	62
1983	69
1955, 1960, 1965 average	73
1970, 1975, 1980, 1983 average	94

Source: Rama, "Crecimiento y estancamiento económico en Uruguay," 206

participation in price-setting decayed as these institutions gradually disappeared—as was the case with the CIE. On the other hand, as explained earlier, authoritarian tendencies expanded and the legitimacy of the party system was increasingly undermined. This is how corporate business's institutionalized access to decision-making gave it a space where it could pursue a strategy oriented toward implementing effective protection.[25]

In this context, the repressive right-wing Jorge Pacheco government (1968–1971) consolidated a technocratic shift in political cadres that had begun in 1958 (see Table 5.2), inviting prominent leaders and high-profile professionals from influential business groups to hold key government positions.[26] By 1972, a new class of technocrats closely linked to major business groups helped the newly installed Bordaberry administration (1971–1976) shift industrial policy toward more systematic export promotion.[27] While the technocratic shift can be seen as part of the government's political strategy to regain legitimacy and authority by integrating

ity of tariffs or subsidies. Changes in the exchange rate only correspond to 1955, since in 1959 the system of multiple changes was eliminated.

[25] Rama, "Crecimiento y estancamiento económico en Uruguay"; Luis Macadar, *Restauración democrática y política económica. Uruguay 1985–1989*. (Montevideo: Ediciones de la Banda Oriental, 1992).

[26] Luis Stolovich & Juan Manuel Rodriguez, (1987). "Gobierno y empresarios: sus vínculos personales." In *¿Hacia dónde va el Estado uruguayo?* Edited by Gerónimo de Sierra, 163–201 (Montevideo: Fondo de Cultura Universitaria, 1987).

[27] Bension & Camount, "Alternative trade strategies and employment." Notaro, *La economía del Uruguay 1998–2014*.

Table 5.2 Uruguay: Business participation in the executive (% of ministries by administration)

Period	*Executive*	*w/business connections*
1951–1958	Colorado Party—Collegiate Executive	26.1%
1959–1966	Nacional Party—Collegiate Executive	51.5%
1967–1973	Colorado Party—Gestido (1967–1968), Pacheco (1968–1971), and Bordaberry (1971–1973) administrations*	44.8%
1974–1976	Military government—Bordaberry administration	52.4%
1976–1981	Military government—Méndez administration	44%
1981–1985	Military government—Álvarez administration	34.8%

*The period 1967–1973 comprises the administration of Oscar Gestido, who died in office; that of Jorge Pacheco Areco, Gestido's vice-president; and of Juan María Bordaberry up until the self-coup of 1973

Note: Business "connections" include businessmen, CEOs, advisors to boards in firms and groups

Source: Based on Stolovich & Rodríguez, "Gobierno y empresarios: sus vínculos personales." For the 1951–1976 period. Authors' elaboration based on administrative records for the period 1976–1985

economic and political power, it presented businesses with an opportunity to operate on the institutional system and seek to cushion some of the effects of the recent liberalization process. As such, the technocratic shift can be understood as a diversification strategy in a context of increasing uncertainty.

The Structure of the Business Community According to a Network Analysis

In order to understand why business groups gladly entered the political arena in those turbulent years, it is paramount to understand the main characteristics of the business community at the time. For this purpose, we offer a network analysis describing the main characteristics of big business circa 1980. We base our analysis in social network methodology because it allows us to unveil the structure of the business network and the relative position of each group within it. Evidence shows that Uruguayan business groups were very tight and closed.

We built our database of business groups from the seminal work on business groups by Stolovich et al. (1987).[28] We used the following criteria for including the groups in the network: first, we included only the 15 groups that Stolovich et al. (1987)[29] classified as belonging to the topmost stratum (the largest groups).[30] We then included all groups directly linked to these 15 groups, as well as their connections, until all the connections were accounted for.[31] The nodes contained in the network are business groups, and the edges between them mean that two business groups had shares in at least one firm in common. Links are unweighted: a group either shared a company with another group or it did not, and the network is undirected, given that the link is reciprocal (that is, it does not indicate the number of shares groups owned).

Figure 5.5 presents the image of the network of business groups. In terms of economic significance, this complex network of alliances covered 256 companies, of which only 50 represented 8.5% of the total sales of the economy in 1987. Beyond the quantitative weight, this network of links between entrepreneurs included oligopolistic control of some strategic value chains (among them, fishing, rice, oil, flour, wool, leather, meat, rubber products, paper and cardboard, the financial sector, and media) at the time.

The network contains 95 nodes (business groups), 220 edges, and a density of 0.05%. This low density is expected given the small size of the business community at the time, and the fact that edges represent a strong bond between the groups (having shares in at least one common firm). Despite the network having a rather low density, other measures such as the average path length and average degree indicate that it was effectively connected. On average, a single node is connected to 4.5 other nodes, meaning that groups shared 4.5 firms with other groups in the network, and it takes 3.5 nodes to reach from any given node to any other node within the network (as Fig. 5.5 shows). In addition, the fact that groups could be linked with each other in ways that this network does not capture

[28] Economic groups classified as big business (the topmost stratum according to the classification of Stolovich et al.) had at least US $20 million in assets and/or annual sales for the same amount. Only 15 of 111 groups identified by Stolovich et al. belong to this stratum.

[29] Stolovich et al., *El Poder económico en el Uruguay actual.*

[30] We included only the 15 groups that Stolovich et al. (1987) classified as belonging to the topmost stratum, which are those whose assets were at least US $20 million.

[31] Only two of the fifteen groups that belong to the topmost stratum did not have any links with other groups. As is customary in network analysis, we excluded isolated nodes (groups).

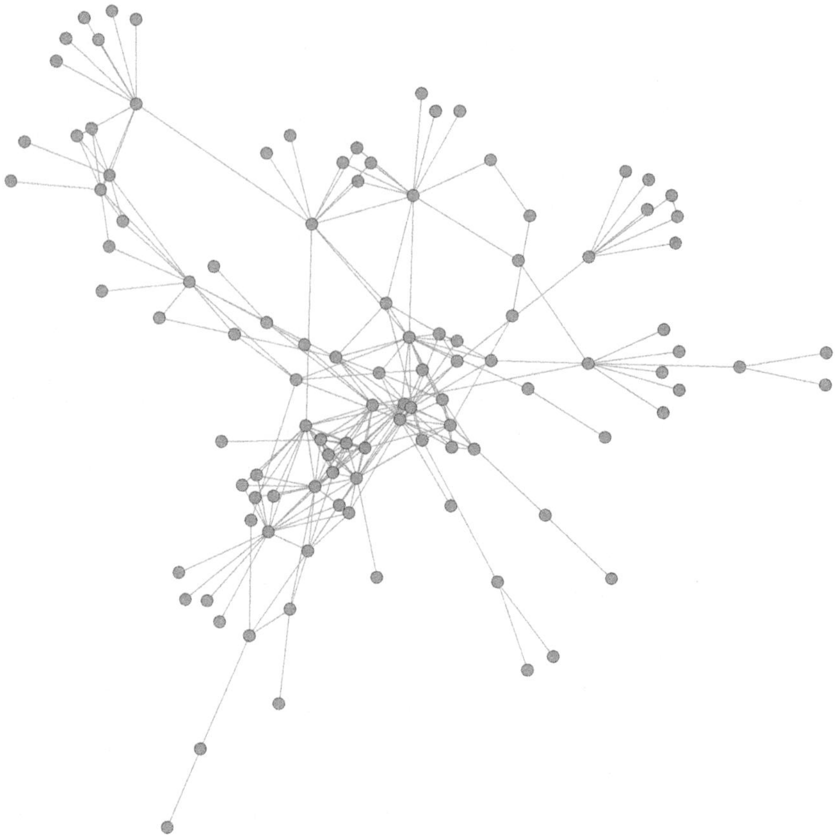

Fig. 5.5 Uruguay: Network of big business group and related groups. (Source: Authors' elaboration based on Stolovich et al., *El Poder económico en el Uruguay actual*)

(such as family/friendship bonds or club membership), suggests that they were capable of exchanging information in a highly effective manner.

Based on the small-worldness index proposed by Humphries and Gurney,[32] our network constitutes a small-world phenomenon (5.8 in our

[32] Mark Humphries & Kevin Gurney, "Network 'small-world-ness': a quantitative method for determining canonical network equivalence" (2008): https://doi.org/10.1371/journal.pone.0002051

network).[33] This results in the distance between nodes being small compared to the number of edges. The key characteristic of this type of network is that it is highly clustered,[34] with information flowing rapidly throughout the network. This is a crucial factor considering that some business groups had direct political influence during the dictatorship.

Thus, our calculations show a tight network with a few important actors. This puts business in a privileged situation within a context of political turmoil. As Bucheli et al.[35] (2018) state, the opening up of a market does not necessarily imply that the importance of interpersonal networks and big business ties will decrease, as the Chilean case also shows.

Further analysis of the distribution of centrality measures for each node suggests that the network had a hierarchical structure. As Fig. 5.6 shows, three measures—centrality degree, betweenness centrality, and eigenvector centrality—have a large number of nodes with low coefficients and a small number of nodes with large coefficients, meaning that a small portion of business groups was crucial to the connectivity of the network. Furthermore, the network's closeness centrality—the extent to which a node can easily reach all other nodes in the network—has a rather normal distribution; that is to say, isolated groups of nodes do not exist in this network.

While our analysis provides evidence of how business groups maintained strong links with each other by sharing the ownership of firms, previous research also suggests it was common practice at the time for business families to form marital bonds.[36] Both elements suggest the existence of shared interests manifested in both formal and informal links, although this does not mean that big business was univocal in its political interests. Nonetheless, the business community did constitute a very small, closed, and interconnected network, with the particularity of some nodes determining the flow of information.

[33] The small-world phenomenon means that the logarithm of the number of nodes converges to the average path length.

[34] Duncan Watts & Steven Strogatz, "Collective dynamics of 'small-world' networks" *Nature*, 393 (1998): 440–442. https://doi.org/10.1038/30918

[35] Marcelo Bucheli, Erica Salvaj & Minyoung Kim, "Better together: How multinationals come together with business groups in times of economic and political transitions." *Global Strategy Journal*, 9 No. 2 (2018): 176–207.

[36] Stolovich et al., *El poder económico en el Uruguay actual*. Raúl Jacob, *Banca e industria: un puente inconcluso* (Montevideo: Fundación de Cultura Universitaria-CIEDUR, 1991).

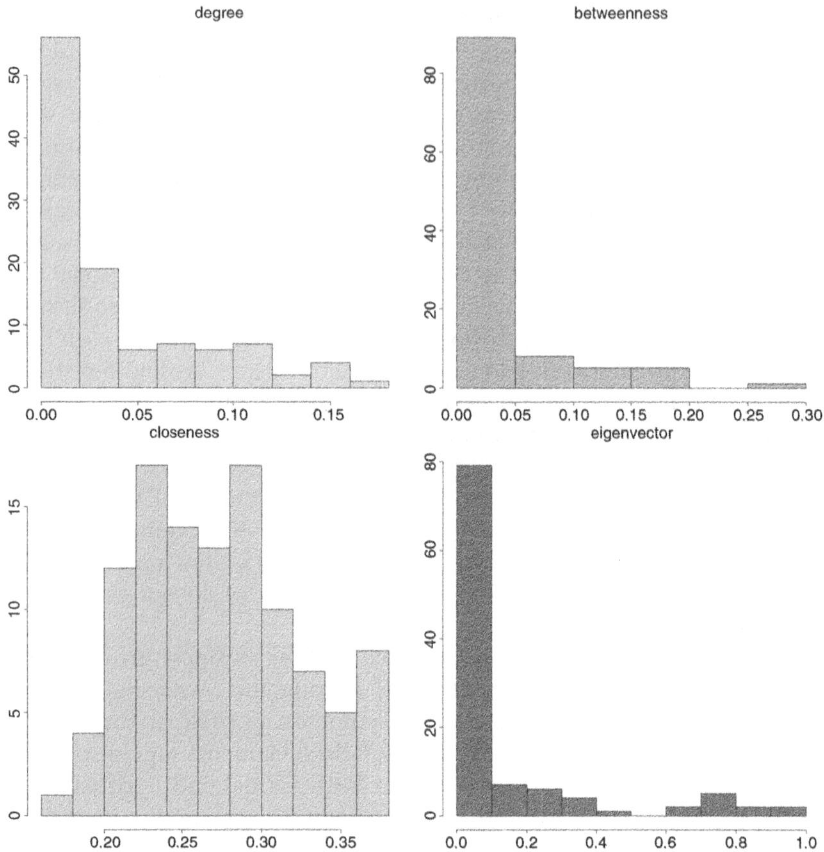

Fig. 5.6 Uruguay: Distribution of centrality measures. (Source: Authors' elaboration based on Stolovich et al., *El Poder económico en el Uruguay actual*)

With the small but highly interconnected and hierarchical structure of the business community in mind, we can better understand how the two main strategies used by business to fight the liberalization process worked out: direct political influence and financial mismanagement. The analysis identifies key business groups—key because of their position in the network—that adopted these new rent-seeking strategies: the Aznárez, Vargas Garmendia, and Cardoso Guani groups.

Direct Political Linkages in Influential Business Groups

We identify key business groups and their position in the network by using different measures. To start with, we identify the cut-points of the network, which are crucial to its articulation. These are the nodes that constitute "a point whose removal would increase the number of components by dividing the sub-graphs into two or more separate sub-sets between which there are no connections."[37] Our network has 19 cut-points. Three of them, the Aznárez, Vargas Garmendia, and Cardoso Guani groups, were those with the most direct links to the military government. In addition, these three groups had familial ties with three other important groups. For instance, the sister of Julio Eduardo Aznárez (the former Minister of Livestock, Agriculture, and Fisheries from 1974 to 1976), Gloria Aznárez Betchold, was married to the head of the Strauch group, Elbio Strauch. Some of Vargas Garmendia's group members were cousins of Soler group members. The Cardoso Guani and Cardoso Cuenca groups had close family ties.[38] As we describe later, these nodes played a crucial role in the business network at the time. In Fig. 5.7, we have illustrated the position of these groups by coloring the edges linked to them.

Soler, Vargas Garmendia, and Aznárez were also among the five most important brokers, with Strauch and Cardoso Cuenca having also been relevant brokers. Brokers' importance lies in their ability to bridge structural holes in the network, making it more efficient at conveying information.[39] This happens because information circulates more within groups than between them, giving nodes that are able to share information with two groups a competitive advantage. Measures of Burt's constraint, which captures whether a node establishes bridges with other nodes,[40] are consistent with cut-point measures.

While information flowed efficiently from node to node due to the structure of the network, our three politically important nodes had a particularly large role in it. In addition to being cut-points and important brokers, they also ranked high in terms of their betweenness (Fig. 5.8),

[37] John Scott, *Social network analysis* (Los Ángeles, Londres, Nueva Dheli, singapure, Washington: Sage, 2017): 118.

[38] Stolovich et al., *El poder económico en el Uruguay actual.*

[39] Ronald Burt, "The network structure of social capital." *Research in organizational behavior*, Volume 22 (2000): 345–423.

[40] Ronald Burt, "Structural holes and good ideas." *American journal of sociology*, Volume *110* (2), (2004): 349–399.

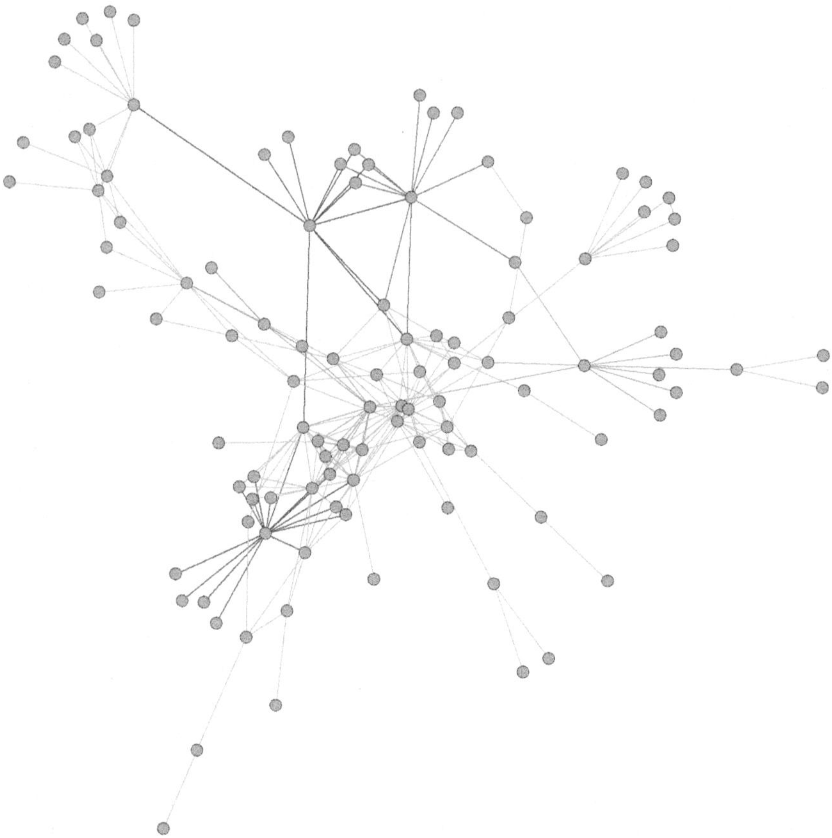

Fig. 5.7 Uruguay: The influence of the Aznárez, Vargas Garmendia, Cardoso Guani, Cardoso Cuenca, Soler, and Strauch groups. Note: Aznárez (red), Strauch (orange), Vargas Garmendia (dark green), Soler (green), Cardoso Guani (blue), and Cardoso Cuenca (violet) groups respectively highlighted. (Source: Authors' elaboration based on Stolovich et al., *El Poder económico en el Uruguay actual*)

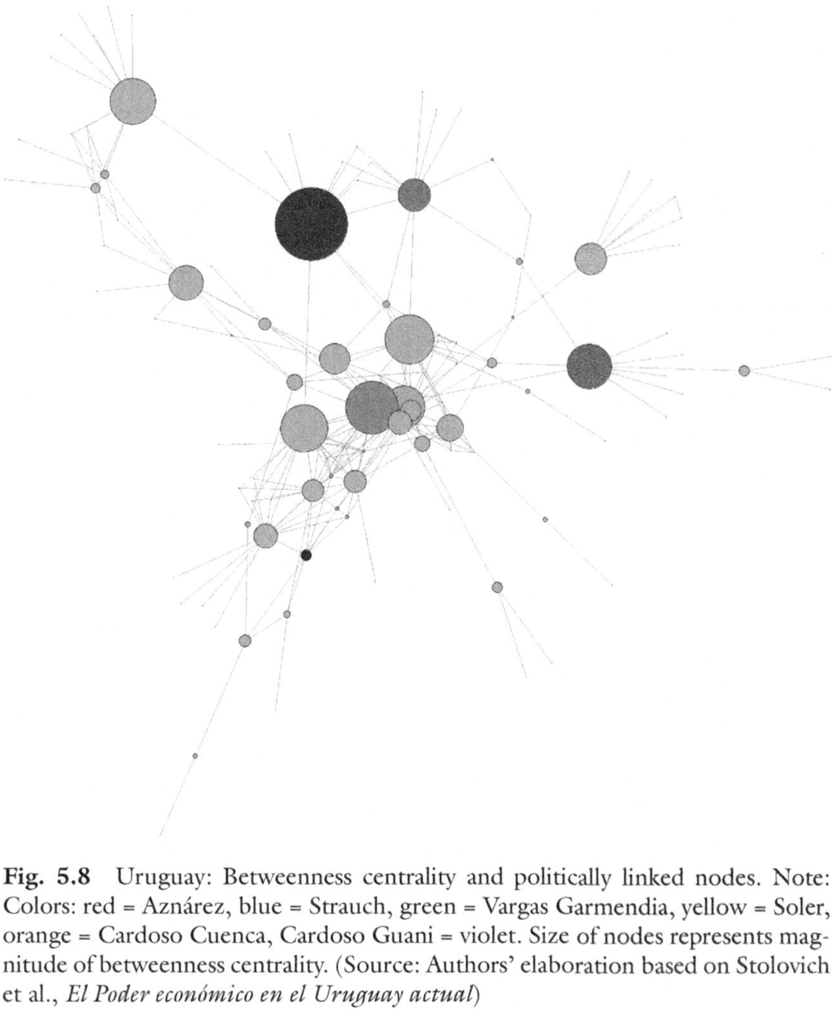

Fig. 5.8 Uruguay: Betweenness centrality and politically linked nodes. Note: Colors: red = Aznárez, blue = Strauch, green = Vargas Garmendia, yellow = Soler, orange = Cardoso Cuenca, Cardoso Guani = violet. Size of nodes represents magnitude of betweenness centrality. (Source: Authors' elaboration based on Stolovich et al., *El Poder económico en el Uruguay actual*)

which measures the number of shortest paths that pass through that node, revealing the extent to which a business group serves as an intermediary "between" other business groups in the network.[41] This implies that the removal of vertices with high betweenness coefficients precipitates a decrease in network connectivity.[42] Figure 5.8 illustrates the high level of betweenness of these groups. The Aznárez group ranks 7/95, Vargas Garmendia 11/95, and Cardoso Guani 17/95.[43] Along with three other groups, with which they had family ties, they were well above the confidence interval of the betweenness centrality mean (0.027 ± 0.011 at 95% confidence): Strauch (1/95), Cardoso Cuenca (4/95), and Soler (6/95).

In order to know how connected a node is with respect not only to its direct links but to a further set of nodes, a measure of closeness centrality was used.[44] Closeness centrality was particularly high for Strauch (1/95), Cardoso Cuenca (4/95), Aznárez (13/95), and Vargas Garmendia (18/95). This indicates that these groups had high levels of information access.

Overall, by any of these measures—cut-points, betweenness, and closeness—the five business groups represented in Fig. 5.8 had direct political influence during the dictatorship, just as those with family ties to them did. This is indicative of the good position big business was in to try to infiltrate the liberalization process for its own benefit. Although it is difficult to establish a quantifiable measure of the extent to which these groups, in particular, and the whole network, in general, benefited from direct political linkages, we provide a case study of three of these groups and analyze qualitative evidence illustrating how the rent-seeking process they engaged in could have developed.

The Aznárez group, one of the biggest at the time (see Diagram 1 in the appendix), whose assets were worth at least US $20 million per year in sales,[45] had two of its board members in key political roles during the dictatorship. Julio Eduardo Aznárez served as Minister of Livestock, Agriculture, and Fisheries from 1974 to 1976, while Walter Lusiardo

[41] Peter Monge & Noshir Contractor, *Theories of communication networks.* (USA: Oxford University Press, 2003).

[42] Linton Freeman, "Centrality in social networks conceptual clarification." *Social networks*, Volume 1 Issue 3 (1978): 215–239.

[43] See Table A1 in the appendix for a complete list of the normalized values.

[44] Stanley Wasserman & Katherine Faust. *Social Network Analysis: Methods and Applications.* (Cambridge: Cambridge University Press, 2005).

[45] Stolovich et al., *El poder económico en el Uruguay actual.*

Aznárez served as Minister of Industry, Energy, and Mining in 1982 and Minister of Economics and Finance from 1982 to 1983. This is of utmost importance given that the Aznárez group was, although highly diversified, an agro-industrial group, closely linked to one of the two biggest Uruguayan groups at the time measured in terms of the ownership of firms (24): Strauch.[46] Apart from family ties, they had solid business connections. The two groups, aided by foreign direct investment, founded an important fishery named Astra in the late 1970s. Our analysis expands the relevance of the fishery in understanding rent-seeking behavior during the military period.

The "Fishing Law" of 1969 provided export rebates and tax-free diesel to the industry. In addition, the state-owned bank (Banco República) granted several loans to the fishing industry, which attracted national and foreign capital. One of the drafters of the law was Marcial Bugallo, who was state counselor at that time. He had formerly worked for Nestle Uruguay and served as Labor Minister under Bordaberry in 1973–1974. Bugallo was also a board member at one of the fishing enterprises that benefited from the "plan pesquero," a plan consisting of a variety of tax exemptions and ease of obtaining credit for the fishing industry.[47,48] That a prominent member of the group served as the head of the Ministry of Agriculture, Livestock, and Fisheries also suggests a conflict of interests.

Besides family ties with the Strauch group, the Aznárez group had joint ventures with foreign and national groups. Among these, the Deambrosis, De Posadas, and Coca Cola Company groups were preeminent. Regarding sugar production—the Aznárez group's main business—the Aznárez established the "sugar trust": an alliance among local sugar companies to distribute production quotas and market segments.[49] The Aznárez group benefited directly from three government conclaves (meetings at which economic guidelines were settled by the military power and the executive branch) at which the sugar industry, a highly protected sector, was given an important position: San Miguel in 1973, Parque Hotel in 1976, and Solís in 1977. The conclaves stated that it was a government priority to ensure the autarkic supply of sugar in Uruguay, even though it was a

[46] Stolovich et al., *El poder económico en el Uruguay actual.*

[47] Executive decree of August 31, 1983.

[48] Miguel Carrió, *País vaciado: dictadura y negociados (1973–1985).* (Montevideo: Monte Sexto, 1987).

[49] Trías, *Reforma agraria en el Uruguay*, 226–227. Seminario Mate Amargo, *Prontuarios,* (Montevideo: Tae Editorial, 1990): 19.

declining industry and was not in the least competitive[50] Overall, the fishing- and sugar-related examples are clear illustrations of how economic groups adapted to the liberalization process by infiltrating the state.

The Vargas Garmendia group was also among the larger and highly diversified groups. It had stakes in the financial sector through bank ownership; in diverse industrial sectors such as textiles, rubber, and beverages; as well as in the newspaper business and the plastic industry. Businesses it owned in relation to these stakes included, respectively, the bank Banco Comercial, the wool company Lanera Santa María, the tire producer FUNSA, the brewing facility Fábricas Nacionales de Cerveza, the paper Diario La Mañana, and the plastic producer Atma. The group was also an important landowner.

The most relevant political linkage the Vargas Garmendia group had with the military government was Luis Vargas Garmendia—a board member at Atma and the brother of Eduardo Vargas Garmendia. Luis integrated several boards such as the previously mentioned FUNSA, Lanera Santa María, Fábricas Nacionales de Cerveza, among others.[51] He was Sub-Secretary of the Interior Affairs Minister from 1974 to 1976, later becoming secretary to the president during the de facto Aparicio Méndez administration (1976–1980). The group had family ties with the Soler group, one of the two biggest ones in Uruguay at the time.[52] While the Soler group had stakes in the production, commercialization, and import of automobiles, advertising, and banking, Daniel Darracq, the Minister of Education and Culture between 1975 and 1981, was married to a member of the Soler Garmendia family.

As in the Aznárez case, Vargas Garmendia comprised an extended network of alliances with joint ventures with other national groups. The most prominent of these included the Otegui group (textiles, media, and banks), Pardo Santayana (rubber, agricultural production, the beverage industry, and media), Fernandez Lladó (the meat industry), and Peirano Veira (mills, construction, and banking).

Unlike Aznárez, Strauch, or Vargas Garmendia, the Cardoso Guani group was comparatively small. However, its family tie with the Cardoso Cuenca group allowed it to have direct access to the financial sector and rice industry. The Cardoso Guani group had shares in one of the most

[50] Stolovich et al., *El poder económico en el Uruguay actual.*

[51] Carrió, *País vaciado: dictadura y negociados.*

[52] Stolovich et al., *El poder económico en el Uruguay actual.*

important supermarket chains in the country (Disco del Uruguay), as well as in other sectors—for example, in textiles (Lavadero Oriental de Lanas). Its most relevant political linkage with the military government was Adolfo Cardoso Guani, who was the Minister of Industry, Energy, and Mining from 1974 to 1976.

Short-Term Budgetary Balance Via Financial Mismanagement

Besides direct political influence, some business groups were able to benefit from state intervention in the private banking sector. As Carrió[53] posits, private investment in this period relied largely on bank loans. However, investors and financiers were usually the same people. A significant portion of the business groups in our network were represented in the board of directors of the main private banks at the time (see Fig. 5.9), which suggests another potential conflict of interest: investors asking for loans were involved in the decision-making process for granting those loans.

This led to an escalating process of "internal debt" and speculation at the expense of "main street" clients and the state. The Latin American debt crisis was a financial crisis in which a huge demand for external funds was associated with increasing trade and fiscal deficits that provoked the worst recession since the 1930s.[54] For instance, it generated a regional GDP recession, and the region's poverty rate increased from 40.5% to 48.3% between 1980 and 1990.[55] In this context, some local banks developed a high amount of uncollectible debt—greater than the 50% of total bank placement—mainly acquired during the economic boom of 1978–1980. In response to this fragile situation, the military government decided to buy out local banks' uncollectible debts, selling them at nominal prices to foreign banks in order to maintain confidence in the local financial system. These operations had a total cost of the equivalent of 10–12% of the Uruguayan GDP at the time, which was assumed by the Central Bank; the number of local banks went from 11 in 1976 to only

[53] Carrió, *País vaciado: dictadura y negociados.*

[54] Luis Bértola & Antonio Ocampo, *El desarrollo económico de América Latina desde la independencia.* (México: Fondo de Cultura Económica, 2013); Diaz Alejandro, *América Latina en los años treinta* (México: Fondo de Cultura Económica, 1988).

[55] Bértola & Ocampo, *El desarrollo económico de América Latina.*

Fig. 5.9 Uruguay: Connection between business groups and financial institutions. Note: Colors represented are: red = business groups that had shares in a bank; gray = the remaining business groups. (Source: Authors' elaboration based on Stolovich et al., *El Poder económico en el Uruguay actual*)

2 in 1983.[56] As Werner[57] states, this procedure strongly damaged the economy of the Uruguayan state even while members of the government sat on the boards of directors of several of the rescued banks.

Five out of the six groups we analyzed in depth in the previous section were directly linked with financial institutions. The Aznárez and Strauch

[56] Carrió, *País vaciado: dictadura y negociados.*

[57] Fabián Werner, "La estrategia y la política económica de la dictadura, 1973–1984," in *El negocio del terrorismo de estado* (Montevideo: Debate, 2016): 183–208.

groups were represented on the board of BAFISUD bank, the Vargas Garmendia and Carodoso Cuenca groups were represented on the board of Banco Comercial, and the Soler group was represented on the board of Surinvest Bank. All three banks eventually had their debt bought by the state by one of two mechanisms. The first mechanism was for the Central Bank (BCU) to buy the debt in order to sell it to a foreign institution—the BCU-incurred cost of bailing out the BAFISUD was around US $94 million, whereas it was sold to NMB Netherland's bank in 1982 for around US $0.015 (1 Nuevo Peso). The second mechanism was for the BCU to buy debt in exchange for the granting of loans by the selling bank to the BCU, as was the case for Banco Comercial and Surinvest.[58]

Although this was not a deliberate strategy of indebtedness across large business groups—only a few of them were strongly involved in these operations and more than 40% of the acquired debt was owned by small or midsize businesses—some clearly used their connections in the financial system and government to access credit irresponsibly. The most notorious case was that of the Soler group, whose debt was acquired by the BCU at a cost of US $37 million (the highest of any business group). Among others, this group owed the BAFISUD (US $14.5 million) and Surinvest (a bank of its own). The Strauch group's debts with BAFISUD and City Bank peaked at US $6.5 million, of which US $2 million was granted solely in the name of Jorge Strauch, a member of BAFISUD's board of directors.[59] The bailout of the Banco Comercial included debts of about US $1.5 million from "Arrozal 33," a rice-producing firm that owned Arrozur, whose board of directors included Jaime Cardoso Cuenca (from the Cardoso Cuenca group), the son of Jaime Cardoso Saavedra (the director of Banco Comercial). Another example of a self-approved unpaid loan was the one granted by the same bank to the Bakirgian group (linked to the Vargas Garmendia group) for US $1.2 million.[60]

[58] Luis Stolovich, Juan Manuel Ródriguez, Daniel Olesker, Luis Porto & Guillermo Pomi, (1986). "*Compra de carteras. Crisis del sistema bancario uruguayo*" (Montevideo: Ediciones de la Banda Oriental, 1986).

[59] Stolovich et al., *Compra de Carteras.*

[60] Carrió, *País vaciado: dictadura y negociados.*

Conclusions

This chapter provided a descriptive account of how big business in Uruguay transited through the liberalization period by perpetuating rent-seeking strategies although it adapted the ones it inherited from the ISI period. The chapter began by filling in the contextual information on the collapse of the ISI model and of democratic institutions, as well as the liberalization process that followed. This included a detailed account of how the ISI incentivized rent-seeking on the part of businesses, and how the perpetuation of rent-seeking became their primary strategy as liberalization advanced.

We described how business strategy for influencing policy outcomes evolved from the ISI to the authoritarian period, moving from institutionalized corporate participation in decision-making to direct participation of businesspersons in government. This adaptation followed the stagnation and collapse of the ISI and the subsequent attempt at liberalization attempt that began in 1974.

By using network analysis methodology, the chapter also provided novel information from an extraordinary database of business networks originally produced by Stolovich et al.[61] Thus, we were able to characterize the network and to illustrate the importance of certain nodes with different measures of centrality. We were able to assess the centrality and influence of key business groups with direct political linkages and domestic bank ownership. The network analysis presented evidence of how business groups maintained strong links with each other by sharing the ownership of firms and how the structure of the business community opened the door for the two adaptive strategies. In particular, the business community structure at the time constituted a very small, closed, and interconnected network, with the particularity of some nodes determining the flow of information. Among them, Aznárez, Vargas Garmendia, and Cardoso Cuenca, as well as Strauch and Soler, stand out because of their economic and strategic importance, along with their close ties with government and domestic banks.

Once the chapter had described the context, the structure of the network, and the main characteristics of its central nodes, it went on to explain how the two main strategies used by businesses to infiltrate—and shelter themselves from—the liberalization process worked. First, they scored

[61] Stolovich et al., *El poder económico en el Uruguay actual*.

political influence by establishing direct political linkages with the authoritarian administration, and, second, they injected short-term capital by means of financial mismanagement. To this end, the chapter recounted case studies of three influential business groups—Aznárez, Vargas Garmendia, and Cardoso Cuenca—based on several secondary sources that we connected to new insights from the network analysis.

The secondary historical evidence helped to better explain how these influential groups managed to infiltrate the inevitable liberalization process that would otherwise have seriously damaged their wealth and industries at the expense of the state's economy and ordinary citizens' well-being, particularly in light of the banking crisis that unfolded after 1982 and how the authoritarian government at the time bailed out banks, business groups, and, ultimately, the few families behind them.

Overall, we used a novel network analysis in order to tie together the rich but not sufficiently connected domestic and international scholarship on corporate business, the breakdown of democracy, and economic liberalization in Uruguay. Our innovation is in improving an already rich descriptive characterization of these processes using network-related metrics that foster an understanding of the relations between big business and the military government in Uruguay from a richer comparative perspective.

References

Astori, Danilo. *La política económica de la dictadura*. Montevideo: Ediciones de la Banda Oriental, 1989.

Bensión, Alberto & Jorge Caumont. "Alternative trade strategies and employment." In *Trade and Employment in Developing Countries*, edited by Anne O. Krueger, Hal B. Lary, Terry Monson, and Narongchai Akrasanee, 495–528. University of Chicago Press Chicago, 1981.

Bértola, Luis & José Antonio Ocampo. *El desarrollo económico de América Latina desde la independencia*. México: Fondo de Cultura Económica, 2013.

Bértola, Luis. *La industria manufacturera uruguaya, 1913–1961: un enfoque sectorial de su crecimiento, fluctuaciones y crisis*. Montevideo: Facultad de Ciencias Sociales-Universidad de la República, 1991.

Bogliaccini, Juan A. "Small Latecomers into the Global Market: Power Conflict and Institutional Change in Chile and Uruguay". PhD diss., University of North Carolina, 2012.

Bogliaccini, Juan A. "The Reconstruction of Business Interests after the ISI Collapse: Unpacking the Effect of Institutional Change in Chile and Uruguay." *Third World Quarterly* 40, no. 7 (2019): 1378–1393.

Bohoslavsky, Juan Pablo. *El Negocio del Terrorismo de Estado. Los cómplices económicos de la dictadura uruguaya*. Montevideo: Debate, 2016.

Bucheli, Marcelo, Erica Salvaj, and Minyoung Kim. "Better together: How multinationals come together with business groups in times of economic and political transitions". *Global Strategy Journal* 9, no. 2 (2018): 176–207.

Burt, Ronald. "Structural holes and good ideas". *American Journal of Sociology* 110, no. 2 (2004): 349–399.

Burt, Ronald. "The network structure of social capital". *Research in organizational behavior* 22 (2000): 345–423.

Caetano, Gerardo. *El asedio conservador: 1925–1929. Series investigaciones CLAEH 42–43*. Montevideo: Centro Latinoamericano de Economía Humana, 1985.

Carrió, Miguel. *País vaciado: dictadura y negociados (1973–1985)*. Montevideo: Monte Sexto, 1987.

Demasi, Carlos. "El apoyo de las cámaras comerciales." In *El negocio del terrorismo de estado,* edited by Juan Pablo Bohoslasvky, 143–161. Montevideo: Debate, 2016.

Díaz, Alejandro. *América Latina en los años treinta*. México: Fondo de Cultura Económica, 1988.

Finch, Henry. *La economía política del Uruguay contemporáneo: 1870–2000.* Montevideo: Ediciones de la Banda Oriental, 2005.

Freeman, Linton. "Centrality in social networks conceptual clarification". *Social networks* 1, no. 3 (1978): 215–239.

García-Repetto, Ulises. "El contralor de exportaciones e importaciones en Uruguay (1941–1959)." *Series de Documentos de trabajo del Instituto de Economía* 13 (2017): 3–41.

Hanson, James, and Jaime De Melo, "The Uruguayan experience with liberalization and stabilization, 1974–1981". *Journal of Interamerican Studies and World Affairs* 25, no. 4 (1983): 477–508.

Humphries, Mark, and Kevin Gurney. "Network 'small-world-ness': a quantitative method for determining canonical network equivalence". PLoS ONE 3, no. 4. https://doi.org/10.1371/journal.pone.0002051

Instituto de Economía- Facultad de Ciencias Económicas y de Administración, Universidad de la República. *El proceso económico del Uruguay contribución al estudio de su evolución y perspectivas.* Montevideo: Fundación de Cultura Universitaria, 1969.

Jacob, Raúl. *Banca e industria: un puente inconcluso.* Montevideo: Fundación de Cultura Universitaria- CIEDUR, 1991.

Jones, Geoffrey, and Asli Colpan. "Business groups in historical perspectives." In *The Oxford Handbook of Business Groups*, edited by Asli Colpan, Takashi Hikino & James Lncoln, 67–96. Oxford: University Press, 2010.

Khanna, Tarun, and Yishay Yafeh. "Business groups in emerging markets: Paragons or parasites?" *Journal of Economic Literature* 45, no. 2 (2007): 331–372.

Macadar, Luis. *Restauración democrática y política económica. Uruguay 1985–1989.* Montevideo: Ediciones de la Banda Oriental, 1992.

Millot, Julio, Carlos Silva, and Lindor Silva. *El desarrollo industrial del Uruguay; de la crisis de 1929 a la posguerra.* Montevideo: Instituto de Economía-Universidad de la República, 1973.

Monge, Peter, and Noshir Contractor. *Theories of communication networks.* USA: Oxford University Press, 2003.

Notaro, Jorge. *La política económica en el Uruguay, 1968–1984.* Montevideo: Ediciones de la Banda Oriental, 1984.

Notaro, Jorge. "La economía del Uruguay 1998–2014. Caracterización e hipótesis explicativas". Accesed February 2017. https://www.researchgate.net/publication/284174297_La_economia_del_Uruguay_1998_-_2014_Caracterizacion_e_hipotesis_explicativas

O'Donnell, Guillermo. *Modernization and Bureaucratic-Authoritarianism: Studies in South American Politics.* Berkeley: University of California, 1973.

Rama, Martín. "Crecimiento y estancamiento económico en Uruguay.". In *Trayectorias Divergentes. Comparación de un siglo de desarrollo económico latinamericano y escandinavo,* edited by Magnus Blomstron & Patricio Meller, 115–144. Chile: Cieplan-Hachete, 1990.

Rama, Martín. *Protección y crecimiento industrial 1975–1980.* Montevideo: Cinve, 1982.

Schneider, Ben Ross. *Business Politics and the State in 20th century Latin America.* Cambridge: Cambridge University Press, 2004.

Scott, John. *Social network analysis.* Washington: Sage, 2017.

Seminario Mate Amargo. *Prontuarios.* Montevideo: Tae Editorial, 1990.

Stolovich, Luis, and Juan Manuel Rodriguez. "Gobierno y empresarios: sus vínculos personales." In *¿Hacia dónde va el Estado uruguayo?*, edited by Gerónimo de Sierra, 163–201. Montevideo: Fondo de Cultura Universitaria, 1987.

Stolovich, Luis, Juan Manuel Rodríguez & Luis Bértola. *El poder económico en el Uruguay actual.* Montevideo: Centro Uruguay Independiente, 1987.

Stolovich, Luis, Juan Manuel Rodríguez, Daniel Olesker, Luis Porto, and Guillermo Pomi. *Compra de carteras. Crisis del sistema bancario uruguayo.* Montevideo: Ediciones de la Banda Oriental, 1986.

Trías, Vivian. *Reforma agraria en el Uruguay.* Montevideo: Ediciones El Sol, 1958.

Wasserman, Stanley & Katherine Faust. *Social Network Analysis: Methods and Applications.* Cambridge: Cambridge University Press, 2005.

Watts, Duncan, and Steven Strogatz. "Collective dynamics of 'small-world' networks." *Nature* 393 (1998): 440–442.
Werner, Fabián. "La estrategia y la política económica de la dictadura, 1973–1984." In *El negocio del terrorismo de estado,* edited by Juan Pablo Bohoslasvky, 183–208. Montevideo: Debate, 2016.
Yaffé, Jaime. "La sociedad uruguaya durante la dictadura." In *El negocio del terrorismo de estado,* edited by Juan Pablo Bohoslasvky, 123–143. Montevideo: Debate, 2016.
Yaffé, Jaime. 2010. "Dictadura y neoliberalismo en Uruguay (1973–1985)." In *Séptimas Jornadas de Historia Económica.* Montevideo: Asociación Uruguaya de Historia Económica, 2010.
Zurbriggen, Cristina. *Estado, empresarios y redes rentistas.* Montevideo: Instituto de Ciencias Políticas-Universidad de la República- Ediciones de la Banda Oriental, 2006.

CHAPTER 6

From Business Associations to Business Groups: Business-Government Relations and Corporate Networks During the Military Dictatorship, Peru 1968–1980

Martín Monsalve Zanatti and Abel Puerta Alarcón

Between 1968 and 1980 Peru, like most South American countries, was governed by a military dictatorship. But unlike their regional counterparts, Peru's military leaders introduced a radical program of social and economic reforms that entailed, among other measures, the nationalization of multinationals engaged in the exportation of raw materials, the creation of a series of new state-run firms, and an agrarian reform process. The military junta transformed Peruvian society in short order, living up

M. Monsalve Zanatti (✉) • A. Puerta Alarcón
Universidad del Pacífico, Lima, Peru
e-mail: monsalve_ma@up.edu.pe

V. Basualdo et al. (eds.), *Big Business and Dictatorships in Latin America*, Palgrave Studies in Latin American Heterodox Economics, https://doi.org/10.1007/978-3-030-43925-5_6

to their self-styling as the "*Revolutionary Government of the Armed Forces* (RGAF)."[1]

In their drive to modernize the nation's economy, the junta equated economic growth with national security. As far as it was concerned, economic growth guaranteed the stability of social order internally, and, on the international front, it protected the country against the interests of the major powers amid the Cold War and against the possible ambitions of neighboring countries. To pursue these ideals, the regime would have to pursue an alliance with the business community. However, business figures were wary of the government's radical discourse and its disregard for private property rights.

Through what channels did the RGAF attempt to dialogue with local businesses? Given that the military envisioned an industrialization project as part of its conception of economic modernization, the ideal conduit for this dialogue was the National Society of Industry (Sociedad Nacional de Industria, SNI). As a symbol of its good faith and resolute support for local industry, the junta awarded subsidies to businesses, as well as tax breaks for the establishment of factories outside the capital, and for the export of manufactured goods.

But at the same time, the military government was suspicious of business associations, which they perceived as political rivals. Thus, the junta implemented a series of measures intended to limit the power of the SNI and secure the political support of the urban working class, such as the passage of the Labor Stability Law and the establishment of the Industrial Community (which allowed union representatives to participate on corporate boards). Medium-sized businesses, as those most affected by these measures, organized themselves into associations in an attempt to channel their opposition to the government. In turn, large businesses, despite their distrust of the military regime, took advantage of the favorable economic measures to enhance their market share and raise the barriers to entry into their industries. These also drew on their personal connections with government agents to obtain privileged information on future proposals.

[1] Julio Cotler, *Clases, Estado y Nación en el Perú* (Lima: Instituto de Estudios Peruanos, 1978); Cynthia McClintock and Abraham F. Lowenthal, *Peruvian Experiment Reconsidered* (Princeton: Princeton University Press, 2016); Daniel Materson, *Fuerza armada y sociedad en el Perú moderno: Un estudio sobre las relaciones civiles militares, 1930–2000* (Lima: Instituto de Estudios Peruanos, 2001); Henry Pease and Gonzalo Romero Sommer, *La Política En El Perú Del Siglo XX* (Lima: Fondo Editorial de la Pontificia Universidad Católica del Perú, 2013).

Focusing on the Peruvian corporate network, this chapter analyzes how the relations of simultaneous collaboration and distrust between Peruvian businesses and the military government (1968–1980) shifted centrality within the network away from Peruvian business associations and toward the economic groups that exploited direct relations with government agents. As such, we hope to contribute to the literature on corporate networks—which tends to overlook analysis of the role of sectoral business associations—and on the relations between government and private enterprise.[2] The special characteristics of the Peruvian military dictatorship (1968–1980) render it a key case study in this context.

Context of the Military Government

The military junta that governed Peru between 1968 and 1980 was composed of military officers who linked the notion of national security with economic development, which it regarded as crucial to avoiding any repeat of the kind of leftist guerrilla activity that had flared in 1965. The junta also believed that government should play a leading role in the organization of the economy and society.

The most radical period of the RGAF fell under the presidency of General Juan Velasco Alvarado (1968–1975). It was during these years

[2] María Inés Barbero, Andrea Lluch, and Erica Salvaj, "Corporate Networks and Business Groups in Argentina in the Early 1970s," *Australian Economic History Review* 54, no. 2 (2014): 183–208; Erica Salvaj and Andrea Lluch, "Estudio Comparativo Del Capitalismo Argentino y Chileno: Un Análisis Desde Las Redes de Directorio a Fines Del Modelo Sustitutivo de Importaciones," *Redes. Revista Hispana Para El Análisis de Redes Sociales* 23, no. 2 (2012): 43–43; Julián Cárdenas, "Why Do Corporate Elites Form Cohesive Networks in Some Countries, and Do Not in Others? Cross-National Analysis of Corporate Elite Networks in Latin America," *International Sociology* 31, no. 3 (2016): 341–63; Adolfo Figueroa, "Competition and Circulation of Economic Elites: Theory and Application to the Case of Peru," *Quarterly Review of Economics and Finance* 48, no. 2 (2008): 263–73; Aldo Musacchio and Ian Read, "Bankers, Industrialists, and Their Cliques: Elite Networks in Mexico and Brazil during Early Industrialization," *Enterprise and Society*, 8 No. 4 (2007), 842–80; Aldo Musacchio, "Drawing Links between Corporate Governance and Networks: Bankers in the Corporate Networks of Brazil, Mexico, and the United States Circa 1910," *Entreprises et Histoire* 54, no. 1 (2009): 16–36; Alejandra Salas-Porras, "Fuerzas centrípetas y centrífugas en la red corporativa mexicana (1981–2001)," *Revista Mexicana de Sociología* 68, no. 2 (October 5, 2006), 331–375. Andrea Lluch and Érica Salvaj, "Fragmentación del empresariado en la época de la industrialización por sustitución de importaciones (ISI) en la Argentina: una aproximación desde el estudio de la red corporativa (1954–1970)," *Apuntes. Revista de ciencias sociales*, 39 No. 70 (2012), 135–66.

that young colonels and generals, with scant links to the corporate elite, implemented most of the program of social and economic reforms now regarded as a milestone in Peruvian history. When the regime began to reveal its economic and political limitations, a conservative section of the army led by General Francisco Morales Bermúdez seized control, ushering in what became known as the "second phase of the RGAF" (1975–1980). This period witnessed fewer social reforms as the junta looked toward a new alliance with local enterprise and multilateral agencies such as the International Monetary Fund. During this stage, the military leaders were pitted against a mounting economic crisis and the political opposition of the urban working classes. This persuaded the RGAF to transition back to civilian rule, a process marked by the election of the Constituent Assembly in 1978 and the organization of presidential elections in 1980.[3]

Eric Hobsbawm, the British historian, classified the military government headed by General Juan Velasco Alvarado as a *"revolution"* because it assimilated, through agrarian reform and cultural policies, the indigenous population into Peruvian politics and society; it snatched control of agricultural assets from the upper classes and transformed the space for political participation; and it transformed the relationship between Peruvian government and foreign capital. Yet Hobsbawm adds that this was a "peculiar revolution" in that it lacked the support of the masses, whether urban or rural. But at the same time, it was not a "top-down" revolution because it did not stamp its authority on the business or working classes. Finally, it did not draw support from any cohesive political movement that might have acted as a bridge between the government and society. Rather, this was a revolution discharged by a group of military officers who swiftly achieved profound reforms at a specific juncture, but without much in the way of representation or capacity to sustain the policies implemented over time.[4] By 1975 the RGAF reforms had reached

[3] Cotler, *Clases, Estado y Nación*; Pease and Romero Sommer, *La política en el Perú del siglo XX*.

[4] Eric Hobsbawm, "The Peculiar Revolution," in *Viva La Revolución. Eric Hobsbawn on Latin America*, ed. Leslie Bethell (London: Abacus, 2016), 334–61; Carlos Aguirre and Paulo Drinot, *The Peculiar Revolution. Rethinking the Peruvian Experiment Under Military Rule* (Austin: University of Texas Press, 2017); Martín Monsalve Zanatti, "'Una Revolución Peculiar', Eric Hobsbawm y El Gobierno Revolucionario de Las Fuerzas Armadas, 1968–1975," in *Eric Hobsbawn: La Historia y América Latina*, ed. Felipe Portocarrero Suárez and Martín Monsalve Zanatti (Lima: Fondo Editorial de la Universidad del Pacífico, 2017), 31–39.

breaking point, and the changes at the top of the military blocked their continued course. In a rightward shift, General Morales Bermúdez proceeded to repress the urban social movement and establish alliances with dictatorships in the Southern Cone. However, he lacked both the political strength and the private-sector confidence needed to undo his predecessor's reforms altogether, sending the revolution into a lengthy spell of stagnation. Therefore, to be specific, the "peculiar" aspect of the revolution and the regime's contradictions awoke among Peruvian businesses a sense of ambivalence that oscillated between opposition and exploitation of the advantages the regime opened to their interests.

Credibility and Trust

Credibility and trust are two key elements in the viability of collaboration between government and business. Schneider and Maxfield argue that the credibility of government in the eyes of business depends, among other factors, on the consistency of the policies implemented, the type of policy, the flow of information, and the reputation of the officials in charge of implementation.[5] The majority of the army officers responsible for the first phase had no links with the private sector, but evidently what most hampered government credibility for the businesses were the policies of nationalization and inconsistencies in the economic program.[6]

The nationalization of agricultural exportation and livestock companies, and of multinationals in the petroleum, mining, railroad, telecommunications, electricity, manufacturing, and banking sectors, created an entrepreneurial state whose management exceeded the capacity of the governing junta.[7] While the junta's developmentalist program anticipated controlling the price of the basket of family goods, wages, and foreign-currency transactions, there was no technocracy capable of overseeing the macroeconomic imbalances that these policies threatened to create.

Schneider and Maxfield note that credibility is a notion applied to certain government policies, but trust implies a more enduring and

[5] Ben Ross Schneider and Sylvia Maxfield, "Business, the State, and Economic Performance in Developing Countries," in *Business and the State in Developing Countries* ed. Sylvia Maxfield and Ben Ross Schneider (Ithaca: Cornell University Press, 1997), 3–35.

[6] Daniel M Schydlowsky and Juan J Wicht, "The Anatomy of an Economic Failure," in *Peruvian Experiment Reconsidered*, 94–143.

[7] Carol Wise, *Reinventando El Estado: Estrategia Económica y Cambio Institucional En El Peru* (Lima: Fondo Editorial de la Universidad del Pacífico, 2003).

multifaceted relationship. Trust between entrepreneurs and the government can reduce transaction costs and political risk while increasing investment.[8] For the government's developmentalist project, fostering a situation of trust was vital to attracting foreign capital and winning over the local manufacturing sector. But once again, the haste and the vertical application of the reforms meant that both domestic and foreign companies were more dissuaded by the political risks than they were persuaded by the prospect of constructing a space for collaboration with the government.

Relations between the military junta and multinational firms hinged on the political and economic plans of the former. Among the first to fall under state control was the International Petroleum Company (IPC), a firm that symbolized the subordination of the Peruvian economy to foreign capital in twentieth-century nationalist discourses. The Peruvian Corporation and its railroads were left in a precarious financial situation, diminishing the firm's bargaining power. On the other hand, Chase Manhattan Bank, Cerro de Pasco Copper Corporation, and W.R. Grace had more room for maneuverer when selling their assets to the Peruvian government. Meanwhile, mining companies, such as Southern Perú (which was largely US-owned), were left intact and furnished with the support of the state bureaucracy, because their operations were indispensable to the developmental plans of the military junta. Similarly, the government opened negotiations with Japanese and European multinationals such as Toyota, Mitsui, Bayer, and Volvo in a bid to attract foreign direct investment to the Peruvian market.[9] Meanwhile, multinational producers of durable and non-durable goods would base their decision as to whether to remain in Peru on their prospects of expansion under the rules imposed by the regime, and on their capacity to manage the political risk that came of operating in the Peruvian economy.

Within Peru, the agrarian reform, the consequent disappearance of the National Agrarian Society (Sociedad Nacional Agraria, SNA), and the

[8] Schneider and Maxfield, "Business, the State, and Economic Performance in Developing Countries," 13.

[9] Shane Hunt, *La formación de la economía peruana: Distribución y crecimiento en la Historia del Perú y América Latina* (Lima: Banco Central de Reserva del Perú e Instituto de Estudios Peruanos, 2011). For Japanese investments in Peru see Isabelle Lausent-Herrera, *Pasado y presente de la comunidad Japonesa en el Perú* (Paris: Institut Français d' Études Andines, 1991).

bankruptcy of the Prado family[10] spelled the end of the business elite that had taken root during the nineteenth century. This gap was filled by upwardly mobile entrepreneurial families such as the Romeros and the Brescias, and by established family-owned companies whose core business lay in sectors other than agricultural exports or mining.[11] These families also took advantage of the withdrawal of certain multinationals. For example, the Romeros bought the interests of Anderson & Clayton in Peru, while the Brescias purchased Minsur (which operated a zinc mine) from W.R. Grace, and Tejidos la Unión from Duncan Fox.[12]

The constant changes to economic policies during this period prompted family businesses to diversify into a range of sectors as a way of mitigating risks and assuring liquidity. This diversification drove the consolidation of economic groups controlled by a holding firm whose majority shareholders belonged to a single family, and which included a financial company among their subsidiaries.[13]

The control or participation of a financial company allowed the groups and their subsidiaries to organize themselves into pyramidal structures,[14]

[10] The Pardo family was one of the most important Peruvian business families from the late nineteenth century. One of its members, Manuel Prado, was president of Peru on two occasions (1939–1945 and 1956–1962). See Felipe Portocarrero Suárez, *El Imperio Prado: 1890–1970* (Lima: Centro de Investigación de la Universidad del Pacífico, 1995).

[11] Grupo Romero and Brescia (now Grupo Breca) are two of the most important Peruvian economic groups. Martín Monsalve Zanatti, "Evolución de La Gran Empresa Familiar Peruana 1890–2012," in *Familias Empresarias y Grandes Empresas Familiares En América Latina. Una Visión de Largo Plazo*, ed. Paloma Fernánde Pérez and Andrea Lluch (Bilbao: Fundación BBVA, 2015), 381–408.

[12] Francisco Durand, *Los doce apósteles de la economía peruana: Una mirada social a los grupos de poder limeños y provincianos* (Lima: Fondo Editorial de la Pontificia Universidad Católica del Perú, 2017); Enrique Vásquez, *Estrategias del poder: Grupos económicos en el Perú* (Lima: Centro de Investigación de la Universidad del Pacífico, 2000).

[13] Ludovico Alcorta, *El nuevo capital financiero: Grupos financieros y ganancias sistemáticas en el Perú* (Lima: Fundación Friedrich Ebert, 1990); Francisco Durand, *Riqueza económica y pobreza política: Reflexiones sobre las élites del poder en un país inestable* (Lima: Pontificia Universidad Católica del Perú: Fondo Editorial, 2003); Vásquez, *Estrategias del poder*.

[14] "In a pyramidal group, and more generally in a business group, the controlling owner has the power to direct the subsidiaries, considering them as a single economic entity. The dominant shareholder, through the controlling parent company at the top of the pyramid, directly exercises the decision-making power of all subsidiaries. In other words, he/she does not only have the power but also exercises that power" Emiliano Di Carlo, "Pyramids and the Separation between Direction and Control of Non-Financial Italian Family Companies," *Journal of Management and Governance* 18, no. 3 (2014): 835–72. See also Randall Morck, "How to Eliminate Pyramidal Business Groups: The Double Taxation of Intercorporate

gain access to cheap credit from the financial sector, and conduct transactions internally. The greater their financial capacity, the better placed these groups were to take advantage of the tax breaks and loans granted by the government to promote the development of a region or economic sector.[15] For example, the joint control of *Banco de Crédito del Perú* by the Romero, Raffo, Brescia, and Nicolini families was fundamental for the diversification and expansion of their respective economic groups.[16]

This business structure demanded an organizational flexibility that would allow companies to adapt to new investments and expand their operations into different markets.[17] Thus, on the one hand, the groups needed professional managers who were not over-specialized and who enjoyed the trust of the family, and on the other hand, their leaders needed to be in constant contact with government agents in order to adapt to changes in economic policies. This pushed the group leaders into constant political activity that, instead of trust and collaboration, promoted an asymmetrical flow of information and raised the barriers to entry still higher.

In this context, it is worth asking what role the business associations played in relations between the government and private enterprises, above all when both the economic groups and the multinationals could obtain greater advantages from dealing directly with state bureaucracy.

Business Associations and the State

Relations between the military government and the business associations were rather complex. Though the agrarian reforms did away with the SNA, the junta initially coveted an alliance with the SNI, which it considered a representative of the modern face of business. Yet when this association gained in prominence, the government threw its weight behind the creation of other sectoral societies to weaken it. Thus, the RGAF did not stimulate the creation of formal institutions as a channel for interaction between business and state bureaucracy.

Dividends and Other Incisive Uses of Tax Policy," *Tax Policy and the Economy*, 19 (2005), 135–179.

[15] Alcorta, *El nuevo capital financiero*; H Campodónico, M Castillo, and A Quispe, *De Poder a Poder: Grupos de Poder, Gremios Empresariales y Política Macroeconómica* (Lima: DESCO, 1994); Vásquez, *Estrategias del poder*.

[16] Monsalve Zanatti, "Evolución de La Gran Empresa Familiar Peruana 1890–2012."

[17] Mauro Guillén, "Business Groups in Emerging Economies: A Resource-Based View," *Academy of Management Journal* 43, no. 3 (2000): 362–80.

According to Schneider,[18] governments in developing countries tend to encourage the formation of encompassing or multisectoral associations at times of economic or political crisis to make up for a lack of information about economic activities or of competent officials. On occasion governments do so actively, by offering such associations (and, thus, their members) access to privileged information, exclusive information channels, and so on, thereby solving the *free rider* problem as theorized by Mancur Olson.[19] At other times they seek to organize these associations indirectly through negative incentives. That is, if a government poses a threat to business, the differences between companies can be obscured by a coalescence of interests. Generally, these threats include intervention in the labor system in favor of workers and/or the curbing of property rights. Both such negative incentives loomed throughout the ten years of the RGAF in Peru. However, it would take another 12 years, and the restoration of democracy, for an encompassing association to be created.

In their studies of the Andean countries, Francisco Durand and Rosemary Thorp[20] propose that to understand the business association formation process, one must consider the external factors analyzed by Schneider and the historical trajectory of associative life in each country. But in the specific case of Peru, they argue that positive or negative government stimuli did not have the effect expected by Schneider's theory because the local entrepreneurial elite was extremely fragmented in regional, economic, and social terms.[21] This atomization prompted firms to negotiate directly with state agents through personal connections or in alliance with multinationals. For this reason, the sectoral associations were of little importance to businesses as channels of communication, much less as encompassing organizations. It was only toward the end of the twentieth century that this situation changed to a sufficient degree to enable the

[18] Ben Ross Schneider, *Business Politics and the State in Twentieth-Century Latin America* (Cambridge: Cambridge University Press, 2004); Ben Ross Schneider, "Organizing Interests and Coalitions in the Politics of Market Reform in Latin America," *World Politics* 56, no. 3 (2004): 456–79; Richard F. Doner and Ben Ross Schneider, "Business Associations and Economic Development: Why Some Associations Contribute More Than Others," *Business and Politics* 2, no. 3 (2000): 261–88.

[19] Mancur Olson, *The Logic of Collective Action: Public Goods and the Theory of Groups* (Cambridge: Harvard University Press, 1965).

[20] Rosemary Thorp and Francisco Durand, "A Historical View of Business-State Relations: Colombia, Peru, and Venezuela Compared," in *Business and the State in Developing Countries*, 216–36.

[21] Maxfield and Schneider, *Business and the State*; Schneider, *Business Politics and the State.*

establishment of the National Confederation of Private Business Institutions (Confederación Nacional de Instituciones Empresariales Privadas, CONFIEP).[22]

Other researchers propose, from a perspective closer to dependency theory, that this very fragmentation of interests meant that the sectoral associations were extremely important in influencing the decisions of the Peruvian government. Indeed, Baltazar Caravedo argues, through meticulous studies of the bulletins published by associations, that the SNA and the SNI are central to understanding the conflicts among entrepreneurial elites.[23]

However, our study of the period between 1940 and 1970 proves that the SNA, despite being a sectoral association, was at the heart of a Peruvian corporate network until the 1969 agrarian reform caused its demise, and that the RGAF catalyzed the fragmentation of business associations by facilitating economic groups that had direct dealings with state officials. Consequently, leading businesses in the Peruvian corporate network seldom participated on the boards of associations, limiting these organizations to a role as public spokespersons during the return to democracy in the 1980s.

Business Associations in the Peruvian Corporate Network Before the Military Junta

To determine the importance of business associations in the corporate network, we have analyzed the board interlocks of major Peruvian firms and sectoral associations. To identify board compositions, we have consulted the *Vademécum Bursátiles* guidebooks published by Banco de Crédito del Perú until 1979, as well as the same instrument published by Bolsa de Valores de Lima in 1981 and 1987.[24] This type of information

[22] Thorp and Durand, "A Historical View of Business-State Relations."

[23] Baltazar Caravedo, *Conflictos interburgueses durante el gobierno de Odría – (1948–1956)* (Lima: Publicaciones CISEPA, 1974); Baltazar Caravedo, *Burguesía e industria en el Perú (1933–1945)* (Lima: Instituto de Estudios Peruanos, 1976).

[24] Banco de Crédito del Perú, *Vademécum del inversionista 1944* (Lima: BCP, Departamento de Estudios Económicos, 1944); Banco de Crédito del Perú, *Vademécum del inversionista 1947* (Lima: BCP, Departamento de Estudios Económicos, 1947); Banco de Crédito del Perú, *Vademécum del inversionista 1952–3* (Lima: BCP, Departamento de Estudios Económicos, 1953); Banco de Crédito del Perú, *Vademécum del inversionista 1956–57* (BCP, Departamento de Estudios Económicos, 1957); Banco de Crédito del Perú,

has some limitations. The most significant is that agricultural companies were not listed on the Lima Stock Exchange before the agrarian reform, as they were family-owned. Moreover, manufacturing companies were not fully represented, but banks and companies involved in finance, public services (such as electricity providers), and real estate were. We analyze the following business associations in the corporate network: the SNA; the SNI; the National Society of Mining and Petroleum (Sociedad Nacional de Minería y Petróleo, SNMP); Lima Chamber of Commerce (Cámara de Comercio de Lima, CCL); the Peruvian Institute of Business Administration (Instituto Peruano de Administración de Empresas, IPAE); the Peruvian Chamber of Construction (Cámara Peruana de Construcción, CAPECO); the Association of Exporters (Asociación de Exportadores, ADEX); the Peruvian Association of Insurance Companies (Asociación Peruana de Empresas de Seguros, APESEG); the Association of Banks of Peru (Asociación de Bancos del Perú, ASBANC); and the CONFIEP.

When analyzing corporate networks, there are various ways of measuring the centrality of a company or director. The indicator of centrality that we have opted to utilize is the *eigenvector*. Under this concept, a node is considered central when it is linked to nodes that are, in turn, well connected.[25] This means that in our sample, an association will be considered central if it is linked with companies and associations that are, in turn, well connected with the rest of the network. This type of centrality is interpreted as an indicator of popularity[26] or of greater influence or power.[27] Because there were no encompassing organizations before 1983, we conduct a sectoral composition analysis of the different associations to determine whether any one of them had greater influence than their sector.

Vademécum del inversionista 1963 (Lima: BCP, Departamento de Estudios Económicos, 1963); Bolsa de Valores de Lima, *Vademécum bursátil 1979* (Lima: Bolsa de Valores de Lima, 1979); Bolsa de Valores de Lima, *Vademécum bursátil 1987* (Lima: Bolsa de Valores de Lima, 1987); Bolsa de Valores de Lima, *Vademécum bursátil 1995* (Lima: Bolsa de Valores de Lima, 1995).

25 For example, if in a network of friends one person has five friends, but these five individuals do not, in turn, have many friends, then under the *eigenvector* the original person is not very central. On the other hand, if a person has three friends, and each of them in turn has between five or six friends, then that person, despite having a lower *degree* than the one in the previous example, will be more central in terms of the *eigenvector*.

26 Stephen Borgatti and Martin Everett, *Analyzing Social Networks* (London: SAGE Publications, 2013).

27 Beth Mintz and Michael Schwartz, *The Power Structure of American Business* (Chicago: University Chicago Press, 1985).

Table 6.1 Peru: Position in the eigenvector ranking, by association, 1944–1963

Year	*SNA*	*SNI*	*SNMP*	*CCL*	*IPAE*	*CAPECO*	*APESEG*	*Sample size*
1944	10	22	13	7				53
1947	6	12	18	5				52
1953	1	9	47	18			54	78
1957	1	8	35	10				81
1963	2	6	40	3	38	72		93

Source: Compiled by authors based on the Vademécum Bursátil, Banco de Crédito del Perú

Table 6.1 shows that the SNA, the SNI, and the CCL are the three top-placed business associations in the corporate network according to the eigenvector indicator. Unsurprisingly, the APESEG, the IPAE, and the CAPECO are lower placed, as organizations founded later with objectives clearly linked to their economic sectors. On the face of it, the lowly position of the SNMP is striking given the importance of the mining sector to the Peruvian economy. But this is explained by the fact that most of this society's member companies were multinationals that had few investments in other economic sectors, and they were only interested in forming alliances with local businesses outside mining. This may be a reason why there was no outcry from local businesses when the oil and mining companies were nationalized by the junta.[28]

Most notable of all is that the SNA was the only society that consistently remained in the top ten from 1944, occupying one of the two highest positions from 1953. This is even more remarkable considering that the sample is made up of trading houses, manufacturing firms and banks, but not agricultural companies (which, as family businesses, were not listed). The data on the sectoral connections of business associations for

[28] For an analysis of local corporate networks and multinationals in Chile see: Marcelo Bucheli and Erica Salvaj, "Adaptation Strategies of Multinational Corporations, State-Owned Enterprises, and Domestic Business Groups to Economic and Political Transitions: A Network Analysis of the Chilean Telecommunications Sector, 1958–2005," *Enterprise and Society* 15, no. 3 (2014): 534–76; Marcelo Bucheli and Erica Salvaj, "Political Connections, the Liability of Foreignness, and Legitimacy: A Business Historical Analysis of Multinationals' Strategies in Chile," *Global Strategy Journal* 8, no. 3 (2018): 399–420; Marcelo Bucheli, Erica Salvaj, and Minyoung Kim, "Better Together: How Multinationals Come Together with Business Groups in Times of Economic and Political Transitions," *Global Strategy Journal* 9, no. 2 (May 2019): 176–207.

Table 6.2 Peru: Sectoral composition of connections by association, 1944

Sector	*SNA*	*SNI*	*SNMP*	*CCL*
Banking	3	4	3	3
Livestock	1	0	0	0
Other associations	3	3	3	3
Guano	1	0	0	0
Manufacturing	3	3	0	2
Real estate	0	0	0	0
Mining	1	0	3	5
Insurance	8	5	2	2
Public services	2	1	1	3
Total	22	16	12	18

Source: Compiled by authors based on the Vademécum Bursátil, Banco de Crédito del Perú

1944 and 1963 (see Tables 6.2 and 6.3) shows that the SNA was the only society that had board interlocks with almost all sectors of the Peruvian corporate network.

The SNA's leading role in the Peruvian corporate network (see also Fig. 6.1) owed to political and economic factors. Agricultural exporters were prominently placed in Peruvian politics from 1890. Several figures from the sector served as deputes, senators, and ministers, and at least three of Peru's presidents were linked to the sector: Eduardo López de Romaña (1899–1903), José Pardo (1904–1908 and 1915–1919), and Augusto B. Leguía (1908–1912 and 1911–1930). This is not to say they acted as a bloc; on the contrary, their political actions were driven by personal projects or factions.[29] Thus, the SNA concerned itself solely with highly technical matters relating to the sector, and its capacity for collective action corresponded to Olson's classification.[30] However, according to Low, the crisis facing the sector at the start of the 1920s, coupled with the Leguía administration's political persecution of some agricultural exporters, meant that businesses preferred to act politically through their association.[31] Thus, starting in 1923, SNA chairs assumed a prominent role in Peruvian politics, opening a direct channel of communication with

[29] Alaine Low, "Agro-Exporters as Entrepeneurs: Peruvian Sugar and Cottom Producers 1890–1945" (1979); Rory Miller, *Empresas Británicas, Economía y Política en el Perú, 1850–1934*(Lima: Banco Central de Reserva del Perú e Instituto de Estudios Peruanos, 2011).

[30] Olson, *The Logic of Collective Action*.

[31] Low, "Agro-Exporters as Entrepreneurs."

Table 6.3 Peru: Sectoral composition of connections by association, 1963

Sector	*SNA*	*SNI*	*SNMP*	*CCL*	*IPAE*
Banking	12	4	4	6	3
Finance	2	1	0	3	1
Livestock	0	0	1	0	0
Other associations	2	2	1	4	2
Guano	1	0	0	0	0
Manufacturing	6	10	1	13	6
Real estate	2	0	1	2	0
Mining	2	1	7	0	0
Insurance	10	7	6	3	2
Public services	2	1	1	2	1
Total	39	26	22	33	15

Source: Compiled by authors based on the Vademécum Bursátil, Banco de Crédito del Perú

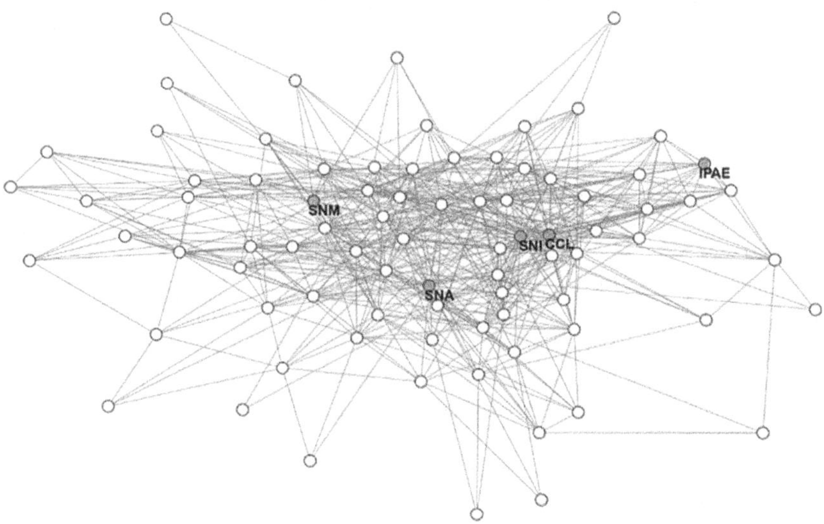

Fig. 6.1 Business association and the core of Peruvian corporate network, 1963. (Source: Compiled by authors based on the Vademécum Bursátil, Banco de Crédito del Perú)

ministers (or even accessing office themselves) and obtaining government benefits for the society. For example, the SNA always had a place on the board of Peru's central bank (and sometimes the position of chair); the Compañía Administradora del Guano, a state-owned firm that sold heavily subsidized fertilizer to businesses in the sector; and the Banco Agrícola del Perú, a state-owned development bank created at the request of the society.[32]

On the economic front, agricultural exporters diversified their surpluses into other sectors, notably manufacturing. As a result, several members of the SNA board also had a seat at the SNI. This was even more common in the case of foreign-owned companies, such as W.R. Grace & Co. and Duncan Fox, which had investments in both sectors. For instance, Luis G. Miranda, an executive at W.R. Grace & Co., was chair of the SNA and vice-chair of the SNI between 1941 and 1943. Similarly, George Bertie, another Duncan Fox representative, occupied important positions at both societies. Thus, as Low points out, the clashes between the two associations reflected more the specific circumstances than they did any division within the business elite. But more importantly, from the second half of the 1920s agricultural exporters invested heavily in banks and insurance, real estate, and service companies and thus had places on the boards of companies in these sectors.[33]

Thus, when the military government opted to include the agricultural export sector in the agrarian reform process, it changed not only the form of agricultural ownership but the entire entrepreneurial system, as well as how businesses communicated with the government. Companies whose core business was manufacturing initially collaborated with the military junta, as its developmentalist discourse convinced these firms that the SNI would occupy the role previously filled by the SNA, but they soon learned that the army officers had a different idea about how to conduct relations with the business community.

[32] Low, "Agro-exporters."

[33] Low, "Agro-exporters;" Alfonso W Quiroz, *Domestic and Foreign Finance in Modern Peru, 1850–1950. Financing Visions Of Development* (London: Macmillan, 1993); Alfonso W Quiroz, *Banqueros en conflicto. Estructura financiera y economía peruana, 1884–1930* (Lima: Fondo Editorial de la Universidad del Pacífico, 1989); Alfonso W Quiroz, *Crédito, inversión y políticas en el Perú entre los siglos XVII y XX* (Lima: Banco Central de Reserva del Perú e Instituto de Estudios Peruanos, 2017); Felipe Portocarrero Suárez, *Grandes fortunas en el Perú, 1916–1960. Riqueza y filantropía en la élite económica* (Lima: Fondo Editorial de la Universidad del Pacífico, 2013).

Business Associations in the Peruvian Corporate Network During the RGAF

As we have noted, relations between the RGAF and the business associations were rather complex, but during both phases these relations were characterized by the vertical and inscrutable nature of the junta's actions. More than the policy of "divide and conquer" that Durand observes,[34] the military regime looked to maintain its autonomy vis-à-vis the business associations and to strengthen its links through "non-institutional" channels with big business. And though in the second phase the RGAF appointed ministers from the business community, these figures never had much influence over the high-ranking officers. As a consequence, the business associations never took the initiative, merely reacting to the policies of the military junta.

Before the coup d'état of 1968, relations between the SNI and the respective governments followed a similar pattern to those involving the SNA. For instance, one SNI representative was a board member of the Central Reserve Bank and the Industrial Bank (the sector's development bank), and members of the association were also on committees linked to trade and industry, customs policies, and social security and employment.[35] Given the RGAF's nationalist discourse of industrial development and the creation of the Ministry of Industry and Commerce in March 1969, the SNI board members might have thought that they would enjoy a prominent position under the new regime. This expectation, added to a disinclination to assume unnecessary political risks under a nationalist dictatorship, may explain the SNI's support for nationalizing the IPC (1968) and its muted reaction to the agrarian reform (1969).

But the first phase of the RGAF was shaped by the strong-handed rule of General Juan Velasco and his Presidential Advisory Committee, who envisioned the state as the driver of industrial policy and as the main agent of development.[36] To build linkages with private enterprise, the army officers relied on a group of businessmen they considered "modern" as informal advisors. Notable among this group were Eduardo Dibós (associated with SNI), Alejandro Tabini (associated with the SNI and the ADEX),

[34] Francisco Durand, *El poder incierto: Trayectoria política y económica del empresariado peruano* (Lima: Fondo Editorial del Congreso de Perú, 2004).

[35] Thomas Bamat, "Peru's Velasco Regime and Class Domination After 1968," *Latin American Perspectives* 10, no. 2–3 (1983): 128–50.

[36] Pease and Romero Sommer, *La Política En El Perú Del Siglo XX*, 248, 256–58.

Luis Banchero, Carlos Raffo, and Pedro Reiser. These business figures and the government preferred the Annual Conference of Executives (Conferencia Anual de Ejecutivos, CADE) as an informal bridging mechanism between executives and the senior RGAF officers.[37]

Conflicts between business associations and the RGAF began in 1970 with the promulgation of the General Industries Law in July. As well as strengthening labor stability and collective bargaining, the law provided for the industrial community, which was to grant workers shares in the companies they worked for as well as participation on their boards (Pease & Romero 256). This latter provision did not feature in the draft law that businesses had been discussing since May, and so they interpreted its inclusion as a betrayal by the government.[38]

The government offensive continued in the following years with a series of expropriations (with compensations) that affected both foreign and local capital. In 1972, the RGAF completed the nationalization of telecommunications and railroad companies (and the SNA was officially wound up). The following year, fish and fishmeal producers followed suit, and then in 1974 the government expropriated cement companies, the media, and the Cerro de Pasco Copper Corporation. This process made the state the biggest economic group in the country and intensified the conflict between the government and the SNI.

The economic policies of the RGAF had the greatest effect on small and medium-sized businesses, which the SNI welcomed as a means of expanding its base and bolstering its representativity. Most of its new members supported the candidacy of Raymundo Duharte for the position of chair in 1972. Following his election, Duharte set his face against the implementation of the Industrial Community and the RGAF's other policies. As a result of this opposition, Duharte was deported by General Velasco and the SNI was forced to change its name to the Society of industries (Sociedad de Industrias).[39]

Meanwhile, the businesses with more sizable investments, including the "modern" ones that advised the RGAF, were also against the efforts to implement the Industrial Community and the expropriation process. But

[37] Durand, *El Poder Incierto.*

[38] Bamat, "Peru's Velasco Regime and Class Domination After 1968," 137; Durand, *El Poder Incierto*, 84–85.

[39] Bamat, "Peru's Velasco Regime and Class Domination After 1968"; Durand, *El Poder Incierto.*

these businesses did not wish to suffer government reprisals or to lose out on benefits such as export subsidies through the Certificate of Tax Refund for Exports (Certificado de Reintegro Tributario por Exportaciones, CERTEX). Thus, they opted for a series of legal and administrative tactics to stall the establishment of the new institution. They also kept open various lines of communication with the government, through the CADE and the creation in 1973 of the ADEX, a new business society, which had the effect of weakening the SNI.

The second phase of the RGAF, led by General Francisco Morales Bermúdez, had to confront the escalating economic crisis and the consolidation of social movements led or channeled by unions linked to the Peruvian left, such as the General Confederation of Workers of Peru (Central General de Trabajadores del Perú, CGTP). Under these circumstances, the military pursued a new rapprochement with private enterprise through an expansion of business subsidy policies, suspension of the Industrial Community, establishment of wage caps for workers, and the frustration of union demands.[40]

To regain the confidence of businesses, Morales Bermúdez appointed civilians with close links to the private sector—such as Luis Barúa and Walter Piazza—as ministers of the economy. However, lacking any real political support and forced to negotiate austerity policies with the IMF that were unpopular with the military leaders and within the burgeoning social and workers' movement, these figures did not last long in post. The inconsistent application of economic policies and a real wage reduction aggravated the economic crisis and sparked the public discontent that led to a national strike on July 19, 1977. The scale of the mass mobilization prompted the military leaders to accelerate their plans for democratic transition, calling elections for a Constituent Assembly in 1978.

Although the transition to democracy was welcome, it did little to resolve the economic crisis or the growth of a popular movement fomented by the left. Thus, the business community eventually decided to unite under a single association that would enhance their scope for negotiation with the government: the Union of Private Businesses (Unión de Empresarios Privados del Perú, UEPP) was formed in December 1977, drawing together all sectoral associations. In the beginning, relations between the government and the new association were characterized by mutual collaboration, allowing the new minister of the economy, Javier

[40] Durand, *El Poder Incierto*, 127.

Silva Ruete, to draw up a plan for navigating the troublesome economic situation. But once a degree of economic and political stability had been reestablished, neither the government nor some sections of the business community believed that the UEPP would endure. Thus, when the association started to oppose certain RGAF measures, the military leadership responded as they had during the first phase: by offering a series of incentives for ADEX to move away from the UEPP, resulting in the closure of the latter institution soon afterward.[41]

In Peru case, the economic crisis and the leftist popular movement were the negative incentives that gave rise, albeit briefly, to the type of business association envisioned by Schneider.[42] But despite what Schneider's proposal might imply, the government, rather than building bridges toward the associations, discouraged attempts at collective business action by resorting to selected positive actions intended to divide their members. The RGAF's policy of weakening business associations was perhaps linked to its aim of maintaining state autonomy from the mass movement and private enterprise. This approach was reflected in the diminished status of business associations in the corporate network under the military regime; as can be seen in Table 6.4, no association achieved the heights previously scaled by the SNA.

This was the point from which the fragmentation of Peruvian business associations quickened, at least until the emergence of the CONFIEP in 1984; none of the associations occupied a top ten position in the Peruvian corporate network under the eigenvector indicator. The SNMP improved

Table 6.4 Peru: Position in the eigenvector ranking, by association, 1979–1995

Year	*SNI*	*SNMP*	*CCL*	*ADEX*	*ASBANC*	*IPAE*	*CONFIEP*	*CAPECO*	*Sample size*
1979	36	19	74	68	13	33		44	78
1981	49	23	89	80	12	57		86	101
1987	55	35	51	110	14	52	74	104	158
1995	47	40	83	97	20	117	45	127	258

Source: Compiled by authors based on the Vademécum Bursátil, Banco de Crédito del Perú and Bolsa de Valores de Lima

[41] Durand, 184–90.

[42] Schneider, *Business Politics and the State*; Maxfield and Schneider, *Business and the State*; Doner and Schneider, "Business Associations and Economic Development."

Table 6.5 Peru: Sectoral composition of connections by association, 1979

Sector	*SNI*	*SNMP*	*CCL*	*ADEX*	*ASBANC*	*IPAE*	*CAPECO*
Banking and finance	1	4	0	1	10	2	2
Miscellaneous	0	1	0	0	2	2	0
Other associations	2	1	1	2	0	2	2
Manufacturing	4	2	0	0	5	3	4
Real estate	0	1	0	0	0	0	0
Mining	1	6	0	1	0	6	0
Insurance	5	4	0	0	3	3	2
Public services	0	0	0	0	0	0	0
Total	13	19	1	4	20	18	10

Source: Compiled by authors based on the Vademécum Bursátil, Banco de Crédito del Perú and Bolsa de Valores de Lima

its position in relative terms from the previous period, while the ASBANC, the society that groups together Peruvian banks and which therefore has links with firms in different sectors, was at the top. Specifically, one of the effects of the RGAF's policies was that the business associations lost their intersectoral connections.

Table 6.5 shows how the SNI retained just one link with the financial sector, and that the CCL lost most of its connections. The predominance of the ASBANC is due to the growth of the banking sector following the consolidation of economic groups. Only the SNMP appears to have maintained its connections, placing it first among the older associations (see also Fig. 6.2).

Major Businesses and Business Associations

One of the measures of the effects of collaboration and conflicts between members of the sectoral associations entails identifying which of the most powerful businesses in the network were represented on the boards of these associations before and after the military government. To this end, taking into account the 25 businesses with the highest eigenvector, we have recorded which of them had a presence on the association boards. We then repeated the excise with the top 50 businesses. The results confirm our hypothesis that the businesses with the highest eigenvector had little interest in association membership after the military government.

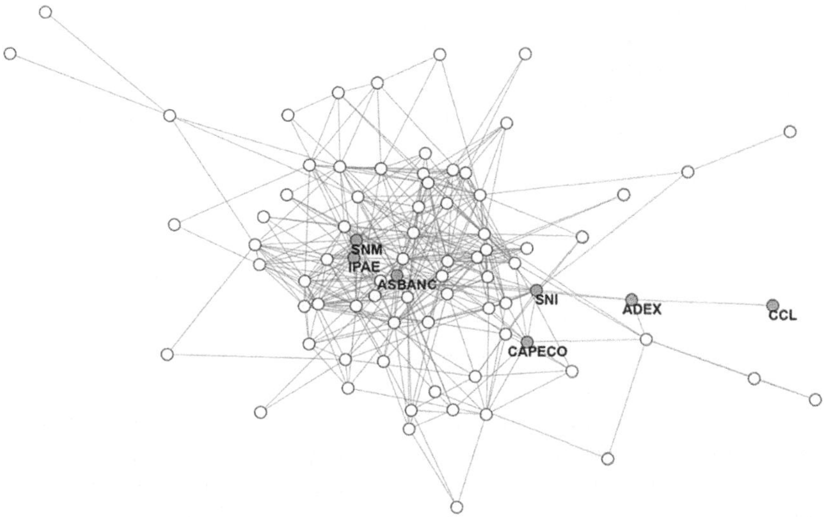

Fig. 6.2 Business association and the core of Peruvian corporate network, 1979. (Source: Compiled by authors based on the Vademécum Bursátil, Banco de Crédito del Perú and Bolsa de Valores)

Table 6.6 shows that from 1979, far fewer of the businesses prominently positioned in the Peruvian corporate network according to the eigenvector participated in business associations. To complement these results, it is worth exploring the profiles of directors who took part in associations before and after the military junta. Thus, we take the years 1944 and 1979. The former year includes Enrique Ayulo (Lima Chamber of Commerce), José Pardo, Héctor Boza Aizcorbe (National Society of Mining and Petroleum), Fernando Wiese (National Society of Mining and Lima Chamber of Commerce), Luis G. Miranda (SNA and SNI), and Andrés F. Dasso (Lima Chamber of Commerce).

In 1979, as far as we could establish, there were just two high eigenvector executives in the associations. These were Francisco Valencia Paz (Arequipa Chamber of Commerce, which we do not include in the calculations due to its low centrality) and Raymundo Morales Urresti (ASBANC). This suggests that from 1968, many of the active directors in the associations did not have much in the way of economic power; rather, their importance lay in their capacity for intermediation, assuming

Table 6.6 Peru: Number of directors with high eigenvector participating in business associations, 1955–1987

Year	*Top 25*	*Top 50*
1944	7	14
1947	9	17
1953	6	17
1957	9	17
1963	8	18
1979	2	6
1981	2	7
1987	2	5

Source: Compiled by authors based on the Vademécum Bursátil, Banco de Crédito del Perú, and Bolsa de Valores de Lima

associative activities in which large businesses are not normally involved. The period of the RGAF introduced a change in relations between businesses and governments: instead of communications being channeled through entrepreneurial associations, the heads of economic groups had a direct line to government. This was a situation that endured until around 2000.

Conclusions

The Revolutionary Government of the Armed Forces (1988–1980) constitutes a special case in Latin America, and the developing world in general, in understanding relations between governments and businesses under nationalist and developmentalist projects. As Shneider has noted, governments in this mold, whether through positive or negative incentives, encourage businesses to form encompassing or multisectoral organizations that serve as a space for interaction between enterprise and the state. In the Peruvian case, the military government, in its pursuit of autonomy from the private sector, first revolutionized the Peruvian corporate network by doing away with the biggest sectoral association, the SNA, and then established (as Durand observes) a policy of divide and conquer against the associations most closely connected with its economic project: the SNI, the IPAE, and the ADEX. Moreover, the looming threat of nationalizations, inconsistent economic administration, and support for the workers' movement all meant that entrepreneurs distrusted in the agents of government.[43]

The option taken by the most powerful businesses was to adapt and conform to political circumstances, pursue personal connections with agents of the state in order to access privileged information, diversify their portfolio of investments to take advantage of state subsidies, and mitigate risk in the event of a change in government policies. To finance this reactive approach to management, companies sought out alliances with financial capital. That is, the government's negative strategies did not result in the creation of a multisectoral or encompassing association, but of business groups. This caused the business associations to lose their central role in the Peruvian corporate network. Therefore, our conclusion in this particular case is that the government did not resolve the difficulties of collective action that Olson identifies[44]; on the contrary, it intensified them.

References

Aguirre, Carlos and Paulo Drinot. *The Peculiar Revolution. Rethinking the Peruvian Experiment Under Military Rule.* Austin: University of Texas Press, 2017.

Alcorta, Ludovico. *El nuevo capital financiero: Grupos financieros y ganancias sistemáticas en el Perú.* Lima: Fundación Friedrich Ebert, 1990.

Bamat, Thomas. "Peru's Velasco Regime and Class Domination After 1968." *Latin American Perspectives* 10, no. 2–3 (1983): 128–50.

Banco de Crédito del Perú. *Vademécum del inversionista 1944.* Lima: BCP, Departamento de Estudios Económicos, 1944.

Banco de Crédito del Perú. *Vademécum del inversionista 1947.* Lima: BCP, Departamento de Estudios Económicos, 1947.

Banco de Crédito del Perú. *Vademécum del inversionista 1952–3.* Lima: BCP, Departamento de Estudios Económicos, 1953.

Banco de Crédito del Perú. *Vademécum del inversionista 1956–57.* BCP, Departamento de Estudios Económicos, 1957.

Banco de Crédito del Perú. *Vademécum del inversionista 1963.* Lima: BCP, Departamento de Estudios Económicos, 1963.

[43] Schneider, *Business Politics and the State*; Doner and Schneider, "Business Associations and Economic Development"; Durand, *El poder encierto*; Thorp and Durand, "A Historical View of Business-State Relations."

[44] Olson, *The Logic of Collective Action.*

Barbero, María Inés, Andrea Lluch, and Erica Salvaj. "Corporate Networks and Business Groups in Argentina in the Early 1970s." *Australian Economic History Review* 54, no. 2 (2014): 183–208.
Bolsa de Valores de Lima. *Vademécum bursátil 1979*. Lima: Bolsa de Valores de Lima, 1979.
Bolsa de Valores de Lima. *Vademécum bursátil 1987*. Lima: Bolsa de Valores de Lima, 1987.
Bolsa de Valores de Lima. *Vademécum bursátil 1995*. Lima: Bolsa de Valores de Lima, 1995.
Borgatti, Stephen, and Martin Everett. *Analyzing Social Networks*. London: SAGE Publications, 2013.
Bucheli, Marcelo, and Erica Salvaj. "Adaptation Strategies of Multinational Corporations, State-Owned Enterprises, and Domestic Business Groups to Economic and Political Transitions: A Network Analysis of the Chilean Telecommunications Sector, 1958–2005." *Enterprise and Society* 15, no. 3 (2014): 534–76.
Bucheli, Marcelo, and Erica Salvaj. "Political Connections, the Liability of Foreignness, and Legitimacy: A Business Historical Analysis of Multinationals' Strategies in Chile." *Global Strategy Journal* 8, no. 3 (2018): 399–420.
Bucheli, Marcelo, Erica Salvaj, and Minyoung Kim. "Better Together: How Multinationals Come Together with Business Groups in Times of Economic and Political Transitions." *Global Strategy Journal* 9, no. 2 (May 2019): 176–207.
Campodónico, H., M. Castillo, and A. Quispe. *De Poder a Poder: Grupos de Poder, Gremios Empresariales y Política Macroeconómica*. Lima: DESCO, 1994.
Caravedo, Baltazar. *Burguesía e industria en el Perú (1933–1945)*. Lima: Instituto de Estudios Peruanos, 1976.
Caravedo, Baltazar. *Conflictos interburgueses durante el gobierno de Odría – (1948–1956)*. Lima: Publicaciones CISEPA, 1974.
Cárdenas, Julián. "Why Do Corporate Elites Form Cohesive Networks in Some Countries, and Do Not in Others? Cross-National Analysis of Corporate Elite Networks in Latin America." *International Sociology* 31, no. 3 (2016): 341–63.
Cotler, Julio. *Clases, Estado y Nación En El Perú*. Lima: Instituto de Estudios Peruanos, 1978.
Di Carlo, Emiliano. "Pyramids and the Separation between Direction and Control of Non-Financial Italian Family Companies." *Journal of Management and Governance* 18, no. 3 (2014): 835–72.
Doner, Richard F., and Ben Ross Schneider. "Business Associations and Economic Development: Why Some Associations Contribute More Than Others." *Business and Politics* 2, no. 3 (2000): 261–88.
Durand, Francisco. *El poder incierto: Trayectoria política y económica del empresariado peruano*. Lima: Fondo Editorial del Congreso de Perú, 2004.

Durand, Francisco. *Los doce apósteles de la economía peruana: Una mirada social a los grupos de poder limeños y provincianos*. Lima: Fondo Editorial de la Pontificia Universidad Católica del Perú, 2017.

Durand, Francisco. *Riqueza económica y pobreza política: Reflexiones sobre las élites del poder en un país inestable*. Lima: Pontificia Universidad Católica del Perú: Fondo Editorial, 2003.

Figueroa, Adolfo. "Competition and Circulation of Economic Elites: Theory and Application to the Case of Peru." *Quarterly Review of Economics and Finance* 48, no. 2 (2008): 263–73.

Guillén, Mauro. "Business Groups in Emerging Economies: A Resource-Based View." *Academy of Management Journal* 43, no. 3 (2000): 362–80.

Hobsbawm, Eric. "The Peculiar Revolution." In *Viva La Revolución. Eric Hobsbawn on Latin America*, edited by Leslie Bethell, 334–61. London: Abacus, 2016.

Hunt, Shane. *La formación de la economía peruana: Distribución y crecimiento en la Historia del Perú y América Latina*. Lima: Banco Central de Reserva del Perú e Instituto de Estudios Peruanos, 2011.

Lausent-Herrera, Isabelle. *Pasado y presente de la comunidad Japonesa en el Perú*. Paris: Institut Français d' Études Andines, 1991.

Lluch, Andrea, and Érica Salvaj. "Fragmentación del empresariado en la época de la industrialización por sustitución de importaciones (ISI) en la Argentina: una aproximación desde el estudio de la red corporativa (1954–1970)." *Apuntes. Revista de ciencias sociales* 39, no. 70 (2012): 135–66.

Low, Alaine. "Agro-Exporters as Entrepreneurs: Peruvian Sugar and Cotton Producers 1890–1945" Ph.D. Diss., Oxford University, 1979.

Materson, Daniel. *Fuerza armada y sociedad en el Perú moderno: Un estudio sobre las relaciones civiles militares, 1930–2000*. Lima: Instituto de Estudios Peruanos, 2001.

McClintock, Cynthia, and Abraham F. Lowenthal. *Peruvian Experiment Reconsidered*. Princeton: Princeton University Press, 2016.

Miller, Rory. *Empresas Británicas, Economía y Política en el Perú, 1850–1934*. Lima: Banco Central de Reserva del Perú e Instituto de Estudios Peruanos, 2011.

Mintz, Beth, and Michael Schwartz. *The Power Structure of American Business*. Chicago: University Chicago Press, 1985.

Monsalve Zanatti, Martín. "'Una Revolución Peculiar', Eric Hobsbawm y El Gobierno Revolucionario de Las Fuerzas Armadas, 1968–1975." In *Eric Hobsbawn: La Historia y América Latina*, edited by Felipe Portocarrero Suárez and Martín Monsalve Zanatti, 31–39. Lima: Fondo Editorial de la Universidad del Pacífico, 2017.

Monsalve Zanatti, Martín. "Evolución de La Gran Empresa Familiar Peruana 1890–2012." In *Familias Empresarias y Grandes Empresas Familiares En*

América Latina. Una Visión de Largo Plazo, edited by Paloma Fernández Pérez and Andrea Lluch, 381–408. Bilbao: Fundación BBVA, 2015.

Morck, Randall. "How to Eliminate Pyramidal Business Groups: The Double Taxation of Intercorporate Dividends and Other Incisive Uses of Tax Policy." *Tax Policy and the Economy*, 19 (2005): 135–179.

Musacchio, Aldo, and Ian Read, "Bankers, Industrialists, and Their Cliques: Elite Networks in Mexico and Brazil during Early Industrialization." *Enterprise and Society*, 8 No. 4 (2007), 842–80.

Musacchio, Aldo. "Drawing Links between Corporate Governance and Networks: Bankers in the Corporate Networks of Brazil, Mexico, and the United States Circa 1910." *Entreprises et Histoire* 54, no. 1 (2009): 16–36.

Olson, Mancur. *The Logic of Collective Action: Public Goods and the Theory of Groups*. Cambridge: Harvard University Press, 1965.

Pease, Henry, and Gonzalo Romero Sommer. *La Política En El Perú Del Siglo XX*. Lima: Fondo Editorial de la Pontificia Universidad Católica del Perú, 2013.

Portocarrero Suárez, Felipe. *El Imperio Prado: 1890–1970*. Lima: Centro de Investigación de la Universidad del Pacífico, 1995.

Portocarrero Suárez, Felipe. *Grandes fortunas en el Perú, 1916–1960. Riqueza y filantropía en la élite económica* Lima: Fondo Editorial de la Universidad del Pacífico, 2013.

Quiroz, Alfonso W. *Banqueros en conflicto. Estructura financiera y economía peruana, 1884–1930*. Lima: Fondo Editorial de la Universidad del Pacífico, 1989.

Quiroz, Alfonso W. *Crédito, inversión y políticas en el Perú entre los siglos XVII y XX*. Lima: Banco Central de Reserva del Perú e Instituto de Estudios Peruanos, 2017.

Quiroz, Alfonso W. *Domestic and Foreign Finance in Modern Peru, 1850–1950. Financing Visions of Development* London: Macmillan, 1993.

Salas-Porras, Alejandra. "Fuerzas centrípetas y centrífugas en la red corporativa mexicana (1981–2001)." *Revista Mexicana de Sociología* 68, no. 2 (October 5, 2009): 331–375.

Salvaj, Erica, and Andrea Lluch. "Estudio Comparativo Del Capitalismo Argentino y Chileno: Un Análisis Desde Las Redes de Directorio a Fines Del Modelo Sustitutivo de Importaciones." *Redes. Revista Hispana Para El Análisis de Redes Sociales* 23, no. 2 (2012): 43–43.

Schneider, Ben Ross, and Sylvia Maxfield. "Business, the State, and Economic Performance in Developing Countries." In *Business and the State in Developing Countries*, edited Sylvia Maxfield and Ben Ross Schneider, 3–35. Ithaca: Cornell University Press, 1997.

Schneider, Ben Ross. "Organizing Interests and Coalitions in the Politics of Market Reform in Latin America." *World Politics* 56, no. 3 (2004): 456–79.

Schneider, Ben Ross. *Business Politics and the State in Twentieth-Century Latin America*. Cambridge: Cambridge University Press, 2004.

Schydlowsky, Daniel M., and Juan J. Wicht. "The Anatomy of an Economic Failure." In *Peruvian Experiment Reconsidered*, edited by Cynthia McClintock and Abraham Lowenthal 94–143. Princeton: Princeton University Press, 1976.

Thorp, Rosemary, and Francisco Durand. "A Historical View of Business-State Relations: Colombia, Peru, and Venezuela Compared." In *Business and the State in Developing Countries*, 216–36.

Vásquez, Enrique. *Estrategias del poder: Grupos económicos en el Perú*. Lima: Centro de Investigación de la Universidad del Pacífico, 2000.

Wise, Carol. *Reinventando El Estado: Estrategia Económica y Cambio Institucional en el Perú*. Lima: Fondo Editorial de la Universidad del Pacífico, 2003.

CHAPTER 7

Banking Southern Cone Dictatorships

Juan Pablo Bohoslavsky

Introduction

This chapter analyzes the role of foreign—in particular, private—lending in the survival and stability of the military dictatorships of Brazil, Argentina, Chile, and Uruguay in the 1970s and 1980s. I argue that the private international financial sector was crucial to the economic and political survival of the dictatorial regimes because it helped them to buy key loyalties and/or maintain a complex and effective repressive apparatus, while there was little oversight and control over the loans they took out. The private sector became the main lender to the dictatorships starting in 1977, when the Carter administration—under U.S. president Jimmy Carter—and some European countries limited the official or publicly backed loans to the dictatorships as a way to pressure them to decrease their human rights violations. This official lending was quickly replaced by loans from private commercial banks, which did not require the dictatorships to make any policy changes as long as they could repay the loans. My findings are consistent with the literature on private lending, direct investment, and authoritarian regimes that has analyzed the cases of Egypt, Haiti, the Philippines, South Africa, and Zaire.

J. P. Bohoslavsky (✉)
Universidad Nacional de Río Negro, Viedma, Argentina

V. Basualdo et al. (eds.), *Big Business and Dictatorships in Latin America*, Palgrave Studies in Latin American Heterodox Economics, https://doi.org/10.1007/978-3-030-43925-5_7

Empirical evidence shows that foreign financial sources may have an important impact on authoritarian regimes' durability in power.[1] Interestingly, if one distinguishes between net transfers on external debt (public and publicly guaranteed external debt) from official creditors and those from private lenders, it is possible to observe the impact of foreign debt provided by private and official creditors on the likelihood of democratization. The results suggest that, although both sources of funds have helped authoritarian regimes endure, loans from private creditors have actually been more likely to stabilize authoritarian regimes than official lending and, thus, are probably also more harmful to human rights.

The different impact of official and private lending might partially be explained by the fact that official creditors—in particular, bilateral lenders—may be subject to some (although frequently limited) political accountability. As most of the world's large bilateral lenders enjoy some form of democratic governance, voters and civil society might resent their governments using taxpayers' money to support states that violate fundamental human rights. Similarly, albeit frequently criticized for their lack of transparency and democratic control, international financial institutions are subject to the scrutiny of public opinion, transnational groups, civil society, and member states.[2]

In contrast, while civil society may monitor corporations, voters exert less control over private lenders operating in international financial markets, and states have so far prohibited private lenders only in exceptional circumstances by means of legal regulation from providing funds to states or state institutions with bad human rights records. Market discipline alone provides insufficient incentives for lending that is sensitive to human rights. It looks mainly at debt sustainability and the likelihood that the loan will be repaid, not at the democratic character of a regime, nor its predisposition to human rights abuses. The market does not prevent loans to dictators. On the contrary, once loans are provided to authoritarian

[1] See Juan Pablo Bohoslavsky and Abel Escribà-Folch, "Rational choice and financial complicity with human rights abuses: policy and legal implications" in *Making Sovereign Financing and Human Rights Work*, Juan Pablo Bohoslavsky and Jernej Letnar (eds.) (Oxford: Hart Publishing, 2013), 15–32.

[2] James Lebovic and Erik Voeten, "The costs of shame: international organizations and foreign aid in the punishing of human rights violators," *Journal of Peace Research*, vol. 46, no. 1 (January 2009), 79–97, found that multilateral development cooperation commitments showed greater sensitivity to criticism of human rights records by the United Nations Commission on Human Rights than bilateral commitments did.

regimes, the market rather provides incentives to grant additional funds to such a regime in order to stabilize it and ensure its repayment capacity. Market logic thus becomes a self-fulfilling prophecy.

In a context of human rights violations, a micro-connection between funds and human rights abuses can frequently be found, such as the one involving the private funding of the repressive *Operação Bandeirante* (OBAN), the multiagency military operation that was in charge of repressing people during the 1964–1985 Brazilian dictatorship, in cooperation with private actors.[3] The same could be said regarding the financing of death camps[4] or transactions to buy weapons to repress the population.[5] However, as will be explored in this chapter, gross and massive violations of human rights are often linked to sovereign financing in less direct and obvious (but still very harmful) ways.

In order to assess if and how such funding contributes to massive crimes, it is necessary to look at the interaction between the structures, processes, and dynamics of sovereign financing and human rights violations. Analyses must take into account both the micro- and macroeconomic data of the country and international markets; internal and external political and institutional processes; the social situation; monetary, budgetary, and industrial policies; and the human rights situation.[6] As part of this analysis, a rational choice approach is useful to better understand whether and how sovereign lending furthers a regime's consolidation (with the human suffering that this implies) by buying loyalties and/or reinforcing repression of the population.[7] Within this theoretical frame-

[3] Marlon Weichert, "O financiamento de atos de violação de direitos humanos por empresas durante a ditadura brasileira," *Acervo* 21, no. 2 (2008), 186.

[4] For example, Deutsche Bank provided loans to construction and chemical companies (such as IG Farben) with contracts for facilities at Auschwitz; see James Harold, *The Nazi Dictatorship and the Deutsche* Bank (Cambridge University Press, 2004), 215.

[5] On how some banks made vast loans to the security forces of the South African apartheid, see First Amended Complaint, *In re South African Apartheid Litigation*, 617 F. Supp. 2d 228 (S.D.N.Y. 2009) (Civ. No. 03-cv-04524), paras. 160–163, available at: http://www.hausfeldllp.com/content_documents/9/KhulumaniClassActionComplai.pdf. See also Hennie van Vuuren, *A Tale of Profit, Guns and Money* (Johannesburg: Jacana Media, 2017).

[6] Antonio Cassese, "Study of the Impact of Foreign Economic Aid and Assistance on Respect for Human Rights in Chile," UN Doc. E/CN.4/Sub.2/412 (1978), vols. I–IV; see also Carlo Edoardo Altamura, "Global Banks and Latin American Dictators," *Business History Review* (2020): 1–32. https://doi.org/10.1017/S0007680519001260

[7] Ronald Wintrobe, *The Political Economy of Dictatorship* (New York: Cambridge University Press, 1998).

work, the aforementioned Latin American dictatorships and the financial support they received will be studied in detail in the next sections.

Argentina[8]

Between 1976 and 1982, Argentina was ruled by a military junta with a notoriously bad human rights record. During these years, Argentina received an increasing volume of credits from states and multilateral bodies during a brief initial period, and later, mostly from major commercial banks based in a range of industrialized countries. While there is no consolidated data available on loan volume and lender identity, some of the banks that granted credits include Lloyd's Bank International Ltd., Citibank N.A., Morgan Guaranty Trust Co., Manufacturers Hanover Trust Co., Chase Manhattan Bank N.A., European Banking Co. Ltd., Bank of Tokyo, Libra Bank Ltd., and Bank of Montreal, among others.[9]

The channeling of such a huge mass of money has been attributed to the expansion of the European market and the massive recycling of "petrodollars." In that context, lending banks implemented a pressure policy to further the indebtedness of states that lacked adequate repayment capacity for the debts they were contracting, and which, in addition, used public resources, in part, to repress their own populations.

In the Argentina of the 1970s, these credits were inserted into a typically monetarist policy, which involved broad economic and financial liberalization, the elimination of tariff protections, high domestic interest rates, and an exchange rate lag, as well as later the overvaluation of the national currency through targeted official policies.[10]

Between 1976 and 1982, Argentina received enormous funds from commercial banks based in developed countries.[11] It can be argued that

[8] See more details in Juan Pablo Bohoslavsky and Veerle Opgenhaffen, "The Past and Present of Corporate Complicity: Financing the Argentinian Dictatorship," *Harvard Human Rights Journal*, 2010, Vol. 23, 166, 157–203.

[9] See Eric Calcagno, "Los bancos transnacionales y el endeudamiento externo en la Argentina," *Cuadernos de la CEPAL*, LC/G.1483 (Santiago, Chile: November 1987), 25 and 108; and Juzgado Nacional en lo Criminal y Correccional Federal no. 2 de la Capital Federal, "Olmos, Alejandro s. denuncia," June 13, 2000, *Jurisprudencia Argentina*, January 31, 2001.

[10] See Jorge Schvarzer, *Argentina 1976–1981: El endeudamiento externo como pivote de la especulación financiera* (Buenos Aires: Cisea, 1983).

[11] See Eduardo Basualdo, "La Reestructuración de la Economía Argentina Durante las Últimas Décadas: De la Sustitución de Importaciones a la Valorización Financiera," in

the banks implemented policies of loan pushing, granting loans to states that did not have the economic capacity to repay these funds[12] and used public resources to repress their own populations. In this general scheme, external finance played a key role in the Argentinean state's economic development and political reality.

The financial dependence was even more acute if we consider that, in its application of an economic policy that involved allocating domestic resources by following the signals of international market prices, the military government adjusted relative domestic prices based on international prices and promoted the de facto dollarization of the economy. With a domestic market demanding dollars and an insufficient foreign trade balance, the state increased its debt with foreign banks in order to supply dollars. Once those dollars were poured into the domestic market, at a value below their real cost through the application of an exchange rate methodology known as the *tablita* (a system that established a calendar of preannounced exchange rates below real values), they initially (1976–1979) swelled the country's international reserves to later feed the capital flight circuit, and, ultimately, they often ended up being deposited in the very same banks that granted the credits, thus benefiting the country's major economic groups. The imported, publicly borrowed funds were withheld from the domestic sphere and served only some elites.

The country's external debt with nonbanking creditors (multilateral and bilateral public lenders) grew by 161% between 1975 and 1981, while the debt with international private banks increased by 615% (measured in US dollars) during that same period. In 1983, bank loans represented more than two-thirds of the external debt, not counting the US$5 billion in bonds that are believed to have been held by banks.[13]

The massive and unrestricted flow of imports in a context of overvaluation of the national currency rapidly led to the drop in domestic demand and industrial activity during the 1976–1983 period, which brought the

Neoliberalismo y sectores dominantes. Tendencias globales y experiencias nacionales, ed. Eduardo Basualdo, Eduardo and Enrique Arceo (Clacso, Buenos Aires, 2006).

[12] See, William Darity and Bobbie Horn, *The loan pushers: The role of commercial banks in the international debt crisis* (Pensacola: Ballinger, 1988); and Cynthia Lichtenstein, "The U.S. Response to the International Debt Crisis: The International Lending Supervision Act 1983," *Virginia Journal of International Law*, 25, no. 2 (1985), 401–435.

[13] Calculated by the author based on data from BAI, the IMF, and Central Bank of Argentina.

country's gross domestic product (GDP) down.[14] Therefore, it is not surprising that the average fiscal deficit from 1976 to 1980 was 7.4% of the GDP, while in the 1981–1983 period (Malvinas/Falklands War) that ratio reached 14.6%.[15] With such deteriorated macroeconomic variables, the external financial support received by the regime appears to have been critical to its survival.

External financing appears to have been instrumental in temporarily sustaining a monetarist system, which, at an extremely high economic and social cost to the country, maintained financial stability, provided the government with liquidity, and enabled it to stave off various domestic economic and social actors, whose demands would grow both in number and in intensity over time, while at the same time buying loyalties from key economic actors. It should be noted, moreover, that the bulk of external debt not only maintained the *tablita* regime and facilitated and funded capital flight; it also furthered the process of deindustrialization and the regressive restructuring of the industrial sector, which benefited certain powerful groups.

There were sectors that profited from the monetarist policy applied by the dictatorship, which was based on external financial aid and distributed funds selectively. One such sector was the financial industry because lenders could obtain large quantities of US dollars at a low price and easily trade them for Argentinean pesos to make huge profits through the state-subsidized interest rate; they could then freely exchange them for US dollars again with no restrictions on leaving the country. The import business also benefited as the complete elimination of tariff protections opened the Argentinean market to the world's goods without restriction.

The impact of external financial aid in Argentina can thus be visualized from two perspectives. The first is a more general, macroeconomic, and political perspective, wherein some leading actors in the country's economy and political life (such as those with access to speculative financial services and importers) benefited from a host of economic instruments

[14] The level of global activity in 1982 was 1.3% lower than 1975, Ernesto Feldman and Juan Sommer, *Crisis financiera y endeudamiento externo en Argentina* (Buenos Aires: CET/IPAL, 1984), 114; Aldo Ferrer, *¿Puede Argentina pagar su deuda externa?* (Buenos Aires: El Cid, 1982), 93.

[15] Mario Damil and Roberto Frenkel, "Restauración Democrática y Política Económica: Argentina 1984–1991," in Juan Morales and Gary McMahon, *La política económica en la transición a la democracia: Lecciones de Argentina, Bolivia, Chile y Uruguay*, (Santiago: Cieplan, 199).

deployed by the government, the feasibility of which rested, to a large extent, on the huge amounts of foreign currency the state made available. These same actors, in turn, compensated for those benefits by giving their support to the regime, thus furthering its political consolidation, with the ensuing costs in terms of human rights.

The other analytical perspective of the impact of financial aid has to do with military spending associated with repression. The loans appear to have financed a policy of greater military spending. In the initial years of the dictatorship—which also involved the most brutal human rights abuses—this spending was not associated with any real hypothesis of war with other countries but rather with internal security issues that, in practice, entailed the repression of the population.[16] In terms of the evolution of military expenditures measured in percentage of the GDP, we found that it was 3.7% in 1975, 4.2% in 1976, 4.3% in 1977, 5% in 1978, 4.9% in 1979, 5.5% in 1980, 5.8% in 1981, and 5.7% in 1982.[17]

During the initial years of the dictatorship, while overall military spending grew, arms imports (to prepare for external military attacks) actually went down.[18] One can infer from this that the increase in military spending was applied, in part, to financing the role assigned to the armed forces in the *war against subversion*, under which the human rights abuses were committed.

The numbers above contradict the idea that the Argentine state took out loans with the sole purpose of buying weapons to defend the country in the event of a military conflict with Chile or with the United Kingdom. The loans and the increase in military spending began before the possibility of these conflicts appeared, and until 1978 the military junta prioritized areas unrelated to external attacks.

The importance of the private financial support Argentina received was explicitly mentioned in a document approved by high-ranking officers of the US Department of State:

> The Argentine strategy for relations with the U.S. has been based on the following assumptions . . . Argentina can survive U.S. hostility because of

[16] See Thomas Scheetz, 'Gastos militares en Chile, Perú y la Argentina', *Desarrollo Económico*, (October–December 1985), 319.

[17] Ibid.

[18] According to conservative estimations, defense imports expenditures evolved as follows: US$1.57 billion in 1975, US$1.19 billion in 1976, and US$626.1 million in 1977, Scheetz, "Gastos miliatares" (data in 1982 US dollars).

> access to alternate suppliers of military aid and economic and financial opportunities... Negative International Financial Institutions votes are a political embarrassment to Argentina, but such votes do not block access to critical financing. The Videla government's economic success in the external sector has ensured the availability of financial opportunities from a variety of foreign sources.[19]

The banks' decision to cease granting credits to Argentina as of 1982, the eruption of the international debt crisis, and the collapse of the domestic economy as a result of the country's recession (which eroded the little social support base that the dictatorship had managed to retain, as more and more domestic businesses went bankrupt and workers faced massive layoffs) coincided with the beginning of the transition to democracy. This shows that even when other factors, of course, influence the possibilities of such a transition to democracy, large-scale financial aid can play a major role in consolidating criminal regimes (and, therefore, in weakening them as well).

Brazil[20]

Juscelino Kubitschek de Oliveira became president of Brazil in 1956, and until 1961 his government's development policies focused largely on major infrastructure projects that all counted on financial support from the United States and the International Monetary Fund (IMF).[21] Between 1961 and 1964, the economic situation worsened. Briefly, with President Janio Quadros and President Joao Goulart, annual inflation rose dramatically[22] while the GDP growth rate decreased.[23]

[19] Department of State Report, "'Evolution' of US Human Rights Policy in Argentina," State Argentina Declassification Project (1975–1984), available at foia.state.gov/documents/Argentina/0000AA65.pdf

[20] This section draws from Juan Pablo Bohoslavsky and Marcelo Torelly, "Financial Complicity: The Brazilian Dictatorship Under the 'Macroscope'" in Dustin Sharp (ed.), Justi*ce and Economic Violence in Transition* (New York, Springer, 2013), 233.

[21] Michael Wallerstein, "The Collapse of Democracy in Brazil: Its Economic Determinants," *Latin American Research Review*, 1980 15:3 15, 3–40.

[22] The annual inflation rate was 26% during the period 1955–1960 and 62% between 1960 and 1963.

[23] Between 1955 and 1960, the GDP per capita growth was 4.8%, while between 1960 and 1963 it was 2.1%.

The economy's poor performance and the lack of unity in leftist parties led to the loss of social support for the government. Pressure on the president from the Brazilian elite, the military sector, and the alleged involvement of the US government[24] ended with a military coup in 1964 under the aegis of a remarkable anticommunist philosophy.[25] Many atrocities were committed after the military takeover.

In attempting to address Brazil's economic woes, after initially trying a *gradualist approach* for a few months, the new military government applied shock treatments.[26] The new military government aimed to control inflation, implement repressive wage policies, eliminate price distortion, give incentives to direct investment, and attract foreign capital.[27] It was only in 1966 that inflation went down and GDP grew by 6.7%.[28]

During the period 1968–1974, Brazil experienced an economic boom: the so-called *economic miracle*.[29] From 1967, Brazil's Strategic Plan of Development aimed at expanding primary exports, maintaining affordable food prices, and reducing the emigration of the rural population. A surge in exports resulted from the government's aggressive policy of tax and credit incentives to favor exports,[30] and the economy continued to grow.[31] Interestingly, by 1969 the dictatorship showed its highest level of repression.[32]

This *economic miracle* helped the military government to create a sense of patriotic euphoria connected to the idea of growth and the destiny of Brazil, allowing the regime to gain support and some legitimacy from key

[24] See Wolfgang Heinz and Hugo Fruhling, *Determinants of Gross Human Rights Violations by State and State-Sponsored Actors in Brazil, Uruguay, Chile, and Argentina (1960–1990)* (The Hague: Kluwer Law International, 1999), 29.

[25] Matias Spektor, *Kissinger e o Brasil*, (Rio de Janeiro: Jorge Zahar, 2009).

[26] Thomas Skidmore, *The Politics of Military Rule in Brazil, 1964–1985* (New York: Oxford University Press, 1988), 30.

[27] Carolina Siqueira Conte, *The Interaction of Economics and Politics in Brazil During the Military Dictatorship* (Ohio University: Master thesis, 2001), 22.

[28] In 1964, it had only been 3.4%.

[29] GDP growth went from 3.7% (1962–1967) to 11.3% (1968–1974), with the industrial sector playing a leading role during those years; Wener Baer, Richard Newfarmer, and Thomas Trebat, "On State Capitalism in Brazil: Some New Issues and Questions," *Inter-American Economic Affairs* 30 (1976): 75–77.

[30] Skidmore, *The Politics*, 140.

[31] Heinz and Fruhling, *Determinants*, 53.

[32] James Green, "Restless youth: the 1968 Brazilian student movement as seen from Washington," in *1968–40 anos depois*, eds. Carlos Fico and Maria Paula Araújo (Rio de Janeiro: 7 Letras, 2011), 31–61.

stakeholders in the country's economic and political life. Particularly during the Emilio Medici government (1969–1974), a period known for great economic performance and stability,[33] the Brazilian bourgeoisie[34] and middle class seemed to have benefited from,[35] accepted, and legitimized the authoritarian regime.[36] This example illustrates how the ***authoritarian bargain*** explained above worked: these classes accepted diminished political freedoms in exchange for public goods.

The *economic miracle* also had another face: growth never extended to the lower classes of the population.[37] Indeed, income concentration increased, and the quality of life remained unchanged for the great majority of Brazilians. Education and health were neither a real political nor economic priority for the military government: no significant part of the total government expenditure was focused on these needs. While the poorest 20% of Brazil's population controlled 3.8% of the country's national income in 1960, by 1970 that figure had dropped to 3.2% and by the end of the 1970s was only 2.8%.[38] By 1969, Brazil had the highest degree of inequality in Latin America. The costs of Brazil's development strategy program were borne, in particular, by the poor, who were not well organized politically[39] and whose collective power was otherwise diminished due to repression.

During the first months of the dictatorship (in 1964), foreign lenders were rather cautious and did not grant financial assistance to Brazil until the United States announced a program loan in June 1964, soon followed by the World Bank, the IMF, and the Inter-American Development Bank. An estimated 80% of the net inflow of long-term capital to the country between 1964 and 1967 was provided by USAID.[40] The renegotiation of

[33] Skidmore, *The Politics,* 109.

[34] Bresser Pereira, Luiz, "Six Interpretations of the Brazilian Social Formation," *Latin American Perspectives* 11, no. 40 (1984): 61.

[35] Salaries among top professionals, technocrats, and managers increased dramatically. Skidmore, *The Politics,* 107.

[36] Celso Lafer, *O Sistema Político Brasileiro* (São Paulo: Perspectiva, 1978), 65–66, 65–66.

[37] Siqueira Conte, "*The Interaction,*" 9, 56.

[38] World Bank, *World Tables,* 48, 423, 426; *see also* Albert Fishlow, "Brazil's Economic Miracle," *The World Today,* no. 29 (1973): 474.

[39] Alfred Stepan, *Authoritarian Brazil: Origins, Policies, and Future* (Hew Haven: Yale University Press, 1973), 70.

[40] Skidmore, *The Politics,* 36, 39, and 55.

the debt and this external financial assistance helped Brazil strengthen its balance of payments, thus giving policymakers more room to maneuver.[41]

The current account balance turned negative in 1967 and remained so.[42] The current account surplus, which amounted to US$1.7 billion in 1973, turned to a deficit of US$7.1 billion in 1974.[43] Brazil was able to finance its current-account deficit through foreign loans.[44] This capital inflow also helped to finance the trade deficit as not only exports but also imports needed to maintain rapid growth.

From 1968, while multilateral and bilateral lending gradually decreased, Brazil turned to private foreign banks for credit to finance a myriad of public works and economic development projects like hydroelectric power plants and transportation infrastructure.[45] The yearly rate of increase of long- and medium-term loans tripled between 1965 and 1969. Brazil was the fourth largest recipient of external resources between 1964 and 1967.[46] From 1965 to 1975, external debt rose more than 400%.[47] Corrupt public officials in the government who benefited from these loans facilitated and accelerated this financial process.[48]

In 1969, external debt began to grow more rapidly. Foreign debt began to rise heavily from 1969 to 1973 at an average yearly rate of 25.1%. From 1968 to 1973, over two-thirds of the increase in foreign debt was due to the growth of foreign exchange reserves ultimately linked to the need to cover the current account deficit.[49] The macroeconomic impact of this indebtedness can be seen in the evolution of the ratio of GDP to external debt during those years.[50] The reasoning was that expanding debt would

[41] Ibid., 92.

[42] Skidmore, *The Politics*, 36, 39, 55, 141.

[43] Baer, Newfarmer and Trebat, "On State Capitalism," 89.

[44] Skidmore, *The Politics*, 36, 39, 55, 141.

[45] José Carvalho Pereira, *Financiamento Externo e Crescimento Econômico no Brasil: 1966/73* (Rio de Janeiro: IPEA/INPES, 1974), 96.

[46] Guilherme Binato Pedras, "History of Public Debt in Brazil: 1964 to the Present," in *Public Debt: The Brazilian Experience*, eds. Anderson Caputo Silva et al. (Brasília: National Treasury, 2010), 64.

[47] Ibid., 64.

[48] James Henry, *The Blood Bankers: Tales from the Global Underground Economy* (New York: Four Walls Eight Windows, 2003), 127–177.

[49] Baer, Newfarmer and Trebat, "On State Capitalism," 93.

[50] 1964: 15.75; 1965: 17.02; 1969: 12.47; 1972: 19.63; 1974: 18.25; 1976: 21; 1979: 25.10; 1982: 31.67; 1984: 54.09. Caputo Silva et al., *Public Debt*, 413.

be paid for with greater exports from a more modern industrial sector in apparent perpetual growth.[51]

The overwhelming majority of the borrowing went, directly or indirectly, to boost production of basic industrial products and raw materials for export, fostering the growth rate. In order to service Brazil's ever mounting debt, the industrial facilities were forced to export a considerable portion of their output. During the dictatorship, the country never generated sufficient internal revenue to pay for such undertakings.[52] The *economic miracle* germinated in a spending deficit and was fertilized heavily with borrowed funds from abroad.

Virtually every major portion of the Brazilian economy came to rely on foreign finance, with state-owned industrial corporations and banks the biggest borrowers, followed by private banks, large domestic industrial firms, and affiliates of multinational corporations.[53] Underlying the economic system was foreign finance.

Brazil's augmented foreign debt arose from two sources: skyrocketing public expenditure and skyrocketing prizes of increased petroleum imports after 1973. After a decade of such practice and the arrival of the world recession in the early 1980s, the accumulated debt was seen as a reckless liability.[54] By 1981, Brazil's parastatals only accounted for US$32.2 billion in foreign debt, which was 46% of Brazil's total foreign debt.[55]

Even after the dramatic oil price shocks, the government kept on borrowing as its main priority was ensuring decent growth rates via increasing imports. It could have drawn down the exchange reserves or borrowed abroad; it did both.[56] Reducing the growth rate of the economy, in the eyes of the government (from 1978), would have been regarded as a major political failure with unforeseeable consequences. The external (both public and private) financial aid was functional in supporting the regime. These funds helped the government to implement economic policies aimed at legitimizing a regime highly dependent on loans, thereby

[51] Marco Aguiar et al., "Economic Dictatorship versus Democracy in Brazil," *Latin American Perspectives* 11, no. 1 (1984), 18.

[52] Eul-Soo Pang and Laura Jarnagin, "Brazilian Democracy and the Foreign Debt," *Current History* (February 1984), 64.

[53] Jeffry Frieden, "The Brazilian Borrowing Experience: From Miracle to Debacle and Back," *Latin American Research Review* 22, no. 1 (1987), 95–6, 100.

[54] Pang and Jarnagin, "Brazilian," 64.

[55] Frieden, "The Brazilian," 104.

[56] Skidmore, *The Politics*, 180.

strengthening it politically. In the end, "[d]ebt-financed industrial growth helped to cement an alliance of the country's economic elites and ensure the passive support of large portions of the middle and working classes pulled upward by the industrialization drive."[57]

With the international debt crisis erupting, foreign financing dried up by 1981.[58] Massive parastatal orders and easy funds were not available anymore: the miracle was over. Departing from an orthodox viewpoint, the regime cut public spending, tightened monetary policies, raised interest rates, and devalued the national currency in order to repay the foreign debt. These measures were disastrous for the industrial sector, and the economy sank into deep recession.[59] The coalition of economic interests that had supported the government from 1964 gradually defected to the opposition.[60] By 1984, the discontent with the regime was almost universal[61]—a fact that accelerated political liberalization.

Some connections are clearer now. The limited legitimacy of the 1964 dictatorship was deeply connected with ensuring the status quo desired by economic elites and promoting concentrated (selective) economic growth.[62] At the same time, the regime also needed funds for welfare and clientelistic policies—such as infrastructure projects of dubious social benefit, like mega football stadiums—that promoted some legitimation among the poor.[63] Economic growth and these clientelistic policies—which were so effective in buying loyalties—were deeply linked to the growth of sovereign debt. However, the only way the military regime could ultimately stay in office was by strongly repressing dissidents, which led to a full range of human rights violations.

While some loyalty could be bought, the dictatorship also needed means to repress dissidents and other resistant social actors. The functions that military expenditure serves will typically evolve according to the role

[57] Frieden, "The Brazilian," 97.

[58] Ibid., 116.

[59] Skidmore, *The Politics*, 237.

[60] *See generally Luiz Bresser-Pereira, O Colapso de uma Aliança de Classes (São Paulo: Brasiliense, 1978), 125.*

[61] Frieden, "The Brazilian," 116.

[62] James Petras, "Political Economy of State Terror: Chile, El Salvador, and Brazil," *Crime and Social Justice*, no. 27–28 (1987), 104.

[63] Tony Addison, "The political economy of the transition from authoritarianism," in Pablo de Greiff and Roger Duthie (eds), *Transitional Justice and Development*, (New York: Social Science Research Council, 2009), 118.

of the military sector in society. Thus, a country in which the military sector focuses very much on domestic stability instead of defense against external attacks will expend more resources in line with this function. In Brazil after 1964, this resulted in the reconfiguration of the fundamental functions of the military sector to focus more on internal security (internal war) than on defense against potential external aggressors.[64]

In data from the Stockholm International Peace Research Institute (SIPRI), a clear trend of increasing military expenditure right after the coup can be discerned. In 1963, the military expenditure of Brazil represented 1.6% of the GDP, and 1.7% in 1964. Interestingly, in 1965 this ratio rose dramatically to 2.5%, reaching its highest point in 1967 at 2.9%. This trend toward increased spending lasted until 1973, consistently exceeding 2%. From 1974 to 1985, this ratio was around 1%.[65] Other sources affirm the sharp increase right after the coup, with this trend lasting several years.[66]

In terms of the national budget, the three military ministries (excluding the Estado-Maior das Forças Armadas) received 16.29% of the overall national budget in 1964, reaching 23.41% in 1965. In the years that followed, this budgetary line remained around 20%, reaching 38.94% in 1971.[67] As the Federal Police was actively involved in the repression,[68] and this organ was functionally under the direction of the Ministry of Justice, it is worth mentioning that the budget of this ministry jumped from 1.31% in 1964, to 3.44% in 1965 and 2.39% in 1966, and then decreased irregularly throughout the subsequent years.[69] These figures do not include the state budgets corresponding to the provincial police agencies also involved in serious human rights violations during the period.[70] The armed-forces-per-capita ratio shows a moderate increase during the 15 years of the dictatorship. While there were 3.91 military persons per 1000 people in

[64] Skidmore, *The Politics*, 4.

[65] SIPRI, "World Armaments and Disarmament," *SIPRI Yearbook*, several years.

[66] Carlos Wellington Leite de Almeida, "Transparência do orçamento de defesa. O caso brasileiro," *Papeles de investigación, RESDAL* (August 2005): 26, http://www.resdal.org/presupuestos/caso-brasil.pdf (accessed April 26, 2018).

[67] Instituto Brasileiro de Geografia e Estatística, "Anuário estatístico do Brasil: 1963–1990," (IBGE: Rio de Janeiro, 1992).

[68] Carlos Fico, *Como eles agiam: os subterrâneos da Ditadura Militar* (Rio de Janeiro: Record, 2001), 200.

[69] Instituto Brasileiro de Geografia e Estatística, "Anuario."

[70] For example, in São Paulo the "Departamento de Ordem Política e Social" (DEOPS) was in charge of coordinating the repression.

1963, there were 4.08 in 1973 and 4 in 1977. In 1983, this ratio dropped to 3.5 per 1000.[71] Imports of light weapons—key to domestic repression—also increased during this same period.[72]

Chile[73]

In 1977, Professor Antonio Cassese was appointed by the UN Commission on Human Rights as a Special Rapporteur to assess the link between the financial aid that the Chilean regime under Augusto Pinochet was receiving at that time and the human rights violations the Chilean people were experiencing.[74] In his 260-page report, Cassese developed a sophisticated methodology to evaluate the impact of the financial aid on the human rights situation, concluding: "[a]s foreign economic assistance largely serves to strengthen and prop up the economic system adopted by the Chilean authorities, which in its turn needs to be based on the repression of civil and political rights, the conclusions warranted that the bulk of present economic assistance is instrumental in consolidating and perpetuating the present repression of those rights."[75]

Although one must make important qualifications when analyzing the evolution of the Chilean economy from September 1973 onward, the military government basically pursued the three following economic objectives: solving the inflation problem, reducing the instability in the balance of payments, and providing incentives to revive the national economy. To reach these goals, the government implemented a set of measures, including restoring the private sector, strategic state enterprises, and lands that belonged to the *Corporación de la Reforma Agraria*; lifting price controls on many items; opening the markets by lowering trade barriers; establishing monetarist policies such as the devaluation of the peso;

[71] US Arms Control and Disarmament Agency, *World Military Expenditures and Arms Transfers*, (1963–193) (Washington, D.C.), 23; and (1985), 55.

[72] Fernando Cordero, "Comercio Exterior e Industria de Armas Livianas en Argentina, Brasil, Colombia, Costa Rica, Chile, República Dominicana, Perú, México y Venezuela. 1970–1980," *Ibero-Americana – Nordic Journal of Latin American Studies* 7, no. 1–2 (1983), 170.

[73] See more details in Juan Pablo Bohoslavsky and Mariana Rulli, "Corporate Complicity and Finance as a 'Killing Agent'. The Relevance of the Chilean Case," *Journal of International Criminal Justice*, 2010, Vol. 8, No. 3, 829–850.

[74] Cassese, "Study."

[75] Ibid., Vol. IV, 24.

and restricting credit expansion, reducing state expenditures, and freezing wages.

The monetarist approach to the balance of payments in a context of decreasing saving and investment rates and an excess of imports contributed to intensifying the need for the import of hard currency in Chile. The excess imports amounted to more than US$7.4 billion between 1977 and 1982, comprising almost three-quarters of the country's total external indebtedness during the same period. Against this backdrop, it is not surprising that the goal of attracting foreign loans, credits, and investment capital played a key role in the formulation of Chilean economic and other policies since the military takeover in 1973. With what was reported to be Latin America's highest per capita debt and its second-highest ratio of debt servicing payments to export receipts in 1976, Chile's need for external financial support was a constant policy preoccupation.[76]

In 1973, Chilean medium- and long-term public external debt added up to US$2862 million, in 1975 it was US$3597 million, in 1979 it was US$4108 million, and in 1983 US$7843 million.[77] Private external debt also steadily increased during the dictatorship: US$399 million in 1973, US$670 million in 1975, US$2.166 million in 1979, and US$6501 million in 1983.[78] The proportion of private and official creditors also changed: while in 1974 only 19% of Chilean foreign debt came from private lenders, in 1981 it reached 80%. Chilean debt with banks grew over 57% between 1977 and 1981, as opposed to most developing countries which saw a 28% rise on average. Chilean dependence on foreign aid was significant, and it became one of the most deeply indebted countries in private international capital markets, going from the 11th place in 1976 to 6th in 1979.

Chile's external financial dependence was notorious. Soon after the coup in 1973, the military government started receiving financial aid from several countries, especially the United States, and multilateral financial institutions, such as the IMF, WB, and IDB.[79] This fact reveals the initial US support of the Pinochet regime, grounded in the geopolitical fight against communism, as happened with other Latin American countries

[76] Ibid, Vol. III, 3,12.

[77] Cental Bank of Chile, "Indicadores Económicos y Sociales de Chile 1960–2000," (Santiago, 2001).

[78] Cental Bank of Chile, "Deuda externa de Chile," (Santiago, 1984).

[79] Cassese, "Study." Vol. III, 5.

like Argentina, Brazil, and Uruguay. As international and US congressional concerns over human rights violations grew from 1976 onward, official financial and military aid decreased dramatically.[80] Some countries and international organizations (like the US Agency for International Development, IDB, and WB) continued to grant aid, claiming it was for concrete humanitarian or developmental goals, but the ways in which the government spent these funds did not, in fact, benefit the needy.[81] Likewise, the government often used this assistance government to replace national resources, which were diverted to other ends, including financing the apparatus of repression.[82]

That the government was thus able to keep the economic scheme in operation had severe repercussions for the population. A concrete representation of this idea is confirmed when we see that, although social expenditures decreased dramatically during the military government, expenditures in the police and military sector grew massively in the national budget from 15% in 1969 to 23.3% by 1982. Military expenditures included salaries, support for the maintenance of concentration camps, help with the implementation of logistics, intelligence, and counterintelligence, the purchase of arms and military equipment, and so on.[83]

According to the Cassese Report: "[this] government economic policy produces to a great extent harmful consequences for the social condition of the vast majority of the population." Therefore, it is not surprising that policy could only give rise to discontent and unrest. In order to keep the people under control, the Chilean authorities needed a repressive system based on the denial of the basic political rights.[84]

From 1976 on, official creditors were replaced by private multinational banks, which started lending enormous sums without expressing any concern for the potential impact of these loans.[85] This allowed the country to

[80] Heinz and Fruhling, "Determinants," 520.

[81] The programs that aimed to finance new houses provide an example of this; Cassese, "Study," Vol. IV, 24.

[82] Ibid.

[83] Scheetz, "Gastos militaes."

[84] Ibid., at 22, 24.

[85] Cassese, "Study," Vol. III, 67. As the article "How Chile Reappeared" said in *Euromoney* in 1977, 101–5: "Both countries [Chile and Argentina] have arguably staged an economic turnaround, which appears to have impressed the international banking fraternity. Although the Carter tirade against those countries infringing on Human Rights prompted a somewhat sticky start to the development of the two countries as a much needed sink-hole for excess

avoid the embarrassing process of renegotiating its external debt in 1976 and 1977. At this same time, following a similar position adopted by the Federal Republic of Germany, the Netherlands, Italy, and Norway, the US government suspended most forms of bilateral economic aid to Chile, expressing disapproval of human rights abuses by the Pinochet government.[86]

According to the Cassese Report, the aforementioned policies supported by the majority in the international community were being rendered ineffective by the lending practices of a small number of private banks. This stubborn reluctance by international financial institutions to be held the least bit accountable for the consequences of their loans helped to prompt the United States to take an unusual step. In 1978, Senator Edward Kennedy (Democrat-Massachusetts) introduced the Foreign Bank Loans Disclosure Act, requiring disclosure of bank loans made to known human rights violators. In proposing this act, Senator Kennedy affirmed that "one of the guiding principles of (US) foreign policy is that except in cases of humanitarian assistance, we shall give no aid to gross violators of human rights."[87] The Institute for Policy Studies submitted a report for the Congressional Record in 1978 and explained how private loans were upholding the Chilean dictatorship:

> Without continual inflow of credit from private banks, Chile will either be forced to return to the Paris Club to seek renegotiation – where it will certainly be held accountable for its massive human rights violations – or to swallow a new dose of austerity like the one Pinochet and Cauas introduced in April 1975. But with the Pinochet regime under attack from both the right and the left, and with the political division within the military junta . . . greater than ever, it would be political suicide for Pinochet to ask a country wracked by poverty and economic austerity to endure another severe depression.[88]

It also led to discussion on the U.S. Senate floor about the capacity of various Latin American dictatorships to retain their stronghold, with his

banking liquidity, it is plain that doubts about the wisdom of lending to countries that contravene Human Rights are fast being dismissed."

[86] Center for International Policy, "Chile: An Analysis of Human Rights Violations and United States Security Assistance and Economic Programmes," 1–2 July 1978.

[87] S 3631-Foreign Loans Disclosure Act of 1978,124 Cong. Rec.376781978.

[88] S 3631-Foreign Loans Disclosure Act of 1978, 124 Cong Rec 37,677 1978.

colleague Senator Frank Church (Democrat-Idaho) commenting that "massive funding such as [what Hanover Trust provided to Chile's Pinochet] may be what enabled five Latin American governments to continue their anti-democratic practices and violations of human rights."[89] During the Carter administration, military and bilateral aid was stopped,[90] but so were multilateral development bank loans to Southern Cone governments when they were not intended to help them meet basic human needs as required by law.[91] In the case of Chile, the United States opposed the loans because of the regime's already disastrous human rights record.[92]

During the Carter administration, the American government expressly warned banks that lending money to Chile would erode US foreign policy, wherein human rights were considered to be a crucial factor for deciding whether to financially support a regime.[93] The chairman of the US House Banking Committee officially told six of the main multinational banks lending to Chile that their actions appeared inconsistent with standards intended to prevent banking practices from interfering with public interest, so he hoped they would provide a full and public explanation.[94] Leaders of the banking community argued that financial institutions should not be impeded from doing their "normal business" regardless of the governments they were engaged with.[95]

[89] Ibid.

[90] S 3631-Foreign Loans Disclosure Act of 1978,124 Cong. Rec.376781978.

[91] S 3631-Foreign Loans Disclosure Act of 1978, 124 Cong Rec 37,677 1978. From January 1977 to August 1980, the United States opposed, either by voting against or by abstaining from voting, 23 loans to Argentina, 5 to Chile, 7 to Paraguay, and 11 to Uruguay.

[92] A detail of US negative votes and abstentions on multilateral development banks' loans for human rights reasons, in Jo Marie Griesgraber, "Implementation by the Carter Administration of Human Rights Legislation Affecting Latin America," (unpublished PhD dissertation, Georgetown University, 1983) (on file with author), 368.

[93] "Rights Policy Not Helped by Loans to Chile From Banks," *The Washington Post*, April 13, 1978, at A19.

[94] "Several US banks Accused of Undercutting Policy on Chile," *The Washington Post*, April 12, 1978.

[95] For example, during his trip to Argentina in March 1979, David Rockefeller—then chair of the US bank Chase Manhattan—made a public speech criticizing President Carter's human rights policy, stressing that "it is not fair to use trade as an instrument to force other nations to do things in the way we think they must be done, because this does not benefit the human rights policy and, in addition, is detrimental to our economy and the one of other countries," "Rockefeller opinó," *Clarín*, March 9, 1979. He went even further by explaining that limiting or curtailing trade as the penalty for nonconformance with human rights standards was not only a wrong-minded approach, but also, at base, antidemocratic as it tried to

Uruguay[96]

Because Uruguay's trade balance and fiscal account were negative during almost the entire dictatorship (1973–1985), an alternative financial source was necessary. As happened with other Southern Cone dictatorships, this source became the inflow of international capital, which financed the Uruguayan economy on a massive scale (see Tables 7.1 and 7.2).[97] Public indebtedness helped the government implement a monetarist policy,[98] keep the financial system flowing, secure a minimum of political support for the regime,[99] and finance public expenditures (including those of the military). The figures in Tables 7.1 and 7.2 vividly show the state's increasing financial dependence on external aid, which became crucial for the country's political and economic well-being.

As the figures show, official aid (both bilateral and multilateral) played an active role in financing the Uruguayan state during the first years of the

Table 7.1 Debt stock evolution (US$ millions)

	1971	*1973*	*1975*	*1977*	*1979*	*1981*	*1983*	*1985*
Public debt stock (including undisbursed)	363	469	1034	1205	1416	1931	3066	3287
Private nonguaranteed debt	29	31	52	83	185	326	158	60

Source: World Bank, *World Debt Tables*

impose American values on other countries; see David Rockefeller, "America's Future: A Question of Strength and Will," *The Atlantic Community Quarterly*, Spring 1979, 14–19; and David Rockefeller, "In Pursuit of a Consistent Foreign Policy: The Trilateral Commission," *Vital Speeches of the Day*, June 15, 517–20. In 1978, the chairman of Lloyds Bank in London responded to criticism for granting loans to the Chilean dictatorship, admitting that this regime was repressive, but also alleging that lending money to Chile was not banned. See "Lloyds bounces Chile protest," *The Guardian*, March 31, 1978.

[96] See more details in Juan Pablo Bohoslavsky, "Another Brick in the Uruguayan Transition: Financial Complicity," Sabine Michalowski (ed.), *Corporate Accountability in the Context of Transitional Justice*, (Routledge, 2012), 189.

[97] Jaime Yaffé, "Proceso económico y política económica durante la dictadura (1973–1984)" in C. Demasi et al., *La dictadura cívico militar. Uruguay 1973–1985* (Montevideo: Ediciones de la Banda Oriental, 2009), 107.

[98] In other words, the economy's performance is determined almost entirely by changes in the money supply.

[99] See Yaffé, "Proceso," 122.

Table 7.2 Main debt ratios

	1971	*1973*	*1975*	*1977*	*1979*	*1981*	*1983*	*1985*
Debt outstanding and disbursed/GNP (%)	10.6	11.9	17.8	17.9	13.2	12	49.5	55.5
Debt outstanding and disbursed/exports of goods and services (%)	137.2	93.1	135.4	104.8	72.9	73	170.3	200.3

Source: World Bank, *World Debt Tables*

Table 7.3 Composition of Uruguay's public debt (US$ millions)

	1971	*1973*	*1975*	*1977*	*1979*	*1981*	*1983*	*1985*
Multilateral	113	156	260	241	346	583	601	731
Bilateral	95	165	234	193	153	225	216	193
Private creditors	155	149	540	771	917	1123	2249	2363

Source: World Bank, *World Debt Tables*

dictatorship. In later years, this aid kept on flowing, but its relevance in Uruguayan finance was gradually superseded by private loans.

This change in the composition of creditors followed a general tendency in international markets for multinational banks to play a leading role in sovereign financing due to the phenomenal development of the Eurodollar market and the recycling of petrodollars (Table 7.3).

During the dictatorship, public expenditures grew both in absolute and relative (15.2% of the GDP in 1973 compared with 20.5% in 1984).[100] These increases were accompanied (except in 1979 and 1980) by a continuous fiscal deficit because the rhythm of the economy did not generate sufficient revenues to cover those expenditures (see the discussion in the previous subsection). Public indebtedness helped finance public accounts and commercial deficits.[101]

Interestingly, the Uruguayan dictatorship managed to maintain a budgetary policy that benefited not only broad corporate sectors of the national economy and the international banks but also, very clearly, the

[100] On state budget and expenditures, see generally Paola Azar et al. *¿De quiénes, para quiénes y para qué? Las finanzas públicas de Uruguay en el siglo XX*, (Fin de Siglo, Montevideo, 2009).

[101] Yaffé, "Proceso," 155.

military sector. This seems to have allowed the state to carry out massive crimes and effective and overwhelming social control in a context of a fiscal deficit, a negative trade balance, and low growth rates.[102] In other words, the external financial aid the civic-military government received provided it with the funds to buy key loyalties from the domestic elite, thus helping to moderate social discontent, and to finance effective repressive measures. Due to its central role during the dictatorship, the financial sector was deemed a "new social actor" in Uruguay.[103]

Once the economy was liberalized and subsidies and other state financial incentives were suppressed, borrowing became more expensive and the recession started to spread. From 1980 onward, the industrial and farming sectors gradually left the governmental coalition, and the financial sector took their place. As the crisis would later dramatically show, the financial sector was already playing a leading role in the economic life of the country.

Particularly during the first phase of authoritarianism (1973–1975) and the subsequent trend toward totalitarianism (1975–1978),[104] the state needed an effective and efficient bureaucratic apparatus capable of keeping civil liberties and political opposition under strict control. As with other dictatorships in Latin America, this phenomenon can be observed in the evolution of Uruguay's public budget, specifically its military expenditures.[105]

During the 1960s, military expenditure[106] as a percentage of the GDP was lower than 2%.[107] This ratio rose considerably during the 1970s,

[102] Ibid.

[103] Jorge Notaro, "La batalla que ganó la economía. 19721984" in Bertoni et al., *El Uruguay del siglo xx. La economía*, Instituto de Economía-Ediciones de la Banda Oriental, Montevideo, 2003, 110.

[104] Alvaro Rico, "Sobre el autoritarismo y el golpe de Estado. La dictadura y el dictador" in Carlo Demasi et al. (eds), *La dictadura Cívico-Militar. Uruguay 1973–1985*, (Montevideo: Ediciones de la Banda Oriental), 231.

[105] Merilee Grindle, "Civil-Military Relations and Budgetary Politics in Latin America," 13 *Armed Forces & Society*, 1987, 262; Scheetz, "Gastos militares," 319.

[106] According to the Stockholm International Peace Research Institute, these figures in principle include, among other things, expenditures on defense ministries and other governmental agencies engaged in defense projects, current military and civil personnel, operations and maintenance, procurement, military research and development, and military construction. *See* www.sipri.org/research/armaments/milex/resultoutput/sources_methods/definitions

[107] SIPRI, "World Armaments," 1979, 56.

alongside the military's increasing role in Uruguayan political life. Military expenditures amounted to 1.9% of the GDP in 1970; 2.4% in 1973; 2.7% in 1978; 4% in 1982; and 2.4% in 1985.[108] This budgetary evolution seems to follow the civic-military government's expectation that increases in defense would increase political stability.[109] It is not surprising that while military expenditures as a whole rose during the Uruguayan dictatorship,[110] the budget line for arms imports (linked to the defense of the territory against external aggressions) did not follow this same pattern,[111] indicating that the increased military resources were spent largely on functions related to internal security.

Concluding Remarks

While the dictatorships of Argentina, Brazil, Chile, and Uruguay received bilateral and multilateral financial assistance right after their respective coups d'état, from 1976 onward, official creditors were replaced by private commercial banks from industrialized countries, which started lending enormous sums to those regimes without expressing any regard for the potential human rights impact of these loans. As statistical data suggest that funding for criminal regimes usually helps them to consolidate, this chapter has analyzed the amount and nature of financial assistance lenders—in particular private banks, because their monies are *more lethal* than public ones[112]—provided to those Latin American regimes and the impact these funds had on their respective economic and political systems as well as on their respective human rights records.

From the point of view of foreign lenders and investors, a country can be considered creditworthy if it shows some positive macroeconomic indicators, even if this state of affairs has been reached thanks to redistribution of income unfavorable to the vast majority of the population, cheap labor, and the suppression of visible social unrest. If creditors charge interest rates linked to the London Inter-Bank Offered Rate (LIBOR), as was the case with the loans to Latin American countries, they can ensure huge

[108] SIPRI, "World Armaments," 1980, 32; 1983, 174; 1984, 30; and 1990, 200.

[109] Brock Blomberg, "Growth, Political Instability and the Defense Burden," *Economica*, 3 (1996), 649.

[110] SIPRI, "World Armaments," 1983, 174.

[111] US Arms Control and Disarmament Agency, *World Military Expenditures and Arms Trade*, 1969–78, 155; 1972–82, 91; 1985, 127; 1987, 123; and 1988, 107.

[112] See findings in Bohoslavsky and Escribà-Folch, "Rational choice," 15–32.

profits for themselves.[113] Without suppressing civil and political rights, authoritarian governments could barely impose and enforce economic and social policies that deeply and continuously disadvantage the interests and needs of the less privileged strata. Granting financial assistance to such regimes can contribute to a vicious circle in which not only civil and political rights but also social, economic, and cultural rights are lost. This happened during the dictatorships in Argentina, Brazil, Chile, and Uruguay.

Latin American dictatorships not only tortured and killed people but imposed economic models that violated fundamental social, economic, and cultural rights as well. The ways in which both groups of rights violations are interlinked is often at the core of most regimes' plans. In this context, foreign investors can be invited to translate these transgressions of human rights into increased profitability. As demonstrated here, economic assistance can contribute to the perpetuation of human rights abuses, and such abuses, in turn, might bring about the necessary conditions to attract and obtain economic assistance.[114]

Unlike his predecessors, US president Jimmy Carter and his administration, along with some European governments, promoted an aggressive foreign policy toward Latin American regimes with the specific objective of using diplomatic pressure and conditional assistance to reduce human rights violations.[115] This led to a policy of explicitly refusing to grant financial and military aid to the dictatorships, which arguably had the goal of provoking political embarrassment and generating some economic and financial drawbacks for the military governments in order to force them to improve their performance in the human rights field. Interestingly, when multilateral and bilateral financing was reduced, commercial banks came to play a prominent role in this criminal-financial game.

President Carter endeavored to drastically alter US policies toward the Southern Cone dictatorships, but the non-holistic approach did not deter private lenders from a number of industrialized countries.[116] The cases in

[113] Salvador Bergel, "Los créditos a interés variable: Su incidencia en la deuda externa latinoamericana," in *Derecho Económico actual. Homenaje al Prof. Manuel A. Laquis,* Depalma, Buenos Aires, 776–781.

[114] Antonio Cassese, "Foreign Economic Assistance and Respect for Civil and Political Rights: Chile, A Case Study," *Texas International Law Journal* 14 (1979): 257.

[115] Cyrus Vance, "Human Rights and Foreign Policy," *Georgia Journal of International and Comparative Law Quarterly*, 1977: 3, 223.

[116] Benjamin Cohen, "International Debt and Linkage Strategies: Some Foreign-Policy Implications for the United States," *International Organization*, (1985) 39(4), 699–727.

this chapter illustrate that even when a powerful state decides to use bilateral and multilateral aid as an incentive to promote human rights, a broad consensus of the international community is needed in order for the initiatives to be effective. The US government failed in its attempt to influence even the nation's own private business sectors.

Studying the role that the financial actors played in the context of the Latin American dictatorships is connected with the human right to the truth. As explained by one the victims of the Argentinean dictatorship who is suing the banks that financed it, "I want to know who gave the money to the military junta that ruled a bankrupted country but had the capability to pay the salaries of the murderers of my parents and buy the machines used to torture them."[117] One of the worst parts of this story is that very little has been learned from the experiences presented in this text. The *Thun Group of Banks*[118] published its second discussion paper in 2017, warning that [a] "bank would generally not be considered to be causing or contributing to adverse human rights impacts arising from its clients' operations because the impact is not occurring as part of the bank's own activities."[119] While UN human rights bodies have strongly responded to this argument,[120] it is clear that the international community is still struggling to develop global standards applied to both official and private lenders in order to prevent loans that consolidate criminal regimes from being granted.[121]

[117] "Los prestamistas de la muerte," *Página 12*, 21 June 2011.

[118] This informal group was established to discuss the implications of the UN Guiding Principles on Business and Human Rights for the banking sector. Its current members are UBS, Credit Suisse, Barclays, BBVA, BNP Paribas, Deutsche Bank, ING, RBS, Standard Chartered, UniCredit, and JP Morgan.

[119] Available at http://www.menschenrechte.uzh.ch/en/publikationen/thun-group-of-banks.html

[120] See the letters of the UN Working Group on Business and Human Rights, http://www.ohchr.org/Documents/Issues/TransCorporations/WG_BHR_letter_Thun_Group.pdf; of the Office of the High Commissioner for Human Rights http://www.ohchr.org/Documents/Issues/Business/InterpretationGuidingPrinciples.pdf; and of the UN Independent Expert on Debt and Human Rights http://www.ohchr.org/Documents/Issues/Development/IEDebt/LetterThunGroup.pdf

[121] Report to the UN Human Rights Council, A/HRC/28/59, 22 December 2014, available at http://www.undocs.org/A/HRC/28/59

References

Addison, Tony. "The political economy of the transition from authoritarianism." In *Transitional Justice and Development*, edited by Pablo de Greiff and Roger Duthie, 110–141 New York: Social Science Research Council, 2009.

Addo, Michael K. Mandate of the Working Group on the issue of human rights and transnational corporations and other business enterprises. February 23, 2017. https://www.ohchr.org/Documents/Issues/TransCorporations/WG_BHR_letter_Thun_Group.pdf

Aguiar, Marco *et al.* "Economic Dictatorship versus Democracy in Brazil." *Latin American Perspectives* 11, no. 1 (1984): 13–25.

Altamura, Carlo E. "Global Banks and Latin American Dictators." *Business History Review* (2020): 1–32. https://doi.org/10.1017/S0007680519001260

Azar, Paola *et al. ¿De quiénes, para quiénes y para qué? Las finanzas públicas de Uruguay en el siglo XX*. Montevideo: Fin de Siglo, 2009.

Baer, Wener, Richard Newfarmer, and Thomas Trebat. "On State Capitalism in Brazil: some New Issues and Questions." *Inter-American Economic Affairs* 30 (1976): 75–77.

Basualdo, Eduardo. "La Reestructuración de la Economía Argentina Durante las Últimas Décadas: De la Sustitución de Importaciones a la Valorización Financiera." In *Neoliberalismo y sectores dominantes. Tendencias globales y experiencias nacionales,* edited by Eduardo Basualdo and Enrique Arceo, 123–177. Buenos Aires: Clacso, 2006.

Bergel, Salvador. "Los créditos a interés variable: su incidencia en la deuda externa latinoamericana." In *Derecho Económico actual. Homenaje al Prof. Manuel A. Laquis,* 776–781. Buenos Aires: Depalma, 1994.

Binato Pedras, Guilherme. "History of Public Debt in Brazil: 1964 to The Present." In *Public Debt: The Brazilian Experience*, edited by Anderson Caputo Silva *et al.*, 64. Brasília: National Treasury, 2010.

Blomberg, Brock. "Growth, Political Instability and the Defense Burden." *Economica* 3 (1996): 649.

Bohoslavsky, Juan Pablo, and Abel Escribà-Folch. "Rational choice and financial complicity with human rights abuses: policy and legal implications". In *Making Sovereign Financing and Human Rights Work*, edited by Juan Pablo Bohoslavsky and Jernej Letnar, 15–32. Oxford: Hart Publishing, 2013.

Bohoslavsky, Juan Pablo. "Another Brick in the Uruguayan Transition: Financial Complicity". In *Corporate Accountability in the Context of Transitional Justice*, edited by Sabine Michalowski, 187–207. New York: Routledge, 2012.

Bohoslavsky, Juan Pablo. "Mandate of the Independent Expert on the effects of foreign debt and other related international financial obligations of States on the full enjoyment of all human rights, particularly economic, social and cultural rights". October 19, 2017. https://www.ohchr.org/Documents/Issues/Development/IEDebt/LetterThunGroup.pdf

Bohoslavsky, Juan Pablo. "Report of the Independent Expert on the effects of foreign debt and other related international financial obligations of States on the full enjoyment of all human rights, particularly economic, social and cultural rights". December 22, 2014. https://www.undocs.org/A/HRC/28/59

Bohoslavsky, Juan Pablo, and Marcelo Torelly. "Financial Complicity: The Brazilian Dictatorship Under the 'Macroscope'". In Justi*ce and Economic Violence in Transition,* edited by Dustin Sharp, 233–262. New York: Springer, 2013.

Bohoslavsky, Juan Pablo, and Mariana Rulli. "Corporate Complicity and Finance as a 'Killing Agent'. The Relevance of the Chilean Case." *Journal of International Criminal Justice* 8, no. 3 (2010): 829–850.

Bohoslavsky, Juan Pablo, and Veerle Opgenhaffen. "The Past and Present of Corporate Complicity: Financing the Argentinian Dictatorship." *Harvard Human Rights Journal* 23, no. 166 (2010): 157–203.

Bresser Pereira, Luiz. "Six Interpretations of the Brazilian Social Formation." *Latin American Perspectives* 11, no. 40 (1984): 35–72.

Bresser-Pereira, Luiz. O Colapso de uma Aliança de Classes. São Paulo: Brasiliense, 1978.

Calcagno, Eric. "Los bancos transnacionales y el endeudamiento externo en la Argentina." *Cuadernos de la CEPAL.* Santiago: Comisión Económica para América Latina y el Caribe, 1987.

Carvalho Pereira, José. *Financiamento Externo e Crescimento Econômico no Brasil: 1966/73.* Rio de Janeiro: IPEA/INPES, 1974.

Cassese, Antonio. "Foreign Economic Assistance and Respect for Civil and Political Rights: Chile, A Case Study." *Texas International Law Journal* 14 (1979): 251–263.

Cassese, Antonio. "Study of the Impact of Foreign Economic Aid and Assistance on Respect for Human Rights in Chile." United Nations Digital Library. https://digitallibrary.un.org/record/556117?ln=en

Center for International Policy. "Chile: An Analysis of Human Rights Violations and United States Security Assistance and Economic Programmes". 1–2. July 1978.

Central Bank of Chile. *Deuda externa de Chile.* Santiago, 1984.

Central Bank of Chile. *Indicadores Económicos y Sociales de Chile 1960–2000.* Santiago, 2001.

Cohen, Benjamin. "International Debt and Linkage Strategies: Some Foreign-Policy Implications for the United States." *International Organization* 39, no. 4 (1985): 699–727.

Cordero, Fernando. "Comercio Exterior e Industria de Armas Livianas en Argentina, Brasil, Colombia, Costa Rica, Chile, República Dominicana, Perú,

México y Venezuela. 1970–1980." *Ibero-Americana – Nordic Journal of Latin American Studies* 7, no. 1–2 (1983): 167–181.

Damil, Mario, and Roberto Frenkel. "Restauración Democrática y Política Económica: Argentina 1984–1991." In *La política económica en la transición a la democracia: Lecciones de Argentina, Bolivia, Chile y Uruguay*, edited by Juan Morales and Gary McMahon, 33–95. Santiago: Cieplan, 1993.

Darity, William, and Bobbie Horn. *The loan pushers: The role of commercial banks in the international debt crisis.* Pensacola: Ballinger, 1988.

Department of State Report, "Evolution of U.S. Human Rights Policy in Argentina." State Argentina Declassification Project (1975–1984). foia.state.gov/documents/Argentina/0000AA65.pdf

Feldman, Ernesto, and Juan Sommer. *Crisis financiera y endeudamiento externo en Argentina.* Buenos Aires: CET/IPAL, 1984.

Ferrer, Aldo. *¿Puede Argentina pagar su deuda externa?* Buenos Aires: El Cid, 1982.

Fico, Carlos. *Como eles agiam: os subterrâneos da Ditadura Militar.* Rio de Janeiro: Record, 2001.

First Amended Complaint. *In re South African Apartheid Litigation.* https://hrp.law.harvard.edu/areas-of-focus/previous-areas-of-focus/in-re-south-african-apartheid-litigation/ Accessed May 12 2020.

Fishlow, Albert. "Brazil's Economic Miracle." *The World Today* 29 (1973): 474.

Frieden, Jeffry. "The Brazilian Borrowing Experience: From Miracle to Debacle and Back." *Latin American Research Review* 22, no. 1 (1987): 95–131.

Green, James. "Restless youth: the 1968 Brazilian student movement as seen from Washington." In *1968–40 anos depois*, edited by Carlos Fico and Maria Paula Araújo, 31–61. Rio de Janeiro: 7 Letras, 2011.

Griesgraber, Jo Marie. "Implementation by the Carter Administration of Human Rights Legislation Affecting Latin America." Unpublished PhD dissertation, Georgetown University, 1983.

Grindle, Merilee. "Civil-Military Relations and Budgetary Politics in Latin America." *Armed Forces & Society* 13 (1987): 255–275.

Harold, James. *The Nazi Dictatorship and the Deutsche* Bank. Cambridge: Cambridge University Press, 2004.

Heinz, Wolfgang, and Hugo Fruhling. *Determinants of Gross Human Rights Violations by State and State-Sponsored Actors in Brazil, Uruguay, Chile, and Argentina (1960–1990).* The Hague: Kluwer Law International, 1999.

Henry, James. *The Blood Bankers: Tales from the Global Underground Economy.* New York: Four Walls Eight Windows, 2003.

"How Chile Reappeared", *Euromoney*, 1977.

Instituto Brasileiro de Geografia e Estatística. *Anuário estatístico do Brasil: 1963–1990.* IBGE: Rio de Janeiro, 1992.

Juzgado Nacional en lo Criminal y Correccional Federal no. 2 de la Capital Federal. "Olmos, Alejandro s. denuncia." *Jurisprudencia Argentina*, June 13, 2000, January 31, 2001.

Lafer, Celso. *O Sistema Político Brasileiro*. São Paulo: Perspectiva, 1978.

Lebovic, James, and Erik Voeten. "The costs of shame: international organizations and foreign aid in the punishing of human rights violators." *Journal of Peace Research* 46, no. 1 (January 2009): 79–97.

Lichtenstein, Cynthia. "The U.S. Response to the International Debt Crisis: The International Lending Supervision Act 1983." *Virginia Journal of International Law* 25, no. 2 (1985): 401–435.

"Lloyds bounces Chile protest", *The Guardian*, March 31, 1978.

"Los prestamistas de la muerte." *Página 12*, June 21, 2011.

Notaro, Jorge. "La batalla que ganó la economía. 19721984." In *El Uruguay del siglo xx. La economía*, edited by Bertoni *et al.*, 95–110. Montevideo: Instituto de Economía-Ediciones de la Banda Oriental, 2003.

Pang, Eul-Soo, and Laura Jarnagin. "Brazilian Democracy and the Foreign Debt." *Current History* (February 1984), 63–67.

Petras, James. "Political Economy of State Terror: Chile, El Salvador, and Brazil." *Crime and Social Justice* 27–28 (1987): 88–109.

Rico, Álvaro. "Sobre el autoritarismo y el golpe de Estado. La dictadura y el dictador." In *La dictadura Cívico-Militar. Uruguay 1973–1985*, edited by Carlo Demasi *et al.*, 179–246. Montevideo: Ediciones de la Banda Oriental, 2009.

"Rights Policy Not Helped by Loans to Chile From Banks", *The Washington Post*, April 13, 1978.

Rockefeller, David. "America's Future: A Question of Strength and Will". *The Atlantic Community Quarterly* (Spring 1979): 14–19.

Rockefeller, David. "In Pursuit of a Consistent Foreign Policy: The Trilateral Commission." In *Vital Speeches of the Day* (June 15, 1980): 517–520.

S 3631-Foreign Loans Disclosure Act of 1978,124 Cong. Rec.376781978.

"Rockefeller opinó", *Clarín*, March 9, 1979.

Scheetz, Thomas. "Gastos militares en Chile, Perú y la Argentina". *Desarrollo Económico* 25, no. 99 (1985): 315–327.

Schvarzer, Jorge. *Argentina 1976–1981: El endeudamiento externo como pivote de la especulación financiera*. Buenos Aires: Cisea, 1983.

"Several US banks Accused of Undercutting Policy on Chile." *The Washington Post*, April 12, 1978.

SIPRI. *SIPRI Yearbook* 1979. Oxford: Oxford University Press, 1979.

SIPRI. *SIPRI Yearbook* 1980. Oxford: Oxford University Press, 1980.

SIPRI. *SIPRI Yearbook* 1983. Oxford: Oxford University Press, 1983.

SIPRI. *SIPRI Yearbook* 1984. Oxford: Oxford University Press, 1984.

SIPRI. *SIPRI Yearbook* 1990. Oxford: Oxford University Press, 1990.

Siqueira Conte, Carolina. "The Interaction of Economics and Politics in Brazil During the Military Dictatorship". Master thesis, Ohio University, 2001.
Skidmore, Thomas. *The Politics of Military Rule in Brazil, 1964–1985*. New York: Oxford University Press, 1988.
Spektor, Matias. *Kissinger e o Brasil*. Rio de Janeiro: Jorge Zahar, 2009.
Stepan, Alfred. *Authoritarian Brazil: Origins, Policies, and Future*. Hew Haven: Yale University Press, 1973.
Thun Group of Banks. "Paper on the Implications of UN Guiding Principles 13b and 17 in a Corporate and Investment Banking Context". December, 2017. http://www.menschenrechte.uzh.ch/en/publikationen/thun-group-of-banks.html
United Nations. OHCHR response to request from BankTrack for advice regarding the application of the UN Guiding Principles on Business and Human Rights in the context of the banking sector. June 12, 2017. https://www.ohchr.org/Documents/Issues/Business/InterpretationGuidingPrinciples.pdf
US Arms Control and Disarmament Agency. *World Military Expenditures and Arms Transfers* (1963–193). 23 and 55. Washington, D.C., 1985.
US Arms Control and Disarmament Agency. *World Military Expenditures and Arms Trade*. 1969–78, 155; 1972–82, 91; 1985, 127; 1987, 123; and 1988, 107.
Vance, Cyrus. "Human Rights and Foreign Policy." *Georgia Journal of International and Comparative Law Quarterly* 7 (1977): 223–225.
Vuuren, Hennie van. *A Tale of Profit, Guns and Money*. Johannesburg: Jacana Media, 2017.
Wallerstein, Michael. "The Collapse of Democracy in Brazil: Its Economic Determinants." *Latin American Research Review* 15, no. 3 (1980): 3–40.
Weichert, Marlon. "O financiamento de atos de violação de direitos humanos por empresas durante a ditadura brasileira." *Acervo* 21, no. 2 (2008): 186.
Wellington Leite de Almeida, Carlos. "Transparência do orçamento de defesa. O caso brasileiro." *Papeles de investigación, RESDAL* (August 2005): 26. Accesed April 26, 2018. http://www.resdal.org/presupuestos/caso-brasil.pdf
Wintrobe, Ronald. *The Political Economy of Dictatorship*. New York: Cambridge University Press, 1998.
World Bank, *World Tables*. Baltimore: Johns Hopkins University Press, 1980.
Yaffé, Jaime. "Proceso económico y política económica durante la dictadura (1973–1984)." In *La dictadura cívico militar. Uruguay 1973–1985*, edited by C. Demasi *et al.*, 117–178. Montevideo: Ediciones de la Banda Oriental, 2009.

CHAPTER 8

Confronting Labor Power: Ford Motor Argentina and the Dictatorship (1976–1983)

Eduardo Basualdo and Victoria Basualdo

Introduction

This chapter analyzes the actions of the automobile manufacturing company Ford Motor Argentina during the 1976–1983 dictatorship in Argentina. First, it summarizes the company's history in Argentina up to the 1970s. Second, it elucidates the process of labor organization and repression in the 1970s. Third, it studies the economic evolution of the company during the dictatorship. Finally, it briefly reviews the judicial process that reviewed the responsibilities of a military chief and two Ford Motor Argentina top officials in the human rights violations perpetrated against twenty-four workers and trade-union delegates who were kidnapped, tortured, and imprisoned between 1976 and 1977. The final remarks of the last section emphasize the close connections Ford Motor

E. Basualdo
Area of Economics and Technology, FLACSO, Buenos Aires, Argentina

V. Basualdo (✉)
Area of Economics and Technology, Facultad Latinoamericana de Ciencias, Sociales-CONICET, Buenos Aires, Argentina

V. Basualdo et al. (eds.), *Big Business and Dictatorships in Latin America*, Palgrave Studies in Latin American Heterodox Economics, https://doi.org/10.1007/978-3-030-43925-5_8

Argentina's leadership had to the regime and its involvement in labor repression, as well as the unprecedented profits the company earned due to the economic and ideological alliance its top officials established with the armed forces.

Ford in Argentina Up to the Mid-1970s

The Ford Motor Company, an American multinational corporation engaged in automotive manufacturing, opened its first branch in Argentina in 1913, initially in La Boca, an industrial neighborhood in the southern part of the city of Buenos Aires.[1] Ford was the first foreign car manufacturer to have offices in Argentina. For several decades, this branch was a subsidiary in charge of importing and assembling vehicles. During the administration of President Arturo Frondizi (1958–1962), and in the context of the second stage of the process of import-substitution industrialization in Argentina, Ford decided to expand its presence in the country.[2] In 1959, when Henry Ford II visited Argentina, the company presented the Pick-Up F100 and announced the creation of Ford Argentina S.C.A., along with an extensive investment plan. The new Ford Motor Argentina automotive manufacturing plant in Pacheco, the northern industrial belt in the province of Buenos Aires, was inaugurated in 1961. By the mid-1970s, the Ford parent company controlled a conglomerate including not only the automotive manufacturing plant (Ford Motor Argentina SA) but also auto-parts firms and other enterprises related to financial activities, as depicted in Table 8.1.

Ford Motor Argentina workers were represented by the Union of Automotive Transport Mechanics and Related Workers (Sindicato de Mecánicos y Afines del Transporte Automotor, SMATA). The firm had prestige: employees wished to be hired by Ford as they considered its wages relatively high; moreover, the automobile industry was one of the most dynamic economic sectors. However, during the 1960s workers put pressure on both the company and their trade-union representatives due

[1] Juan Sourrouille, *El complejo automotor en la Argentina: transnacionales en América Latina* (Mexico City: Instituto Latinoamericano de Estudios Transnacionales, 1980).

[2] Eduardo Basualdo, *Estudios de historia económica argentina. Desde mediados del siglo XX hasta la actualidad* (Buenos Aires: Siglo Veintiuno Editores, 2006); and Eduardo Basualdo, Juan Santarcángelo, Andrés Wainer, Cintia Russo, and Guido Perrone, *El Banco de la Nación Argentina y la dictadura. El impacto de las transformaciones económicas y financieras en la política crediticia, 1976–1983* (Buenos Aires: Editorial Siglo Veintiuno, 2016).

Table 8.1 Ford conglomerate in Argentina in the mid-1970s

Activities	*Firms*
Automotive manufacturing industry (terminal plant)	Ford Motor Argentina
Auto-parts production	
Melting and molding	Metalúrgica Constitución S.A. (Metcon S.A.)
Metallurgical components	Transax S.A.
Valves and switches	Acosol S.A.
	Coradel S.A.
Financial activities	Cía. Financiera Ford S.A.
	Fimue S.A.
	Corporación Financiera de Boston S.A.

Source: Eduardo Basualdo, technical report submitted as evidence during Ford trial, November 2006, based on the Área de Economía y Tecnología of FLACSO database

to several persistent labor grievances, such as difficult and unhealthy working conditions that generated work-related health issues.[3] In 1968, two trade-union leaders, Dirck Henry Kloosterman and José Rodríguez, formed a new group to participate in the trade-union elections, the National Movement for Automobile Unity (Movimiento Nacional de Unidad Automotriz). As their campaign capitalized on workers' existing dissatisfaction, they won, and Kloosterman was elected General Secretary of SMATA. In the late 1960s and early 1970s, the trade-union organization grew substantially, expanded medical coverage for workers, and bought a recreational center in Vicente Casares and other recreational facilities in other regions of the country.[4] At the same time, guerrilla and other left-wing organizations began to confront some trade-union leaders, accusing them of favoring employers and having strong connections with American networks and the "free trade-union movement," which sought

[3] Valeria Ianni, "La acción sindical en el marco de las negociaciones colectivas en Ford Motor Argentina durante la segunda etapa de la industrialización por sustitución de importaciones," paper presented at the 10th National Congress of Labor Studies, Asociación Argentina de Especialistas en Estudios del Trabajo (ASET), Facultad de Ciencias Económicas, Universidad de Buenos Aires (UBA), June 2011.

[4] María Florencia Lascano Warnes, "Cambios y continuidades en la historia de los trabajadores industriales argentinos (1973–1983). Una aproximación a través del caso de Ford Motor Argentina" (MA thesis, Universidad Nacional de General Sarmiento, Argentina, 2012), 43–44.

to stop the increasing radicalization of the working class in Argentina and other South American countries. In May 1973, in the context of these growing tensions and conflicts, Kloosterman was assassinated by a guerrilla organization and José Rodríguez became the general secretary of SMATA.

The struggles continued and deepened between 1973 and 1975 as workers demanded higher wages during a phase of inflation, and the employees of the many factory cafeterias came to be included within SMATA's collective agreement. Moreover, the union opposed changes in the organization of production that demanded more intense labor worsening the already serious health problems related to labor conditions that workers had been confronting and denouncing over the previous years.[5] However, conflict was simultaneously growing within the union as groups of workers became ever more disgruntled with the leadership of José Rodríguez, whom they saw as increasingly distanced from the rank and file.[6]

This cycle of labor unrest and mobilization took place as significant groups within the labor movement were becoming more radicalized, and it peaked in June and July 1975. Toward the mid-1970s, following a period of growth in the country's automotive industry, workers at the Pacheco plant began mobilizing and organizing at the rank-and-file level, represented by nearly 200 factory delegates who not only stepped up their demands to management but also increasingly confronted their own national leadership at SMATA. The northern industrial belt of the province of Buenos Aires was a central territory in this process of labor protest, with Ford workers likewise playing a crucial role in fostering resistance to the austerity plan that the Minister of Economy Celestino Rodrigo implemented in June 1975 during the presidency of María Estela Martínez de Perón. They also demanded that collective bargaining, which had been frozen in 1973 due to a social pact promoted by the government, begin once again. In 1975, Ford workers formed a Claim Committee (Comisión de Reclamos) at the plant, aiming to pressure both the labor representatives and the company to address these issues.[7]

In this context, Ford Motor Argentina workers decided to become part of the inter-factory coordination committee of the northern industrial

[5] Héctor Löbbe, *La guerrilla fabril. Clase obrera e izquierda en la Coordinadora de Zona Norte del Gran Buenos Aires (1975–1976)* (Buenos Aires: Ediciones Razón y Revolución, 2006), 113.

[6] Interview with Pedro Troiani, September 2012, quoted in Lascano Warnes, *Cambios y continuidades*, 45.

[7] Héctor Löbbe, "Las 'desmemorias' de José Rodríguez," *El Aromo*, N° 15, 2004, 3.

belt, together with the shipyards of Tigre and San Fernando, Squibb Chemical Laboratories, and the industrial factories of Del Carlo and Terrabusi, among many others.[8] On June 6, 1975, the adjunct secretary of SMATA, Mercado, compelled rank-and-file workers to accept a negotiated agreement and denounced the existence of "subversive" militants at the factory.[9] Ten days later, on June 16, 1975, a massive assembly of workers decided to march toward the central headquarters of the General Confederation of Labor. Five thousand workers marched for six hours along a 17-kilometer stretch of the Pan-American Highway, mobilizing workers at many other factories on their way.[10] This was one of the largest and most visible episodes in a period of intense labor mobilization, in a context of increasing social and political unrest. But these events of June and July 1975 had a paradoxical result for Ford workers. On the one hand, labor protest succeeded in defeating the economic program that sought to impose austerity measures, instead making clearly beneficial collective agreements with employers, among which the one Ford workers signed was one of the best. On the other hand, the company management responded to this labor mobilization by firing nearly 400 workers in the ensuing days and weeks, as well as by going on the offense against the functions and power of trade-union delegates at the factory. At the same time, managers distanced themselves from the leadership of José Rodríguez, whose power was growing more concentrated due to the extraordinary funds the general secretary of SMATA gained from a 2 percent contribution of automotive manufacturing companies' sales on behalf of the workers they represented. Therefore, by the end of 1975 and beginning of 1976, the situation at the Ford Motor Argentina plant was extremely tense and complex, and yet workers and their representatives on

[8] Lascano Warnes, *Cambios y continuidades*, 51; and Yolanda Colom and Alicia Salomone, "Las coordinadoras inter-fabriles de Capital Federal y Gran Buenos Aires. 1975–1976," *Razón y Revolución*. No. 4, 1998. See also Omar Abdala, "Rupturas y continuidades en las formas de acción y resistencia de los trabajadores. El caso Ford Motor Argentina. 1970–1985" (BA thesis in Sociology, Instituto de Altos Estudios Sociales, UNSAM, December 2015).

[9] Löbbe, *La guerrilla fabril*, 114. See also Victoria Basualdo, "Contributions for the Analysis of the Participation of Sectors of the Trade-union Leadership in Labor Repression in Argentina during the 1970s," in *The Economic Accomplices of the Argentine Dictatorship: Outstanding Debt*, ed. Horacio Verbitsky and Juan Pablo Bohoslavsy (Cambridge: Cambridge University Press, 2015).

[10] Löbbe, "Las 'desmemorias' de José Rodríguez," 3.

the shop floor still had considerable power to mobilize and make demands.[11]

Labor Repression Against Ford Workers During the Last Dictatorship in Argentina (1976–1983)

The repressive policies Ford Motor Argentina implemented with increasing force after the military coup that took place on March 24, 1976, need to be analyzed in the context of previous labor mobilization at Ford, the northern industrial belt of Buenos Aires and Santa Fe, as well as within the political struggles in the country. A comprehensive report that investigated the case of Ford along with twenty-four other firms in the country registered a total of thirty-seven victims of human rights violations during the 1976–1983 dictatorship in Argentina related to Ford Motor Argentina.[12] However, this chapter focuses predominantly on twenty-four Ford workers who were kidnapped between 1976 and 1977, most of whom were members of the trade-union delegates commission ("Comisión interna"), while almost all of them were labor activists with no active or militant political affiliation.[13] Many of them "disappeared" for thirty to sixty days. Some of them were kidnapped from their homes and taken to two police stations, Tigre and Maschwitz, which operated as clandestine detention centers. Others were seized directly at the factory, where they were held for hours, tortured, and then taken to the Tigre or Maschwitz police stations, staying there for weeks in extremely precarious conditions. After this initial time, they were transferred to various penitentiaries throughout the country, where they spent nearly a year in prison without

[11] Victoria Basualdo, "Complicidad patronal-militar en la última dictadura argentina: Los casos de Acindar, Astarsa, Dálmine Siderca, Ford, Ledesma y Mercedes-Benz," *Engranajes* (Buenos Aires: Federación de Trabajadores de la Industria y Afines, 2006).

[12] Área de Economía y Tecnología (AEyT) de la Facultad Latinoamericana de Ciencias Sociales (FLACSO), Centro de Estudios Legales y Sociales (CELS), Programa Verdad y Justicia (PVJ) and Secretaría de Derechos Humanos (SDH) del Ministerio de Justicia y Derechos Humanos de la Nación, *Responsabilidad empresarial en delitos de lesa humanidad. Represión a trabajadores durante el terrorismo de Estado* (Buenos Aires: Infojus, 2015).

[13] Victoria Basualdo, Tomás Ojea Quintana and Carolina Varsky, "The Cases of Ford and Mercedes-Benz Argentina," in *The Economic Accomplices of the Argentine Dictatorship: Outstanding Debts*, ed. Horacio Verbitsky and Juan Pablo Bohoslavsky (Cambridge: Cambridge University Press, 2015).

any formal charges being brought against them. All twenty-four of these workers were eventually released at different moments during 1977, but they had to endure years of security forces watching them in their homes afterward. In some cases, such as that of Ismael Portillo, security forces continued the surveillance of their homes until a couple of years after the transition to democracy in 1983. Workers were extremely damaged by the effects of violence, many of them suffering illnesses to date. They also found it nearly impossible to find work in the same line of business after their release from jail. Their families, too, paid a high price for this process, as the detention of workers left them with no financial support. The wives had to provide for the children and also lead the search for their husbands, visit them in prison afterward, and endure the extreme violence perpetrated within the penitentiaries against the prisoners' families, as well as suffer from the long-term effects of this persecution.

The relationship between the company and the armed forces in this process of repressing workers became apparent in different ways in the Ford Motor Argentina case. For one thing, military personnel were constantly present on factory premises, as other employees confirmed. Daniel Hagelin, who worked at the factory during the dictatorship, stated, for example:

> There was a strong military presence on the premises, in fact, the sports area, which included the football ground, tennis courts, barbecue area, and workers' changing rooms, was turned into a military barracks; this section was off-limits to workers. But, in addition to that, the plant cafeteria had a specific time in which it only opened for the members of the military posted there; there were even young men doing military service in the factory, as if it were just another unit. I can't say there was a regiment, but there were more than 100 people posted there, there was at least a military company in the factory, and they weren't exactly manufacturing cars. (...) They weren't providing security in the installations, the company itself took care of that; their task was specifically repression. The military acted at the request of management, and the one calling the shots there was Galarraga, the institutional relations manager. We can't say that the military gave orders to the workers, but they were there in case any wage demands or other forms of trade union complaints came up. The company's management was pro-military. The situation in the internal commission hit by the coup was notorious: months before the government of Isabel [Martínez de Perón] collapsed, they had an argument with Galarraga, who told them verbatim: "I'm not arguing with you people anymore; from now on take it up with

Camps." No one knew who this Camps guy was; after the coup he became chief of police of the province of Buenos Aires, and was responsible for the disappearance of two members of the internal commission.[14]

But aside from the connections between the armed forces and the company and the general provision of infrastructure, fuel, food, and support, there were many concrete ways the company leadership was directly involved in the human rights violations. First, most of the kidnappings took place within the plant in broad daylight and in the presence of Ford personnel. In some cases, such as Pedro Troiani's, workers were explicitly instructed to stay at their workstations until the armed forces came for them. In most cases, they were seized by military personnel in front of their whole work sections. The company's top personnel were aware of these actions and even planned meticulously for them, having their replacements standing ready so that the factory never stopped working. Among those detained on factory premises was Juan Carlos Conti, a SMATA delegate who had worked for Ford since 1965 and was kidnapped on April 14, 1976. After his kidnapping, as happened with most of the kidnapped workers, the company accused him of "walking out on the job." When his wife responded by explaining what had happened, which the company necessarily had to know about, he was fired.[15]

A second link between the company and the armed forces was that the company supplied F100 pickup trucks to the military for carrying out many of the kidnappings. The aforementioned Conti, for example, was abducted with his hands bound together with wire in one of these trucks. So not only were workers kidnapped in broad daylight and in front of their fellow workers, but they were also transported in the company's vehicles. Third, numerous testimonies indicate that, in addition to supporting the armed forces, the company asked the military to kidnap individual workers and trade-union delegates. Arcelia Luján Ortiz de Portillo, one victim's wife, testified that a military officer named Molinari who was responsible for the kidnappings had, during a meeting with her, "opened a drawer and

[14] Quoted in F. Domínguez and A. Sayus, "La sombra de Campo de Mayo," section "Testimonies," sub-section "Repression. The factory of fear," available at www.desaparecidos.org/nuncamas/web/investig/saydom/lasombra/lasombra.htm (accessed April 10, 2020).

[15] See the report filed in 1998 by the Federation of Workers of Argentina (Central de Trabajadores Argentinos, CTA) in the trial conducted in a Spanish court by Judge Baltasar Garzón for the forced disappearance of persons during Argentina's last dictatorship.

pulled out a list typed on a sheet of paper with the Ford logo, which he told me had 'all the names that the company gave us of workers they wanted us to kidnap.'"[16] Several testimonies indicate that the company had "marked" the workers who were to be kidnapped using this list but also by providing the workers' photo IDs, so the military could identify them. Additional testimonies, such as that by Jorge Ernesto Berguier, a young man who was doing his military service during the years of the dictatorship, provided a picture of the exchange of favors between the company and the armed forces.[17]

Fourth, the company's participation in the repression was not limited to providing logistical support or requesting the detention of some of its own workers. As in other extreme cases, such as the Acindar steel mill in Villa Constitución, in the province of Santa Fe, the support was highly organized. It has been proven that a military unit operated on factory premises, set up in the sports grounds, particularly in the quincho, or enclosed barbecue area, with the alleged purpose of combating "subversion." This was part of the criminal plan that was proven to have existed in "Causa 13/84," the military junta trial whose oral proceedings started in 1985 in the Federal Court of the city of Buenos Aires. Many of the workers were detained and tortured in the quincho, and then they were brought either to the Tigre First Police Station or to the Ingeniero Maschwitz police station in the province of Buenos Aires.

Fifth, Ford personnel participated in the interrogations and torture of the kidnapped delegates to extract information regarding trade-union activities in the factory. One such interrogation was that of detainee Francisco Guillermo Perrotta, who was not a factory worker but an administrative employee. This category of employees was not represented by a union until the mid-1970s. As an employee in the cost, material, and inventory analysis division, Perrotta had access to key information about

[16] Request for preliminary statements in the case "Molinari, Antonio, personal Ford s. privación ilegal de la libertad," brought by Troiani with the legal counsel of Tomás Ojea Quintana. The statement by Arcelia Luján Ortiz de Portillo appears on folio 44 of the case file. Numerous additional testimonies are included, such as that of Elisa Josefa Charlin, the wife of another kidnapping victim who met with Molinari, "who had a list with approximately twenty or thirty typewritten names. I remember the paper had the Ford logo on it." Molinari made it clear then that "'this is the list they gave me,' putting his hand on the list mentioned above" (465–66).

[17] Testimony by Berguier, given on August 25, 2005, on folio 712 of the case "Molinari, Antonio, personal Ford s. privación ilegal de la libertad."

the factory's internal matters. Perrotta's interrogators hid their identity from him by putting a hood over his head while they tortured him with an electric prod. Nevertheless, they mentioned details and names that only very well-informed employees of the firm could know, and, moreover, Perrotta was able to identify the voice of the factory's security chief, Héctor Francisco Sibilla, among them. Sibilla was a member of the armed forces, and on July 26, 1978, after the workers had been kidnapped, he was promoted to the rank of lieutenant colonel. After his time in the company, he was hired to work in security at the US embassy, a position he held until 2004.[18]

These elements show a clear pattern of cooperation between the company and the armed forces. In sum, they included company permission for the military to operate on its private property and direct company involvement in determining the targets, thus providing crucial infrastructure for the military to carry out the kidnappings, top company officials' direct participation in some cases, and authorizing the military to use a sector of the company's premises to hold and torture workers who were later transported off company grounds with the permission of the armed guards at the company gates.

The Evolution of the Company During the Dictatorship (1976–1983)

Ford Motor Argentina had been a prominent company in the country since the 1960s, but it became the second largest firm in the country in terms of sales during the dictatorship, particularly between 1979 and 1980. It was also the top-selling foreign corporation in Argentina, accounting for the 3.2 percent and the 3.6 percent, respectively, of sales in the 200 bestselling companies in Argentina. Ford had never reached these positions before, and it never did again afterward. It is also particularly significant that this took place in 1979 and 1980, when the financial sector was becoming more important in the economy and the industrial sector was experiencing stagnation at levels similar to those of 1974. The automobile industry was no exception within the industrial sector. On the contrary,

[18] Alejandra Dandan, "Ford Falcon modelo 76," Página/12, Buenos Aires, February 26, 2006. One of the lines of investigation followed by the workers and their legal representatives is the relationship between the Argentine branch and the parent company, with the aim of determining the latter's degree of knowledge and participation in the repression.

Table 8.2 Participation of Ford Motor Argentina in the top 200 companies in terms of sales and participation within the top foreign corporations in Argentina, 1975–1985 (position number and percentages)

	1975	*1976*	*1977*	*1978*	*1979*	*1980*	*1981*	*1982*	*1983*	*1984*	*1985*
% of the sales of the top 200 companies	1.6	1.6	2.0	2.3	3.2	3.6	2.8	2.0	2.0	1.6	1.1
Position among the 200 bestselling companies	9	10	8	8	2	2	6	10	10	10	17
Position among the foreign companies within the 200 top companies	2	2	2	4	1	1	3	3	4	3	7

Source: Eduardo Basualdo, technical report submitted as evidence during Ford trial, November 2006, based on the Área de Economía y Tecnología of FLACSO database

major foreign firms like General Motors had left the country in 1978 when many foreign companies decided to leave or sell to national companies, as Peugeot and Fiat did.[19] In these critical years for industrial production in Argentina, Ford Motor Argentina was among the subsidiaries with the highest profitability in the world (see Table 8.2).

Another key variable for understanding the evolution of Ford Motor Argentina during this period was the growth in its level of external indebtedness, which was crucial to increasing its profits by means of financial valorization.

As the Table 8.3 shows, Ford occupied the 44th place in the list of private companies with external debt, and the fourth place within foreign companies in the country, with an external debt of 80.4 million dollars in 1983.

In sum, Ford Motor Argentina's extremely favorable financial performance during the military dictatorship, even at a time of aggregated deindustrialization, can be explained in connection with three main processes or factors. First, the financial valorization of assets obtained through the

[19] Eduardo Basualdo, technical report submitted as evidence during Ford trial, November 2006.

Table 8.3 External debt of Ford Motor Argentina 1983 and its place within the ranking of top companies of Argentina and within the top industrial foreign companies in Argentina, 1983 (in thousands of dollars)

		External debt in 1983			
Position in ranking of top companies in Argentina	*Companies*	*Capital*	*Interests*	*Total*	*Kind of company*
30	Swift Armour	79,102	35,645	114,747	ET
31	IBM	100,765	7748	108,513	ET
35	Mercedes-Benz	91,881	241	92,122	ET
44	Ford Motor	71,071	9349	80,420	CE
48	Deere y Co. Suc.	67,133	1693	68,826	ET
54	Macrosa	47,744	13,231	60,975	ET
61	Industrias Pirelli	49,126	6948	56,074	CE
62	Esso Argentina	47,320	7188	54,508	CE
75	Pirelli Platense	31,495	14,860	46,355	CE
76	Renault Argentina	43,580	2668	46,248	CE
79	Indupa	34,560	10,832	45,392	CE
82	Petrosur	34,616	8938	43,554	ET
83	Volkswagen Argentina	42,422	420	42,842	ET
85	Hughes Tool Co.	32.671	9736	42,407	ET
91	Ducilo	37,833	774	38,607	ET

Source: Eduardo Basualdo, technical report submitted as evidence during Ford trial, November 2006, based on the Área de Economía y Tecnología of FLACSO database

Note: ET: Foreign companies with less than six subsidiaries in the country. CE: Foreign conglomerates with more than six subsidiaries in the country

process of external indebtedness and through financial companies controlled by Ford allowed the company to earn high profits through financial activities. Second, its level of production in its specific industrial activity, automobile manufacturing, boosted its performance. It was able to increase its production because its market grew on account of the elimination of some of its competitors, such as General Motors, and the existence of a "captive market" connected to the military-controlled state's demand for vehicles. Mercedes-Benz also served this demand, producing other types of vehicles, such as trucks, for the dictatorship. Third, the dictatorship brought about profound changes in labor relations and trade-union rights, activities, and liberties. In the repressive atmosphere described earlier, with severe restrictions on or the elimination of trade-union activity on the shop floor and beyond, workers had to labor more intensively and longer each workday as their wages declined and their working conditions worsened considerably.

To contextualize the extremely favorable evolution of Ford Motor Argentina during the dictatorship, it is useful to take public statements into account, such as the one the company's president, Juan María Courard, made in an interview with *The New York Times* in February 1976. At that time, shortly before the military coup, he argued that "the terrorists are not only the guerrilla members in the mountains or the streets. They are also at the assembly line, threatening workers and telling them how they have to produce every day."[20] At the end of the article, the executive expressed his belief that ensuring productivity on the shop floor required "the success of the current efforts by the armed forces."

Far from changing these views, Courard continued to express support for the armed forces even after they engaged in mass human rights violations. One example is the public statement he made at an event on May 13, 1980, to announce the construction of a new truck manufacturing plant on the premises of Ford Motor Argentina in the presence of Minister of Economy José Alfredo Martínez de Hoz, State Secretary of Industrial Development Lic. Alberto Luis Grimoldi, Chief of the Federal Police General Dr. Juan Bautista Sasiaiñ, Director of Military Institutes General D. Cristiano Nicolaides, and various representatives of the military junta, among other authorities of the dictatorship, officers of the Catholic Church, and representatives of the business community. Courard remarked that it had become clear beginning in March 1976 that it was necessary to change the system, as well as the state's philosophy and the mentality of the people:

> In our case, it was necessary to make a business decision, and with our actions and procedures we showed what that decision was. Ford Motor Argentina agreed that the changes had to be made. And when the changes came and they affected the firm, we adapted and worked as hard as possible

[20] Interview by Juan María Courard in *The New York Times*, on February 22, 1976, fs. 1910/2 of Trial 2358, quoted in Tribunal Oral en lo Criminal Federal N° 1 of San Martín, integrated by Dr. Osvaldo Alberto Facciano, Mario Jorge Gambacorta, and Eugenio J. Martínez Ferrero, and the Chamber Secretary Déborah E. Damonte, Basis for the verdict for trials N° 2855 and 2358, March 15, 2019, p. 201.

> to make the most out of this new situation, in favor of the company and of the source of employment for thousands of people. In sum, in favor of the country. Ford Motor Argentina believed in the *Proceso de Reorganización Nacional* because it saw in it a vehicle for the country to find its true path, within the regional and the international framework. The change that was under way demanded us to do the things we do, better and better.[21] (...) This new truck manufacturing plant means that we put a lot of faith in this country, as a company. Faith in the country because we saw it shaking, and then we saw it recovering from chaos towards a new way of life. And we saw that with the help of the healthy population, the governing team first put the country on its feet—not only economically, which was almost a miracle, but also morally, which was even more difficult, and then, it put it into motion. There are many reasons to feel proud.[22]

The speech also included references to people deemed a positive influence because they build, and those deemed a negative influence as they have "no homeland, no God," and "work to divide," "who have been so difficult to eradicate."[23] In other words, utilizing a wide variety of sources, one can document the role Ford Motor Argentina's leadership played in the repression of workers, as well as an economic and ideological alliance between the company's top officials and the armed forces. In fact, the Ford Falcon, the Ford model manufactured since 1963, went from being the most popular to a notorious model when the security forces, both regular and irregular, began to use it most often for kidnappings and acts of violence from the mid-1970s. A disarmed Ford Falcon is exhibited today at the former ESMA (The Navy School of Mechanics), which was the largest extermination camp in Argentina, to represent the confluence of business and the armed forces during the 1976–1983 dictatorship.

[21] The military junta named the regime that started on March 24, 1976 "Proceso de Reorganización Nacional" (National Reorganization Process).

[22] Document "Información de Prensa," appendix in "FORD la idea que hizo historia," publication included as evidence in box 3, document number 212 of trial 2358, quoted in the statement made at the criminal trial by the legal team of the Secretary of Human Rights of the Province of Buenos Aires headed by Maximiliano Chichizola, Buenos Aires, November 12–13, 2018 (translation mine).

[23] Statement by the SHR of PBA, p. 11 (translation mine).

Prosecuting Human Rights Violations Perpetrated Against Ford Workers

In Argentina, the history of the legal actions brought by workers is lengthy and began as soon as the dictatorship came to an end. After the return to democracy, Pedro Troiani, a worker who was a victim of repression, sued Ford Motor Argentina for wrongful dismissal because his family had received a telegram a few days after his kidnapping notifying them that he had been fired for walking off the job, like the other people abducted. The Supreme Court of Justice rejected the lawsuit in the 1980s, arguing that the statute of limitations had expired. In other words, the court held that Troiani should have sued Ford during the military dictatorship. Despite the fact that legal action appeared to be impossible because of the Full Stop and Due Obedience Acts, passed during President Raúl Alfonsín's administration (1983–1989), other trade-union delegates also sued Ford for wrongful dismissal. These other cases, however, were successful, as the Supreme Court modified its judgment by applying interruptions to the statute of limitations. Although the lawsuits involved labor claims, they were underpinned by the conviction that Ford was responsible for abductions and torture. Judge Juan Carlos Morando's concluding argument in Conti's labor trial made this clear:

> Dr. Capón Filas, with his vote, has shown that the defendant corporation acted, in the emergency, with exemplary bad faith. What is more, in the course of the proceedings, it attempted to assume the inadmissible position of a disinterested third party with regard to the circumstances in which the claimant and the other delegates were detained, an episode in which, as these proceedings have established to a moral certainty, its officials acted as instigators.[24]

After the Full Stop and Due Obedience laws, known as the "impunity laws," were ruled unconstitutional in 2001, it once again became possible to bring charges against the perpetrators of the crimes, and Pedro Troiani became a plaintiff in a criminal case brought before the courts in November 2002.[25] From the start, the main aim of the case put forward by Troiani,

[24] See the court ruling in "Conti, Juan Carlos c. Ford Motor Argentina SA s. cobro de pesos," court file 26,091.

[25] Regarding the unconstitutionality, see Juzgado Federal en lo Criminal y Correccional no. 4, "Simón, J. H. y otros," resolution of March 6, 2001.

accompanied by the rest of the trade-union delegates, aimed mainly at underlining the role Ford managers played in the crimes committed. The case, labeled "Müller, Pedro and Others Concerning Illegal Arrest" (known as the "Ford" case, N. 2855), sought to determine what, exactly, the military and civilians had been responsible for in the kidnapping, torture, and illegal captivity of twenty-four former Ford workers—some of them also trade-union representatives—between 1976 and 1977. The judicial process started in 2002, deriving from the investigation focused on military chief Santiago Omar Riveros, who was in charge of the defense zone "Campo de Mayo," where the Ford plant is located, among other responsibilities, between 1976 and 1978. Throughout these years, when the victims and their families constantly demanded justice in every forum and from every authority they could find, the "Ford" case was tried in three different departments of the federal justice system and took over eleven years to be brought to trial. In 2014, the case was assigned to Federal Oral Court N.1 in San Martin (in the province of Buenos Aires), and the trial finally began on December 19, 2017.[26]

Meanwhile, in 2004, a U.S. law firm represented by Paul Hoffman agreed to sue Ford Motor Company under the Alien Tort Claims Act (ATCA), which enables foreigners to seek remedies in the U.S. courts for violations committed by individuals and companies abroad. This firm worked with the Argentine lawyers privately prosecuting the case, and together they prepared a lawsuit on behalf of the trade-union delegates, filing it in a California court of first instance. This filing raised expectations, but these were dashed when the U.S. lawyers decided to withdraw shortly before the company was notified of the lawsuit. Their decision had been prompted by a U.S. Supreme Court ruling that seriously limited future ATCA cases. From Buenos Aires, the workers insisted on moving forward with the lawsuit, but the American lawyers' decision was final; this attempt to sue ended with no results.[27]

When the oral proceedings of the criminal trial finally started in Buenos Aires in December 2017, there were three different plaintiffs along with the public prosecution (Ministerio Público Fiscal): the Human Rights Secretariat at the national level, that of the Province of Buenos Aires, and the victims' lawyers, Dr. Tomás Ojea Quintana and Dr. Elizabeth Gomez

[26] Basualdo, Ojea Quintana and Varsky, "The Cases of Ford and Mercedes-Benz Argentina" 163–64.

[27] Ibid., 165.

Alcorta. In addition to Riveros, four civilians had been identified as responsible in this trial, but only two stood trial. The president of the company, Juan María Courard, died before the trial began, while Guillermo Galarraga, the manager of the Labor Relations department, passed away as the case was being prepared. The two top executives of Ford Motor Argentina who stood trial, therefore, were Pedro Müller, the production manager, who filled in for the president in Courard's absence, and Héctor Francisco Jesús Sibilla, who was the Chief of Security and Protection at the time.

The oral proceedings included the testimonies of the surviving victims, their spouses, some of their children, and other relatives, as well as of the expert witnesses including both authors of this chapter, Eduardo and Victoria Basualdo, Federico Vocos, a sociologist and Silvio Feldman, an expert in labor relations. The defense lawyers called witnesses as well. Besides the testimonies, the trial also included visual inspections of the two police headquarters where the workers had been detained and the Ford Motor Argentina plant; the space used as a detention and torture center for some of the kidnapped workers within the premises was inspected particularly carefully. Defense lawyers did not dispute the facts concerning the human rights violations but argued that the armed forces alone had been responsible for them. Disputing different parts of the evidence presented against the two accused business executives, they denied that their clients had been involved in any of these crimes. Moreover, Ford Motor Argentina made no official statement concerning this trial, about which it had only issued a press release when directly addressed by The Business & Human Rights Resource Centre in 2007.[28]

After a year of hearings, forty-two years after the events and sixteen years after the legal proceedings had begun, the verdict was announced on December 11, 2018, at a venue packed with victims, their families, important political leaders, and trade unionists, as well as a massive crowd waiting in an adjacent room and on the street. The three presiding judges found the three defendants guilty, sentencing them to various terms in prison. Santiago Omar Riveros received 15 years of effective prison time (not house arrest), Sibilla 12, and Müller 10. The judges considered Sibilla and Müller "necessary participants" in the illegal detentions and tortures,

[28] https://www.business-humanrights.org/en/ford-statement-regarding-legal-claims-brought-by-former-employees-who-say-they-were-kidnapped-and-tortured-on-ford-argentina-premises-during-the-1976-83-military-dictatorship%22/1%22c36643%22

a fact that generated immediate repercussions around the world and silence in significant segments of the Argentine media.

The judges released their reasoning behind this landmark decision on March 15, 2019. First, the judges explained that these acts qualified as crimes against humanity. They invoked rulings by the Argentine Supreme Court and also referred to the verdicts of several international tribunals to clearly affirm that civilians could, indeed, be perpetrators of such crimes. Further, they carefully analyzed the ways that Ford Motor Argentina officials had gotten involved in the repression. The judges considered that Ford authorities and top officials had made "a specific contribution of information about the workers to be kidnapped."[29] On the one hand, they had given the military forces the personnel files, and, on the other hand, it was proven that the information Ford top officials had handed over to the military in order for it to carry out the kidnappings took the form of lists of people to be detained.

Second, the judges also held that company officials' logistical assistance to the armed forces for carrying out the abductions had been proven with the same degree of certainty. Such help included material resources like vehicles, food, and gasoline, among other things. The judges also explained that the evidence showed that Ford authorities and top executives had contributed to the organizational structure and the territorial infrastructure on behalf of the military in charge of the abductions. In particular, they underlined that after March 24, 1976, a sector of the recreational facilities "became a clandestine detention center with the particularity of being located within private property. Workers detained and kidnapped from their workplaces were brought to these facilities, where they were kept in the condition of having 'disappeared.'"[30]

Third, in regard to the motives behind these criminal actions, the judges ruled that the elimination of the trade-union delegates commission ("comisiones internas") of the trade-union organizations within the factories, "which were symbols of the working-class strength and resistance to the demands of higher efficiency, was a common goal between business leaders and the military who seized the government." Furthermore, they

[29] Criminal Federal Court N° 1 of San Martín, integrated by Dr. Osvaldo Alberto Facciano, Mario Jorge Gambacorta, and Eugenio J. Martínez Ferrero, and the Chamber Secretary Déborah E. Damonte, Basis for the verdict for trials N° 2855 and 2358, March 15th, 2019, p. 201.

[30] Tribunal Oral en lo Criminal Federal N° 1, Basis for the verdict, p. 218.

considered that the dynamic of the labor market was yet another dimension of the project of social and economic transformation put into motion by both the military and a sector of the business leadership. This highlights the common denominator among the twenty-four victims, which was "their labor relation with Ford." The judges added that there was "a strategic relationship between the military and a sector of the business leadership" because the two groups had interests in common, namely, to ensure a "normalization" of labor relations and the profound transformation of the economic and social structure they sought to promote.[31]

Fourth, the judges found particular types of evidence admissible, and it is important to pay attention to what these were. They granted central importance to the testimonies of the victims and their families, taking into account that the crimes had been perpetrated in a clandestine manner involving the systematic destruction of proof and documentation. They also cited a wide array of sources in the decision, including the oral presentations, written reports, and conclusions provided by the expert or "context" witnesses, describing them as "clarifying and conclusive." In addition, the judges particularly valued the book *Responsabilidad empresarial en delitos de lesa humanidad. Represión a trabajadores durante el terrorismo de estado* (Corporate Responsibility in Crimes Against Humanity. Repression of Workers Under State Terrorism), and also cited a variety of company-produced sources, such as the minutes of the board of directors meetings, publications and public statements, and interviews conducted with various business leaders, among many others.

In the verdict, the court concluded that the two top business officials were "responsible for complicity by means of necessary participation." This implies that while the judges considered that responsibility for the crimes relied on public officials—in this case the military chief Santiago Omar Riveros—they also found that Müller and Sibilla were functionally co-authors. That is, Müller and Sibilla were not direct perpetrators of the crimes, but they made effective contributions to the perpetrators who had control over the criminal act. The crimes against the twenty-four employees were illegitimately holding them captive, aggravated by violence and threats, and in fifteen cases extending this captivity for over a month. In all cases, there was also torture aggravated by political persecution. The judges underlined that these crimes had been possible thanks to the use of state resources in the hands of the military, but also thanks to the use of

[31] Ibid., p. 247.

the factory's resources and facilities, that is, the everyday workplace of the victims, who considered it a vital part of their development, their lives, and the lives of their family members. It was through the factory that Ford business officials "contributed to the repressive apparatus of the state, providing information, means and facilities for the execution of crimes against humanity."[32]

In the yearly mass demonstration in Buenos Aires in remembrance of the victims of the dictatorship and to demand Memory, Truth, and Justice, the central speech at this event highlighted the need for courts to find ways to prosecute not only individuals but corporations themselves and called for the immediate activation of the Congressional Commission to Investigate Economic and Financial Crimes during the dictatorship.[33] The congress had approved this commission in 2015, but it had never been convened. In this context, the basis for the verdict provides not only a solid foundation for the Ford case, which, needless to say, concerns one of the most prominent multinational corporations in contemporary history. It is also a reminder of the importance of trade-union organization and activity in the defense of labor rights, and it paves the way for future trials and for other truth-and-justice initiatives that address business involvement in human rights violations.

Conclusion

In sum, the case of Ford Motor Argentina constitutes an example of a company and its top leadership becoming extremely involved in the repression of its workers. In this case, the company's motive was strongly connected to a drastic change in labor relations within the plant and beyond, a severe loss of labor rights and possibilities for effective protest and organization among workers, and also to an extraordinary increase in the company's profits. Judicial progress in the "Ford" case was only possible thanks to a collective long-term effort of many sectors and actors. In many other cases, the obstacles and shortcomings of the judicial system in analyzing these issues become apparent. This case, therefore, shows that progress could be made in the judicial system by mobilizing and organizing the

[32] Ibid., p. 364.

[33] "Marcha del 24 de marzo: el documento completo leído en la Plaza de Mayo," *Página/12*, March 24, 2019.

victims within the context of other social movements, such as trade-union and human rights organizations, as well as by conducting academic research and providing legal advice and opportunities for strategic litigation. But even the major achievement of obtaining guilty verdicts in this case only implied the prosecution of individual responsibilities, while corporate involvement and participation remained out of reach. Therefore, this case is particularly relevant for illustrating in depth the complex alliance between a business sector and the armed forces in the 1976–1983 dictatorship in Argentina and for understanding how the expansion of labor repression increased the company's profits. At the same time, it also serves as a reminder that the company's very centrality and power in the economy seems key to understanding the obstacles that, for decades, prevented the perpetrators of these criminal acts from being brought to justice.

References

Archival Sources

Argentina, Ministerio de Justicia y Derechos Humanos. Secretaría de Derechos Humanos de la Nación. Archivo Nacional de la Memoria.

Bibliography

Abdala, Omar. "Rupturas y continuidades en las formas de acción y resistencia de los trabajadores. El caso Ford Motor Argentina. 1970–1985." BA thesis in Sociology, Instituto de Altos Estudios Sociales, Universidad Nacional de San Martín, December, 2015.

Área de Economía y Tecnología de la Facultad Latinoamericana de Ciencias Sociales, Centro de Estudios Legales y Sociales, Programa Verdad y Justicia and Secretaría de Derechos Humanos del Ministerio de Justicia y Derechos Humanos de la Nación, coord. *Responsabilidad empresarial en delitos de lesa humanidad. Represión a trabajadores durante el terrorismo de Estado.* Buenos Aires: Infojus, 2015.

Basualdo, Eduardo. *Estudios de historia económica argentina. Desde mediados del siglo XX hasta la actualidad.* Buenos Aires: Siglo Veintiuno Editores, 2006.

Basualdo, Eduardo, and Juan Santarcángelo, Andrés Wainer, Cintia Russo, and Guido Perrone. *El Banco de la Nación Argentina y la dictadura. El impacto de las transformaciones económicas y financieras en la política crediticia, 1976–1983.* Buenos Aires: Editorial Siglo Veintiuno, 2016.

Basualdo, Victoria. "Complicidad patronal-militar en la última dictadura argentina: Los casos de Acindar, Astarsa, Dálmine Siderca, Ford, Ledesma y Mercedes-Benz." *Revista Engranajes*, no. 5 (Buenos Aires: Federación de Trabajadores de la Industria y Afines, 2006).

Basualdo, Victoria. "Contributions for the Analysis of the Participation of Sectors of the Trade-union Leadership in Labor Repression in Argentina during the 1970s." In *The Economic Accomplices of the Argentine Dictatorship: Outstanding Debt*, edited by Horacio Verbitsky and Juan Pablo Bohoslavsy. Cambridge: Cambridge University Press, 2015.

Basualdo, Victoria, and Tomás Ojea Quintana and Carolina Varsky, "The Cases of Ford and Mercedes-Benz Argentina." In *The Economic Accomplices of the Argentine Dictatorship: Outstanding Debts*, edited by Horacio Verbitsky and Juan Pablo Bohoslavsy. Cambridge: Cambridge University Press, 2015.

Colom, Yolanda, and Alicia Salomone, "Las coordinadoras inter-fabriles de Capital Federal y Gran Buenos Aires. 1975–1976," *Razón y Revolución*, no. 4 (1998).

Dandan, Alejandra. "Ford Falcon modelo 76." *Página/12*, February 26, 2006.

Domínguez, Fabián, and Alfredo Sayus. "La sombra del campo de mayo." *Proyecto Desaparecidos*, accessed April 10, 2020. http://www.desaparecidos.org/nuncamas/web/investig/saydom/lasombra/lasombra.htm

Ianni, Valeria. "La acción sindical en el marco de las negociaciones colectivas en Ford Motor Argentina durante la segunda etapa de la industrialización por sustitución de importaciones." Paper presented at the 10th National Congress of Labor Studies, Asociación Argentina de Especialistas en Estudios del Trabajo, Facultad de Ciencias Económicas, Universidad de Buenos Aires, Buenos Aires, June 2011.

"Marcha del 24 de marzo: el documento completo leído en la Plaza de Mayo." *Página/12*, March 24, 2019.

Lascano Warnes, María Florencia. "Cambios y continuidades en la historia de los trabajadores industriales argentinos (1973–1983). Una aproximación a través del caso de Ford Motor Argentina." MA thesis, Universidad Nacional de General Sarmiento, Argentina, 2012.

Löbbe, Héctor. "Las 'desmemorias' de José Rodríguez." *El Aromo*, no. 15 (2004).

Löbbe, Héctor. *La guerrilla fabril. Clase obrera e izquierda en la Coordinadora de Zona Norte del Gran Buenos Aires (1975 – 1976)*. Buenos Aires: Ediciones Razón y Revolución, 2006.

Sourrouille, Juan. *El complejo automotor en la Argentina: transnacionales en América Latina*. Mexico City: Instituto Latinoamericano de Estudios Transnacionales, 1980.

CHAPTER 9

A Typology of the Collaboration Between Multinational Corporations, Home Governments, and Authoritarian Regimes: Evidence from German Investors in Argentina

Meta Stephan

Introduction

Between 1976 and 1983 Argentina was ruled by one of the most notorious dictatorships in the Western Hemisphere. This regime developed an agenda that coincided in several respects with the interests of major domestic and foreign corporations alike. The nature of the regime, its alliance with the Western bloc, and the policies affecting these firms make this country a good case for analyzing the strategies large firms employed in their relationships with authoritarian regimes during the Cold War. In this chapter, I discuss the collaboration between multinational subsidiaries and authoritarian regimes and suggest a typology of analytical categories for

M. Stephan (✉)
Humboldt University, Berlin, Germany

V. Basualdo et al. (eds.), *Big Business and Dictatorships in Latin America*, Palgrave Studies in Latin American Heterodox Economics, https://doi.org/10.1007/978-3-030-43925-5_9

studying that collaboration. Using the case of the German multinationals Siemens and Daimler-Benz in Argentina during the military regime, I suggest that they pursued the following four types of strategies in their collaboration with the regime:

(a) Doing business directly with the military regime
(b) Promoting acceptance of the military regime in their home country
(c) Promoting the home country's support of the military regime
(d) Directly collaborating with the military regime's repressive apparatus

The analysis begins with a brief overview of the events of the 1970s. Next, I set the scene of German corporate involvement in Argentina. By classifying collaboration into four types, I embark on a deeper analysis of the relations between German companies, the government of the German Federal Republic, and the Argentine military dictatorship. Here, I will not use the term "collaboration" in the sense of the German word *Kollaboration*, with its negative connotation in the dichotomy of "collaboration and resistance" under Nazi occupation. Breaking out of this oversimplified dichotomy allows for a more nuanced exploration of the variety of complex and subtle forms that "collaboration" can take. Given that the subsidiaries were dependent on the parent companies, as well as on German government support, it is important to examine Germany's economic relations with Argentina and economic policy instruments, such as federal insurance, that are used to promote business relationships. Companies, and multinationals, in particular, are not just economic actors. They are also political actors trying to influence the terms of trade they depend on. In the case of multinationals, companies have to navigate the economic and political situations of both the country in which the headquarters is located and the country housing their operations. The multinationals are limited by macropolitical conditions, but they also have a certain freedom of action.

The relationship between German multinationals and the Argentine dictatorship has already been studied by journalists, human rights activists, and lawyers.[1] However, a number of sources that can provide a good

[1] See, for example, Wolfgang Kaleck, *Kampf gegen die Straflosigkeit. Argentiniens Militärs vor Gericht* (Berlin: Klaus Wagenbach, 2010); Gaby Weber, *Die Verschwundenen von Mercedes-Benz* (Hamburg: Assoziation A, 2001); Rechtsweg ausgeschlossen? Mercedes-Benz Argentina – ein Präzedenzfall produced by Gaby Weber, aired July 22, 2014, on

historical account of these events have not been studied in detail; they also serve as the basis of this research. This chapter is based primarily on three different kinds of sources: documents from corporate archives,[2] state archives, and archives of social movements and NGOs.[3]

A secondary focus of this research is the remarkable shift in international awareness and attention to collaboration with authoritarian regimes that occurred beginning in the 1970s. At that time, there was a substantial increase in activism under the banner of human rights campaigns. This was also a time when business negotiations and companies in Germany started to be scrutinized for social injustice and human rights concerns.[4] I find that this new focus on human rights triggered changes in the practices of German businessmen, diplomats, and politicians in the ensuing years.

Siemens and Daimler-Benz were among the largest German companies operating in Argentina, so they had a significant economic and political position as well as access to policymakers.[5] The subsidiaries of both companies were important employers in Argentina and dominated parts of their

Deutschlandfunk; Koalition gegen Straflosigkeit, ed., *Menschenrechte und Außenpolitik. Bundesrepublik Deutschland – Argentinien 1976–1983* (Bad Honnef: Horlemann Verlag, 2006).

[2] The records regarding the business activities of Daimler-Benz in Argentina at the Daimler Archive are currently not available for scholars. Therefore, the report of Christian Tomuschat, *Mercedes-Benz Argentina zur Zeit der Militärdiktatur (1976–1983)* (Berlin: Humboldt Universität, Juristische Fakultät, Institut für Völker- und Europarecht, 2003), is of particular interest for the research and for gaining access to sources about the activities of Daimler-Benz in Argentina during the last Argentine dictatorship. Nevertheless, it is important to review this report critically, first, because it was commissioned by Daimler-Benz itself. Tomuschat denies any responsibility on the part of the company in the cases of Mercedes Benz Argentina workers who disappeared, while the majority of journalists, human rights activists, and experts on the topic believe that Mercedes Benz Argentina and Daimler-Benz (Germany) definitely played a role in the disappearances. Another point of criticism is the author's selection of sources. The main sources used are minutes of meetings of the board of directors while the witness testimonies of ex-workers, arrested workers, and relatives of those who disappeared are almost never included.

[3] The chapter is largely based on archival sources in the German Federal Archives (BArch), the Archive of the German Federal Foreign Office, and the Political Archive (PA AA); other sources are from the Siemens Corporate Archives (SA), the Forschungs und Dokumentationszentrum Chile-Lateinamerika e.V. (FDCL), and the Archive of the "Koalition gegen die Straflosigkeit" at ECCHR. The focus of my research is on the German perspective, so I used only sources from German archives for this chapter.

[4] Claudia Olejniczak, "Dritte Welt Bewegung," in *Die sozialen Bewegungen in Deutschland seit 1945*, ed. Roland Roth and Dieter Rucht (Frankfurt a. M.: Campus Verlag, 2008), 319–346.

[5] See the compilation by Hervé Joly, "Ende des Familienkapitalismus? Das Überleben der Unternehmerfamilien in den deutschen Wirtschaftseliten des 20. Jahrhunderts," in *Die*

business branches. Mercedes-Benz Argentina ("Mercedes") was founded in 1951, during the first Peronist government, and was the first subsidiary from Germany. Between 1952 and 1955 Argentina was the most important country for Daimler-Benz's exports. Daimler gained permanent access to the Argentine market in the 1950s by establishing assembly and production facilities there.[6] Until the 1970s it was the only important German investor in the Argentine automobile sector.[7] Its primary business was the construction of trucks, omnibuses, and engines. In the omnibus sector, Mercedes dominated the market in the late 1970s with an almost 100% market share.[8] Another important branch was the production of the UNIMOG (a four-wheel drive vehicle used for military purposes), which was sold to the Argentine military especially and on the international market to Cuba and Chile.[9] Mercedes built houses where selected members of the company could live with their families, and it established a learning center in the 1960s that provided training opportunities.[10]

Siemens started operations in Argentina in 1857 and opened its first Argentine branch office in 1908. The firm was involved in different industries, such as construction, medical and military equipment, power generation, and electrical engineering. For decades Siemens maintained a 40% market share in the Argentine telephone sector.[11] In addition, Siemens built the first Latin American nuclear power station in Argentina between 1968 and 1974.[12]

deutsche Wirtschaftselite im 20. Jahrhundert. Kontinuität und Mentalität, ed. Volker R. Berghahn and Stefan Unger (Essen: Klartext Verlag, 2003), 75–91.

[6] Hans Pohl, "Exporte und Auslandsaktivitäten der Daimler-Benz AG in den Jahren des Wiederaufbaus (1945–1955)," in *Wirtschaft, Unternehmen, Kreditwesen, soziale Probleme. Ausgewählte Aufsätze.* Teil 1, ed. Pohl (Stuttgart: Franz Steiner Verlag, 2005).

[7] Daimler-Benz Aktiengesellschaft, Memorandum, October 23, 1975 (BArch, B 102/215091).

[8] Tomuschat, *Mercedes-Benz Argentina*, 29.

[9] Florencia Rodriguez, "Estrategias de lucha en industrias dinámicas durante la segunda ISI. Un análisis a partir del estudio de caso de Mercedes Benz Argentina," in *La clase trabajadora Argentina en el siglo xx: Experiencias de lucha y organización*, ed. Victoria Basualdo (Buenos Aires: Atuel, 2011), 125.

[10] Rodriguez, "Estrategias de lucha en industrias dinámicas durante la segunda ISI," 128–30.

[11] Referat W/VI 1, December 9, 1971 (BArch, B 102/149881, Bd. 5).

[12] See articles and documents at the Archive of the German Federal Foreign Office (PA AA, Zwischenarchiv, Bd. 100473) and the German Federal Archives (BArch, B 102/195445).

On the Eve of the Military Coup

On March 24, 1976, a section of the Argentine army staged a coup against President María Estela Martínez de Perón (Isabel). The coup d'état ended the third Peronist government. Prior to this, Juan Domingo Perón had died in July 1974, whereupon his wife and successor as president inherited a politically disordered and economically unstable country. María Estela Martínez de Perón did not have any government experience, and the situation in the country grew steadily worse. The Minister of Social Welfare, José López Rega, gained influence within the government and organized the Triple A (Argentine Anticommunist Alliance), a paramilitary death squad responsible for murdering alleged opponents of the government even before the military came to power.[13] Fights between right- and left-wing Peronists, as well as increasing guerrilla actions and economic instability, were indicative of the country's catastrophic political situation. Siemens and Daimler-Benz complained about inflation, the increase in material costs and wages, and mandatory price limits set by the state.[14] At the same time, major companies became a popular target of guerrilla groups. The companies were considered to be "places of exploitation," and several members of these companies' management were kidnapped.[15]

Altogether, the Argentine subsidiaries of Siemens and Daimler-Benz regarded the economic and political climate during the early 1970s as disruptive. At that time, Siemens Argentina got into a major conflict with the public Argentine telephone company (Empresa Nacional de Telecomunicaciones: ENTel). The state made threats ranging from canceling existing contracts to nationalizing (i.e., "Argentinizing") parts of the company. ENTel accused Siemens of maintaining an excessive profit margin, of presenting incorrect or double invoices, and of obscuring the real costs of its products. Siemens, in turn, denied the accusations and rebuked ENTel for not paying for supplies. In fact, Siemens stated that it had incurred losses in deals with ENTel and that loans already granted to the Argentine telephone company had not been repaid. Overall, Siemens

[13] Sandra Carreras and Barbara Potthast, *Eine Kleine Geschichte Argentiniens* (Berlin: Suhrkamp, 2013), 216.

[14] Furthermore, the Peronist government started an economic program that included protective measures, such as setting sales prices (Daimler-Benz to Hermes-Kreditversicherungs-Aktiengesellschaft, July 17, 1975 [BArch, B 102/215091]).

[15] See, for example, PA AA, Zwischenarchiv, 102019 or PA AA, Zwischenarchiv, 103590.

had invested a great deal in Argentina during the preceding years.[16] Due to the conflict, the Argentine parliament canceled a very profitable telecommunications contract in 1974. This caused Siemens to lose an order worth around DM360 million (about $140 million), forcing it to reduce the number of Argentine employees and to shut down parts of its branch factories.[17]

Shortly before the coup, the situation at Mercedes had become very complex. In October 1975, many Mercedes workers went on strike, denouncing the labor conditions and low wages, among other things. Within the Argentine automobile industry, which was controlled by eight foreign companies, the tradition of labor protests was very strong, and the workers at Mercedes-Benz Argentina were considered to be very well organized. Since the end of the 1960s, conflicts at the plant had steadily increased, peaking during the 1970s. Mercedes workers complained about unhealthy labor conditions, the lack of air-conditioning on the shop floor, increased working speed, mandatory overtime, and the implementation of a productivity bonus system.[18] Dissatisfied, politically active employees were encouraged to leave the firm voluntarily or otherwise were fired in the context of staff cuts. Workers protested with stoppages, sabotage, occupying small parts of the plant for several hours, calling assemblies, and distributing pamphlets.[19]

The conflict-laden situation reached its peak in October 1975 when most of the workers of Mercedes-Benz Argentina went on strike for 22 days. Aside from the aforementioned complaints against the company, another major reason for the strike was that most employees did not consider themselves adequately represented by the "employer-friendly"[20]

[16] Informationen Argumente. Für den oberen und mittleren Führungskreis des Hauses Siemens, Nr. 11/74, November 8, 1974 (BArch, B 102/211542).

[17] Internal letter to the Federal Minister of Economic Affairs, September 15, 1976 (BArch, B 102/312829).

[18] According to witness testimonies of former Mercedes employees, the workers were consistently opposed to any kind of working speed increases or overtime. See, Dirección Nacional del Sistema Argentino de Información Jurídica, *Responsabilidad empresarial en delitos de lesa humanidad. Represión a trabajadores durante el terrorismo de Estado. Tomo I* (Buenos Aires: Ministerio de Justicia y Derechos Humanos de la Nación, 2015), 497.

[19] For more information, see *Responsabilidad empresarial*; Rodriguez, "Estrategias de lucha en industrias dinámicas durante la segunda ISI"; Tomuschat, *Mercedes-Benz Argentina.*; Weber, *Die Verschwundenen von Mercedes-Benz.*

[20] Wolfgang Kaleck, "Die verschwundenen Gewerkschafter von Mercedes-Benz," in *Menschenrechte und Außenpolitik. Bundesrepublik Deutschland – Argentinien 1976–1983*, ed. Koalition gegen Straflosigkeit (Bad Honnef: Horlemann Verlag, 2006), 27.

trade union of mechanics (SMATA). They wanted to vote for their representatives in free elections.[21] They appointed an independent internal labor commission composed of nine elected employee representatives, which was called the "group of the nine."[22] After this cycle of labor protest, the management ultimately fired 117 people, among them the members of the "group of the nine." A memo composed by manager Klaus Oertel shows how Mercedes managers viewed these strikers. He described them as "known activists, extreme elements." Even the German ambassador in Argentina, Jörg Kastl, assumed that the company had specifically laid off the workers who directly opposed SMATA.[23] Moreover, the company and the regional secret police would have kept track of the workers' political orientation since the late 1960s.[24] In the middle of the strike, after the dismissals, production manager Heinrich Metz was kidnapped, probably by a Peronist guerrilla group called Montoneros,[25] or a faction thereof. This was not the first incident of this kind: his predecessor, Herbert Pilz, had been kidnapped the year before.[26] The kidnappers demanded, among other things, that the fired employees be rehired. After Mercedes rehired them, paid the wages they had lost, accepted the freely elected committee as representatives of the workers, and paid a huge

[21] According to an open letter published by the Mercedes strikers in 1975, the working atmosphere was very bad because of the SMATA policies that the company had accepted: "The slogan of the company always was 'the big family of Mercedes-Benz Argentina' and because of bad bosses and bad (union) leaders we end up as a 'broken family'" ("El slogan de la Empresa siempre fue 'La gran familia de Mercedes-Benz Argentina' y por culpa de malos jefes y malos dirigentes terminamos siendo una 'familia desmembrada'" (Open letter "A la excelentisima señora presidente de la nación Argentina y a la opinión pública en general," signed by the workers and employees of Mercedes (Private document collection).

[22] *Responsabilidad empresarial*, 500; Tomuschat, *Mercedes-Benz Argentina*, 39.

[23] "Bekannte Aktivisten, extreme Arbeiter" (Note, October 28, 1975, cited by Tomuschat, *Mercedes-Benz Argentina*, 40). Deutsche Botschaft to Auswärtiges Amt, October 16, 1975 (PA AA, Zwischenarchiv, Bd. 102019).

[24] Rodriguez, "Estrategias de lucha en industrias dinámicas durante la segunda ISI," 131.

[25] Montoneros was one of the Argentine leftist armed guerilla groups that arose during the late 1960s. Its origins lay in the leftist Peronist movement. Montoneros was known for a series of bank robberies, kidnappings, occupations of police stations, and raids on military bases. One of its most notable actions was the kidnapping and assassination of former Argentine dictator and President General Pedro Eugenio Aramburu in 1970.

[26] "Herrliche Menschen," *Der Spiegel*, no. 45 (1975): 109–10; Tomuschat, *Mercedes-Benz Argentina*, 34.

ransom,[27] Metz was released on December 24, 1975. The Ministry of Labor, and especially SMATA, criticized the Mercedes management for cooperating with the "industrial guerrilla" and paying a ransom to the kidnappers; consequently, they demanded a national intervention.[28] The lawyer of the company, Rubén Pablo Cueva, had reported the kidnapping to a department of the Argentine federal police that was in charge of political matters, handing over the names and addresses of several politically active employees.[29] Management also hired army forces to solve the kidnapping, and SMATA sent armed groups during the strike.[30] The measures Mercedes took during the kidnapping and the strike should be kept in mind when examining the cases of workers who disappeared after the coup d'état.

Both Siemens and Mercedes were considering leaving Argentina when the coup was announced because the precarious political situation and the uncertain economic climate had created an unstable business environment.[31] Siemens, just like Mercedes, had transferred its German board of directors to Montevideo, Uruguay, for security reasons after a Siemens manager had been kidnapped as well. Uruguay had been ruled by a military regime since 1973 and received the managers of the companies with open arms. Altogether, Siemens withdrew 45–50 staff and their families to this neighboring South American country.[32] Still, both companies were highly interested in retaining the Argentine market for their business.

[27] Up to this day, the exact sum remains unknown (something between $2 and $7 million).

[28] See, for example, Tomuschat, *Mercedes-Benz Argentina*, 41–9; *Responsabilidad empresarial*, 502–3; Deutsche Botschaft to Auswärtiges Amt, November 6, 1975 (PA AA, Zwischenarchiv, Bd. 102019). Almost two months passed from the time the workers were rehired until Metz was released.

[29] *Responsabilidad empresarial*, 502; Tomuschat, *Mercedes-Benz Argentina, 44.*

[30] Tomuschat, *Mercedes-Benz Argentina*, 44–8; and "Juzgado Federal en lo Criminal y Correcional N 1 de San Isidoro. Provincia de Buenos Aires. Metz, Heinrich" (Archive of "Koalition gegen die Straflosigkeit" at ECCHR, Signature No 132 Tasselkraut, Juan [Fall Mercedes-Benz]). The cited minutes of the phone conversation could be interpreted as evidence that Mercedes also expected a military coup; December 21, 1975 (Tomuschat, *Mercedes-Benz Argentina*, 48).

[31] Daimler-Benz to Hermes-Kreditversicherungs Aktiengesellschaft, July 17, 1975 (BArch, B 102/215091); and Tomuschat, *Mercedes-Benz Argentina*, 2, 34.

[32] See, for example, several news articles (BArch, B 102/211542) and ZVA—Rundschreiben Nr. 7/75 (SA 68.LI 260).

The Coup of 1976 and the Argentine Regime's New Policies

The military junta that seized political power in 1976 was comprised of the Joint Chiefs General of the Armed Forces,[33] with the head of the army, Jorge Rafael Videla, also assuming the presidency. The ideological basis of the new regime was the so-called National Security Doctrine, as was the case for other Latin American dictatorships as well. Former Argentine dictator Juan Carlos Onganía (from 1966 to 1970) had already shaped the idea of national security and the need to fight the Argentine "subversion" (meaning left-wing opposition). At that time, different left-wing guerilla groups had also emerged to fight against the military regime. The goal of the dictatorship of 1976 was not only to fight the guerilla groups that were already weakened by that time but also to crack down on any potential protest and to discipline all of society. The junta had started a war against its own population. The "Process of National Reorganization" was based on a combined political and economic agenda,[34] resulting in "one of the bloodiest dictatorships of Latin America."[35] According to human rights organizations, about 30,000 people "disappeared," were tortured, and ultimately assassinated.[36] Economic policy was handed to "neoliberals" who, under the leadership of Economy Minister José Alfredo Martínez de Hoz, advocated "tight monetary controls and orthodox anti-inflationary measures."[37]

Following the coup d'état, the violence of paramilitary death squads and fighting against "subversion" increased. The new regime prohibited trade union activities and terminated the right to strike indefinitely. The military regime's "dirty war" focused particularly on unions and workers,

[33] In discussing the last Argentine dictatorship, it is important to note that the regime went through different political phases. There were changes within the political leadership of the junta. The various leaders and branches of the military services pursued different strategies in their dealings with foreign countries. A detailed account of this variability would exceed the scope of this chapter.

[34] Peter Birle, *Argentinien: Unternehmer, Staat und Demokratie* (Frankfurt a. M.: Vervuert Verlag, 1995), 145–6; Carreras and Potthast, *Eine Kleine Geschichte Argentiniens*, 218–22.

[35] Birle, *Argentinien: Unternehmer, Staat und Demokratie*, 21.

[36] Additionally, it is not known where around 500 children of people who disappeared wound up.

[37] Michael Goebel, *Argentina's Partisan Past: Nationalism and the Politics of History* (Liverpool: Latin American Studies LUP [Book 11], 2011), 186.

as well as on leftist or allegedly leftist students and intellectuals.[38] The main form of repression was forced disappearance. In most of these "disappearance cases," family and friends never heard from the arrested individual again. This system of repression was visible and secret at the same time: everybody knew more or less what happened to those who disappeared, but it was almost impossible to get any information about them or to locate anyone in charge of these secret arrests.

One day before the coup, Walter Boos, the CEO of Siemens Argentina, wrote the following to the German Federal Ministry for Economic Affairs: "Although I do not think much of military governments, I do think that a strong military government is the only solution for this poor country at this point."[39] This statement raises at least three questions: First, why did he think that a military government was the "only solution"? Second, did the military coup affect German-Argentine business relations? And third, if so, how? Siemens was not the only large German company in Argentina that seemed to welcome the coup. Mercedes-Benz Argentina was also hoping that a strong hand might improve the political and economic situation there. Western diplomats, such as the German[40] and British ambassadors in Argentina, as well as some members of the international and Argentine media, praised the overthrow as a chance to restore law and order. They believed that the majority of Argentinians would feel the same way.[41]

Since the companies already had a good relationship with the military before the coup, they had high expectations for improving business with

[38] Iain Guest, *Behind the Disappearances. Argentina's Dirty War against Human Rights and the United Nations* (Philadelphia: University of Pennsylvania Press, 1990), 21–2; Birle, *Argentinien: Unternehmer, Staat und Demokratie*, 146.

[39] "Obwohl ich von Militaerregierungen nicht viel halte, so glaube ich doch, dass jetzt fuer dieses arme Land eine strenge Militaerregierung die einzige Loesung darstellt" (Walter Boos, March 23, 1976 [BArch, B 102/211542]).

[40] For example, the German embassy in Buenos Aires reported at that time to the Foreign Office: "The military leadership of Argentina is searching for our understanding and active support. We can count on sympathy for the satisfaction of our justifiable wishes, but we have to understand as well that the intervention of the military offers another chance for this country. If we close ourselves off from this development, we risk losing an important partner: as a friend, as a host country of a big German minority and important investments, as a sales market, raw material supplier and as a cornerstone in the Western Hemisphere" (Report of the German Embassy Buenos Aires to the Foreign Office, March 25, 1976 [PA AA, Zwischenarchiv, Bd. 103 579]).

[41] PA AA, Zwischenarchiv, Bd. 103579; Goebel, *Argentina's Partisan Past*, 181.

the new regime once it came to power. The dictatorship only partly fulfilled these expectations; for example, the state never gave up control of the economy, and the economic situation in Argentina never stabilized, as the companies had hoped.[42] But the junta and its new Minister of the Economy made some promises and some free market compromises that enticed these companies to work with the regime. A Siemens memorandum from July 1976 highlighted the military regime's announcement that it did not want to nationalize foreign firms but would instead reprivatize state-owned companies.[43] In this case, the regime's promises exceeded its actions. Siemens and Daimler-Benz hoped that their Argentine subsidiaries could operate without disruptions. According to the Tomuschat report, the management of Mercedes-Benz Argentina had not only expected the coup d'état but rather endorsed it primarily because of the country's unstable situation. Managers expected the regime's fight against subversion to stop the disruptive activities of labor agitators, thus decreasing production losses from long-lasting strikes.[44] The companies also anticipated that conflicts from the Perón era would finally be resolved, including, for example, an end to the imminent risk of Siemens Argentina being nationalized.[45]

The military blamed the interventionist policies of the previous governments for the country's catastrophic economic situation, and the new regime announced a more liberal economic policy, not least for the purpose of attracting foreign capital.[46] Shortly after the military coup, Argentina received "special drawing rights" from the International Monetary Fund (IMF) worth over $100 million and then a supplementary loan worth over a quarter of a billion dollars. This was the largest IMF

[42] Birle, *Argentinien: Unternehmer, Staat und Demokratie*, 373–4.

[43] Memorandum, July 12, 1976 (BArch, B 102/312829).

[44] See the quote by Walter Boos. In a meeting with the Federal Ministry of Economic Affairs in May 1976 Walter Boos emphasized the "complete change of mood" ("totale[n] Stimmungsumschwung") since the military had come into power. The rate of absenteeism at Siemens Argentina had dropped from 30% to 1.8% after the coup (Ergebnisvermerk, Bonn, May 6, 1976 [BArch, B 102/211542]). See also Tomuschat, *Mercedes-Benz Argentina*, 69, 123.

[45] The conflict between ENTel and Siemens Argentina was one of the first that the new Minister of Economic Affairs, Martínez de Hoz, put on the political agenda (Memorandum, July 12, 1976 [BArch, B 102/312829]).

[46] See Birle, *Argentinien: Unternehmer, Staat und Demokratie*, 149–50. Martínez de Hoz quickly became very popular among international trade partners. See also the records of the Political Archive and the German Federal Archives.

loan ever granted to a Latin American nation and the first one it had given Argentina in five years.[47] In addition, Argentina received loans from private US banks and European countries, including Germany. Deutsche Bank gave a DM100 million loan (about $43 million) in 1977.[48] Among the multinationals, such financial support was seen as a positive indication of growing business opportunities.

The previous two sections have provided the context of the events leading up to the military coup and the operations Siemens and Daimler-Benz developed during that period. In the next sections I offer a typology of the collaboration between the multinationals and authoritarian regimes that I inductively derived from the case of the German corporations in Argentina.

Doing Business Directly with the Military Regime

During the Argentine dictatorship, both the Siemens and Daimler-Benz subsidiaries worked directly with the regime. At Siemens Argentina, this translated into steadily increasing annual investment and employment throughout this period.[49] Siemens' cooperation began when it came to an agreement with the dictatorship over its previous conflict with the telephone company ENTel.[50] A Siemens memorandum from May 1980 contained the following note: "After the change of government in 1976, conflict settlement with full rehabilitation of the house of Siemens."[51] Even though the negotiations with the new regime took longer than expected and were not as easy as they appeared in retrospect, in the end, Siemens was satisfied with the outcome. In addition, Siemens received an order in January 1977 to deliver telecommunications worth DM35

[47] The country received an additional loan of over $1 billion from the international private finance sector (Birle, *Argentinien: Unternehmer, Staat und Demokratie*, 151); see also Deutsche Botschaft to Auswärtiges Amt, September 23, 1976 (PA AA, Zwischenarchiv, Bd. 103584).

[48] Banker Hermann J. Abs, who had a close relationship with the Argentine junta, was in charge (Lothar Gall, *Der Bankier Hermann Josef Abs. Eine Biographie* [Munich: C.H. Beck, 2004], 315).

[49] "Investments and Employees of Siemens Buenos Aires" (BArch, B 102/312829).

[50] Memorandum, July 12, 1976 (BArch, B 102/312829); Letters from the German Ambassador (PA AA, Zwischenarchiv, Bd. 103584).

[51] "Nach Regierungswechsel 1976 Beilegung Konflikt mit voller Rehabilitierung Haus Siemens" (Note, May 20, 1980 [BArch, B 102/312829]). In May 1976, Siemens had prospective deals worth around DM220–290 million (about $87–115 million).

million (about $15 million) for the FIFA World Cup in 1978.[52] Another important branch of business for Siemens besides telecommunications was nuclear energy. Siemens had built the first nuclear plant in Latin America, which opened in 1974. Then, Siemens formed a joint venture with Allgemeine Elektricitäts-Gesellschaft AG (AEG) named KWU, which began the construction of a second plant in June 1981. In 1979, the German nuclear power industry was relieved to get its first order in two years. The KWU had outcompeted its Canadian business rival (Atom Energy of Canada Ltd.) and had received the order to deliver a nuclear plant. In its invitation to tender, Argentina emphasized the importance not merely of a nuclear power reactor but rather of establishing its own heavy water production plant as well. The US government, in particular, criticized the nuclear deal with Argentina since the country did not take part in the Nuclear Non-Proliferation Treaty (NPT), had not yet ratified the Treaty of Tlatelolco (Latin American Nuclear-Free Zone), and had refused to allow international inspectors to view its nuclear facilities in their entirety. The US feared that if Argentina were able to complete the nuclear fuel cycle, it would eventually be able to produce nuclear weapons. One cannot rule out the possibility that Argentina's decision to take the German offer instead of the Canadian one may have had something to do, among other things, with Canada's insistence on "full scope safeguards" for supplying a nuclear power reactor.[53] The German federal government, by contrast, insisted only on project-based safeguards and consequently on less extensive international interventions in the Argentine nuclear power industry.[54]

Mercedes, for its part, worked directly with the regime by supplying the Argentine police and military as well as the Chilean forces.[55] In February 1976, Mercedes had already received an important order from the

[52] Prüfungsbericht. Konsultation D 169/76, February 16, 1977 (BArch, B 102/312829).

[53] German media and politicians had serious concerns when the company was charged with building the first nuclear power plant in Argentina in 1968 since the country had not joined the "Treaty on the Non-Proliferation of Nuclear Weapons" (see articles and documents at the Archive of the German Federal Foreign Office, PA AA, Zwischenarchiv, Bd. 116007).

[54] See BArch, B 102/195446-195449.

[55] Tomuschat, *Mercedes-Benz Argentina*, 117–8. Mercedes was among the 20 companies with the highest revenue generation, and it owned one of the most important industrial parks in the country (Victoria Basualdo, "Complicidad patronal-militar en la última dictadura argentina: Los casos de Acindar, Astarsa, Dálmine Siderca, Ford, Ledesma y Mercedes-Benz," *Revista Engranajes*, no. 5 [March 2006]: 16).

Argentine army, which was valued at DM100 million (about $40 million): the delivery of 1300 Unimogs (a type of all-wheel drive, multi-purpose truck), specially reinforced for military use.[56] By 1977, Mercedes had 4257 employees, the highest number to date. In 1980, sales reached a high of DM1.14 billion (about $620 million). During the following years, however, the company experienced a slump in production and revenue, as well as a reduction in the number of employees.[57] Nevertheless, German direct investments in Argentina and the Argentine-German trade exchange doubled between 1976 and 1983.[58] In other words, German business did well under the Argentine dictatorship.

Promoting Acceptance for the Military Regime in the Home Country

Based on their statements to ministries of the German federal government, it is clear that both Siemens and Mercedes-Benz painted a positive picture of the new regime and made every effort to communicate it to German authorities. In May 1976, in a meeting with members of the German Federal Ministry for Economic Affairs, Walter Boos, the CEO of Siemens Argentina, characterized the political climate after the coup in Argentina as completely changed. According to his report, worker morale had improved and efficiency at Siemens Argentina was up by almost 100%. The management of both companies emphasized the positive political and economic changes since the coup of 1976 and that the effective crackdown on "subversive elements" was steadily improving the business environment in Argentina.[59] Siemens and Daimler-Benz warned of the potential for unemployment even in Germany should the economic and political situation hinder business in Argentina.[60] On the other hand, the

[56] Deutsche Botschaft to Auswärtiges Amt, February 19, 1976 (PA AA, Zwischenarchiv, Bd. 103584).

[57] Tomuschat, *Mercedes-Benz Argentina*, 30, 67.

[58] Kaleck, *Kampf gegen die Straflosigkeit*, 56.

[59] The memo says: "Extremism [is] currently very active. About 10 dead daily. Military forces are taking drastic measures. [There is] hope that terrorism will be overcome by the end of the year" ("Extremismus z. Z. noch sehr aktiv. Täglich rd. 10 Tote. Militär greift hart durch. Hoffnung, daß bis Ende des Jahres der Terrorismus überwunden ist") (Ergebnisvermerk, May 6, 1976, Bonn [BArch, B 102/211542]); Tomuschat, *Mercedes-Benz Argentina*, 59.

[60] See, for example, Bundesministerium für Wirtschaft (BMWi) to the Bundesminister der Finanzen, Dr. Hans Apel, September 1976; and Note, May 20, 1980 (BArch, B 102/312829).

junta representatives reacted with indignation whenever German politicians and diplomats criticized the political situation in Argentina, in spite of good economic cooperation between the two countries. They seemed to believe that if Germany was one of the biggest beneficiaries of the economic agreements, it should not distance itself politically from the junta. In some cases, the junta even threatened to cancel existing economic contracts, although it never carried this out.[61]

In the 1960s, human rights became an important topic on the international political agenda. Non-governmental organizations such as Amnesty International became critical observers and important global actors. The rising power of international human rights campaigns was clearly visible in the case of the Chilean dictatorship. Argentine dictators tried to avoid such campaigns from the beginning. Consequently, the military regime saw the FIFA World Cup of 1978 as an important opportunity to improve its international as well as domestic image. Hosting the soccer World Cup in Argentina was crucial to the junta's ideological battle and to reinforce national pride in the Argentine society. Argentina had tried several times to host the games, but FIFA repeatedly rejected its request due to security concerns.[62] Due to their direct business deals with the junta, Siemens and Daimler-Benz implicitly supported these plans. Siemens delivered electricity, sound, and communication technology for the event.[63] Mercedes provided 128 vehicles free of charge for transporting soccer teams and their delegations. The German parent company gave the order for the vehicles, and the Argentine media welcomed this as an act of friendship.[64]

Promoting the Home Country's Support of the Military Regime

Doing business in Argentina would not have been possible for Siemens and Daimler-Benz without the support of German politicians and state-backed export risk insurance. For example, Siemens was able to sign a

[61] See, for example, Deutsche Botschaft to Auswärtiges Amt, October 2, 1979 (PA AA, Zwischenarchiv, Bd. 116007); Deutsche Botschaft to Auswärtiges Amt, July 12, 1978 (PA AA, Zwischenarchiv, Bd. 111044).

[62] See, for example, Jürg Ackermann, *Fußball und nationale Identität in Diktaturen. Spanien, Portugal, Brasilien und Argentinien* (Zürich/Berlin: Lit Verlag, 2013).

[63] Siemens Mitteilungen, H. 5, Mai 1978 (SA 68LI, 260).

[64] Deutsche Botschaft to Auswärtiges Amt, May 22, 1978 (PA AA, Zwischenarchiv, Bd. 107941).

contract with ENTel to deliver and install telecommunications hardware with an order value of DM72 million (about $31 million) in 1977 because the German state insured the financial risk.[65] Shortly before the coup of 1976, the German Federal Ministry of Finance had actually made it clear to Siemens that its chances of increasing insurance against financial risk in Argentina were slim to none.[66] On account of Argentina's unstable political and economic situation and its lack of foreign exchange, the benchmark of the export credit guarantee ("Hermesdeckung") was capped at one million DM.[67] A review of the Argentine balance of payments was planned only after the IMF completed its reassessment in March or April of 1976. Even in May 1976, the German Federal Ministry of Finance was not able to provide confirmation of risk coverage. Only after the IMF gave Argentina new loans, the conflict between Siemens and ENTel was settled, and Siemens received new orders could the business risk be accurately assessed and an increase in the amount of insurance be made possible.[68] At the same time, since German politicians were supporting German business in Argentina, the German ambassador informed the German Foreign Office that a contract between Argentina and the Swedish telephone company Ericsson had not been finalized. The Argentine side was considering canceling it due to Swedish criticism of the Argentine human rights situation.[69] In the course of my research, I could not find any case where similar problems with German companies were discussed.

Nevertheless, there was a public movement within Germany that brought attention to human rights abuses in Argentina. This German "Argentine solidarity movement" opposing the military junta peaked during the 1978 World Cup when political campaigns were founded in response to German "disappearances" within Argentina.[70] The foreign business deals of Daimler-Benz and Siemens became a topic of public

[65] Siemens to BMWi, January 28, 1977 (BArch, B 102/312829).

[66] BMWi to Deutsche Botschaft, February 4, 1976 (BArch, B 102/211542).

[67] BMWi to the Bundesminister der Finanzen, Dr. Hans Apel, September 1976 (BArch, B 102/312829).

[68] VB5 – 953 202/2 Bonn, January 26, 1976 (BArch, B 102/211542); Siemens to BMWi, January 28, 1977 and BMWi to Bundesminister der Finanzen, September 1976 (BArch, B 102/312829); Ergebnisvermerk, May 6, 1976, Bonn (BArch, B 102/211542).

[69] Memorandum, June 16, 1976 (BArch, B 102/312829); Deutsche Botschaft to Auswärtiges Amt, September 23, 1977 (PA AA, Zwischenarchiv, Bd. 107922).

[70] Among those who disappeared during the dictatorship were Germans and descendants of German immigrants. According to various studies, there were about 80 cases, with that of Elisabeth Käsemann being one of the most known.

debates. Relatives of Germans who disappeared in Argentina asked for German corporations' support in gaining information about their loved ones and reproached them for their ongoing business relationship with the military regime.[71] Politicians and diplomats had to acknowledge these campaigns and the questions they raised, and at least talk to members of organizations such as Amnesty International. This development changed the public discourse. In general, the German Federal Foreign Office did not disavow the head of the military regime in public, so it was able to announce that there was no reason to forego business with Argentina. Compared to the US, which restricted negotiations with Argentina due to human rights concerns under the Carter administration in 1977, German-Argentine relations—both political and business ones—actually improved.[72]

On the whole, German diplomats did not allow the disappearances of German citizens to disturb political and economic relations with Argentina. The head of the diplomatic division for Argentina at the Foreign Office, Karl-Alexander Hampe, clearly prioritized business as usual over human rights in his comments on the Argentine situation: "Our commitment to human rights issues should not go so far as to lead to a crucial and permanent impairment of our German-Argentine relationship."[73] In particular, the German ambassador was an important supporter of German

[71] See, for example, Vermerk, Auswärtiges Amt, September 25, 1977 (PA AA, Zwischenarchiv, Bd. 107937); see also PA AA, B 83, Bd. 1139. The mother of missing Argentine-German Klaus Zieschank asked in a letter addressed to the German Federal President that he use economic pressure on Argentina to find her son (A. Zieschank to Bundespräsident Walter Scheel, June 27, 1976 [PAAA, B 83, Bd. 1139]).

[72] Vermerk Auswärtiges Amt, July 6, 1978 (PA AA, Zwischenarchiv, Bd. 111044); Deutsche Botschaft to Auswärtiges Amt, March 25, 1977 (PA AA, Zwischenarchiv, Bd. 107923); several reports (PA AA, Zwischenarchiv, Bd. 111044); Amnesty International report, May 31, 1982 (Forschungs- und Dokumentationszentrum Chile-Lateinamerika e.V. [FDCL], Argentinien. Repression: Verschwundene, Proteste Int. 1979–1986).

[73] The Foreign Office's answer was similar to Hampe's. "Unser Einsatz in der Menschenrechtsfrage sollte nicht so weit gehen, daß er zu einer entscheidenden und nachhaltigen Beeinträchtigung des deutsch-argentinischen Verhältnisses führte [sic]" (Auswärtiges Amt, note, October 11, 1977 [PA AA, Zwischenarchiv, Bd. 107921]). In June 1977, the Federal Ministry for Economic Cooperation asked the Federal Foreign Office if—following Käsemann's unexplained death—it had any reservations or objections regarding business collaborations with and financial support for the Argentine fishing sector (Bundesminister für Wirtschaftliche Zusammenarbeit to Auswärtiges Amt, June 28, 1977). Its answer was: "In our view, the mentioned case of Käsemann should not obstruct the initiation of negotiations." ("Der von Ihnen erwähnte Fall Käsemann sollte hiesigen Erachtens die Aufnahme

business interests and was consistently willing to represent the interests of German companies to its Argentine interlocutors.[74] Visits by, for example, the Argentine Minister of Economic Affairs, Martínez de Hoz, to Germany were crucial to clarifying German companies' interests.[75] During these business meetings, human rights concerns were discussed only in passing.[76] Critical voices from the public and NGOs were not yet part of any business calculations, even if the multinationals could not simply ignore them.

Corporate Direct Collaboration with the Military Regime's Repressive Apparatus

It is crucial to companies' economic growth that they collaborate with the government of countries in which they operate. If the government is a dictatorship that systematically violates human rights, and if a company collaborates with the repressive apparatus responsible for the crimes, it is necessary to clarify whether that company itself can be held accountable for human rights violations.

In the cases of Siemens and Daimler-Benz operating within the last Argentine dictatorship, it is evident that the management of both companies communicated closely with the military forces at times. Both companies were informed about actions against guerilla groups, and they

der Verhandlungen nicht hindern" (Auswärtiges Amt to Bundesminister für Wirtschaftliche Zusammenarbeit, July 27, 1977 [PA AA, Zwischenarchiv, Bd. 107932]).

[74] See, for example, Deutsche Botschaft to Auswärtiges Amt, August 9, 1978 (PA AA, Zwischenarchiv, Bd. 111046); or Deutsche Botschaft to Auswärtiges Amt, July 7, 1976 (PA AA, Zwischenarchiv, Bd. 103584).

[75] Consider, for example, Martínez de Hoz's visit to Germany in July 1976. Important talking points for the meeting between the Minister of Economy, Hans Friderichs, and Martínez de Hoz included the conflict between Siemens and ENTel and Siemens's interest in providing Argentina with a nuclear power plant (Deutsche Botschaft to Auswärtiges Amt, June 23, 1976, PAAA, Zwischenarchiv, 103584); internal letter to the Federal Minister of Economy, September 15, 1976 (BArch, B 102/312829).

[76] For example, the German Minister of Economy, Otto Graf Lambsdorff, wanted to bring up Siemens's business concerns during a phone conversation with Martínez de Hoz about the release of a German who had disappeared (Vermerk, August 11, 1980, Bonn [BArch, B 102/312829]).

accepted that violence and even killings were part of the effort to restore law and order.[77]

Looking first specifically at Mercedes-Benz, it is evident that armed soldiers frequently were present at the manufacturing plant in Argentina to ask whether there were any problems or disturbances.[78] The management discussed union concerns and workers' discipline with members of the military regime.[79] Furthermore, Mercedes-Benz's management was informed about details it could only have received from those involved in the arrests. For example, in the minutes of the board of directors meeting, it was stated that banned Marxist literature had been found in the home of one arrested worker.[80] At the same time, the human resources management of Mercedes-Benz Argentina shared personal information about workers—like addresses, photos, and information about their involvement in political activities—with the military forces, which they then used in undertaking their repressive actions.

Altogether, between 10 and 17 Mercedes workers disappeared between 1976 and 1977.[81] Hardly any of them were over 30, and the majority disappeared during a single week in August 1977. Just prior to their disappearance, the head of Mercedes-Benz Argentina noted in meeting minutes that the situation at the plant was critical. In a July 1977 meeting between director Pedro de Elías and the company's lawyer Rubén Pablo Cueva

[77] "Security has improved substantially. Recently further important successes have been achieved by military actions against the guerilla. Among other things, one of those responsible for kidnapping Metz was eliminated. [...] In general, the results of the governmental activities of the first year have been favorable and are opening up good chances for the further development of the country." ("Die Sicherheit hat sich wesentlich gebessert. In diesen Tagen wurden weitere wichtige Erfolge in der Militäraktion gegen die Guerilla erzielt, u. a. wurde einer der Verantwortlichen für die Entführung von Metz eliminiert. [...] Im allgemeinen waren die Ergebnisse der Regierungsmaßnahmen während ihre ersten [sic] Jahres günstig und eröffnen gute Aussichten für die weitere Entwicklung des Landes," Direktoriumsprotokoll 13/77, March 22, 1977, cited by Tomuschat, *Mercedes-Benz Argentina*, 59); and BArch, B 102/211542.

[78] Testimony of Tasselkraut (December 2001, Archive of "Koalition gegen die Straflosigkeit" at ECCHR, Signature No 132 Tasselkraut, Juan [Fall Mercedes-Benz]).

[79] Tomuschat, *Mercedes-Benz Argentina*, 54, 60.

[80] Ibid., 73; and *Responsabilidad empresarial*, 491.

[81] This figure varies depending on how one counts disappearances. Two workers were released after their disappearance, while others no longer worked at Mercedes when they were arrested. One of the few who disappeared and returned alive was Héctor Aníbal Ratto. He has been one of the most important eyewitnesses in lawsuits against production manager Juan Tasselkraut and Mercedes.

with the minister for employment, General Horacio Tomás Liendo, the "discipline" at the plant was discussed as well.[82] The number of workers who voluntarily quit out of fear of arrest, or who were forced to quit, is unknown. A large number of the workers who disappeared had been fired in 1975 and later rehired. After the disappearances, Mercedes continued to pay the workers' salaries to their relatives for years, even exceeding ten years in one case. Acts of sabotage and worker protests continued even after the coup d'état, but the company likewise continued to dismiss workers for disciplinary reasons. Nevertheless, as the military regime's repression increased, such activities carried a higher risk, so they decreased significantly, especially after the wave of arrests in August 1977. At that time, the board of directors noted a "normalization of everyday work" in the minutes of their meeting.[83]

Different witnesses testified that the factory management gave information to the security forces in several cases, as outlined in Tomuschat's report. Héctor Aníbal Ratto has been one of the most important eyewitnesses. He was one of those who disappeared, yet he returned alive after being held in a torture camp for one and a half years. Several times after the dictatorship ended, Ratto reported that the production manager of Mercedes, Juan Tasselkraut, had given the name and address of worker Diego Eustaquio Nuñez to the civil security forces; Nuñez had subsequently been arrested and murdered. Concerning his own disappearance, Ratto stated that Tasselkraut had been involved in trying to trick him into going home for a family emergency so that he could be arrested secretly, away from the factory. In the end, his life was saved by the fact that he became suspicious, refused to leave, and was finally arrested in front of a number of coworkers who served as witnesses. The board of directors knew that the workers who disappeared had been arrested by security forces, even when they were arrested at home. In one case, an arrested worker did not subsequently disappear, and, the company gave him ten days off, sending his wife a telegram with details of his release before it even occurred. Thus, Mercedes-Benz must have been informed by the security forces about the duration of the illegal arrest. On another occasion, there was a mix-up, and the wrong worker was arrested by uniformed persons when he left to go home on the factory bus. Civil forces had been standing by outside, and they then tied him up and blindfolded him. It

[82] Tomuschat, *Mercedes-Benz Argentina, 60.*

[83] See: Tomuschat, *Mercedes-Benz Argentina* and *Responsabilidad empresarial.*

took one hour for the kidnappers to realize their mistake, during which they apparently abused him so severely that he lost consciousness. He awoke later in the factory's own ambulance. Did the security forces bring him back to the ambulance or had he been bound and blindfolded the whole time on factory grounds? Christian Tomuschat's report does not give this information, but either scenario serves to illustrate the prevailing climate of the time and the existing connection between the military forces and the company.[84]

Mercedes also collaborated with security forces in employing Rubén Luis Lavallén, who had been an inspector at the police station in San Justo, which was also home to a clandestine detention center. Relatives of people who disappeared have identified Lavallén in their testimonies as one of those involved in the kidnappings and torture. Lavallén was recruited by Mercedes in 1978 and became the new head of the company's security guard unit.[85] Even if Lavallén was indisputably identified as a torturer only after the dictatorship ended, the decision of Mercedes management to recruit an inspector from such a police station was questionable from the beginning.

At Siemens Argentina, by contrast, there are no known incidents of arrests having taken place on the plant grounds or of employees who disappeared. But the reports of increased operational efficiency that we already noted indicate that Siemens benefited from the climate of fear surrounding union or political activism. Obviously management was willing to turn a blind eye to human rights violations in Argentina for the sake of business.

The Corporate Gains of Collaboration

Business partners, banks, and the International Monetary Fund considered the new military regime capable of improving the economic climate in Argentina. For this reason—and in the hope that the regime might clamp down on guerrilla groups and workers' protests—Siemens and Mercedes, as we have seen in this chapter, were among the companies that welcomed the Argentine dictatorship. They benefited from doing business with the junta and from overcoming the administrative barriers of the

[84] Tomuschat, *Mercedes-Benz Argentina*, 73–96; *Responsabilidad empresarial*, 512.
[85] Tomuschat, *Mercedes-Benz Argentina*, 132; *Responsabilidad empresarial*, 525.

Perón era. This was the case even if, in the end, the military regime did not accomplish all of the economic changes they had hoped for.

Given the marked reduction in the number of strikes and incidents of sabotage due to workers' fear of repression or even assassination by the military regime, as well as the increased control over union activities, it is apparent that the companies aligned themselves with the new political realities by turning a blind eye toward the daily routine of kidnapping, murdering, and torturing individuals involved in union activities and labor agitation. Such human rights violations were part of the Argentine reality that surrounded these German subsidiaries. Moreover, as is becoming clear in the case of Mercedes-Benz Argentina, the company was involved in the regime's violation of human rights by passing information on to the repressive apparatus. Siemens Argentina and Mercedes-Benz Argentina did not just benefit from good business relations with the new regime but also from the repressive system that "disciplined" their plant workers and ended potentially disruptive protest activities.

There were several political reasons that companies might have considered suspending or restricting business with the Argentine dictatorship, particularly the disappearances of Germans in Argentina. However, in the climate of the 1970s, human rights campaigns were not yet able to apply sufficient pressure on international business relations and companies to effect such a shift in business relations. The German Federal Government presented maintaining the economic relationship with the regime as a way to influence the junta in the interest of Germans who had disappeared or been arrested. At times, German partners marginally addressed these cases during trade negotiations and in the companies' investment agreements. However, in no case did the German Federal Government put consistent economic pressure on the Argentine government, for example, by refusing to conclude contracts. Nevertheless, the reference material makes frequent note of the fact that the corporate actors and German diplomats were increasingly confronted with human rights issues until they could no longer ignore them. International political behavior and economic relationships began to change. Members of the German Foreign Office began to ask whether trade negotiations could continue unabated despite German disappearances. The German ambassador called for clarification of Elisabeth Käsemann's disappearance, for example, even in the midst of important trade talks. Still, the context during the 1970s—characterized by terrorism, guerrilla groups, and the Cold War—allowed the focus to remain narrow and on business imperatives. It was not until the late 1980s that Western democracies came to a general political agreement that foreign policy must rest on universal values. Even today, when human rights issues form an indisputable part of most Western democracies' foreign policy, one can find multiple examples demonstrating that violations of human rights do not automatically entail a disruption of economic and political relationships. For the 1970s, though, this was certainly even more the case. As we saw in this chapter, Siemens Argentina and Mercedes-Benz Argentina at that time made the military dictatorship even more acceptable to the German government with their statements to members of the Federal Ministry of Economic Affairs about the improved political and economic situation after the coup d'état and with their business relations with the regime.

Conclusion

German industry played an important role in some key sectors of the Argentine economy before, during, and after the 1976 coup. German companies' expectations of economic change and improved economic policy were decisive factors in their support and endorsement of the juntas, even though they recognized that it was an authoritarian regime that did not fulfill all of their expectations. Corporations must now question the political impact of their past actions, their responsibility toward their employees, and the appropriateness of their having reaped profits under a repressive dictatorship and having maintained close contact with the forces of repression. The four types of collaboration identified and examined in this chapter demonstrate that collaboration with and support of a dictatorship can encompass not just direct actions, such as presenting a death list or allowing torture, but also indirect political support. No government exists in an isolated bubble. Every government, including any dictatorship, depends on international acceptance and economic exchange. Likewise, no company can operate in an economic sphere detached from politics. Siemens and Daimler-Benz could have suspended their engagement in Argentina based on ethical, moral, or political grounds, but their drive to do business—the inherent logic of capitalism—was the decisive factor. Nor was the German federal government willing to restrict or end business relations with the Argentine dictatorship. Hopefully the typology put forward in this chapter will serve as a starting point for other studies on the collaboration between big businesses and authoritarian regimes.

References

Archival Sources

European Center for Constitutional and Human Rights. Archive of "Koalition gegen die Straflosigkeit" [ECCHR], Berlin, Germany.
Forschungs- und Dokumentationszentrum Chile-Lateinamerika e.V. [FDCL], Berlin, Germany.
German Federal Archives [BArch], Koblenz, Germany.
German Federal Foreign Office. Political Archive [PA AA], Berlin, Germany.
Siemens. Siemens Corporate Archives [SA], Berlin, Germany.

Bibliography

Ackermann, Jürg. *Fußball und nationale Identität in Diktaturen. Spanien, Portugal, Brasilien und Argentinien.* Zürich, Berlin: Lit Verlag, 2013.

Basualdo, Victoria. "Complicidad patronal-militar en la última dictadura argentina: Los casos de Acindar, Astarsa, Dálmine Siderca, Ford, Ledesma y Mercedes-Benz." *Revista Engranajes*, no. 5 (Buenos Aires: Federación de Trabajadores de la Industria y Afines, 2006).

Birle, Peter. *Argentinien: Unternehmer, Staat und Demokratie.* Frankfurt a. M.: Vervuert Verlag, 1995.

Carreras, Sandra, and Barbara Potthast. *Eine Kleine Geschichte Argentiniens.* Berlin: Suhrkamp, 2013.

Dirección Nacional del Sistema Argentino de Información Jurídica. *Responsabilidad empresarial en delitos de lesa humanidad. Represión a trabajadores durante el terrorismo de Estado. Tomo I.* Buenos Aires: Ministerio de Justicia y Derechos Humanos de la Nación, 2015.

Gall, Lothar. *Der Bankier Hermann Josef Abs. Eine Biographie.* Munich: C.H. Beck, 2004.

Goebel, Michael. *Argentina's Partisan Past: Nationalism and the Politics of History.* Liverpool: Latin American Studies LUP (Book 11), 2011.

Guest, Iain. *Behind the Disappearances. Argentina's Dirty War against Human Rights and the United Nations.* Philadelphia: University of Pennsylvania Press, 1990.

"Herrliche Menschen". *Der Spiegel*, no. 45 (1975): 109–110.

Joly, Hervé. "Ende des Familienkapitalismus? Das Überleben der Unternehmerfamilien in den deutschen Wirtschaftseliten des 20. Jahrhunderts." In *Die deutsche Wirtschaftselite im 20. Jahrhundert. Kontinuität und Mentalität*, edited by Volker R. Berghahn and Stefan Unger. Essen: Klartext Verlag, 2003.

Kaleck, Wolfgang. "Die verschwundenen Gewerkschafter von Mercedes-Benz." In *Menschenrechte und Außenpolitik. Bundesrepublik Deutschland – Argentinien 1976–1983*, edited by Koalition gegen Straflosigkeit. 27. Bad Honnef: Horlemann Verlag, 2006.

Kaleck, Wolfgang. *Kampf gegen die Straflosigkeit. Argentiniens Militärs vor Gericht.* Berlin: Klaus Wagenbach, 2010.

Koalition gegen Straflosigkeit, ed. *Menschenrechte und Außenpolitik. Bundesrepublik Deutschland – Argentinien 1976–1983.* Bad Honnef: Horlemann Verlag, 2006.

Olejniczak, Claudia. "Dritte Welt Bewegung." In *Die sozialen Bewegungen in Deutschland seit 1945*, edited by Roland Roth and Dieter Rucht. Frankfurt a. M.: Campus Verlag, 2008.

Pohl, Hans. "Exporte und Auslandsaktivitäten der Daimler-Benz AG in den Jahren des Wiederaufbaus (1945–1955)". In *Wirtschaft, Unternehmen, Kreditwesen, soziale Probleme. Ausgewählte Aufsätze. Teil 1*, edited by Hans Pohl. Stuttgart: Franz Steiner Verlag, 2005.

Rodriguez, Florencia. "Estrategias de lucha en industrias dinámicas durante la segunda ISI. Un análisis a partir del estudio de caso de Mercedes Benz Argentina". In *La clase trabajadora Argentina en el siglo xx: Experiencias de lucha y organización*, edited by Victoria Basualdo. Buenos Aires: Atuel, 2011.

Tomuschat, Christian. *Mercedes-Benz Argentina zur Zeit der Militärdiktatur (1976–1983).* Berlin: Humboldt Universität, Juristische Fakultät, Institut für Völker- und Europarecht, 2003.

Weber, Gaby. *Die Verschwundenen von Mercedes-Benz.* Hamburg: Assoziation A, 2001.

Weber, Gaby. "Rechtsweg ausgeschlossen? Mercedes-Benz Argentina – ein Präzedenzfall," produced by Gaby Weber. *Deutschlandfunk.* July 22, 2014.

CHAPTER 10

Class Conflict and the Ascent of Globalized Business Groups Under Chile's Dictatorship: A Case Study of the Copper Manufacturing Industry

Joel Stillerman

Introduction

The Pinochet dictatorship ushered in a new era of state–business relations in Chile. The junta's neoliberal policies departed from the import substitution industrialization (ISI) model developed in the late 1930s and continued until the 1973 coup. The policies facilitated the transformation of traditional business groups that added nontraditional exports, services, and international financial partnerships to the traditional foci of mining and manufacturing present among business groups prior to the coup. The junta also promoted growing concentration of wealth and businesses' increasing political power under subsequent civilian administrations. This

J. Stillerman (✉)
Grand Valley State University, Allendale, MI, USA
e-mail: stillejo@gvsu.edu

V. Basualdo et al. (eds.), *Big Business and Dictatorships in Latin America*, Palgrave Studies in Latin American Heterodox Economics, https://doi.org/10.1007/978-3-030-43925-5_10

transformed business sector was made possible in part through the brutal repression of trade unions and the political left as well as the adoption of labor laws that maximized labor flexibility while sharply restricting unions' capacity to organize and collectively bargain on behalf of their members.[1]

Analysts have developed important case studies and survey analyses of unions during the dictatorship and under post-authoritarian rule, yet few have examined the long-term trajectory of a single union organization.[2] In this context, this study asks: How did state policies shape the trajectories of firms and workers under Chile's democratic, authoritarian, and post-authoritarian governments? I answer this question through a case study of Manufacturas de Cobre (MADECO) (now-Nexans), Chile's largest copper manufacturer. The study is based on 100 interviews with managers, workers, and political officials; analysis of archival documents; and ethnographic observation.[3] The MADECO case illustrates national patterns of industrial change across ISI and neoliberal policy periods as well as unions' rise and decline across democratic and authoritarian regimes. Nonetheless, it is an emblematic case due to the firm's importance to Chile's housing,

[1] Carlos Huneeus, *El régimen de Pinochet* (Santiago: Editorial Sudamericana, 2001), 437–498; Ricardo Ffrench-Davis, *Economic Reforms in Chile: From Dictatorship to Democracy* (Ann Arbor, MI: University of Michigan Press, 2002), 30–35; Manuel Gárate Chateau, *La revolución capitalista en Chile (1973–2003)* (Santiago: Ediciones Universidad Alberto Hurtado, 2012), 181–238; Marcelo Bucheli, Erica Salvaj, and Minyoung Kim, "Better Together: How Multinationals come Together with Business Groups in Times of Economic and Political Transitions." *Global Strategy Journal*, 9, No 2 (2019): 1–32; Peter Winn, "The Pinochet Era," in *Victims of the Chilean Miracle: Workers and Neoliberalism in the Pinochet Era, 1973–2002*, edited by Peter Winn (Durham, NC: Duke University Press, 2004), 14–70.

[2] For case studies of unions in the textile, copper mining, agricultural, forestry, and fisheries sectors under the dictatorship, see Peter Winn, ed. *Victims of the Chilean Miracle* (Durham, NC: Duke University Press, 2004). Studies of unions since the dictatorship include Alberto J. Armstrong V. and Rafael A. Águila B., *Evolución del conflicto laboral en Chile, 1961–2002* (Santiago: Ediciones Universidad Católica de Chile, 2006), 315–326; Carolina Bank-Muñoz, *Building Power from Below: Chilean Workers Take on Walmart* (Ithaca, NY: Cornell University Press, 2017), 86–133; Antonio Aravena and Daniel Núñez, eds., *El Renacer de la Huelga Obrera en Chile* (Santiago: Instituto de Ciencias Alejandro Lipschutz, 2009), 1–100.

[3] Documentary evidence includes union contracts, press releases, and pamphlets housed at the union hall; newspaper and magazine articles accessed at the Biblioteca Nacional and the Servicio de Recortes de la Biblioteca del Congreso; congressional hearings from the Biblioteca del Congreso; company annual reports, administrative documents, and legal documents housed at the Superintendencia de Valores y Seguros; union complaints against the firm filed with the Dirección del Trabajo; industry analyses accessed while the author was employed as a financial proofreader at J.P. Morgan; a company study available at the CORFO library; firm managers' personal notes; and local history documents at the Municipalidad de San Miguel.

mining, and energy sectors, the firm's purchase by the Luksic business group (today Chile's most profitable), and the dictatorship's efforts to crush the union due to unfounded allegations that workers there planned an armed uprising prior to the military coup.

My analysis demonstrates that the company and its owners have operated under the shadow of the state during both ISI and neoliberal periods, in contrast to the dictatorship's claims that its policies required firms to compete on the free market. ISI policies facilitated the firm's early development, the dictatorship's neoliberal labor policies increased the firm's profitability, and post-authoritarian governments' provision of loans to the Luksic Group facilitated its meteoric rise during the 2000s. The dictatorship reinforced preexisting patterns of wealth concentration within business groups rather than creating open competition among efficient economic actors.[4] Notwithstanding business groups' economic power and political influence, MADECO unions' dogged persistence continues to today, as a successful 2018 lawsuit against the firm attests. Nonetheless, the union's weakened state reflects labor's national political and organizational decline. Union density peaked at 34% in 1973, rebounded to 18% in 1991 after a sharp decline, and then dropped to 14% by 2013. The number of strikes peaked at 3000 in 1972, descended to 82 under the dictatorship in 1981 once collective bargaining was permitted, and rose again to 379 walkouts in 1994 under civilian rule.[5]

The following analysis explores the development of the MADECO firm and union from 1944 to present. Prior to 1970, management and the industrial union developed close ties to state officials and figured

[4] Fernando Leiva, "Chile's Grupo Luksic and the 'New Spirit of Capital,'" (unpublished manuscript) https://rca.ucsc.edu/images/Leiva-Chiles-Luksic-Economic-Conglomerate (accessed March 7, 2019); Bucheli et al., "Better Together," 13; Tomás Undurraga, *Rearticulación de grupos económicos y renovación ideológica del empresariado en Chile 1980–2010*. Working Papers ICSO-UDP (Santiago: Universidad Diego Portales, 2011) http://www.icso.cl/wp-content/uploads/2011/03/Working-paper-elites-Tomas-Undurraga1.pdf (accessed March 8, 2019), 21–22.

[5] For union density, see Gonzalo Durán and Marco Kremerman, *Sindicatos y Negociación Colectiva* (Santiago: Fundación Sol), 3, http://www.fundacionsol.cl/wp-content/uploads/2015/04/Fundaci%C3%B3n-SOL-2015-Negociaci%C3%B3n-Colectiva.compressed.pdf (accessed March 11, 2016); for strike data, see Armstrong and Águila, *Evolución del conflicto laboral*, 367–68, and Rodrigo Medel Sierralta and Domingo Pérez Valenzuela. "Tres modelos de conflicto laboral en Chile: El peso de la economía, la organización sindical y el régimen de trabajo en las tendencias de la huelga extralegal." *Revista Colombiana de Sociología* 40, 2 (2017): 173–195.

prominently in discussions of development policy and partisan rivalries. Allende's Popular Unity government (1970–73) took control over the firm due to its strategic importance as part of its "Chilean road to socialism." The military junta's dual policies of labor repression and economic liberalization profoundly reshaped the firm and union. In 1979, after a period of downsizing, the Luksic Group purchased the firm. Thanks to labor policies benefitting managers, the Luksic family oversaw the firm's growth, technological advancement, and acquisition of competitors at home and abroad. The Luksic Group continued to grow in wealth, political influence, and international stature under post-authoritarian governments, while MADECO and its industrial union diminished in importance. The conclusion revisits some of the study's key insights and implications.

MADECO's Origins and Development Prior to the 1973 Coup

MADECO was the product of Chile's state-led industrialization policies following the collapse of export markets for Chilean goods during the Great Depression of the 1930s. Import substitution industrialization (ISI) as an explicit state policy began during the first Popular Front administration led by the centrist Radical Party with the 1939 establishment of the State Development Corporation (CORFO). The plan for CORFO followed a devastating earthquake in Southern Chile and responded to an import shortage sparked by World War II. CORFO allocated funds from a variety of sources to sponsor industrial development projects through either direct investment or subsidized credit. The policies witnessed a dramatic increase in industry's share of the economy: from 1938 to 1961, the employment share of agriculturally based firms dropped from 47% to 35% of the workforce, while from 1940 to 1970 the number of workers in industry doubled. CORFO also engaged in large-scale infrastructure planning projects, making it a model for other Latin American governments seeking to industrialize. CORFO's policies were supplemented by price controls and import tariffs that shielded industry from global competition.[6]

[6] Brian Loveman, *Chile: The Legacy of Hispanic Capitalism 2nd. Ed.* (New York: Oxford University Press, 1988), 231–32; Eduardo Silva, "Import Substitution: The Chilean Model in Comparative Perspective," *Latin American Perspectives* 34, 3 (May 2007), 73–74.

Chile's industrial development coincided with the rise of legal protections for trade unions and the development of a politicized labor movement. After unions' early history of unregulated conflicts and legalization through the 1924 labor laws and 1931 Labor Code, the labor movement unified via the Chilean Workers' Confederation (CTCh) under Pedro Aguirre Cerda's Popular Front administration (1938–1941). Despite internal fissures and the 1948–1957 anti-communist law the government used to attack leftist union leaders, the union movement grew beginning in 1953 under the National Labor Confederation (CUT). From the early 1950s until the coup, the union movement became more politically powerful and organizationally strong. Beginning in 1957, a majority of unions supported the communist-socialist electoral alliance that in 1970 carried socialist Salvador Allende to the presidency. During the 1960s, the CUT increased its influence while union militancy grew.[7]

The 1931 Labor Code permitted the formation of industrial, professional, and (in 1967) agricultural unions. Public employee associations gained considerable de facto power though they could not legally form unions or strike. Industrial unions uniting blue-collar workers (*obreros*) represented the majority of all union members. The law limited these organizations to the plant level (with a few important exceptions), set a minimum of 25 workers to form a union, exerted supervision and financial control over unions, and limited strike opportunities through compulsory conciliation and preventing the accumulation of strike funds. However, the law offered the closed shop, profit sharing, and other benefits. Because industrial unions operated at the plant level, lacked significant monetary resources, and had lasting traditions of leftist ties, they allied with Communist and Socialist parties, who offered political and legal support.[8]

[7] Alan Angell *Politics and the Labour Movement in Chile* (London: Oxford University Press), 83–145; Julio Samuel Valenzuela, "The Chilean Labor Movement: The Institutionalization of Conflict," in *Chile: Politics and Society*, eds. Arturo Valenzuela y Julio Samuel Valenzuela (New Brunswick, NJ: Transaction Books), 135–71; Armstrong and Águila, *Evolución del conflicto laboral*, 34–35.

[8] Ibid.

Industry Origins and Early Labor Conflicts

In 1944, two Italo-Chilean artisans, Aurelio and Américo Simonetti, founded Manufacturas de Cobre (MADECO) S.A.[9] The brothers began as small artisans, and in the late 1930s, through partnerships with other small entrepreneurs and government support, they created MADEMSA, a home appliance firm. Thanks to loans from the US Eximbank and a one-third stock ownership from CORFO, MADECO was founded as an offshoot of MADEMSA. The firm initially supplied the domestic construction and mining industries, though it exported wire rod (a minimally processed intermediate good), especially during the Korean and the Vietnam War booms.[10] In 1958, MADECO sold its CORFO stock but still benefited from import tariffs bolstering domestic industry.

In 1945, socialist union leaders at MADEMSA formed the Sindicato Industrial at MADECO, though communist leaders quickly took control of the organization. The party affiliations of union leaders varied during the 1950s, though by the 1960s communist and socialist militants controlled most leadership posts. Because MADECO was a profitable firm and union leaders gained congressional officials' support, union officials negotiated high salaries.[11]

MADECO's first major conflict emerged after management laid off 200 workers in 1956 following President Ibañez's anti-inflation policies recommended by the US-based Klein-Saks mission. Ibañez, a former dictator who was elected in 1952 on a populist platform, shifted rightward during his presidential term as evident in the stabilization program. These

[9] Entrevista: Aurelio Simonetti." *Revista MADECO: MADECO 50 Años*, Año II, Número 5, April 1994, 4–5; MADECO, "Don Aurelio Simonetti: Un Viaje Hacia la Historia de MADECO," *MADECO 50 Años: Desarrollando Futuro*, April 1994, 6, Chile, Ministerio de Economía, Superintendencia de Valores y Seguros (hereafter MESVS).

[10] Manufacturas de Cobre, MADECO, S.A. "Estatutos," April 3, 1944, 2, MESVS; MADECO, "Modificación de Estatutos, Aumento de Capital, y Mandatos," March 14, 1945, 3, MESVS; Theodore Moran, *Multinational Corporations and the Politics of Dependence: Copper in Chile* (Princeton, NJ: Princeton University Press, 1974), 46–47, 66–67; Chile, Cámara de Diputados, "-Conflicto que afecta al personal de la industria MADECO.-Inserción de documentos.-Proyecto de acuerdo," Sesión 20, November 18, 1965, 1863–1870.

[11] Joel Stillerman, *from Solidarity to Survival: Transformations in the Culture and Styles of Mobilization of Chilean Metalworkers under Democratic and Authoritarian Regimes, 1945–1995*. PhD dissertation (New York, New School for Social Research, 1998), 79–89.

layoffs reflect the end of the easy phase of ISI when industrial growth slowed and inflation increased.[12]

In 1958, conservative presidential candidate and former entrepreneur Jorge Alessandri narrowly defeated Salvador Allende. In 1960, Alessandri proposed an anti-inflation wage freeze. MADECO workers joined a national strike to oppose the wage freeze and secure a better severance payment upon dismissal in light of the 1956 mass layoffs. Strikers engaged in bloody confrontations with strikebreakers and the police during the two-month illegal walkout. Congressional allies gained their release from jail after arrests, and eventually brokered their return to work after a shooting outside the union hall. While union members regained their jobs, they did not win the increased severance payment.[13]

In 1964, the Christian Democratic (PDC) candidate, Eduardo Frei, was elected president. The PDC replaced the Radicals as the main centrist party. Unlike the Radicals, who alternated alliances with left- and right-wing parties, the Christian Democrats rejected party alliances. Frei's administration sought to expand Chile's economic development through agrarian reform, foreign investment, and expanded exports and to mobilize shantytown dwellers, women, and peasants to compete with the left. Radicalization on the left and internal conflict between technocratic and progressive members of the party led to a split and the creation of two small left-wing Christian parties (Christian Left, IC, and the United Popular Action Movement, MAPU), which later joined Allende's Popular Unity coalition.[14]

In 1965, the MADECO industrial union conducted a legal strike, this time with the white-collar union's participation. Union leaders won accolades during a special congressional session for their careful analysis of the firm's capacity to afford their severance payment, and Congress (now with a majority of leftist and centrist members) asked Frei's labor minister to intervene with management on the union's behalf. During the debate, congressional officials also considered nationalizing the firm alongside copper mines to capture more profits from manufacturing copper rather

[12] Silva, "Import Substitution," 74–75; Loveman, *Chile*, 262–63.

[13] Joel Stillerman, "Space, Strategies and Alliances in Mobilization: The 1960 Metalworkers' and Coal Miners' Strikes in Chile." *Mobilization: An International Journal* 8, 1 (February 2003), 65–85.

[14] Silva, "Import Substitution," 76; Loveman, *Chile*, 270–92.

than exporting the metal for its production elsewhere.[15] Because workers were able to shut down the firm, management felt more economic pressure to settle with the union and the organization won its key demand.[16]

In 1966, MADECO entered a joint venture with CEAT (Italy) and General Cable (the United States) to build a telephone cable plant in Antofagasta near the Chuquicamata copper mines.[17] This formed part of the Frei administration's efforts to establish joint ventures with multinationals in the copper mining industry. The policy of *chilenización* would be a first step toward the full nationalization of the *Gran Minería de Cobre* (GMC) under Salvador Allende's socialist administration. The Frei administration hoped the new plant would help MADECO export to neighboring Andean Pact countries to unload the firm's excess capacity that had already saturated Chile's small market. As part of this effort, Fernando Pérez and José Zabala, college-trained managers with long-term ties to the firm, took charge of MADECO. In addition to the telephone cable plant, they hoped to downsize the company and make production more efficient. With the Frei administration's 1966 job security law that prohibited dismissals without due cause, they had to negotiate these changes. They reduced the workforce from 1600 to 1300 and cut some slack in production processes.[18]

Government Control Under Popular Unity

Salvador Allende's 1970 presidential election was both a sea change in Chilean politics and the culmination of a process of radicalization and electoral success on the left beginning in the late 1950s. Allende defeated Jorge Alessandri and progressive Christian Democrat Radomiro Tomic. Elected with support of left-wing parties and unions, Allende pledged to follow the "Chilean road to socialism" through legal means. While the president attempted to move his program of nationalization of strategic industries and a deeper agrarian reform through Congress, opposition by the PDC and rightist National Party led him to take control of industries

[15] "Comisión investigadora de la industria manufacturera del cobre acordó la Cámara," *El Mercurio*, November 23, 1965, 33.

[16] Stillerman, "Explaining Strike Outcomes in Chile," 107–108.

[17] "'MADECO' puso en práctica un vigoroso plan de expansión de sus actividades," *La Nación*, January 15, 1967, 14; "Préstamo de 12 millones de dólares conceden a MADECO," *El Diario Ilustrado*, 17 Aug. 1967, 7.

[18] Joel Stillerman, *From Solidarity to Survival*, 54, 196–203.

through decree laws dating back to the 1930s. The presidential coalition proposed social, mixed, and private property areas, with the first given priority for nationalization. However, in practice, workers, peasants, and migrants to cities took over factories, farms, and vacant land and demanded that the government take control of them. The proposed nationalizations, direct action, and growing inflation radicalized opposition among the middle and upper classes. The opposition organized with support from the US government, which had also established an economic blockade and planned assassinations of constitutionalist generals upon Allende's election. The polarization and external interference eventually paved the way for the 1973 military coup.[19]

In 1971, Salvador Allende's Popular Unity (UP) socialist administration used a presidential decree to take control of MADECO so that it could be co-managed by workers and government administrators as part of the mixed-property sector.[20] Allende's goal to create full employment led MADECO to hire more workers, increasing the workforce to 2000 by 1973. Groups of workers organized by section served on production committees with an advisory role in relation to the firm's new chief executive, a former union leader, and state-appointed managers. Fernando Pérez remained as production manager, and Jaime Deischler, a retired military official hired in the late 1960s, stayed on as personnel manager. There is not firm evidence to measure the efficiency of production under Allende, and both workers and managers have conflicting memories of the experience of co-management. The unions' growing politicization beginning in the late 1960s was evident in union activists' campaigning in support for Allende's candidacy, demand for the firm's intervention after his election, active involvement in implementing co-management at the firm, and participation in volunteer work and other activities in support of the Allende administration. This increasing politicization would ultimately place leaders and activists in harm's way after the September 11, 1973, coup.[21]

[19] Peter Winn, *Weavers of Revolution: The Yarur Workers and Chile's Road to Socialism* (New York: Oxford University Press, 1986), 139–252; Loveman, *Chile*, 292–309.

[20] Pío García, interview with author, March 12, 1995. Interviewees who preferred to remain anonymous identified by first name only.

[21] Stillerman, *From Solidarity to Survival*, 203, 210–223, 251–273, 281–285.

MADECO Under the Dictatorship and Subsequent Civilian Administrations

After the September 11, 1973 military coup, the junta systematically repressed leftist militants and activists. Following the US-based National Security Doctrine, the junta sought to purge Chile of Marxism. The regime's initial years were characterized by the imprisonment, torture, assassination, exile, firing, and blacklisting of thousands of Chileans. Additionally, the generals suspended centrist and rightist parties as well as parliament to address perceived dysfunctions of Chilean politics. Moreover, the generals appointed military officials to lead government agencies and publicly controlled firms. The military replaced leftist union leaders with the oldest workers in each firm and suspended all union activities except for information sharing.[22]

The junta did not initially have an economic plan. The Navy had commissioned a plan for economic reconstruction in 1972, led by the so-called "Chicago Boys," a group of economists based primarily, though not exclusively, at the Catholic University, who gained key posts in the Economy and Planning Ministries early under the dictatorship. These individuals had done postgraduate work at the University of Chicago and adopted the monetarist approach favored by Milton Friedman and others there. Shortly after the coup, the group provided their plan, "the brick" (*el ladrillo*) to the junta. The plan did not offer a coherent blueprint for the Chilean economy, but it did include ideas that were later adopted by the dictatorship such as the privatization of pensions. While some members of the junta and cabinet officials initially criticized monetarist policies because they strayed from the Keynesian approach adopted in Chile since the 1940s, Pinochet and his allies worked to marginalize these critics in the regime's first few years. The Chicago Boys initially focused on reducing Chile's high inflation, though they later implemented tariff reduction, privatization, the elimination of subsidies and price controls, liberalization of financial markets, and market-based social policies. The Chicago Boys had free reign to apply these policies because the military insulated them from interest groups or other forms of democratic accountability. These policies had world historical significance because they later became the

[22] Winn, "The Pinochet Era," 19–29; Huneeus, *El régimen de Pinochet,* 96–108; Gárate, *La revolución capitalista,* 181–83.

doctrine of the Reagan and Thatcher governments, respectively, in the United States and the United Kingdom.[23]

The Chicago Boys' economic policies have been grouped into "radical neoliberal" (1973–1982) and "pragmatic neoliberal" (1982–1989) phases. During the first phase, economic policymaking officials applied monetarist policies without consulting leaders with business peak associations or other groups. While they adopted numerous market-based policies, we focus here on privatization. From 1974 to 1980, the government reduced its holdings from 400 to 45 firms. A first phase in 1974 returned about 250 firms to their owners. Then, from 1974 to 1978, the government auctioned off firms. Because the government sold large packages of shares and only required buyers to post 10–20% of the firms' value, the sales favored further concentration of wealth among existing and new business groups. The process was not transparent, as some purchasers relied on insider information or privileged access to foreign credit due to their links to economic policymakers.[24]

Chile experienced a speculative financial bubble from 1978 to 1981 driven by easy access to foreign credit and the government's adherence to a fixed exchange rate of 39 pesos/dollar. The economy collapsed in 1982 amid the global recession and its failed foreign exchange policy, and the government was compelled to adopt pragmatic policies including once again nationalizing failing banks and firms controlled by the two largest business groups, Cruzat-Larraín and BHC; currency devaluation; modest countercyclical measures; and later in 1986–1988, the second privatization of these firms alongside the sale of public utilities and telecommunications companies. The government implemented these policies with greater consultation with business peak associations. The last phase of privatization included greater foreign investment. By the mid-1980s, the economy had entered a period of sustained growth.[25]

[23] Huneeus, *El régimen de Pinochet*, 389–413; Gárate, *La revolución capitalista*, 181–252; Juan Gabriel Valdés, *Pinochet's Economists: The Chicago School in Chile* (Cambridge, UK: Cambridge University Press, 1995), 16–28; David Harvey, *A Brief History of Neoliberalism* (Oxford: Oxford University Press, 2005), 8–9.

[24] Huneeus, *El régimen de Pinochet*, 437–498; Patricio Meller, *Un siglo de economía política chilena (1890–1990)* (Santiago: Editorial Andres Bello, 1996), 185–88, 267–72; Eduardo Silva, "The Political Eocnomy of Chile's Regime Transition: From Radical to 'Pragmatic' Neo-liberal Policies," in *The Struggle for Democracy in Chile* (rev. ed.), edited by Paul Drake and Iván Jaksić, 98–127 (Lincoln: University of Nebraska Press, 1996).

[25] Ibid.

Repression and Industrial Restructuring, 1973–1978

Because MADECO played a critical role in the UP's mixed property area and its union strongly identified with the UP government, 270 union members and political militants were swiftly arrested and dismissed after the coup.[26] However, two factors intensified the regime's attack against MADECO workers. First, some workers had used a motorized forklift to patrol the streets around the factory after a bombing attempt by a far-right organization late in the UP administration. Days after the coup, photos appeared in national newspapers of the forklift alleging that it was used as a "mini-tank" as part of an alleged (though never proven) armed conspiracy against the military. Second, since Jaime Deischler had served as personnel manager since the late 1960s, he compiled a list of left-wing leaders and militants ready to use once the coup occurred. These individuals were disappeared, arrested, tortured, blacklisted, and/or exiled.[27]

After these arrests, Deischler hired Osvaldo Romo, who had been a left-wing activist under the UP and worked for the intelligence service (DINA) after the coup. He assembled a team whose spying led to additional workers' arrest. In 1992, after the dictatorship ended, Romo was extradited to Chile from Brazil and interviewed by several media outlets during which he noted his short tenure at MADECO. After his extradition, he was convicted for human rights violations and died in prison in 2007. Deischler retired from MADECO shortly after Romo's return.[28]

While the military officials at MADECO could fire and arrest known party militants based on the junta's emergency decrees promulgated shortly after the coup, these individuals only represented a fraction of the workforce of 2000. The firm's CEO, Fernando Pérez, who claimed not to know about the political firings and arrests, faced the larger challenge of drastically cutting the workforce to pay off MADECO's debts so that they could sell the state's share in the firm. During the UP, CORFO had exercised an option to purchase a majority of MADECO's shares and took

[26] "Primer discurso del interventor en MADECO, pos-golpe," mimeo, December 26, 1973, 9.

[27] "26 'tanquetas' construyó un agitador brasileño en MADECO," *La Tercera*, September 27, 1973, 5; Achié, interview with author, November 20, 1996; and Roberto, interview with author, December 21, 1994.

[28] "Osvaldo Enrique Romo Mena: Agente DINA," Accessed October 27, 2018. https://www.memoriaviva.com/criminales/criminales_r/romo_mena_osvaldo.htm; "Entrevista de Carmen Castillo: Habla Romo," *Agencia Publicitaria de Servicios Informativos (APSI)* 503, May 1995, 8.

physical possession of those shares; the purchase was never completed. Management and members of the company's board had attempted to identify buyers, but none was interested given the firm's debts. In 1975, MADECO asked the U.S. copper mining company, Anaconda, which had owned mines in Chile, to analyze MADECO's prospects and to consider purchasing the firm, but Anaconda only offered technical assistance.[29]

Given the currency stabilization measures in 1975 and tariff reductions from 1977 to 1979, MADECO, like other firms, faced a harsh competitive environment on domestic and foreign markets. Stiff competition heightened the urgency of cost-cutting measures and a swift sale of the firm. After eliminating leftist party activists, the firm faced a challenge in further workforce reductions. Labor policy did not face radical reforms until the late 1970s. Collective bargaining and union elections were banned, but the labor law remained intact, putting the brakes on mass layoffs and voiding union contracts.

Consequently, management had to encourage voluntary retirements by offering workers 125% of their contractual severance payment. Barring the emergency decrees permitting dismissal of party activists, if companies fired workers without cause, labor courts could award a double severance payment to complainants. Thus, the firm could not engage in mass layoffs and workers had a minimal degree of bargaining power regarding dismissals. However, Deischler often threatened individual workers he viewed as troublemakers with imprisonment if they did not accept voluntary retirement. Through this policy, MADECO cut the workforce in half by 1978.[30]

In addition to workforce reductions, management negotiated benefit givebacks with union leaders. While the leaders had little experience and feared management retribution, they extracted one-time bonuses in exchange for accepting reduced production incentives and profit sharing payments. The crux of these changes was to shift the proportion of wages from blue- to white-collar and administrative staff and to reduce the firm's liability regarding profit sharing.[31]

How did MADECO workers experience these changes? Jaime Deischler had purged union leaders and leftist party militants immediately after the

[29] Fernando Pérez B., interview with author, December 6, 1994.

[30] Stillerman, *From Solidarity to Survival*, 309.

[31] Joel Stillerman, "Disciplined Workers and Avid Consumers: Neoliberal Policy and the Transformation of Work and Identity among Chilean Metalworkers," in *Victims of the Chilean Miracle*, 169–171.

coup and continued with more targeted dismissals throughout the 1970s. The junta installed the workers with the greatest seniority in union posts to serve as information conduits for management, but these leaders lacked adequate experience, legitimacy among workers, and authority to engage in collective bargaining.[32]

An independent group of union members emerged after 1976, when two former student activists, Héctor Velásquez and Guillermo Gómez, were hired along with others. Velásquez met secretly with union members with leftist or pro-union sympathies in the firm's daycare center, where he worked in his early years, and after sports games. Additionally, because the union still had an organizational presence even if it had no power, section delegates and committee members of the union's summer resort adopted leadership roles that would later bear fruit when union elections and collective bargaining began again.[33]

Privatization, Industrial Conflict, and Technological Modernization, 1979–1992

By 1979, downsizing, benefit givebacks, and growing exports helped MADECO attract a buyer. The Luksic family, which had operated in Chile since the 1950s and owned shares in MADECO, purchased the firm.[34] The Luksics had begun in auto sales and mining, and gradually expanded their holdings prior to the coup. The family's patriarch opted to sell most of his assets under the UP and leave for England. Some businessmen resented their departure, insisting that they should have stayed and fought against Allende's administration. However, they returned after the coup and gained a reputation for buying firms at low prices and making them profitable. They were one among several business groups that expanded their holdings during the first phase of privatization.[35]

The Luksic group had a freer hand than their predecessors to modify the firm due to labor law changes from 1978 to 1982. A series of decree

[32] René Gutierrez, author interview, May 5, 1994.

[33] Stillerman, "Explaining Strike Outcomes in Chile," 108–111.

[34] MADECO, *Memoria Annual,* 1979, 5. The Luksic Group had long-term connections with MADECO. In 1970, it owned 5% of MADECO's stock: Fernando Dahse, "El poder de los grandes grupos económicos nacionales." Working Paper #18. (Santiago, Chile: Facultad Latinoamericana de Ciencias Sociales, 1983), 23.

[35] "La saga de los Luksic: La consolidación del imperio," *Qué Pasa* (October 16, 1993), 37–40.

laws became known as the Plan Laboral and were part of the junta's efforts to institutionalize its rule via the 1980 Constitution and the "seven modernizations" that applied the Chicago Boys' market principles to social policy areas such as labor, health, pensions, and education. The Plan Laboral emerged after the AFL-CIO threatened to boycott Chilean exports due to the absence of union elections and collective bargaining. Under Labor Minister José Piñera, the junta did include elections and bargaining to prevent the boycott but used the opportunity to wipe out many labor protections dating back to the 1931 Labor Code and subsequent amendments. Most importantly, the laws permitted massive layoffs, allowed firms to hire replacement workers after a one-month strike, limited strikes to 59 days, allowed firms to void previous wage commitments in new contracts, eliminated labor courts, and allowed firms to modify contractually negotiated job descriptions.[36] The Luksics used these changes to engage in massive layoffs during the 1981–1983 recession, reduce wages, subcontract nonproduction functions (food service, security), modify job descriptions, and eliminate internal subcontracting (a firm tradition of hiring workers' family members).[37]

When the junta called for elections in 1979, the clandestine group of workers described above identified Manuel Espinoza, who had served as a section delegate, as a viable leader. Through word of mouth and the distribution of tiny paper messages, the activists persuaded a majority of workers to support Espinoza's candidacy. During the next election cycle, Espinoza was reelected, alongside Velásquez and Carlos Vargas, who had served on the summer resort committee and was a MAPU militant.[38]

Velásquez and Vargas adopted a more forceful leadership role. They began to circulate a newsletter among members. They also led efforts to thwart benefit givebacks management attempted to unilaterally impose by isolating individual workers and demanding they sign away those benefits. Additionally, in 1982, MADECO union leaders began coordinating with other Santiago unions with the goal of organizing a citywide conference in May 1983. An initial planning meeting in May 1982 had 300 in attendance and fostered discussions among plant-level union leaders.[39]

[36] Winn, "The Pinochet Era," 31–38.

[37] Stillerman, "Disciplined Workers and Avid Consumers," 172–73.

[38] Stillerman, "Explaining Strike Outcomes in Chile," 108–111.

[39] Stillerman, "Explaining Strike Outcomes in Chile," 108–111.

These efforts took on greater urgency during the 1982 recession when MADECO laid off workers and reduced wages in light of new legal provisions. While this context gave the union little to no bargaining leverage, in early 1983 members decided to strike to defend their organization and demand better wages and benefits. The conflict gained national visibility as one of the few walkouts in the early years of the Plan Laboral.[40]

The union was at a distinct disadvantage because of legal changes limiting strikes to 59 days and permitting firms to hire strikebreakers. Additionally, police officials arrested marching strikers who sought to discourage job seekers from applying for jobs. During the arrests, police interrogated and tortured union leaders. Even as some strikers returned to work after the strike had continued for one month, the remaining strikers decided to continue "until the final consequences" and stayed off the job until the 59th day. After the strike, management fired 100 strike activists. Additionally, when a few of the union leaders were not reelected shortly after the strike's completion, management fired them as they no longer enjoyed immunity from dismissal.[41]

The union was severely damaged after the strike and Velásquez, who was reelected and became president, urged strikers to forgive coworkers who crossed the picket line to retain the union's members. In addition to mass layoffs, management encouraged members of the more militant blue-collar union to switch affiliation to the weaker white-collar union in an effort to destroy the organization. Additionally, management made several efforts to remove Velásquez from office. They offered him promotions or cash settlements to step down from his position. Additionally, a bomb was planted outside the firm during the night shift, and Velásquez was arrested, interrogated, and tortured under suspicion of planting the bomb. When he was released two days later and reported for work, Deischler threatened to fire him for abandonment of the workplace, but Velásquez retorted that Deischler knew exactly where he was, and the personnel manager desisted. The union again attempted to coordinate with other plant-level unions and spoke out against efforts to build a new labor peak organization based on political accords rather than a

[40] Stillerman, "Explaining Strike Outcomes in Chile," 108–111; Winn, "The Pinochet Era," 39–41.

[41] "Dirigentes de Madeco quieren hablar con Mardones," *Las Ultimas Noticias* February 18, 1983, 10; Juan Fuentes, interview with author, March 9, 1995.

democratic process involving plant-level unions, though they were unable to persuade the CUT leadership to change course.[42]

During the late 1980s and 1990s, MADECO began purchasing labor-saving machinery and other copper manufacturers in Chile and abroad. From 1991 to 1995, MADECO increased its profits from $23 million to $47 million and increased investment in related firms from $33 million to $145 million while keeping the headcount at its Santiago location at 900.[43] As the company's portfolio expanded, MADECO was converted into a holding company headquartered at its original Santiago location. The introduction of new machinery allowed the company to adopt some dimensions of Japanese-style managerial techniques—Just-in-Time production and Total Quality Management. These techniques aim to reduce excess raw material storage and to identify product failures while they are still on the production line. In principle, they also give line workers greater authority to stop production to address machine failures and product defects. However, MADECO adopted techniques introducing greater efficiency without giving line workers greater authority, as has been noted in other Chilean firms and Japanese transplant factories in international locations. An additional dimension of these changes was management's requirement that workers become polyvalent—that each machine tender learns to operate multiple machines to reduce downtime. In 1993, MADECO was one of the first Chilean firms to sell shares (American Depository Receipts, ADRs) on the NY Stock Exchange, raising $90 million in stock purchases.[44]

Democratic Transition, Globalization, and the Luksic Group's Ascent, 1992 to Present

As the economy grew in the mid-1980s and MADECO began to hire more personnel, the union was able to negotiate some improved benefits. It is possible that management sought to build more pacific relations with the organization to improve morale and productivity. However, another conflict emerged after the 1990 transition to civilian rule in Chile. The

[42] Stillerman, *From Solidarity to Survival*, 339–341.

[43] INVEXANS, "Historia: 1944–2005." Accessed October 27, 2018. https://invexans.cl/nosotros/historia/: "US $ 90 millones sumó el aumento de capital completado por MADECO," *El Mercurio*, August 25, 1993, D5; MADECO, *Memoria Anual* (Santiago: MADECO, 1995).

[44] Stillerman, "Disciplined Workers and Avid Consumers," 173–178.

union had already effectively sued the firm for inadequate payment of overtime work after a modest labor reform promulgated by the elected Concertación administration. They advanced a second suit alleging that the firm had underpaid quarterly bonuses from 1989 to 1991. Management sought to pressure the blue-collar, white collar, and supervisory unions to modify the clause in their contract that was the basis of the lawsuit. Office employees in the white-collar union and members of the supervisory union desisted, but the blue-collar union stood firm and planned a strike to defend their contractual clause.[45]

The firm responded to the planned strike by forming nonunion negotiating groups (permitted under the law) to lure away union members with bonuses. As noted above, office workers in the white-collar union exited en masse, but only a handful of blue-collar members left their organization. While during the 1983 strike, the union had been confined to the union hall located a few blocks from the factory; during the 1993 conflict, they camped out at a Federation building the union owned located across the street from the firm. The strike's protagonists were younger workers who did not hold union office. Many had participated in Chile's 1983–1986 pro-democracy street protests based in Santiago's shantytowns. They used tactics prevalent during the protests like tooting on cornets, banging on garbage cans, and stoning buses transporting replacement workers. Additionally, small groups of workers sabotaged company equipment during the night shift. Management eventually accepted the union's demand after strikers marched to the Presidential Palace located across the street from a hotel owned by the Luksic Group. Strikers inferred that company officials were meeting with foreign investors (likely linked to MADECO's ADR issue on the NYSE) and used this meeting as leverage to bring the company to the negotiating table.[46]

After the strike, management fired 40 workers who overturned their lunch trays to protest a bonus offered to workers who had not participated in the walkout. The union's lawsuit proceeded and the Supreme Court ruled in the union's favor two years later. However, management dragged its feet until 2002, when the union secured an asset seizure order against MADECO through the National Comptroller's General Office, at which time the two sides reached a settlement to pay 60% of the funds owed the union to eligible workers upon retirement or departure from the firm. The

[45] Stillerman, "Disciplined Workers and Avid Consumers," 189–192.
[46] Stillerman, "Disciplined Workers and Avid Consumers," 189–192.

union had won, but the firm used its extensive resources and institutional connections to drag out the settlement for nearly a decade.[47]

The firm's expansion and modernization yielded positive results until the mid-1990s, when warning signs indicated that their international investments were not successful. The firm eventually divested from most of its international operations. By 2002, the price of MADECO ADRs dropped below $1.00 for more than 30 days on the NYSE, requiring corrective action. The company first tried to comply with SEC regulations to continue to list its stock on the NYSE, but in 2009 decided to delist its stock on the NYSE because it only represented a small portion of total stock and being listed cost additional expenses to the company.[48]

In 2003, Héctor Velásquez, who had been a major force in rebuilding the union since the mid-1970s, and had served continuously in union office since 1981, died of colon cancer in his early 50s. He had worked tirelessly to regain lost benefits at MADECO and also led several attempts to coordinate rank and file unions in Santiago and outside the CUT's bureaucratic structures. Immediately preceding his death, Velásquez had attempted to form a coordinating body of workers employed by Luksic companies, but this organization did not prosper. His death was an important loss for both the MADECO organization and the labor movement.[49]

By 2008, the Luksic Group sold its wire operations to the French firm, Nexans, and simultaneously purchased a controlling interest in the firm. The firm brought in French managers to the Santiago plant with an initially more conciliatory managerial approach. In 2013, after the final MADECO brand asset, the Santiago brass mill, was unable to compete with cheaper Mexican goods, the Luksic Group shuttered the plant. They retained the MADECO name to market products but eliminated it on the

[47] Stillerman, "Disciplined Workers and Avid Consumers," 193–194.

[48] MADECO, S.A. "For Immediate Release: Madeco announces intent to delist from the NYSE, and terminate its ADR program in the United States." https://www.sec.gov/Archives/edgar/data/899296/000089929609000011/madeco.pdf (accessed March 8, 2019).

[49] Stillerman, "Explaining Strike Outcomes in Chile: Associational Power, Structural Power, and Spatial Strategies." *Latin American Politics and Society* 59, no. 1 (2017): 96–118" 109; Leiva, "Flexible Workers, Gender, and Contending Strategies for Confronting the Crisis of Labor in Chile," 117–118; Coordinadora de Sindicatos del Grupo Luksic Vol. 10. 2004 https://lae.princeton.edu/catalog/95c3f770-6ea5-46cc-80b9-e07bcbd50bcc?locale=en#?c=0&m=0&s=0&cv=0&xywh=-2447%2C-1%2C8452%2C5165 (accessed March 8, 2019).

production side. With the brass mill closed, the Luksics changed the name of the multinational to Invexans, essentially burying the MADECO name.[50]

The final challenge to the union's long-term vitality came after the wire mill's 2008 sale to the French consortium, Nexans. Because the wire mill workers were no longer employed by MADECO, which still owned the brass mill, the change led to complications for the union. While the law clearly stated that the union could continue to operate as a single entity representing workers in the two factories, brass mill union leaders claimed that since the wire mill union members were not employed by MADECO, they should be expelled from the union and denied access to union facilities and services. The president of the Nexans union, who had worked with Velásquez, attempted to negotiate with the leaders, but to no avail. The Nexans union retained an attorney to sue the brass mill union for access to the union's facilities. They eventually won their case, but it was a pyrrhic victory, as the Luksic group shut down the brass mill in late 2013 because it was unable to compete with cheap Mexican imports. The MADECO brand name was still used to market products, but the firm itself had ended.[51]

The Nexans union continues to operate. Union leaders initially had a honeymoon with the French management, which began with a more respectful tone toward the organization reflecting the industrial relations system in France. However, after a few years, they began to emulate their Chilean counterparts—laying off workers at the end of the year when many union members were on vacation and unable to stage a protest and engaging in union busting tactics. The Nexans union, with 127 members, remained a shadow of the once mighty MADECO organization of the 1960s and 1970s with over 1000 members. Nonetheless, the union successfully sued the firm in late 2018 for union busting practices whereby

[50] Stillerman, "Disciplined Workers and Avid Consumers," 196; Invexans, "Historia: 1944–2005."

[51] Invexans, "Historia." Accessed October 27, 2018. http://www.invexans.cl/invexans/historia/; Manuel, personal communications, Facebook messages to author, August 15, 2010, December 18, 2010, June 23, 2013, February 13, 2014; "Cierre de Madeco Mills enciende inquietud," *Minería Chilena*, December 19, 2013. Accessed October 27, 2018. http://www.mch.cl/2013/12/19/cierre-de-madeco-enciende-inquietud-por-el-futuro-manufacturero-del-cobre-en-chile/

the firm agreed to end the practice of hiring new staff as temporary workers without the option to gain permanent contracts.[52]

While the union was weakened like other organizations in industry and mining during the 2000s, the Luksic Group soared. A 2002 loan from the Banco del Estado during the presidential administration of Socialist Ricardo Lagos allowed the group to purchase the Banco de Chile and create one of its largest sources of revenue. Like some other business groups that began to adopt a more pragmatic approach to government alliances rather than offering the political right steadfast loyalty, the Luksics' ties to the Lagos and later Bachelet administrations were evident in the receipt of loans and the group's strategic use of campaign contributions and employment of former government ministers, which may have shielded it from regulatory control. This pragmatic attitude toward center-left governments has borne fruit. From 2002 to 2012, growing wealth from banking and mining operations allowed the group's asset value to increase from \$2 billion to \$15 billion. In 2017, the group was ranked first in Chile in stock wealth, earnings, and assets, and a few years earlier the family was ranked 27th on the *Forbes* list of the world's wealthiest individuals and families. While since its inception, the group had holdings in several economic sectors, it significantly expanded into banking, communications, food, and mining during the 1990s and 2000s.[53]

Conclusion

The trajectory of MADECO and its blue-collar unions since the September 1973 military coup illustrate broader patterns of state–business relations under the Pinochet dictatorship and afterward. The MADECO union was viciously targeted by the military as part of its broader attack on union leaders and leftist party activists during its first five years. While union elections and collective bargaining were frozen until the 1978 Plan Laboral,

[52] Manuel, personal communication via Facebook message, October 27, 2018; Avenimiento. Juzgado de Letras del Trabajo de San Miguel. El Sindicato de Trabajadores de la Empresa Nexans y Nexans, S.A. December, 2018.

[53] Leiva, *Chile's Grupo Luksic*, 11, 21–22, 28–35; Bucheli et al., "Better Together," 17; Undurraga, "Rearticulación de grupos económicos," 13–14; M. Leiva and P. Poblete, "Luksic lideró el Ranking de Grupos Económicos de 2017 impulsado por el alza del precio del cobre" (October 15, 2018). Accessed October 27, 2018. https://www.latercera.com/pulso/noticia/luksic-lidero-ranking-grupos-economicos-2017-impulsado-alza-del-precio-del-cobre/361873/

the firm's personnel manager used force, surveillance, and intimidation to root out union activists, while the general manager negotiated benefit givebacks to resolve the firm's debts and competitive challenges on the workers' backs. Businesses were important venues for the state to exert its repressive power.

MADECO went through a lengthy process of privatization because investors were reluctant to assume the firm's debts and to take control of the firm with what they perceived as an excessive workforce. By the late 1970s, the combination of repression, benefit givebacks, and voluntary retirements allowed management to halve the workforce. Additionally, MADECO avoided collapse by pursuing export opportunities amidst the junta's trade liberalization policies. The firm was ripe for the picking, and the Luksic Group was back on the scene after abandoning Chile during the UP.

The firm's privatization and further downsizing in the early 1980s were permitted by Plan Laboral provisions permitting mass layoffs and wage cuts, both made necessary by Economy Minister Sergio de Castro's stubborn adherence to monetarist doctrine through dollar parity currency policies that worsened the effects of the global economic slowdown. Like many other Chilean firms that survived the crisis, MADECO benefited from the economy's rebound, facilitating new machinery purchases and acquisition of competing firms in Chile and abroad.[54]

The union's reorganization, election of pro-democracy activists, and 1983 strike followed similar patterns among other organizations. Copper mining unions had initiated walkouts in the late 1970s, followed by textile and construction workers.[55] The union's 1983 walkout resulted from management provocation, and while union members ended the two-month strike with their heads held high, subsequent layoffs of strike activists and union-busting strategies nearly crushed the organization. With a steady hand, Velásquez and other leaders and activists kept the organization afloat, aided by a growing economy and a wave of new hires in the mid-1980s.

[54] Martínez and Díaz, *Chile: The Great Transformation* (Geneva: Brookings Institution, 1997), 70–72; Winn, "The Pinochet Era," 28; Claudio Ramos Zincke, *La transformación de la empresa chilena: Una modernización desbalanceada* (Santiago: Ediciones Universidad Alberto Hurtado, 2009), 20–21.

[55] Winn, "The Pinochet Era," 37.

Aided by the 1992 departure of the hated personnel manager and a modest labor reform under the first Concertación administration, in 1993 the union sought to settle scores with management regarding benefit give-backs dating to the 1970s. While the Supreme Court upheld the union's lawsuit against the firm, management's ability to drag out the settlement for nine years reflected the economic, legal, and political power of big business.[56]

The union's weakened state was mirrored in other organizations. After the early 1990s, union density declined, most unions negotiated collective agreements rather contracts, and strikes declined with a few important exceptions (civil servants, retail workers, subcontracted export workers, and dockworkers). The MADECO union's decline was part of a longer process of political repression, economic transformation, and legal reform that had profoundly diminished unions' negotiating power and influence on public policy.[57]

While unions languished, new and reorganized business groups flourished thanks to the privatization waves of the 1970s and 1980s, deregulation, and labor laws favoring business. The Luksic Group's meteoric rise in the 2000s reflects this broader process of business's growing economic, legal, and political power thanks to favorable state action. These large business groups and their subsidiaries are distinct from the firms that grew in the ISI era. They are internationally networked in their ownership structure, markets, and financial backing, and relatively independent of state support via subsidies and ownership. Nonetheless, like the ISI firms, these business groups benefited from state privatization, pro-business labor laws, the loosening of investment restrictions, and close ties to elected officials. While business arguably has greater power than the state, its economic and political muscle result from state policies that benefited capital and sharply diminished labor's bargaining power and institutional presence.

[56] On this point, see, for example: Paul W. Posner, "Labor Market Flexibility, Employment, and Inequality: Lessons from Chile," in *Labor Politics in Latin America: Democracy and Worker Organization in the Neoliberal Era*, ed. Paul W. Posner, Viviana Patroni, and Jean Francois Mayer (Gainesville: University of Florida Press, 2018), 56–58.

[57] Gonzalo Durán, and Marco Kremerman. *Sindicatos y negociación colectiva* (Santiago: Fundación Sol, 2015). Accessed October 27, 2018. http://www.fundacionsol.cl/wp-content/uploads/2016/05/Sindicatos-y-Negociaci%C3%B3n-Colectiva.pdf

References

Archival Sources

Chile, Biblioteca Nacional.
Chile, Servicio de Recortes, Biblioteca del Congreso.
Chile, Congressional Hearings, Biblioteca del Congreso.
Chile, Ministerio de Economía, Superintendencia de Valores y Seguros.
Chile, Dirección del Trabajo.
Chile, CORFO Library.
Chile, Municipalidad de San Miguel.
Sindicato #1, MADECO.

Bibliography

"26 'tanquetas' construyó un agitador brasileño en MADECO." *La Tercera*, September 27, 1973.

Angell, Alan. *Politics and the Labour Movement in Chile*. London: Oxford University Press, 1972.

Aravena, Antonio, and Daniel Núñez, eds. *El Renacer de la Huelga Obrera en Chile*. Santiago: Instituto de Ciencias Alejandro Lipschutz, 2009.

Armstrong V., Alberto J., and Rafael A. Águila B. *Evolución del conflicto laboral en Chile, 1961–2002*. Santiago: Ediciones Universidad Católica de Chile, 2006.

Bank-Muñoz, Carolina. *Building Power from Below: Chilean Workers Take on Walmart*. Ithaca, NY: Cornell University Press, 2017.

Bucheli, Marcelo, Erica Salvaj, and Minyoung Kim. "Better together: How Multinationals come Together with Business Groups in Times of Economic and Political Transitions." In *Global Strategy Journal*, 9, No 2 (2019): 1–32.

"Cierre de Madeco Mills enciende inquietud." *Minería Chilena*, December 19, 2013, accessed October 27, 2018. http://www.mch.cl/2013/12/19/cierre-de-madeco-enciende-inquietud-por-el-futuro-manufacturero-del-cobre-en-chile/

CHILE, Cámara de Diputados, "-Conflicto que afecta al personal de la industria MADECO.-Inserción de documentos.-Proyecto de acuerdo," Sesión 20, November 18, 1965.

"Comisión investigadora de la industria manufacturera del cobre acordó la Cámara." *El Mercurio*, November 23, 1965.

Coordinadora de Sindicatos del Grupo Luksic Vol. 10. 2004. Digital Archive of Latin American and Caribbean Ephemera. Princeton University Library. Accessed March 8, 2019. https://lae.princeton.edu/

catalog/95c3f770-6ea5-46cc-80b9-e07bcbd50bcc?locale=en#?c=0&m=0&s=0&cv=0&xywh=-2447%2C-1%2C8452%2C5165

Dahse, Fernando. "El poder de los grandes grupos económicos nacionales." Working Paper #18. Santiago, Chile: Facultad Latinoamericana de Ciencias Sociales, 1983.

"Dirigentes de Madeco quieren hablar con Mardones." *Las Ultimas Noticias*, February 18, 1983.

"Don Aurelio Simonetti: Un Viaje Hacia la Historia de MADECO," *MADECO 50 Años: Desarrollando Futuro*, April 1994.

Durán, Gonzalo, and Marco Kremerman. *Sindicatos y negociación colectiva*. Santiago: Fundación Sol, 2015, accesed October 27, 2018. http://www.fundacionsol.cl/wp-content/uploads/2016/05/Sindicatos-y-Negociaci%C3%B3n-Colectiva.pdf

Ffrench-Davis, Ricardo. *Economic Reforms in Chile: From Dictatorship to Democracy*. Ann Arbor, MI: University of Michigan Press, 2002.

Gárate Chateau, Manuel. *La revolución capitalista en Chile (1973–2003)*. Santiago: Ediciones Universidad Alberto Hurtado, 2012.

Harvey, David. *A Brief History of Neoliberalism*. Oxford: Oxford University Press, 2005.

Huneeus, Carlos. *El régimen de Pinochet*. Santiago: Editorial Sudamericana, 2001.

"La saga de los Luksic: La consolidación del imperio." *Qué Pasa*, October 16, 1993, 37–40.

Leiva, Fernando. "Chile's Grupo Luksic and the 'New Spirit of Capital,'" (unpublished manuscript, accessed March 7, 2019), https://rca.ucsc.edu/images/Leiva-Chiles-Luksic-Economic-Conglomerate

Leiva, M., and P. Poblete, "Luksic lideró el Ranking de Grupos Económicos de 2017 impulsado por el alza del precio del cobre" (October 15, 2018). Accessed October 27, 2018. https://www.latercera.com/pulso/noticia/luksic-lidero-ranking-grupos-economicos-2017-impulsado-alza-del-precio-del-cobre/361873/

Loveman, Brian. *Chile: The Legacy of Hispanic Capitalism*. 2nd, Ed. New York: Oxford University Press, 1988.

MADECO, *Memoria Anual*. Santiago: MADECO, 1995.

MADECO. *Memoria Anual*. Santiago: MADECO, 1979.

"'MADECO' puso en práctica un vigoroso plan de expansión de sus actividades." *La Nación*, January 15, 1967, 14.

Martínez, Javier, and Alvaro Díaz. *Chile: the Great Transformation*. Geneva: Brookings Institution, 1997.

Medel Sierralta, Rodrigo, and Domingo Pérez Valenzuela. "Tres modelos de conflicto laboral en Chile: el peso de la economía, la organización sindical y el régimen de trabajo en las tendencias de la huelga extralegal." *Revista Colombiana de Sociología* 40, 2 (2017): 173–195.

Meller, Patricio. *Un siglo de economía política chilena (1890–1990)*. Santiago: Editorial Andres Bello, 1996.

Moran, Theodore. *Multinational Corporations and the Politics of Dependence: Copper in Chile*. Princeton, NJ: Princeton University Press, 1974.

Posner, Paul W., "Labor Market Flexibility, Employment, and Inequality: Lessons from Chile." In *Labor Politics in Latin America: Democracy and Worker Organization in the Neoliberal Era*, edited by Paul W. Posner, Viviana Patroni, and Jean Francois Mayer. Gainesville: University of Florida Press, 2018.

"Primer discurso del interventor en MADECO, pos-golpe," mimeo, December 26, 1973.

Proyecto Internacional de Derechos Humanos. "Osvaldo Enrique Romo Mena: Agente DINA", accessed October 27, 2018. https://www.memoriaviva.com/criminales/criminales_r/romo_mena_osvaldo.htm

Ramos Zincke, Claudio. *La transformación de la empresa chilena: Una modernización desbalanceada*. Santiago: Ediciones Universidad Alberto Hurtado, 2009.

Silva, Eduardo. "The Import-Substitution Model: Chile in Comparative Perspective." *Latin American Perspectives* 34, no. 3 (May 2007): 67–90.

Silva, Eduardo. "The Political Eocnomy of Chile's Regime Transition: From Radical to "Pragmatic" Neo-liberal Policies." In *The Struggle for Democracy in Chile* (rev. ed.), edited by Paul Drake and Iván Jaksić, 98–127. Lincoln: University of Nebraska Press, 1996.

Stillerman, Joel. "Disciplined Workers and Avid Consumers: Neoliberal Policy and the Transformation of Work and Identity among Chilean Metalworkers." In *Victims of the Chilean Miracle. Workers and Neoliberalism in the Pinochet Era, 1973–2002*, edited by Peter Winn. Durham, NC: Duke University Press, 2004.

Stillerman, Joel. "Explaining Strike Outcomes in Chile: Associational Power, Structural Power, and Spatial Strategies." *Latin American Politics and Society* 59, no. 1 (2017): 96–118.

Stillerman, Joel. *From Solidarity to Survival: Transformations in the Culture and Styles of Mobilization of Chilean Metalworkers under Democratic and Authoritarian Regimes, 1945–1995*. PhD Diss., New York, New School for Social Research, 1998.

Stillerman, Joel. "Space, Strategies and Alliances in Mobilization: The 1960 Metalworkers' and Coal Miners' Strikes in Chile." *Mobilization: An International Journal* 8, no. 1 (February 2003): 72–76.

Undurraga, Tomás. *Rearticulación de grupos económicos y renovación ideológica del empresariado en Chile 1980–2010*. Working Papers ICSO-UDP. Santiago: Universidad Diego Portales, 2011. Accessed March 8, 2019. http://www.icso.cl/wp-content/uploads/2011/03/Working-paper-elites-Tomas-Undurraga1.pdf

"US $ 90 millones sumó el aumento de capital completado por MADECO." *El Mercurio*, August 25, 1993, D5.

Valdés, Juan Gabriel. *Pinochet's Economists: The Chicago School in Chile*. Cambridge, UK: Cambridge University Press, 1995.

Valenzuela, Julio Samuel. "The Chilean Labor Movement: The Institutionalization of Conflict." In *Chile: Politics and Society*, edited by Arturo Valenzuela and Julio Samuel Valenzuela. New Brunswick, NJ: Transaction Books.

Winn, Peter, ed. "The Pinochet Era". In *Victims of the Chilean Miracle*. Durham, NC: Duke University Press, 2004.

Winn, Peter. *Weavers of Revolution: The Yarur Workers and Chile's Road to Socialism*. New York: Oxford University Press, 1986.

CHAPTER 11

The Limits of Repression: State-Owned Enterprises, Corruption, Environmental Activism, and the Brazilian Tucuruí Dam (1974–1984)

Frederik Schulze

Introduction

After World War II, many Latin American countries tried to overcome the colonial legacy of their national economies, especially their export dependency on primary commodities such as agricultural goods and ores and the unequal distribution of income and means of production. As in other regions of the Global South, national governments fostered industrialization and economic development and often referred to economic ideas inspired by US modernization theory. During the Cold War, the United States utilized this theory to promote its economic and democratic model as universal and promised growth and prosperity to the so-called

F. Schulze (✉)
Westfälische Wilhelms-Universität Münster, Münster, Germany
e-mail: frederik.schulze@uni-muenster.de

V. Basualdo et al. (eds.), *Big Business and Dictatorships in Latin America*, Palgrave Studies in Latin American Heterodox Economics, https://doi.org/10.1007/978-3-030-43925-5_11

underdeveloped countries, an idea that generated great interest among Latin American elites.[1] Since domestic business activities in many Latin American countries in the 1940s were mostly limited to the production of primary goods, these countries attracted foreign industrial companies to enhance industrialization. When national elites assumed a more nationalistic approach in the late 1950s, propagated by the United Nations Economic Commission for Latin America and the Caribbean (ECLAC) under the banner of import substitution industrialization (ISI), the focus shifted to internal industrialization efforts and, subsequently, to stronger state participation in business activities. A crucial vehicle for this was state-owned enterprises, which began to assume an important role in the expansion of infrastructure and the exploitation of raw materials.[2]

From the 1940s, Brazil figured as one of the key actors in the state-owned enterprise sector, with powerful companies such as Companhia Vale do Rio Doce (1942), Petrobras (1953), and Eletrobrás (1962). Under the military dictatorship (1964–1985), these corporations were critical to the success of the authoritarian development policy; the nation's huge annual economic growth rates helped to legitimize the dictatorial regime. The military considered the expansion of the energy supply and the economic valorization of the Amazon region particularly relevant. To achieve both of these aims, the regime founded the state-owned company Eletronorte as a subsidiary of the national energy supplier Eletrobrás in 1973. Under the direction of the military, Eletronorte implemented huge dam projects in the Amazon, among them the Tucuruí Dam on the Tocantins River in Pará state (1974–1984). From a technical standpoint, the company was successful in building and operating hydroelectric plants, thus fulfilling its task in the national development program.

At first glance, the dictatorship created a successful state-owned company that helped to legitimize its economic policy. This chapter, however, argues the exact opposite. The relationship between the military and Eletronorte turned out to be a source of conflict and an open flank for criticism and resistance on the part of civil society from the late 1970s onward. While the state tried to implement a successful development policy, personal interests, corruption, a lack of business skills, and disregard

[1] David Ekbladh, *The Great American Mission: Modernization and the Construction of an American World Order* (Princeton: Princeton University Press, 2010).

[2] For an overview, see Victor Bulmer-Thomas, *The Economic History of Latin America since Independence* (Cambridge: Cambridge University Press, 1995).

for human and environmental rights thwarted that goal. First, the military's business interests complicated the work of Eletronorte and jeopardized its positive image among the public. The military tried to make a fortune by selling precious tropical wood from the future reservoir of the Tucuruí Dam through the private firm Agropecuária Capemi. Due to incompetence and corruption, however, the project failed, severely damaging Eletronorte's reputation. Second, the authoritarian implementation of the Tucuruí Dam provoked local resistance, which gained momentum precisely because the residents perceived Tucuruí and Eletronorte as symbols of the military dictatorship. Third, the destruction of the rainforest by the dam's huge reservoir resulted in a local and national debate on environmental protection that even mobilized global environmental movements and worsened the image of the Brazilian regime abroad.

The potential for conflict regarding the business activities in Tucuruí was a consequence not just of the government's misjudgments and misbehavior but also of competing interests among the military and the companies involved. State-owned enterprises in authoritarian Brazil had a subversive potential because they tempted the leading actors to pursue personal interests and to enrich themselves illegally. The attempts of the national intelligence service Serviço Nacional de Informações (SNI) to control and contain the resulting conflicts and resistance failed. Business proved a much more complicated field of operation than the military expected, so that Eletronorte and the business activities relating to it became, in the end, one of many factors that led to the downfall of the regime in 1985.

By highlighting conflicts and erosion of control, this chapter aims at rethinking the relation between the Brazilian military dictatorship and private and state-owned enterprises, contributing to a fresh understanding of Latin American business history. In the last decades, this field has become firmly established as a distinct line of research.[3] Against the backdrop of dependency theory and criticism of imperialism, two diverging interpretations emerged in Brazilian economic and business history in the 1970s

[3] For an introduction, see Rory M. Miller, "The History of Business in Latin America," in *The Routledge Companion to Business History*, ed. John F. Wilson, Steven Toms, Abe de Jong and Emily Buchnea (London and New York: Routledge, 2017), 187–201; Carlos Dávila and Rory Miller, eds., *Business History in Latin America: The Experience of Seven Countries* (Liverpool: Liverpool University Press, 1999); María Inés Barbero, "Business History in Latin America: A Historiographical Perspective," *The Business History Review* 82, no. 3 (2008): 555–75.

and 1980s, and both are still influential today. On the one hand, scholars inspired by dependency theory criticized the exploitative behavior of foreign enterprises and condemned the collaboration of national elites and businesses that helped to strengthen social inequality in Brazil.[4] Peter Evans, for instance, suggested the concept of a "triple alliance" between a strong state, political elites, and "international capital" that pursued an industrialization policy based on personal and selfish interests.[5] According to Evans, state-owned enterprises had an important function in this system and worked relatively successfully.[6] José Paulo Netto recently pointed to the significance of repression for this specific model of development and called attention to the participation of private companies such as VW in "state terrorism."[7] On the other hand, a second strand of scholarship, inspired by US modernization theory, was less critical of business and asked instead whether and why Brazilian industrialization was successful for the purpose of developing future policies.[8]

Recent historiography has tried to overcome such politically motivated interpretations and, thus, has expanded our understanding of Brazilian business activities by looking closely at the history of specific corporations. For instance, in his study on the multiple local, national, and international entanglements of a British gold mining company in Minas Gerais, Marshall C. Eakin was able to demonstrate the limitations of foreign influence while Oliver Dinius, in his work, traced the economic and political agency of Companhia Siderúrgica Nacional's steel workers.[9] These studies typify the

[4] Octavio Ianni, *Ditadura e agricultura: o desenvolvimento do capitalismo na Amazônia: 1964–1978* (Rio de Janeiro: Civilização Brasileira, 1986); Peter Evans, *Dependent Development: The Alliance of Multinational, State, and Local Capital in Brazil* (Princeton: Princeton University Press, 1979); José Paulo Netto, *Pequena história da ditadura brasileira (1964–1985)* (São Paulo: Cortez, 2014).

[5] Evans, *Dependent Development*, 11.

[6] Ibid., 217–9.

[7] Netto, *Pequena história da ditadura brasileira*, 160.

[8] Thomas J. Trebat, *Brazil's State-Owned Enterprises: A Case Study of the State as Entrepreneur* (Cambridge: Cambridge University Press, 1983); Judith Tendler, *Electric Power in Brazil: Entrepreneurship in the Public Sector* (Cambridge: Harvard University Press, 1968); Nathaniel H. Leff, *The Brazilian Capital Goods Industry 1929–1964* (Cambridge: Harvard University Press, 1968).

[9] Marshall C. Eakin, *British Enterprise in Brazil: The St. John d'el Rey Mining Company and the Morro Velho Gold Mine, 1830–1960* (Durham: Duke University Press, 1989); Oliver Dinius, *Brazil's Steel City: Developmentalism, Strategic Power, and Industrial Relations in Volta Redonda, 1941–1964* (Stanford: Stanford University Press, 2010).

new research agenda in Latin American business history in general, pointing to the heterogeneous negotiation processes between private companies and states, emphasizing Latin American agency, thereby questioning the dependency theory's assumption that foreign businesses could easily advance their interests in Latin America and generate profit by counting on the collaboration of the national elites.[10]

While more and more research is being done on the 1950s and early 1960s, business history during the Brazilian military dictatorship and, more specifically, the role state-owned enterprises played within it remain understudied fields.[11] Publications on Eletronorte still reproduce the dichotomy between Marxist critique and uncritical praise that has thus far characterized Brazilian business history: journalistic and political science-oriented studies have rebuked Eletronorte for its negative behavior toward the environment, local residents, and indigenous populations,[12] whereas official publications appreciate the company's achievements in engineering.[13] This chapter, by contrast, sheds light on the complex and conflict-laden facets of the history of state-owned businesses during the Brazilian dictatorship. The first section explains the historical context of Brazilian economic and business policies, and the second looks at Eletronorte and its control by the intelligence service SNI. The vast documentation by the SNI about problems, conflicts, and resistance in Tucuruí provides the basis for the empirical analysis that follows. This formerly classified source material allows for unique insight into the regime's concerns about difficulties in business and related fields. It is now accessible for research at

[10] Miller, "Business History in Latin America," 7 and 13; Ben Ross Schneider, *Business Politics and the State in Twentieth-Century Latin America* (Cambridge: Cambridge University Press, 2004).

[11] Miller, "Business History in Latin America," 16.

[12] Maria Gracinda C. Teixeira, *Energy Policy in Latin America: Social and Environmental Dimensions of Hydropower in Amazônia* (Aldershot: Avebury, 1996); Elizabeth Monosowski, *Institutional Capacities for Assessing Impacts and Trade-offs of Large Hydro Power Dams in the Tropics and Subtropics: the Case of Tucuruí Dam in Brazilian Amazonia: Final Report* (Rio de Janeiro: manuscript, 1990); José Carlos de Assis, *Os mandarins da República: anatomia dos escândalos da administração pública* (Rio de Janeiro: Paz e Terra, 1984); Sebastião Pinheiro, *Tucuruí: o Agente Laranja em uma república de bananas* (Porto Alegre: Sulina, 1989).

[13] Centro da Memória da Eletricidade no Brasil, *Eletronorte: 25 anos* (Rio de Janeiro: Centro da Memória da Eletricidade no Brasil, 1998.

Brazil's National Archives in Brasília.[14] After an overview of the diverse problems documented by the secret service, the main section focuses on Agropecuária Capemi's logging activities in Tucuruí. The Capemi case provides an example of the complexity of business activities during the Brazilian dictatorship and demonstrates the multiple entanglements between the state, private business, state-owned enterprises, and civil society, as well as the divergent interests of different military and governmental actors. By tracing this complexity, the chapter grounds its approach in Marcelo Bucheli's and Jin Uk Kim's call for historians to examine the relationship between politics and business more closely.[15]

Business and Economics Under the Brazilian Dictatorship

Cold War thinking enabled the emergence of military dictatorships in Latin America during the 1960s and 1970s, with the Brazilian dictatorship (1964–1985) being one of the first and most persistent of its kind. The right-wing military embraced the thinking in terms of ideological blocs and argued that only authoritarian measures could hinder the spread of communism and guarantee national security. In the eyes of the military, the overthrow of João Goulart's leftist government and the struggle against opposition and guerillas legitimized the abolition of democratic rights and the use of repression and torture.[16] The military also adopted the idea of economic development and claimed that only an authoritarian regime would enable Brazil to develop quickly into "a modern industrial society," as the Segundo Plano Nacional de Desenvolvimento (II PND, Second National Development Plan) of 1975 suggested, and, in so doing, overcome inflation and the stagnant economy of the Goulart government.[17] The military regime adopted US modernization theory, which maintained that underdeveloped countries could finally reach the living

[14] Acervos dos Órgãos de Informação do Regime Militar: Série SNI, Arquivo Nacional, Brasília.

[15] Marcelo Bucheli and Jin Uk Kim, "The State as a Historical Construct in Organization Studies," in *Organizations in Time: History, Theory, Methods*, ed. Marcelo Bucheli and R. Daniel Wadhwani (Oxford: Oxford University Press, 2013), 241–262.

[16] For an introduction, see Netto, *Pequena história da ditadura brasileira*; Elio Gaspari, *As ilusões armadas*, 5 vols. (Rio de Janeiro: Intrínseca, 2014–2016).

[17] República Federativa do Brasil, *II PND: II Plano Nacional de Desenvolvimento (1975–1979)* (Rio de Janeiro: Centro de Serviços Gráficos do IBGE, 1975), 16.

standard of Western countries by generating economic growth through planning, infrastructure programs, and industrialization.[18] Since the regime pursued a nationalistic agenda, it also incorporated the economic thinking of the United Nations Economic Commission for Latin America and the Caribbean (ECLAC), which suggested that Latin American economies industrialize by means of import substitution to become less dependent on world markets.[19] The government founded planning authorities, drew up several five-year plans (among them the II PND for the years 1975–1979), tried to acquire loans abroad, and attracted foreign investors and experts. Its overall goal, however, continued to be developing a strong national economy without too much dependency on foreign actors.[20]

Brazil's developmentalist thinking did not exclusively originate in an international context, whether shaped by the United States or ECLAC. Brazilian politicians and economists produced their own economic knowledge while trying to understand how economic development was possible. Under the influence of the Great Depression, the authoritarian regime of Getúlio Vargas (1930–1945) was the first Brazilian government that intervened actively in the economy by promoting the country's industrialization and founding state-owned enterprises to diminish Brazil's dependency on the export of agrarian commodities; John Wirth called this policy "economic nationalism."[21] President Juscelino Kubitschek (1956–1961) expanded this policy even further. He implemented economic plans, promoted infrastructure, including the new capital of Brasília, and influenced the global debate on development by stimulating US President John F. Kennedy's development aid program Alliance for Progress.[22] To put it briefly, what the military did after 1964 was linked to a much longer tradition of Brazilian economic thought.[23] Indeed, criti-

[18] Ekbladh, *The Great American Mission*.

[19] Kathryn Sikkink, "Development Ideas in Latin America: Paradigm Shift and the Economic Commission for Latin America," in *International Development and the Social Sciences: Essays on the History and Politics of Knowledge*, ed. Frederick Cooper and Randall Packard (Berkeley: University of California Press, 1997), 228–256.

[20] An overview offers Werner Baer, *The Brazilian Economy: Growth and Development* (Boulder and London: Lynne Rienner, 2014).

[21] John D. Wirth, *The Politics of Brazilian Development 1930–1954* (Stanford: Stanford University Press, 1970), 7; Dinius, *Brazil's Steel City*, 14–38.

[22] Rafael R. Ioris, *Transforming Brasil: A History of National Development in the Postwar Era* (New York and London: Routledge, 2014).

[23] Ricardo Bielschowsky, *Pensamento econômico brasileiro: o ciclo ideológico do desenvolvimentismo* (Rio de Janeiro: Contraponto, 2004).

cism of development thinking originated in Latin America as well, and Brazilian sociologists such as Fernando Henrique Cardoso were crucial to the emergence of dependency theory.

Under President Emílio Garrastazu Médici (1969–1974), the military regime's economic efforts seemed to succeed. The economy grew at an annual average rate of 11%, and industry expanded to such an extent that the regime celebrated and touted the "Brazilian miracle."[24] Yet the wage level remained low, and the regime's economic policy resulted in increasing social inequality. Under Médici's successor Ernesto Geisel (1974–1979), the oil crisis of 1973 led to a trade deficit and to declining economic indicators. Geisel gave priority to infrastructure projects such as large dams to reduce "dependency" on petroleum.[25] He and the last military President João Figueiredo (1979–1985) failed to revitalize the economy and instead accumulated huge debts for infrastructure projects. While this policy fostered social inequality, political repression was decreasing only slowly, resulting in protests in civil society, which finally helped to overthrow the regime in 1985.

The unexploited Amazon region was one of the main targets of development policy during the dictatorship. In 1973, Médici announced that his government aimed to "occupy our empty space and valorize, without distinction, all regions of the Brazilian territory."[26] The II PND called for the "productive occupation of Amazonia" by means of road construction, colonization, the development of the agricultural and timber industries, as well as the exploitation of iron and bauxite deposits.[27] A state-run planning authority, the Superintendência do Desenvolvimento da Amazônia (SUDAM), implemented the aims of the II PND on the ground: the plan sought to "accelerate regional growth," "intensify the integration of Amazonia into the national economy," "contribute substantially to the

[24] For the following, see Werner Baer, *The Brazilian Economy: Growth and Development* (Boulder and London: Lynne Rienner, 2014), 73–9; Netto, *Pequena história da ditadura brasileira*, 152–160 and 189–190.

[25] República Federativa do Brasil, *II PND*, 17.

[26] Discurso do Presidente Médici, perante reunião do Ministério, anunciando, entre outras media descoberta de novos potenciais hidrelétricas no região Amazônica, 6 June 1973, Principais Realizações e Discursos do Governo Médici, Brasília 1974, Arquivo e Coleção Particular Emílio Garrastazu Médici, Instituto Histórico e Geográfico Brasileiro, Rio de Janeiro, 9.

[27] República Federativa do Brasil, *II PND*, 18.

increase of the national foreign exchange revenue," and "increase the salaries of the population."[28]

Foreign investments and the activities of multinational corporations played a crucial role in Brazil's economic policy. At the same time, the state invested heavily in infrastructure and state-owned enterprises that controlled the petroleum, steel, and energy sectors.[29] However, private domestic firms remained rather weak. In 1974, of the 200 biggest companies in Brazil, 41.6% were foreign, 35.3% were state-owned, and only 23.1% were private domestic ones.[30] During a speech in 1977, Geisel outlined the relevance of all three sectors. Foreign business, he insisted, "brings us a supply of capital and technology and helps us to develop more quickly," while state-owned business was important since it "pioneers or acts in areas that are particularly interesting for national security and development."[31] Numerous state-owned companies backed Brazil's development policy—for instance, the national petroleum producer Petrobras and the national energy supplier Eletrobrás. The problem child was private Brazilian business, which Geisel regarded as highly relevant to the growth of exports. Private domestic firms, he highlighted in 1974, "with modern, efficient and dynamic economic organization, comply with the functions that the national strategy assigns to them."[32] Therefore, the government strove to enable such companies to have better access to capital.[33]

[28] Superintendência do Desenvolvimento da Amazônia, *II Plano Nacional de Desenvolvimento: programa de ação do governo para a Amazônia. 1975–79* (Belém: SUDAM, 1976), 52.

[29] Baer, *The Brazilian Economy*, 77.

[30] Netto, *Pequena história da ditadura brasileira*, 149.

[31] Geisel, "Discurso," in *Apoio à empresa privada nacional: discursos pronunciados na solenidade realizada no Palácio do Planalto em 30 de março de 1977: medidas aprovadas* (Brasília, 1977), 5.

[32] Ernesto Geisel, "Aumento das exportações (30.9.1974)," in *As diretrizes governamentais do presidente Ernesto Geisel: subsídios e documentos para a história do Brasil contemporâneo*, ed. Fernando Jorge (São Paulo, 1976), 276.

[33] Ernesto Geisel, "Setor empresarial (10.3.1974)," in *As diretrizes governamentais do presidente Ernesto Geisel: subsídios e documentos para a história do Brasil contemporâneo*, ed. Fernando Jorge (São Paulo, 1976), 342.

Eletronorte, a State-Owned Company, and the Secret Service

Large dams and hydroelectric plants represented a key component of the military's industrialization efforts. The state-owned holding Eletrobrás, founded in 1962, coordinated the energy supply.[34] During the dictatorship, the company turned into an energy planning authority tasked with expanding Brazil's energy output. From 1967 to 1976, the installed hydropower capacity increased from 5,787 MW to 17,675 MW.[35] In the mid-1970s, the regime commissioned large dams such as the Itaipu and Tucuruí Dams as part of the II PND.[36] The downside of this expansion in infrastructure was that the government accrued US $15 billion in debts in 1982.[37] Several of Eletrobrás's regional subsidiaries were responsible for the construction and operation of these plants, and in June 1973, Eletronorte (short for Centrais Elétricas do Norte do Brasil S.A.) started to serve northern Brazil, including the Amazon region.[38]

Eletronorte developed a hydrologic inventory of the tributaries of the Amazon River and identified several suitable places for dam construction. The most important project was the gigantic Tucuruí Dam, but the company also implemented several smaller dams to power the urban centers in northern Brazil. Tucuruí provided highly subsidized electricity for large-scale projects in the Amazon such as Carajás. The main customers were two new aluminum smelters, joint ventures with Japanese firms and the US firm Alcoa.[39]

The Tucuruí Dam is located on the Tocantins River, an Amazon tributary, 300 kilometers south of Belém, the capital of Pará.[40] Reflecting the military's desire to be economically and technologically independent, it was almost entirely a Brazilian project. The Brazilian engineering firms Engevix and Themag designed the dam and, together with Eletronorte,

[34] For the following, see. José Lima, *Políticas de governo e desenvolvimento do setor de energia elétrica: do Código de Águas à crise dos anos 80 (1934–1984)* (Rio de Janeiro: Centro da Memória de Eletricidade no Brasil, 1995), 81–123.

[35] Netto, *Pequena história da ditadura brasileira*, 152.

[36] República Federativa do Brasil, *II PND*, 84.

[37] Lima, *Políticas de governo e desenvolvimento do setor de energia elétrica*, 123 and 126.

[38] On the following, see Centro da Memória da Eletricidade no Brasil, *Eletronorte: 25 anos*.

[39] Eletrobrás, *UHE Tucuruí: estudo de caso* (Rio de Janeiro: Eletrobrás, 1992), 24–5.

[40] For an introduction to the dam's history, see Centro da Memória da Eletricidade no Brasil, *Eletronorte*, 58–75 and 113–54.

supervised its implementation by the Brazilian construction company Camargo Corrêa. In addition, national financiers covered the main share of needed credits. Only some turbines and part of the loans came from France. During the first building phase from 1975 to 1984, the Brazilians built a dam 11 kilometers long and 78 meters high; it had a powerhouse containing 12 turbines with a capacity of four million kilowatts. The second phase doubled energy production, making Tucuruí the fifth largest hydropower plant in the world.

Eletronorte seemed to be a typical state-owned technocratic company in the era of high modernism, relying on engineering expertise, science, and planning. The company's military director, Raul Garcia Llano, highlighted in an official publication from 1977 that Eletronorte and Tucuruí were integral parts of the military's development project. He recognized that "the inspiration and capacity of the government and the Brazilian people [...] chose to construct Tucuruí not just because of its energetic scale and value [...], but also because it embodies priorities that are shaped by relevant geopolitical aspects. It deploys actions for the productive occupation and the rational use of the riches of Amazonia and constitutes an important goal of the program for socio-economic development and national integration."[41]

However, the company's organization and developmentalist approach were not typical of an authoritarian regime. As mentioned, the mother company Eletrobrás had already been founded before the coup, and the developmental ideas dated back to the 1940s. A closer look at other Latin American countries reveals that this type of state-owned enterprise existed in non-authoritarian countries as well. Like Eletronorte, the Venezuelan state-owned energy supplier Edelca, just to name an example, built several dams to provide hydroelectric energy for the country's industrialization.[42] Although Venezuela was governed by a democratic system, Edelca was almost entirely comparable to Eletronorte. Both provided energy for industrialization projects and relied on technical planning; they cooperated with private companies and accumulated huge debts; both had a military officer as their first president, exploited natural resources in peripheral regions, and ignored negative impacts on the local population and the environment.

[41] Eletronorte, *Usina Hidrelétrica de Tucuruí* (Brasilia: Eletronorte 1977), 1.

[42] For an overview, see Jesús Sanoja Hernández, *A las puertas de El Dorado: CVG 30 años* (Caracas: Editorial Binev, 1990).

Still, Eletronorte differed in two respects from other non-authoritarian state-owned enterprises. First, the military had the company monitored by its secret service, and second, Eletronorte, as a representative of the regime, faced an array of criticism and resistance, which the intelligence services again policed. Shortly after the coup, in June 1964, the Brazilian regime installed a new secret service, the Serviço Nacional de Informações (SNI, National Information Service), with the support of the CIA.[43] The SNI intended "to conduct and coordinate, in the entire national territory, the activities of intelligence and counterintelligence, especially those that are important for national security."[44] Its mastermind and first director, Golbery do Couto e Silva, was one of the chief ideologists of the military regime and formulated the Brazilian doctrine of national security, for which security, order, progress, geopolitics, and the fight against the so-called communist subversion were central objectives.[45]

The SNI worked under the direct authority of the Brazilian president without any external control and provided him with all the necessary information. Most members of the staff were military. In December 1964, the SNI established its Agência Central (Central Agency) with around 2000 employees and several regional bureaus. In 1967, the agency founded divisions at ministries and other institutions and corporations such as Eletrobrás.[46] The SNI's importance is evident in the fact that two later presidents, Médici and Figueiredo, served as directors. Its information procurement was highly standardized.[47] The reports, called informes and informações, had specific formats and codes—for instance, to classify the credibility of the informant. The reports referred to up to 250,000 suspects and a wide range of political and social issues, including the Tucuruí Dam. Due to their confidentiality and their extremely prosaic and clear content, these reports are valuable historical sources. Since the agents

[43] On the following, see Lucas Figueiredo, *Ministério do Silêncio: a história do serviço secreto brasileiro de Washington Luís a Lula (1927–2005)* (Rio de Janeiro and São Paulo: Editora Record, 2005), 121–164; Priscila Carlos Brandão Antunes, *SNI & ABIN: uma leitura da atuação dos serviços secretos brasileiros ao longo do século XX* (Rio de Janeiro: Editora FGV, 2002).

[44] Figueiredo, *Ministério do Silêncio*, 125.

[45] Golbery do Couto e Silva, *Geopolítica do Brasil* (Rio de Janeiro: Olympio, 1967).

[46] Figueiredo, *Ministério do Silêncio*, 156–7.

[47] On the following, see Carlos Fico, *Como eles agiam: os subterrâneos da Ditadura Militar: espionagem e polícia política* (Rio de Janeiro and São Paulo: Editora Record, 2001), 95–9.

collected material and viewpoints from the opposition, such as pamphlets or interviews, they are characterized by multi-perspectivity.

Resistance to Eletronorte

Eletronorte faced a wide spectrum of resistance and protest since the company implemented its infrastructure projects in a technocratic and authoritarian setting.[48] The Tucuruí project had unwanted subversive potential because of its massive impacts on the environment—it flooded a huge area of rainforest—and required the resettlement of the local population and indigenous groups. Several NGOs, unions, local groups, and even the Catholic Church protested the construction of the dam, shaping national and global environmental and human rights debates, and finally helping to undermine the image of the dictatorship in the country and abroad.

SNI agents traveling to Tucuruí and staff members in the local agency in Belém documented every facet of the problems in Tucuruí.[49] The intelligence service collected NGO brochures, critical newspaper articles, and personal information about human rights activists. The problems ranged from labor disputes at the dam's construction site, sabotage, local protests, and demonstrations against Eletronorte's resettlement and environmental policy to the so-called communist subversion. Since the regime was interested in maintaining a positive public image abroad, the SNI also took notice of the tremendous international response to the issues surrounding the Tucuruí project. The military directed attention toward the following main problems of the dam:

1. Resettlement. The creation of a huge artificial lake made it necessary to resettle around 16,000 people and 2 indigenous villages. Eletronorte was overwhelmed with the task, underestimating local agency and committing innumerable errors during the implementation of the resettlement program. The SNI reported extensively on these protests and the participants, criticizing Eletronorte for mistakes in the construction of the new settlements, such as precarious

[48] For an overview, see Teixeira, *Energy Policy in Latin America*, 181–252.

[49] Acervos dos Órgãos de Informação do Regime Militar: Série SNI, Arquivo Nacional, Brasília.

or inadequate infrastructure.[50] Eletronorte also mismanaged the program for compensating local residents. Many locals had opted to receive a compensation payment but spent their money without investing in new homes and complained about their situation.[51] The military tried to suppress opposition but had little success. In the end, Eletronorte had to increase its commitment to those who were resettled without solving the problem completely.

2. Environment. Activists and journalists further denounced the ecological damage caused by the reservoir and the usage of toxic defoliants during the construction of the long transition lines.[52] A pamphlet by the NGO Movimento em Defesa da Vida (Movement for the Defense of Life) illustrates how harsh the criticism was. It condemned the "absurd aggression against humanity and the environment," as well as "crimes" and "irresponsible acts of Eletronorte."[53] As so often happened, the SNI suspected that "leftist 'intellectuals,' militant communists and 'progressive' clergy" were involved[54] Nonetheless, Eletronorte had to respond to the criticism,[55] which it did by commissioning an environmental report by World Bank expert Robert Goodland, launching an environmental program, and conducting various studies, for instance, on vegetation, diseases, and water quality, though it ignored the social impacts of environmental destruction. All these measures were

[50] See, for instance, Ministério de Justiça. Departamento de Polícia Federal. Superintendência Regional no Estado do Pará. Serviço de Informações: Informe No. 0173/83-SI/SR/DPF/PA, K0032098-1983, Acervos dos Órgãos de Informação do Regime Militar: Série SNI, Arquivo Nacional, Brasília; Movimento dos Expropriados pela Eletronorte—Repartimento Novo, 14 November 1984, Informe COMAR No. 256/84, BR NA BSB VAZ 117 0216, Acervos dos Órgãos de Informação do Regime Militar: Série CISA, Arquivo Nacional, Brasília.

[51] MME. DSI. Informação No. 40/197/81/DSI/MME, 23 October 1981, A0366055-1983, Acervos dos Órgãos de Informação do Regime Militar: Série SNI, Arquivo Nacional, Brasília.

[52] Cf. Philip M. Fearnside, "Environmental Impacts of Brazil's Tucuruí Dam: Unlearned Lessons for Hydroelectric Development in Amazonia," *Environmental Management* 27, no. 3 (2001): 377–396.

[53] SNI. ABE. Informação No. 0611/19/ABE/84, 20 July 1984. Anexo: Movimento em Defesa da Vida, Manifesto ao povo brasileiro, Belém, 15 July 1984, 2, K0047466-1984, Acervos dos Órgãos de Informação do Regime Militar: Série SNI, Arquivo Nacional, Brasília.

[54] SNI. ABE. Informação No. 0801/14/ABE/84, 1, K0048665-1984, Acervos dos Órgãos de Informação do Regime Militar: Série SNI, Arquivo Nacional, Brasília.

[55] On the following, see Monosowski, *Institutional Capacities.*

meant to be "an answer to the increasing opposition to the project."[56] Although the program failed to predict all the consequences for the environment and lacked concrete action steps, the Tucuruí project marked a turning point in Brazilian environmental policy. Not least because of the international outcry about the destruction of the rainforest, Brazil adopted environmental legislation and made it obligatory for dam projects to implement environmental programs as early as during their planning phase.

3. Capemi. Environmental concerns, corruption, business ambitions, civil unrest, and the SNI's containment efforts all came together in the scandal involving the private firm Agropecuária Capemi.

Corruption and Dilettantism: The Case of Capemi

Since the reservoir of the Tucuruí Dam would flood a huge area of rainforest, World Bank expert Robert Goodland, in his commissioned environmental report, recommended clearing the area of biomass to prevent greenhouse gases from being generated and to protect the dam from acid water and trunks that could damage the turbines. He referred to bad experiences with the Brokopondo Dam in Suriname, where acid water had pummeled the facility.[57]

Already in 1977, the SUDAM had produced an inventory of the forest in the space of the future reservoir and recommended that precious wood be extracted and sold.[58] The government asked the Instituto Brasileiro de Desenvolvimento Florestal (IBDF), the national authority for forest development, to organize the extraction and exportation of the timber. In 1980, the institute estimated the market value of the wood, identified suitable tracts of land for logging, and published the results in a feasibility study.[59] It claimed that approximately 43% of the wood could easily be

[56] Monosowski, *Institutional Capacities*, 63.

[57] Robert J. A. Goodland, *Environmental Assessment of the Tucuruí Hydroproject, Rio Tocantins, Amazonia, Brazil* (s.l.: manuscript, 1978), 81–98.

[58] Superintendência do Desenvolvimento da Amazônia, *Madeira derrubada para construção da hidrelétrica de Tucuruí: possibilidades de aproveitamento* (Belém: SUDAM, 1977).

[59] Instituto Brasileiro de Desenvolvimento Florestal, *Aproveitamento da madeira da área do reservatório da Usina Hidrelétrica de Tucuruí: síntese avaliativa da situação: volume 1: estudos básicos* (Brasília: IBDF, 1980).

sold[60] and that this clearing of the reservoir could boost economic development and the "dynamization of business activities in the timber sector."[61] At the same time, it would prevent uncontrolled environmental destruction since the forest would have disappeared in the reservoir anyway.

Private logging companies did not share SUDAM's enthusiasm for this extraction because they did not consider the pricing framework and the overall plan to be realistic.[62] In January 1980, the IBDF solicited offers for the extraction of precious wood and the clearing of the biomass across an area of 65,000 hectares. However, nobody delivered an offer, although 14 national timber companies had consulted the documentation. In retrospect, the responsible Ministry of Agriculture admitted that companies did not wish to take a risk and hoped that a new invitation with guaranteed revenues would be issued.[63] Indeed, the potential contractors knew that the exportation of trunks was prohibited by law.[64] They also doubted that it would be possible to clear the area by the time the lake was to be dammed in 1983, a reservation shared by employees of the IBDF and local timber companies in Tucuruí.[65]

Nevertheless, the IBDF issued a second invitation for tenders, and this time, Agropecuária Capemi Indústria e Comércio tendered an offer and won as the only bidder. The parent group Capemi, the Caixa de Pecúlio dos Militares, a pension insurance company for the military, guaranteed the solvency of the undertaking. Since the military founded Agropecuária Capemi just shortly after the first invitation, it was evident that it wished to make a profit with the tropical wood from the reservoir, which was allegedly worth US $400 million.[66] In August, IBDF and Capemi signed a contract, and the Ministry of Agriculture took control of the project. In November, Capemi concluded another contract with the French company Maison Lazard Frères (hereafter "Lazard") for technical assistance and

[60] IBDF, *Aproveitamento da madeira*, 122–4.

[61] IBDF, *Aproveitamento da madeira*, 4.

[62] "Tucuruí: pouco interesse na exploração madeireira," *Revista da Madeira* 29, no. 342 (1980): 33.

[63] On the following, see Ministério da Agricultura, *Tucuruí: um projeto pioneiro de desmatamento* (Brasília: Ministério da Agricultura, 1983), 10–7.

[64] SNI. AC. Informação No. 064/51/AC/80, 16 December 1980, 3, A0208991-1981, Acervos dos Órgãos de Informação do Regime Militar: Série SNI, Arquivo Nacional, Brasília.

[65] Ministério de Agricultura. DSI. Informação No. 2/DSI/MA/80, 12 February 1980, 1, A0208991-1981, Acervos dos Órgãos de Informação do Regime Militar: Série SNI, Arquivo Nacional, Brasília.

[66] Figueiredo, *Ministério do Silêncio*, 305.

marketing. The deal included loans over US $100 million, provided by the Banque Nationale de Paris (BNP), for the purchase of French equipment.[67] The Banco Nacional de Crédito Cooperativo promoted the project in Brazil, where Capemi hired several subcontractors to support the logging.[68] In addition, Capemi persuaded the National Council of Foreign Trade to permit the exportation of trunks, although economic associations in Pará protested this preferential treatment.[69] Shortly thereafter, the IBDF published advertising material for selling the timber abroad, for instance, in Germany.[70]

Despite the government's support, it quickly became evident that Agropecuária Capemi was completely incompetent concerning the project's logistics, and that it was mismanaged. The SNI registered numerous problems as early as in late 1981.[71] Within the first 30 months, Capemi had five different project coordinators.[72] The Capemi managers in charge preferred to travel to Europe and deal with side projects, such as the production of alcohol from timber, rather than address the problems in Tucuruí. Necessary equipment was missing or broken, and a lack of fuel precipitated a weeks-long standstill of the works.[73] Subcontractors did not receive payment. Moreover, Capemi forgot to register the wood for sale so that it was unable to present export permits at the port. The company even failed to appropriately receive the president of the European timber industry during his visit in Tucuruí. In addition to all this, BNP withdrew its commitment and granted only US $25 million in loans.[74]

The situation generated very long delays, which threatened not just the schedule but also the job as a whole. Capemi's military staff traced the problem back to delays in the shipment of machinery, so that the

[67] Ministério da Agricultura, *Tucuruí*, 11 and 23.

[68] SNI. AC. Apreciação No. 005/50/AC/82, 25 January 1982, 2, A0373722-1983, Acervos dos Órgãos de Informação do Regime Militar: Série SNI, Arquivo Nacional, Brasília.

[69] SNI. AC. Apreciação No. 005/50/AC/82, 2; SNI. AC. Informação No. 064/51/AC/80, 3.

[70] Instituto Brasileiro de Desenvolvimento Florestal, *Madeiras de Tucuruí: características e utilização: Hölzer aus Tucuruí: Merkmale und Anwendung* (Brasília: IBDF, 1981).

[71] SNI. AC. Apreciação No. 005/50/AC/82, 1–5.

[72] Ministério da Agricultura, *Tucuruí*, 20.

[73] Diretor da Divisão de Segurança e Informações do MME to Chefe da AC do SNI, Brasília, 22 September 1982. Anexo: Ministério de Minas e Energia. DSI. Relatório de viagem, 5, A0279304-1982, Acervos dos Órgãos de Informação do Regime Militar: Série SNI, Arquivo Nacional, Brasília.

[74] Ministério da Agricultura, *Tucuruí*, 24.

responsible project coordinator Colonel Lício Maciel simply halved the amount of wood to be logged in January 1982. The SNI still doubted the practicability of this less ambitious plan and the profitability of the project: "the results are not very stimulating."[75] The intelligence branch declared that Capemi had lost sight of the overall goal: the protection of the dam.[76] Similarly, in August 1982 the journal of the Brazilian timber industry cruelly pointed out that Capemi had extracted only 1% of the predicted amount of wood and that the company should concede "that at least one part of the failure of this operation stems from its own mistakes. And still discover who could do the job correctly."[77] Even the wood that had been extracted could not be sold since there was little interest in the world market. Capemi traded only US $350,000 worth of timber.[78]

The whole situation jeopardized Capemi's contract with Lazard. Capemi had promised to pay Lazard with precious wood and established a contractual compensation of US $1 million if it failed to deliver.[79] As soon as it became clear that Capemi would not hand over the wood and Lazard had the right to compensation, the SNI and the Ministry of Agriculture intervened. Already in November 1980, the Ministry contacted Capemi and asked for a statement concerning the delay.[80] The following year, those requests became more frequent. In December, the responsible officials in the ministry declared that they were "worried with the progress of the work" and proposed specific measures for improvement.[81] In the meantime, the press started to discuss the matter. As early as October 1981, federal deputy Hélio Duque from the opposition party PMDB had made critical remarks about the project, indicating in a speech that there were signs of "an entrepreneurial disaster."[82]

[75] Diretor da Divisão de Segurança e Informações do MME to Chefe da AC do SNI, 4; SNI. ABE. Informação No. 0175/118/ABE/82, 1–3, K0019367-1982, Acervos dos Órgãos de Informação do Regime Militar: Série SNI, Arquivo acional, Brasília.

[76] MME. DSI. Informação No. 40/197/81/DSI/MME, Anexo: Ministério de Minas e Energia. DSI. Relatório de viagem, 2–4.

[77] "Projetos da Capemi," *Revista da Madeira* 31, no. 368 (1982): 36.

[78] Ministério da Agricultura, *Tucuruí*, 24.

[79] SNI. AC. Informação No. 064/51/AC/80, 2–4.

[80] Roberto Ferreira da Amaral to Fernando José Pessoa dos Santos, Brasília, 14 November 1980, in Ministério da Agricultura, *Tucuruí*, 81–2.

[81] Roberto Ferreira da Amaral to [Fernando José Pessoa dos Santos], Brasília, 2 December 1981, in Ministério da Agricultura, *Tucuruí*, 84.

[82] Ministério da Agricultura. DSI. Encaminhamento No. 30/DSI/MA/81, 13 October 1981. Anexo: Discurso de Hélio Duque, 7 October 1981, 1, A0195870-1981, Acervos dos

In November and December 1981, the SNI and the ministry organized several crisis meetings with Capemi and Lazard to increase pressure and issue instructions, but without success.[83] Furthermore, the SNI documented a series of corruption allegations against military personnel at Agropecuária Capemi, among others against the acting director Fernando Pessoa. The secret service recommended that Capemi's president, General Aragão, restructure the staff. Disregarding this advice, Aragão put together a new board of directors that included military officers charged with corruption. At the same time, the SNI learned about the firm's huge debts and cash flow problems and asked the government to look into these issues.[84]

After Capemi and Lazard dissolved their contract by mutual agreement, the SNI suggested in August 1982 that Capemi be given a second chance since no other company could carry out the job.[85] After all, there was more time available because Eletronorte faced similar financial problems and was behind on its own schedule, too. The SNI recommended that the government guarantee loans, since Capemi's bankruptcy could provoke a negative reaction in the media. This, however, was a vain hope. On March 1, 1983, the ministry canceled the contract with Capemi due to "failure to perfect and execute the services," and in April 1983, Agropecuária Capemi declared bankruptcy.[86] This resulted in protests in Tucuruí, where former workers sat on wage claims, trying to enforce their demands by blockading roads and Capemi's machine park.[87]

The Capemi scandal made press headlines and became a PR disaster for Eletronorte and the government.[88] The Minister of Agriculture and the director of Eletronorte had to justify themselves before the Senate and the Chamber of Deputies. When the opposition criticized the government for

Órgãos de Informação do Regime Militar: Série SNI, Arquivo Nacional, Brasília.

83 On the following, see SNI. AC. Apreciação No. 005/50/AC/82.

84 SNI. AC. Apreciação No. 018/50/AC/82, 2 August 1982, 3–4, A0373722-1983, Acervos dos Órgãos de Informação do Regime Militar: Série SNI, Arquivo Nacional, Brasília.

85 On the following, see SNI. AC. Apreciação No. 018/50/AC/82.

86 Ministério da Agricultura, *Tucuruí*, 27.

87 Ministério de Justiça. Departamento de Polícia Federal. Superintendência Regional no Estado do Pará. Serviço de Informações: Informe No. 0173/83-SI/SR/DPF/PA.

88 On the following, see Ministério da Agricultura. DSI. Encaminhamento No. 16/DSI/MA/83, 29 April 1983. Anexo, A0333219-1983, Acervos dos Órgãos de Informação do Regime Militar: Série SNI, Arquivo Nacional, Brasília. Examples for investigative journalism on the Capemi scandal are Assis, *Os mandarins da República*, 167–225 and Pinheiro, *Tucuruí*.

having "acted at least in a terribly irresponsible way" by privileging Capemi and not informing the parliament, Minister Amaury Stabile denied responsibility.[89] If there had been corruption at the company, he objected, the shareholders would have to investigate it. The director of Eletronorte also rejected any responsibility and underlined the fact that Eletronorte had warned Capemi.[90] Eletronorte, for its part, was annoyed that it was now associated in public opinion with the Capemi scandal, although the IBDF and, later on, the ministry, had been in charge of the deal.[91]

In addition, the director of SNI's Central Agency, Newton Cruz, denied that his family was involved in the affair in an interview.[92] However, a secret report by the SNI reveals how close the entanglements between the military regime and Capemi were. The report warned explicitly that there could be "a national scandal that possibly could involve family members of the president of the Republic."[93] Concerning this scandal, historian Lucas Figueiredo stated that the SNI had exerted pressure to make the Capemi deal happen, and that Capemi had business contacts with President Figueiredo's son and Newton Cruz's brother.[94] A journal article from 1983 even alleged that Capemi had won the tender "in exchange for help for the election campaign fund of General Octávio Aguiar de Medeiros, head of the SNI, for the presidency of the republic."[95] The journal article further affirmed that, in exchange for machinery from the indigenous affairs agency FUNAI in Tucuruí, Capemi had paid for the agency's former president to take a trip to France.

Soon after Capemi's bankruptcy, an environmental scandal added to the disaster. At the end of 1983, some activists and the press accused Capemi of having used Agent Orange during the logging, endangering the local population. Similar accusations involved Eletronorte and the

[89] Ministério da Agricultura. DSI. Encaminhamento No. 16/DSI/MA/83, 29 April 1983. Anexo, 1, A0333219-1983, Acervos dos Órgãos de Informação do Regime Militar: Série SNI, Arquivo Nacional, Brasília.

[90] Depoimento do presidente da Centrais Elétricas do Norte do Brasil S/A – Eletronorte, na Comissão Parlamentar de Inquérito – CPI da Capemi, Brasília, 4 August 1983, A0367692-1983, Acervos dos Órgãos de Informação do Regime Militar: Série SNI, Arquivo Nacional, Brasília.

[91] Eletrobrás, *UHE Tucuruí*, 69.

[92] Ana Lagôa, *SNI: como nasceu, como funciona* (São Paulo: Editora Brasiliense, 1983), 28.

[93] SNI. AC. Informe No. 1052/30/AC/83: Situação atual de Tucuruí, 1, A0326136-1983, Acervos dos Órgãos de Informação do Regime Militar: Série SNI, Arquivo Nacional, Brasília.

[94] Figueiredo, *Ministério do Silêncio*, 306.

[95] "Há algo de podre no reino da Capemi," *Porantim* 49 (1983).

construction of the power lines through the jungle.[96] Critics claimed that the use of toxic defoliants had killed or injured rubber tappers and livestock. Eletronorte denied the use of dioxin, but no one knew exactly what Capemi had done. Upon questioning, the chemical company Jimo Química informed Eletronorte that it had delivered 21,840 liters of a product containing pentachlorophenol to Capemi, which was supposed to protect the logged wood from pests. The product, Jimo alleged, decomposed quickly and did not pose a risk to humans.[97]

However, Eletronorte preferred to conduct a survey and seize possible remnants of agrotoxics in the abandoned logging areas.[98] In April 1984, an agronomist inspected Capemi's deserted camps, interviewing their residents, activists, and former Capemi employees, and found several barrels with chemicals. He also documented rumors that Capemi had used dioxin-containing Tordon 101, which had been used during the Vietnam War as Agent Orange to poison Brazil nut trees so that they could be cut down more easily.[99] During this and several other field trips from April to July 1984, Eletronorte found 464 barrels, almost all of them empty.[100] While working in the jungle, three staff members contracted malaria, which shows how precarious the working conditions in the Capemi camps must have been. A toxicological examination of the reservoir and its residents revealed only slight contamination, leading toxicologists to conclude that

[96] SNI. ABE. Informação No. 1058/19/ABE/83, 6 December 1983, K0042237-1983, Acervos dos Órgãos de Informação do Regime Militar: Série SNI, Arquivo Nacional, Brasília. Cf. also Pinheiro, *Tucuruí*.

[97] Jimo Química Industrial Ltda. to Eletronorte, Telex, Curitiba, 27 April 1984, Relatório: metodologia de trabalho adotada com nossos produtos na preservação de madeiras, na área do projeto Tucuruí, Relatórios da Superintendência de Meio Ambiente, Eletronorte, Biblioteca da Eletronorte, Brasília.

[98] Douglas Souza Luz to Mauro da Silva Reis, Brasília, 10 April 1984, Relatório: metodologia de trabalho adotada com nossos produtos na preservação de madeiras, na área do projeto Tucuruí, Relatórios da Superintendência de Meio Ambiente, Eletronorte, Biblioteca da Eletronorte, Brasília.

[99] João Basílio Costalonga Seraphim, "Relatório de viagem, 09/04/84–19/04/84," Relatório: metodologia de trabalho adotada com nossos produtos na preservação de madeiras, na área do projeto Tucuruí, Relatórios da Superintendência de Meio Ambiente, Eletronorte, Biblioteca da Eletronorte, Brasília.

[100] Ministério de Minas e Energia. DSI. Informação No. 35/0457/84, 10 August 1984. Anexo II/III, A0535000-1986, Acervos dos Órgãos de Informação do Regime Militar: Série SNI, Arquivo Nacional, Brasília.

Capemi had not used any dioxin.[101] Thus, for the SNI, it was evident that the Agent Orange case was "one more plot designed with the intention of denigrating the government, by ELETRONORTE."[102] Similarly, in a white book that Eletronorte used to downplay the environmental impacts of Tucuruí, it lamented that "political reasons, sometimes with an ideological background, caused a stir and exacerbated public opinion against the construction of the hydroelectric plant." Although damage had occurred, it alleged, "disasters, tragedies, apocalypses had not."[103] In March 1985, environmental activists succeeded in getting the United Nations Environment Program to conduct a survey, which demonstrates just how considerable the prejudice against Eletronorte was. Still, the UN expert was not able to prove that Agent Orange or any other toxin had been utilized in Tucuruí.[104]

Conclusion

In the end, Eletronorte's close ties with the military regime damaged the reputation of both actors. The corporation represented an important pillar of the military's centralist development policy, an authoritarian policy that resulted in conflicts about land ownership and environmental damage in Tucuruí. Therefore, Eletronorte quickly became a negative symbol of the dictatorship and the target of resistance. As a result, the state-owned company was forced to engage in social programs like those for resettlement. In some cases, Eletronorte tried to outsource non-engineering tasks, such as the logging of the rainforest in the reservoir. This again led to new problems: Eletronorte's cooperation with state agencies and private companies created a confusing network of different actors without clear responsibilities, from which military actors could personally profit. This

[101] Ministério de Minas e Energia. DSI. Informação No. 42/0268/85, 12 August 1985, A0561186-1986, Acervos dos Órgãos de Informação do Regime Militar: Série SNI, Arquivo Nacional, Brasília. Beim Bau der Stromtrassen kam allerdings Tordon zum Einsatz, cf. Ministério de Minas e Energia. DSI. Informação No. 35/0214/84, 26 April 1984, 1, A0535000-1986, Acervos dos Órgãos de Informação do Regime Militar: Série SNI, Arquivo Nacional, Brasília.

[102] SNI. ABE. Informação No. 1058/19/ABE/83, 5.

[103] Eletronorte, *Livro Branco sobre o meio ambiente na usina hidrelétrica Tucuruí* (Brasília: Ministério das Minas e Energia, 1987), 7 and 9.

[104] Denúncia de uso de agrotóxicos na área da Usina Hidrelétrica de Tucuruí (UHE), K0052425-1985, Acervos dos Órgãos de Informação do Regime Militar: Série SNI, Arquivo Nacional, Brasília.

undermined Eletronorte's efficacy and presented problems to the SNI, because the secret service could no longer manage the situation. In fact, the whole situation ran counter to the development policy and power of the regime.

Problems swiftly came back to Eletronorte. It had to organize the hasty clearing of the forest close to the dam itself to avoid damage to the structure. The company endured protests and had to learn social responsibility. Subsequently, it had to deal with activities beyond its expertise and engage in a learning process. As Elizabeth Monosowski has highlighted, Eletronorte "became the most important governmental agency in the region" and "was required to fulfill other regional needs, far beyond the environmental management scope, such as operating a modern hospital and schools at Tucuruí, installing and operating sewage systems, maintaining feeder roads, etc."[105]

This case study demonstrates that different stakeholders were fighting for their own interests during the dictatorship, creating a situation beyond the regime's control. Aside from the political and operational mistakes made by the responsible actors, three important factors transformed the state-owned business sector into such a conflict-laden field. First, state-owned enterprises such as Eletronorte often implemented huge infrastructure and factories. These projects did not just represent the authoritarian approach of the regime but also drew criticism and enabled different opposition groups to join forces. In the case of Tucuruí, journalists, human rights activists, environmentalists, trade unions, and the Church, all with specific interests, joined the local population in their fight against Eletronorte and the regime. Second, the centralist implementation of infrastructure projects, often conceived as measures against nature and "backward" indigenous groups, engendered international criticism and coincided with the rise of global human rights and environmental movements. Local and global critique against Eletronorte mutually strengthened each other. Third, the second phase of the Brazilian dictatorship under Geisel and Figueiredo was characterized by decreasing control and repression, facilitating the rise of oppositional voices. This change was partly initiated by the regime itself and partly resulted from the negative outcomes of its development policy, such as environmental destruction, social inequality, and corruption. The business sector constituted a crucial arena in which most of these problems intermingled and became visible.

[105] Monosowski, *Institutional Capacities*, 63.

References

Archival Sources

Acervos dos Órgãos de Informação do Regime Militar: Série SNI, Arquivo Nacional, Brasília.

Arquivo e Coleção Particular Emílio Garrastazu Médici, Instituto Histórico e Geográfico Brasileiro, Rio de Janeiro.

Relatórios da Superintendência de Meio Ambiente, Eletronorte, Biblioteca da Eletronorte, Brasília.

Bibliography

Assis, José Carlos de. *Os mandarins da República: anatomia dos escândalos da administração pública*. Rio de Janeiro: Paz e Terra, 1984.

Baer, Werner. *The Brazilian Economy: Growth and Development*. Boulder and London: Lynne Rienner, 2014.

Barbero, María Inés. "Business History in Latin America: A Historiographical Perspective." *The Business History Review* 82, no. 3 (2008): 555–75.

Bielschowsky, Ricardo. *Pensamento econômico brasileiro: o ciclo ideológico do desenvolvimentismo*. Rio de Janeiro: Contraponto, 2004.

Brandão Antunes, Priscila Carlos. *SNI & ABIN: uma leitura da atuação dos serviços secretos brasileiros ao longo do século XX*. Rio de Janeiro: Editora FGV, 2002.

Bucheli, Marcelo, and Jin Uk Kim, "The State as a Historical Construct in Organization Studies." In *Organizations in Time: History, Theory, Methods*, edited by Marcelo Bucheli and R. Daniel Wadhwani. Oxford: Oxford University Press, 2013.

Bulmer-Thomas, Victor. *The Economic History of Latin America since Independence*. Cambridge: Cambridge University Press, 1995.

Centro da Memória da Eletricidade no Brasil. *Eletronorte: 25 anos*. Rio de Janeiro: Centro da Memória da Eletricidade no Brasil, 1998.

Couto e Silva, Golbery do. *Geopolítica do Brasil*. Rio de Janeiro: Olympio, 1967.

Dávila, Carlos, and Rory Miller, eds. *Business History in Latin America: The Experience of Seven Countries*. Liverpool: Liverpool University Press, 1999.

Dinius, Oliver. *Brazil's Steel City: Developmentalism, Strategic Power, and Industrial Relations in Volta Redonda, 1941–1964*. Stanford: Stanford University Press, 2010.

Eakin, Marshall C. *British Enterprise in Brazil: The St. John d'el Rey Mining Company and the Morro Velho Gold Mine, 1830–1960*. Durham: Duke University Press, 1989.

Ekbladh, David. *The Great American Mission: Modernization and the Construction of an American World Order*. Princeton: Princeton University Press, 2010.
Eletrobrás. *UHE Tucuruí: estudo de caso*. Rio de Janeiro: Eletrobrás, 1992.
Eletronorte. *Livro Branco sobre o meio ambiente na usina hidrelétrica Tucuruí*. Brasília: Ministério das Minas e Energia, 1987.
Eletronorte. *Usina Hidrelétrica de Tucuruí*. Brasilia: Eletronorte, 1977.
Evans, Peter. *Dependent Development: The Alliance of Multinational, State, and Local Capital in Brazil*. Princeton: Princeton University Press, 1979.
Fearnside, Philip M. "Environmental Impacts of Brazil's Tucuruí Dam: Unlearned Lessons for Hydroelectric Development in Amazonia." *Environmental Management* 27, no. 3 (2001): 377–396.
Fico, Carlos. *Como eles agiam: os subterrâneos da Ditadura Militar: espionagem e polícia política*. Rio de Janeiro and São Paulo: Editora Record, 2001.
Figueiredo, Lucas. *Ministério do Silêncio: a história do serviço secreto brasileiro de Washington Luís a Lula (1927–2005)*. Rio de Janeiro and São Paulo: Editora Record, 2005.
Gaspari, Elio. *As ilusões armadas*, 5 vols. Rio de Janeiro: Intrínseca, 2014–2016.
Geisel, Ernesto. "Aumento das exportações (30.9.1974)" In *As diretrizes governamentais do presidente Ernesto Geisel: subsídios e documentos para a história do Brasil contemporâneo*, edited by Fernando Jorge. São Paulo, 1976.
Geisel, Ernesto. "Setor empresarial (10.3.1974)". In *As diretrizes governamentais do presidente Ernesto Geisel: subsídios e documentos para a história do Brasil contemporâneo*, edited by Fernando Jorge. São Paulo, 1976.
Geisel, Ernesto. "Discurso". In *Apoio à empresa privada nacional: discursos pronunciados na solenidade realizada no Palácio do Planalto em 30 de março de 1977: medidas aprovadas* (Brasília, 1977), 5–7.
Goodland, Robert J. A. *Environmental Assessment of the Tucuruí Hydroproject, Rio Tocantins, Amazonia, Brazil*. (s.l.: manuscript, 1978), 81–98.
"Há algo de podre no reino da Capemi," *Porantim* 49 (1983).
Ianni, Octavio. *Ditadura e agricultura: o desenvolvimento do capitalismo na Amazônia: 1964–1978*. Rio de Janeiro: Civilização Brasileira, 1986.
Instituto Brasileiro de Desenvolvimento Florestal. *Aproveitamento da madeira da área do reservatório da Usina Hidrelétrica de Tucuruí: síntese avaliativa da situação: volume 1: estudos básicos*. Brasília: IBDF, 1980.
Instituto Brasileiro de Desenvolvimento Florestal. *Madeiras de Tucuruí: características e utilização: Hölzer aus Tucuruí: Merkmale und Anwendung*. Brasília: IBDF, 1981.
Ioris, Rafael R. *Transforming Brasil: A History of National Development in the Postwar Era*. New York and London: Routledge, 2014.
Lagôa, Ana. *SNI: como nasceu, como funciona*. São Paulo: Editora Brasiliense, 1983.
Leff, Nathaniel H. *The Brazilian Capital Goods Industry 1929–1964*. Cambridge: Harvard University Press, 1968.

Lima, José. *Políticas de governo e desenvolvimento do setor de energia elétrica: do Código de Águas à crise dos anos 80 (1934–1984)*. Rio de Janeiro: Centro da Memória de Eletricidade no Brasil, 1995.

Miller, Rory M. "The History of Business in Latin America." In *The Routledge Companion to Business History*, edited by John F. Wilson, Steven Toms, Abe de Jong and Emily Buchnea. London and New York: Routledge, 2017.

Ministério da Agricultura. *Tucuruí: um projeto pioneiro de desmatamento*. Brasília: Ministério da Agricultura, 1983.

Ministério de Justiça. Departamento de Polícia Federal. Superintendência Regional no Estado do Pará. Serviço de Informações: Informe No. 0173/83-SI/SR/DPF/PA.

Monosowski, Elizabeth. *Institutional Capacities for Assessing Impacts and Trade-offs of Large Hydro Power Dams in the Tropics and Subtropics: the Case of Tucuruí Dam in Brazilian Amazonia: Final Report*. Rio de Janeiro: unpublished manuscript, 1990.

Netto, José Paulo. *Pequena história da ditadura brasileira (1964–1985)*. São Paulo: Cortez, 2014.

Pinheiro, Sebastião. *Tucuruí: o Agente Laranja em uma república de bananas*. Porto Alegre: Sulina, 1989.

"Projetos da Capemi," *Revista da Madeira* 31, no. 368 (1982): 36.

República Federativa do Brasil, *II PND: II Plano Nacional de Desenvolvimento (1975–1979)*. Rio de Janeiro: Centro de Serviços Gráficos do IBGE, 1975.

Sanoja Hernández, Jesús. *A las puertas de El Dorado: CVG 30 años*. Caracas: Editorial Binev, 1990.

Schneider, Ben Ross. *Business Politics and the State in Twentieth-Century Latin America*. Cambridge: Cambridge University Press, 2004.

Sikkink, Kathryn. "Development Ideas in Latin America: Paradigm Shift and the Economic Commission for Latin America." In *International Development and the Social Sciences: Essays on the History and Politics of Knowledge*, edited by Frederick Cooper and Randall Packard. Berkeley: University of California Press, 1997.

Superintendência do Desenvolvimento da Amazônia. *II Plano Nacional de Desenvolvimento: programa de ação do governo para a Amazônia*. 1975–79. Belém: SUDAM, 1976.

Superintendência do Desenvolvimento da Amazônia. *Madeira derrubada para construção da hidrelétrica de Tucuruí: possibilidades de aproveitamento*. Belém: SUDAM, 1977.

Teixeira, Maria Gracinda C. *Energy Policy in Latin America: Social and Environmental Dimensions of Hydropower in Amazônia*. Aldershot: Avebury, 1996.

Tendler, Judith. *Electric Power in Brazil: Entrepreneurship in the Public Sector*. Cambridge: Harvard University Press, 1968.

Trebat, Thomas J. *Brazil's State-Owned Enterprises: A Case Study of the State as Entrepreneur*. Cambridge: Cambridge University Press, 1983.

"Tucuruí: pouco interesse na exploração madeireira." *Revista da Madeira* 29, no. 342, (1980): 33.

Wirth, John D. *The Politics of Brazilian Development 1930–1954*. Stanford: Stanford University Press, 1970.

CHAPTER 12

Business as Usual Under a Military Regime? Volkswagen Do Brazil and the Military Dictatorship in Brazil (1964–1980)

Christopher Kopper

Introduction

Historians have not systematically researched large-scale investments of foreign multinationals—and particularly of European ones—in Latin American countries. This omission is far from self-evident, since Brazil became one of the most important destinations for German foreign direct investments during the 1960s. During the 1960s and 1970s, the Brazilian affiliate of the Volkswagen (VW) AG grew to become Brazil's biggest foreign and biggest nonpublic industrial corporation with a workforce of more than 40,000 employees and annual production of 500,000 vehicles.

In contrast to current conventional economic wisdom, foreign direct investments in Brazil and other Latin American countries took place in highly state-controlled and protectionist economic environments that

C. Kopper (✉)
Universität Bielefeld, Bielefeld, Germany
e-mail: christopher.kopper@uni-bielefeld.de

V. Basualdo et al. (eds.), *Big Business and Dictatorships in Latin America*, Palgrave Studies in Latin American Heterodox Economics, https://doi.org/10.1007/978-3-030-43925-5_12

would not be considered conducive to foreign investment. The steep growth of VW do Brasil's equity, output, and profit rates indicates that emerging industrial nations like Brazil benefited from a strictly coordinated variety of capitalism. During the decade of military dictatorships in the 1970s and early 1980s, German managers were confronted with massive human rights violations that neither stopped at the factory gates nor spared some of their local employees.

In 2014, the National Truth Commission of Brazil (Comissão Nacional de Verdade) presented preliminary evidence of collaboration between the management of VW do Brasil and the Political Police.[1] The mass media coverage that followed in Brazil and Germany prompted the chief compliance officer of Volkswagen to commission the author of this article to write a detailed report about the relations between the military dictatorship of Brazil and VW, that is, both VW do Brasil and its parent company. I enjoyed unrestricted access to the corporate archives of VW in Germany and Brazil and freedom from any interference into my results and the publication. But this report comes with a caveat: The archive of VW do Brasil was not established before 2013 and contains only a few insignificant original documents. In his research about Volkswagen's collaboration with the military regime, the author had to rely on the surviving documents of the Political Police (DOPS).

The history of the Brazilian Volkswagen affiliate VW do Brasil started only eight years after the end of World War II. On March 23, 1953, the Volkswagen GmbH founded its first Brazilian affiliate as an operating company to assemble the Volkswagen Beetle.[2] Its purpose was to assemble the Volkswagen from imported parts from Germany, a procedure that insiders in the automotive industry called "Completely Knocked Down" (CKD). Volkswagen's Brazilian assembly plant was located in São Paulo, the emerging industrial heartland of Brazil.[3] From VW's perspective, the decision to establish an assembly plant in Brazil was nothing less than a pioneering investment. Its Brazilian assembly plant was the first German

[1] Comissão Nacional de Verdade, Relatório, 3 vols., Brasilia 2014.

[2] At that time, Volkswagen still was a state-owned enterprise and did not become a joint-stock company (*Aktiengesellschaft*) until 1960. Even now, the state remains a major shareholder.

[3] For the early history of VW do Brazil, see its website (www.vwbr.com/ImprensaVW/page/Historia.aspx). Volker Wellhöner, *"Wirtschaftswunder", Weltmarkt, Westdeutscher Fordismus: Der Fall Volkswagen* (Münster: Westfälisches Dampfboot, 1996) is still a fundamental work on the history of VW do Brasil up through the early 1960s.

automobile manufacturing plant in Brazil—and Volkswagen's first investment in a factory outside Germany.

At this time, Volkswagen had just started selling cars in foreign markets. The decision to assemble cars in a remote Latin American country looked audacious. At first sight, the Brazilian automotive market was small. Car sales in Brazil still ranked below those in Argentina, but the most populated Latin American country offered significant growth potential for automobile manufacturers. An average GDP growth of 5.2% between 1939 and 1953 demonstrated Brazil's rapid and uninterrupted economic takeoff during and after World War II and contributed to the perception of Brazil as a major market of the future.[4]

VW's decision to assemble the Volkswagen Beetle with imported CKD kits was mainly based on Brazil's foreign trade policies. Exports of ready-made cars to Brazil collided with high import duties. In addition, the low wage rates for semiskilled assembly-line workers created an economic incentive to transfer the assembly process to Brazil. Until the 1990s, the Brazilian government and the government-controlled Central Bank (Banco Central do Brasil) set fixed exchange rates and maintained the right to set separate exchange rates for essential and for nonessential imports. From the perspective of a Brazilian manufacturer, imported CKD kits benefited from a 40% lower exchange rate for foreign currency than ready-made vehicles.[5]

The Establishment of a Car Factory in Brazil

Right from the time VW do Brasil was established, Volkswagen's executive board considered constructing a complete manufacturing plant in Brazil. In 1956, the Brazilian government's industrialization policy forced Volkswagen to make a quick decision between two opposite alternatives: to build a complete car factory and to abandon the Brazilian market altogether. The so-called target plan of the democratically elected government of Juscelino Kubitschek set the ambitious goal of establishing a domestic automotive industry by 1960 in order to replace almost all imports of cars and trucks. President Kubitschek coined the proverbial slogan "50 years of

[4] Francisco Vidal Luna and Herbert S. Klein, *The Economic and Social History of Brazil since 1889* (Cambridge: Cambridge University Press, 2014), Table A3, 368.

[5] Helen Shapiro, *Engines of growth. The state and transnational auto companies in Brazil* (Cambridge: Cambridge University Press) 1994, 48–51.

progress in a five-year term" to mobilize the national pride and the ambition of his fellow countrymen. This target plan bore some superficial resemblances to Mao Tse Tung's concept of the "Great Leap Forward" of China but did not result in a mass famine. Instead, it really accelerated Brazil's transition from an agricultural to an industrial society.

As a consequence, the predominantly foreign owners of car assembly plants in Brazil were confronted with a government directive to manufacture complete cars in Brazil from 1960. In 1956, an interministerial steering group for the development of the automotive industry (Grupo Executivo da Industria Automobilistica—GEIA) set up a detailed target plan for gradually replacing foreign car parts with domestically manufactured ones and demanded nothing less than 95% local components by July 1, 1960.[6] Under these conditions, Volkswagen's executive board decided on the opt-in solution and acquired a large site for a new plant located about 20 km south of São Paulo. Optimistic estimates of future car sales in the Brazilian market and growing confidence in the political stability of Brazil were certainly decisive in the establishment of Volkswagen's first full-scale plant abroad. The new plant at São Bernardo do Campo was already operational by January 1959, at a time when VW do Brasil was still transitioning from German to domestically produced engine parts.[7]

VW's high investment cost in the Brazilian plant was mitigated by a set of different trade, foreign exchange, and credit policy incentives. The Brazilian authority for foreign exchange and credit control (Superintendencia da Moeda e do Credito—SUMOC) exempted foreign automotive manufacturers from advance deposit requirements for equipment imports, reducing VW do Brasil's liquidity needs. In addition, foreign investors were generally exempted from import duties on investment goods. Advantages of this kind were at least helpful, if not essential, for maintaining foreign investors' confidence, but they were not direct monetary subsidies.

Brazilian affiliates of foreign investors were also relieved of the obligation to buy foreign currency at SUMOC auctions above the official exchange rate. VW do Brasil received a portion of the Deutschmark amounts for capital goods imports from Germany at a favorable fixed rate. Volkswagen's overall savings through the preferential exchange rate

[6] Wellhöner, *Wirtschaftswunder*, 272–274.

[7] Volkswagen Archive Wolfsburg (UVW), Z 1184, no. 355/3.

amounted to 11.9 million Deutschmarks (DM) from 1956 to 1960.[8] In addition to subsidized foreign exchange, VW do Brasil received generous low-interest loans from SUMOC amounting to 18.1 million DM in 1959 and 1960.[9] Brazilian government loans reduced the funding requirements of the Volkswagen parent company (since 1960: Volkswagen AG). In 1958, the national economic development bank of Brazil (Banco National do Desenvolvimento Economico—BNDE) granted VW do Brasil an additional loan amounting to about the equivalent of 5.9 million DM to be repaid between 1958 and 1963. Since the BNDE lent the money at a reduced interest rate of 11%, whereas the annual inflation rate averaged 39.5% from 1958 to 1963, VW do Brasil benefited from a negative interest rate of 28.5% that equaled an overall benefit—or subsidy—of 8.4 million DM.[10] However, this cheap loan was not a precondition of Volkswagen's investment but rather an unexpected surprise bonus. The BNDE had obviously underrated the inflationist tendency of the Brazilian economy and forgotten to set an inflation-adjusted interest rate. VW do Brasil received this bonus at a time when the German parent company had already signed contracts for the construction of the new plant in São Bernardo do Campo. The preferential exchange rate and the cheap loan amounted to an overall indirect subsidy of 20.3 million DM with the parent company expecting total expenses of 70 million DM for the new factory.[11] Indirect subsidies were quite significant from a cost-benefit and a cash flow perspective but not decisive for the decision to invest.

[8] Werner Baer, *The Brazilian Economy. Growth and Development* (Boulder: University of Colorado Press, 2008), 55–60: Shapiro, *Engines of growth*, 52, 142–143.

[9] Shapiro, *Engines of growth*, 145–148.

[10] Calculated in accordance with the numbers from Shapiro, *Engines of growth*, 152–153 and the exchange rate charts of the Institute of Brazilian Business & Management Issues at the George Washington University, Washington D.C. (www2.gwu.edu/˜ibi/database/Exchange_Rate_1954-present.pdf). The peso-dollar exchange rates were converted into DM using the exchange rate statistics of the Deutsche Bundesbank; the average inflation rate was calculated in Baer, *Brazilian Economy*, 410.

[11] Wellhöner, *Wirtschaftswunder*, 274. Due to inflation and expansions, this estimate from 1956 was certainly lower than the actual costs after completion in 1959.

A Profitable Investment: Volkswagen and the Motorization of Brazil

During the negotiations between VW do Brasil and the Brazilian government, government officials held an equal position to that of their German counterparts, if not a stronger one. SUMOC maintained the right to set the timeline for the "Brazilianization" of the Brazil-made Volkswagen. Volkswagen's biggest foreign investment by far during the 1950s and early 1960s took place in a country where the Ministry of Finance wielded strict controls over money and capital transfers abroad. Transfers of profits and royalties from VW do Brasil to the German parent company needed prior approval and were subject to potential restrictions in cases of balance of payments deficits.

VW's establishment of a full-scale car factory already paid off within the first four years after it opened in 1959. In 1958, VW do Brazil only assembled 4800 cars from CKD kits. In 1959, production nearly quadrupled to 16,800 cars and minibuses (VW Kombi) and tripled to 53,800 units in 1962. Gross profits (*Bruttogewinne*) before taxes were more than handsome: The turnover profit after tax (*Umsatzrendite*) reached an impressive 20.4% in 1959, 17.7% in 1960, and 15.6% in 1961—and these figures were even understated. In its annual reports, VW do Brasil overstated its equity in order to reduce the profit rate. The motive for this, which was legally possible through an overadjustment to the high inflation rate, was to reduce excess corporate taxes for profit rates beyond 30% (of equity). Despite this deliberate overstatement of equity, annual profit rates (profits after taxes: equity) amounted to 40.8% (1959), 44.8% (1960), 50.3% (1961), and even 58.1% in 1961.[12]

Profit rates of this size were extraordinary at that time and remain so today. The low wage level in Brazil was one reason for this, but not the only one. The rapid rise in consumer demand and Brazilian consumers' limited choice were equally crucial to generating VW do Brasil's high profits and turned Brazil into a sellers' market. In contrast to its performance in the open markets in the United States and in Europe, VW do Brasil drew significant profits from the protectionist policies of the Brazilian government and from its position as a prime mover in the Brazilian market. In 1959, bureaucratic red tape in the GEIA delayed the start of potential competitors like Renault and Simca. This helped VW do Brasil to gain the

[12] Numbers quoted in ibid., 261, based on the annual reports of VW do Brasil.

pole position on the Brazilian market. Until the 1980s, the Brazilian market remained mostly closed to foreign manufactured cars. As a consequence, competition was limited to rather few companies and stayed low during the 1960s and 1970s.

In 1962, VW do Brazil sold 42% of all new cars in the country, overtaking former market leaders Ford and General Motors.[13] Volkswagen was not the first automobile manufacturer in Brazil to produce compact cars in the low-price segment, but it was the first European one. Unlike GM and Ford's car models, the VW Beetle matched the requirements of the Brazilian market nearly perfectly. The Beetle was sold at a lower price than its American competitors and was considerably cheaper to operate and maintain. The technological backwardness of the Beetle—in comparison to the Mini and the Renault R 4—proved to be a benefit in disguise on the Brazilian market. Its noisy, air-cooled, heat-proof engine and robust but unsophisticated technology were significant assets in a subtropical country with many unpaved roads. The Beetle's simple and repair-friendly technology was absolutely adequate considering the limited vocational training of most car mechanics there. Even though Brazil had been a member of the anti-Hitler coalition in World War II, German products and German corporations benefited from a positive image from the beginning of domestic car production. Unlike GM, Ford, and the big US oil companies, Volkswagen did not suffer from the negative *gringo* image of Americans and US multinationals. The Kubitschek government and large swaths of Brazilian society were concerned about the country's economic dependency on the United States and were particularly interested in foreign direct investments from Europeans.

Consequently, Brazilians were quick to embrace the Volkswagen as a Brazilian product. After a short time, Brazilians coined the friendly nickname (or pet name) *fusca* (literally: wild duck) for the Beetle. This was a clear indicator that Volkswagen's only available car model at this time had made its way into Brazilian popular culture and gained the affection of many Brazilians, whether they were car owners or not. One reason for this affectionate attitude might be that the Beetle was the first car middle-class Brazilians could afford and a symbol of their start into a motorized life.

The German Volkswagen managers in Brazil were not left on their own when they started to conquer the Brazilian market. Already in 1953, Volkswagen passed a 20% minority partnership to the Aranha and the

[13] Ibid., 259.

Monteiro families, two wealthy family clans with close ties to the administrative, political, and business elites of Brazil. Despite occasional frictions about the power of attorney to represent VW do Brasil, the German CEO of VW do Brasil and his fellow German executives drew plentiful benefits from their partnership with Aranha and Monteiro. Their Brazilian partners' ability to mediate helped the German CEO of VW do Brazil Friedrich Schultz-Wenk (1914–1968) navigate through the unfamiliar and rather unpredictable seas of Brazilian politics and through tedious negotiations with GEIA and SUMOC.[14] During the crucial stage of factory construction in 1958, Schultz-Wenk needed his partners' political connections to ensure that the Brazilian bureaucracy would approve import permits and currency allowances in time to prevent a delay of the factory construction. The high inflation rate in Brazil confronted Volkswagen managers in Germany and Brazil with previously unknown concerns about the devaluation of profits and potential losses from customer loans.[15]

Volkswagen and the Perception of the Military Coup

VW managers' concerns increased when the left-leaning new president João Goulart (1961–1964) demonstrated his intention to nationalize large plantations ("fazendas") along the federal roads and US oil companies. VW do Brasil was not directly affected by Goulart's populist agenda, but managers became increasingly worried about the decline in economic growth and the steep rise of inflation. GDP growth fell from 8.6% in 1961 to a poor 0.6% in 1963, whereas inflation grew from 50% to 78% during the same period. The Brazilian Ministry of Finance restricted the transfers of profits and royalties to the German parent company in order to curb a growing balance of payments deficit. By November 1963, VW do Brasil was waiting for approval to transfer the equivalent of 80 million DM from its accounts in Brazil to Germany.[16] Moreover, due to public utility capacity deficits, VW do Brasil experienced periodic blackouts and had to cut its production by 15%.[17]

[14] Ibid., 272–273.

[15] Ibid., 284–285.

[16] Minutes of the VW AG executive board meeting on November 14, 1963, in: UVW, Z 373, no. 455/2.

[17] Annual report of VW do Brasil for 1963, in: UVW, Z 174, no. 559/1.

Like many members of the Brazilian business elite, the managers of VW do Brazil became increasingly worried about the country's economic performance and their impression of a political swing to the left. Goulart's intention to enfranchise illiterate citizens prompted uneasiness that there could be a solid left majority after the next elections.[18] Since VW do Brasil did not keep any records from the time before 2000, historians are left to make educated guesses about whether the management was willing to support a coup d'etat against the Goulart government. Historians have found sufficient evidence that the Industrial Association of the State of São Paulo (FIESP) wielded considerable political influence and was in favor of a regime change. Since VW do Brasil had become one of the biggest industrial enterprises in the state of São Paulo, the industrial heartland of Brazil, and a significant contributor to FIESP, Friedrich Schultz-Wenk would certainly have been informed about attempts to support a military coup against Goulart.

The conspirators in the military elite faced little resistance from the Brazilian population and only needed two days (March 31 and April 1, 1964) to overthrow the government. On April 2, 1964, the Brazilian armed forces started a massive "clean-up operation" (Operaçao Limpeza, literally "operation clean-up") and arrested 7000 left-leaning supports of the overthrown Goulart government. By enacting an emergency decree (Ato Instituçional No. 1), the military elite installed General Castelo Branco as president. During the following months, this emergency decree served as a pseudo-legal basis for purging the public service and the military of pro-constitutional loyalists of the former government.

How did the management of VW do Brasil and the Volkswagen AG react to the coup and the regime change? Friedrich Schultz-Wenk was in no way shocked and reacted positively; he was even euphoric. In a long letter of April 16, 1964, to Volkswagen CEO Heinrich Nordhoff, he did not hide his satisfaction about the coup against "the distinct leftward swing of the Goulart government."[19] Schultz-Wenk welcomed the arrest of trade union leaders and of alleged sympathizers of the Communist Party of Brazil (PCB). He remarked, "I was astounded by the sincere joy with which the government's fall was welcomed," expressing both his mood and the opinion of Brazil's business elites. A 100% rise in the stock

[18] In Brazil, illiterate adults were not entitled to vote until 1985.

[19] Letter from Schultz-Wenk to Nordhoff, April 16, 1964, in: UVW, Z 174, no. 559/1.

market within a few weeks of the coup was a clear indicator of their confidence in the military government.

Schultz-Wenk did not hesitate to justify the violence after the coup. He commented that "What is currently taking place is a hunt such as we did not even see back in 1933 in Germany," but this expressed respect and awe rather than than horror. Born in 1914, Schultz-Wenk was old enough to have firsthand memories of the Nazi seizure of power. Although he did rhetorically question the regime, stating, "Whether it's alright can be questioned, because pressure does of course generate counter-pressure," this was not an objection on principle but a warning of a potential uprising of the left. Schultz-Wenk's boss Heinrich Nordhoff did not share his optimism about the coup, but not because he harbored any general reservation about military regimes.[20] Nordhoff was concerned that VW do Brasil might be caught in a civil war between the military and its opponents. He encouraged his colleagues in Brazil not to publicly support the military government out of fear that a foreign company like VW do Brasil might jeopardize its position if it interfered in Brazilian politics. He also remarked on the instability of Brazilian politics, but this indicated that Nordhoff perceived the military coup as a natural consequence of the unstable democracy in Brazil.

Nevertheless, VW AG's senior management did not share Nordhoff's caution and reticence regarding the military government. The managers of Volkswagen's Group Foreign Investment Department expected a business-friendly turn and judged that "the political change in Brazil has given grounds for hoping that fruitful collaboration with the country's authorities can be maintained. So we very much welcome the fact that, just in this period of the restoration of a rational political order, German development aid is beginning to flow."[21] Both Schultz-Wenk and the management in Wolfsburg expected the new government to adopt a stiff austerity policy in order to curb inflation, the major concern of Brazil's business elite. Since the German president Heinrich Lübke did not cancel his official visit to Brazil in May 1964, the Volkswagen managers were reassured that their positive attitude toward the military regime did not provoke any human rights-related objections on the part of the German government. The status of Volkswagen as a semipublic company had no

[20] Letter from Nordhoff to Schultz-Wenk, May 15, 1964, in: UVW, Z 174, no. 559/1.

[21] Letter from VW AG (Novotny/Siebert) to the German Federal Minister for Economic Cooperation, June 11, 1964, in: UVW, Z 174, no. 479/1.

visible impact on managerial decisions concerning its Brazilian affiliation. The state government of Lower Saxony held 50% of all Volkswagen shares at that time, but did not get involved in managerial decisions about VW do Brasil.

The Impact of the Military Dictatorship on Labor Relations and Economic Performance

The executive board of VW do Brasil expected a positive change from the new military government. Since high inflation had been the greatest source of concern, Schultz-Wenk and his colleagues were ready to accept a rigid austerity policy, even at the price of a temporary slowdown of growth. The new government responded in an accommodating manner. At the request of VW do Brasil, the Ministry of Economic Affairs (Ministro do Planejamento) temporarily reduced the sales tax on cars when sales briefly collapsed in 1965.[22] VW do Brasil and the Volkswagen AG considerably benefited from the government's decision to ease restrictions on capital transfers abroad, of profits, royalties, and consulting fees.

The military coup of 1964 also had significant repercussions on industrial relations at VW do Brasil. On June 1, 1964, the government enacted the Strike Act (Lei de Greve), abolished the constitutional right to strike, declared strikes "of a political or social nature" illegal, and threatened strike leaders with prison sentences of 6 to 12 months.[23] Even before the coup, trade unions (*sindicatos*) were weakened by being legally limited to a single industry and a single region, which impeded them from amalgamating into a nationwide Metalworkers' Union. In order to depoliticize the unions, the military government removed opposing trade union executives.

Employers like VW do Brasil profited from the Labor Code that had been established under the Vargas dictatorship (1937–1945). The Labor Code remained valid during the era of parliamentarian governments (1945–1964) despite its origins in the authoritarian corporatism of the Vargas Era and strong similarities with other authoritarian regimes like the Estado Novo in Portugal. Collective wage agreements between unions and employers required approval by the Ministry of Labor before they

[22] *Der Spiegel* 39/1966.

[23] Maria Helena Moreira Alves, *State and Opposition in Military Brazil* (Austin: Texas University Press, 1985), 51–53; Law 4.330 of June 1, 1964 (www.planalto.gov.br/ccivil_03/leis/1950-1969/L4330.htmimpressSao.htm).

came into force.[24] From 1964, the Ministry of Labor unilaterally favored employers and used its arbiter role to keep wages below the market level. Despite the methodological problems of counterfactual hypotheses, it seems safe to assume that wages would have increased significantly faster in a free labor market with autonomous unions and a strictly neutral government. Real wage increases after inflation remained low even during the economic boom from 1966 to 1973. In order to curb inflation, the government made sure that pay raises stayed below the growth of labor productivity.

VW do Brasil and the automotive industry in general paid the highest wages in the manufacturing industries in Brazil. Nevertheless, Volkswagen workers did not harvest the fruits of their increasing productivity. From 1960 to 1972, labor productivity at VW do Brazil grew by a factor of three (1960: 100; 1972: 344). The increase in real wages lagged considerably behind the productivity gains (1960: 100, 1972: 180).[25] Even during Brazil's boom years, at a time when the country enjoyed double-digit annual GDP growth rates, the shortage of qualified staff did not generate pressure for pay raises in the automotive industry.

Therefore, the managers of VW do Brasil were never confronted with any kind of labor militancy. The Brazilian Labor Code did not contain any rules for shop floor representation of workers or for the recognition of union representatives. In an interview with the German illustrated magazine *Stern*, CEO Schultz-Wenk declared in an authoritarian manner: "I am my own trade union here." His PR manager João Corduan added: "There are no strikes, and if anyone incites the workers to strike, he will be dismissed."[26] This announcement expressed an uncompromising anti-union approach to labor relations. VW do Brasil benefited from the fact that many employees were first-generation industrial workers with absolutely no experience in labor representation. The Volkswagen managers pacified their Brazilian workforce with social benefits far above the

[24] Kenneth P Erickson, *The Brazilian Corporative State and Working-Class Politics* (Berkeley/Los Angeles: University of California Press, 1977), 153–174; Youssef Cohen, *The manipulation of consent. The state and working-class consciousness in Brazil* (Pittsburgh: University of Pittsburgh Press, 1989).

[25] Internal memo from the Economics Department of the VW AG to the Investment Department, July 13, 1973, in: UVW, Z 1199, no. 167/2. Wage statistics from VW do Brasil in response to a query from the General Workers Council (*Gesamtbetriebsrat*) of the VW AG to VW do Brasil, June 30, 1978, in: UVW, Z 947, no. 662/1.

[26] *Stern*, Oktober 16, 1966.

Brazilian average: cheap but rich meals in the factory canteen, very inexpensive transportation from home to the factory, a cooperative food shop and department store with considerably discounted prices and, above all, free healthcare for employees, their spouses, and children.[27] This was the benevolent side of the authoritarian paternalism that Schultz-Wenk bluntly expressed. However, some social benefits for employees had a hidden repressive side. The factory hospital and Volkswagen's cooperation with general practitioners kept sick leave low. Physicians working for VW do Brazil were restrictive in writing sick notes and wielded additional control over the staff.

In 1967, the military government provided employers with additional benefits. First, the government abolished the legal job guarantee after ten years of employment at one enterprise (*stabilidade*). Second, employers were granted permission to reduce severance payments by a single lump-sum payment. Since Brazil had no public unemployment insurance, employees had been entitled to a severance payment of one month for every year of employment at their current company. The reduction of severance payments reduced the costs of layoffs to the benefit of VW do Brazil but at the expense of its staff.

Since car sales and employment in the automotive industry rose steeply during the 1960s and the early 1970s, layoffs were only a minor concern for employers. During this period, VW do Brasil earned very substantial profits and managed to transfer sizable gains to the parent company. The average annual return of investment (ROI) of VW do Brasil from 1968 to 1973 amounted to an impressive 42.2%. The average return of sales during the same period reached an extraordinary level of 15.5%.[28] Even in 1974, when VW AG was severely hit in the wake of the oil price crisis by the first postwar slump and had to bear losses of 800 million DM, VW do Brasil still scored a 14.6% return on investment and a 4.6% return on sales. Annual data about profit and royalty transfers from VW do Brasil to VW AG have only survived for the three consecutive years from 1971 to 1973, but these numbers are impressive. During these years, the parent company received payments of 135 million DM, a weighty contribution to keeping VW afloat during the disastrous year of 1974, when VW AG suffered an

[27] See the Social Report of VW do Brasil for 1982, in. UVW, Z 947, no. 308/1.

[28] Statistics from VW AG, International Investments Department I, in: UVW, Z 587, no. 6/229.

annual loss of more than 800 million DM.[29] During the entire period from 1962 to 1980, VW AG received a total of 594 million DM in dividends, as well as in licensing and consulting fees, from its Brazilian subsidiary, or an annual amount of 31.3 million DM.[30]

The Economic Order of Brazil and the Dependency Theory

Brazil's so-called economic miracle (*milagre economico*) differed distinctly from the Ricardian textbook narrative of export-generated economic growth. The Brazilian economy resembled a strictly coordinated market economy under the firm guidance of a powerful public administration. Foreign trade controls and high tariffs on nonessential imports were the primary elements of this heterodox economic model. But import restrictions worked well for VW do Brasil as they prevented importers from challenging its position as Brazil's market leader. From the early 1970s, the Brazilian government reacted to growing balance of payments deficits with an export subsidy program. Manufacturers like VW do Brasil received hefty export subsidies as rewards for their export efforts but incurred financial disadvantages if they failed to meet the government's export targets. VW do Brasil had no choice but to accept a long-term export commitment of US$1 billion for the period from 1973 to 1982. This use of sticks and carrots prompted the Volkswagen Group to revise internal supply chains in order to increase VW do Brasil's export performance. As a consequence, VW do Brasil became the designated deliverer to markets in Africa and the Middle East and supplied the Volkswagen factories in Mexico and the United States with engines and gearboxes for the new Passat. VW do Brasil even received a limited contract to supply the German Volkswagen factory in Baunatal in order to guarantee the fulfilment of the Brazilian export plan.[31] In 1979 and 1980, the Brazilian government resorted to a policy of financial incentives and political pressure to reduce

[29] Overview in UVW, Z 69, no. 345/1. These transfers included dividends and consulting fees.

[30] Overview of VW AG, International Investments Dept. I, May 22, 1981, in: UVW, Z 1184, no. 361/2.

[31] Minutes of the executive board meetings on August 31, 1972, and June 5, 1973, in: UVW, Z 69, no. 730/1; draft resolution for the executive board meeting on August 21, 1973, in: UVW, Z 1199, no. 167/2; internal memo from the Economics Department to the Investments Department, July 13, 1973, in: ibid.

dependence on increasingly costly oil imports. Car manufacturers received financial support to manage the introduction of ethanol-fueled engines but had to accept a rigid timeline for implementing the shift toward energy autarchy.

The second element of Brazil's economic model was strict control of currency and capital transfers through the Central Bank (Banco Central do Brasil). Despite general permission to transfer dividends and consulting and licensing fees to Germany up until 1974, monetary transfers abroad were subject to discretionary limitations by the national monetary authorities. Since the Brazilian government did not allow dividend transfers beyond 12% of the share capital, VW do Brasil had to reinvest a significant part of its profits in the Brazilian capital market.[32] The red tape of Brazilian bureaucracy did have its costs for Volkswagen: The Central Bank took several months to decide on Volkswagen's transfer applications. This delay resulted in a partial devaluation of transferable profits on account of inflation and a declining exchange rate between Cruzeiro and Deutschmark. In 1979, at the beginning of the second oil price crisis, VW do Brasil and other car manufacturers had no choice but to accept the government's rigid fuel conservation policy, which resulted in a significant drop in sales. The Brazilian Association of Vehicle Manufacturers (Anfavea) had no means to negotiate a lower increase of the VAT for cars (from 24% to 30%), of the registration fee (from 3% to 7%), and the limitation on bank loans for car purchases to as little as 12 months.[33]

The third element of the Brazilian economic model was government interference in managerial decisions. VW do Brasil did not have the freedom to set car prices as it saw fit. Mandatory government approval for price increases did not allow VW do Brasil to maximize sales revenues, yet it did not prevent high returns on investments, either.[34] Apart from price controls, large industrial enterprises like VW do Brasil needed the government's consent for major investments in equity. In light of these observations, dependency theory's postulate that lesser developed nations are unilaterally dependent on fully developed countries and their multinationals merits a closer look. The example of Brazil proves the Prebish-Singer

[32] Briefing by the VW AG Investments Department, undated (1973), in: UVW, Z 69, no. 345/1.

[33] Analysis of the International Investments Dept. of VW AG about the economic policy of the Brazilian government, June 2, 1980, in: UVW, Z 1184, no. 390/1.

[34] Report of Wolfgang Sauer (CEO of VW do Brasil) to Rudolf Leiding (CEO of VW AG), August 24, 1973, in: UVW, Z 1184, no. 577/1.

thesis about the beneficial effects of a protectionist development policy right. Companies' need to invest in Brazilian factories to conquer the market resulted in a steep increase in foreign direct investments and caused high growth in domestic industrial output from the late 1950s to 1973. During the 1970s, the Brazilian government maintained its protectionist strategy but recognized the necessity of growing industrial exports to keep the payment balance under control. The strategy of boosting exports with subsidies was definitely incompatible with the GATT agreements and the concept of fair trade but was justified by concerns about a permanent payment deficit.

Some prior observations raise doubts about whether dependency theory applies to Brazil.[35] On the one hand, the Brazilian government needed foreign multinationals like VW for the implementation of national development programs and the success of its industrial development. The import substitution strategy would not have succeeded without investments from multinational corporations, but the government wielded significant discretionary power to steer foreign investors into the direction it chose. On the other hand, the privileges multinationals enjoyed, like exemptions from import duties on foreign capital goods, needed to be renewed periodically and could be revoked if relations between senior Brazilian officials and foreign CEOs deteriorated. For this reason, the CEOs of the Volkswagen AG were anxious to maintain good relations with the Brazilian ministers of finance. On their annual visits to VW do Brasil, Volkswagen CEOs even paid courtesy visits to the presidents of Brazil. Surviving documents in the Volkswagen archive in Wolfsburg do not indicate that they talked about details of customs regulations and foreign currency transfers.[36] The major purpose of these visits was to assure the presidents that VW do Brazil's biggest foreign manufacturer at that time, was still fully committed to the development of its production sites in Brazil. In 1974, VW AG had no choice but to accept that Brazil's payment imbalance forced the Central Bank to restrict transfers of royalties and licensing fees.

Since the 1970s, economic historians and political scientists have done a great deal of research into the macroeconomic policies of the Brazilian

[35] On dependency theory, see Fernando Henrique Cardoso/Enzo Faletto, *Abhängigkeit und Entwicklung in Lateinamerika* (Frankfurt: Suhrkamp, 1976).

[36] Telex from Werner P. Schmidt (CEO of VW do Brasil) to Rudolf Leiding (CEO of VW AG), February 2, 1973, in: UVW, Z 174, no. 576/1.

government and their effects on economic growth, balance of payments, and social inequality, but they have not researched government–business relations on the micropolitical level and the influence of business associations on political decision-making. Historians have not conducted research with the files of the Ministry of Finance and the Ministry of Economic Planning and have been unable to assess the formal and informal influence of Brazilian business elites, in general, and foreign multinationals, in particular. This case study on VW do Brasil allows us at least to conclude that the structures and objectives of the Brazilian economic order remained non-negotiable. But the executive managers of VW do Brasil and its parent company had the power to negotiate occasional favors such as export subsidies as a reward for their loyal support in Brazil's pursuit of key macroeconomic objectives.

Doing Business in a Dictatorship: The Attitude of the Volkswagen Management

For the period of 1964–1978, the files of the Volkswagen AG executive board and the CEO do not reveal any concerns about human rights violations in Brazil. After their return from business trips to Brazil, VW's CEOs informed their fellow executives about the general economic situation and the performance of VW do Brasil but never mentioned the political situation in general. When German journalists and human rights organizations started to question human rights abuses in Brazil in 1972, Volkswagen executives spoke up publicly in defense of the military government. Werner P. Schmidt, the CEO of VW do Brasil from 1971 to 1973, was interviewed by the liberal newspaper *Süddeutsche Zeitung*, which asked him about human rights violations like torture and murder, but he justified some of these means, such as interrogation under torture, as a legal and legitimate defense of Brazil's political order ("You can't make progress without being tough. And progress is being made").[37] In one of his monthly reports to Volkswagen CEO Rudolf Leiding, Schmidt condemned a critical article by the influential magazine *Der Spiegel* for its

[37] Interview in *Süddeutsche Zeitung*, February 16, 1972, quoted in Werner Würtele, *Auf dem Weg zu einer authentischen Gewerkschaftsbewegung in Brasilien* (Heidelberg: Esprint, 1982), 334.

sharp criticism of social inequality in Brazil and the military government.[38]

In a letter to a leading member of Brazils's governing pro-military party ARENA (Aliança Renovadora Nacional) from October 1973, Leiding expressed his disapproval of the German press and its critical reports on Brazil and encouraged his interlocutor to disclose his praise of Brazil to the Brazilian public. Leiding stated: "I have noticed in the course of many contacts with journalists and leading personalities in Germany (...) that many people are not yet aware of the true nature of Brazilian life (...) It will take a long time and a lot of patience to disseminate a more positive image of Brazil."[39] In an interview with a Brazilian journalist, he lauded Brazil as "the most stable country in Latin America" and characterized Brazilians as people "who are not envious (...), and [are] satisfied with their lot if they can always be certain that their living conditions might slowly but surely improve. Brazilians are also willing to work, even if they hate doing heavy labor."[40] His praise of political stability in Brazil indicated his full approval of the military dictatorship, which he blended with benevolent but rather colonialist stereotypes of Brazilian workers. VW even tried to counter public criticism of the political regime in Brazil with a whitewashing brochure about the beneficial aspects of German investments in a country that was developing well.[41]

Leiding's knowledge of Brazil was based on annual business trips and his former firsthand experience as CEO of VW do Brasil. Since Leiding had been at the top of Volkswagen's Brazilian affiliate from 1968 to 1971, he firmly believed that his judgment about Brazil was superior to that of German journalists. During his tenure in Brazil, the country went through a radicalization of repression. In 1968, the military government of president General Medici enacted the infamous Executive Order No. 5 (Ato Instituçional No. 5), which suspended habeas corpus and allowed the Political Police to arrest and detain political opponents without arrest warrants from the judiciary power. Due to his lack of Portuguese skills, Leiding probably did not notice that the military government tightened

[38] "Unser Kapitalismus kennt keine Scham", *Der Spiegel* 36/1972, September 18, 1972.

[39] Letter from Leiding to the Brazilian congressman Alberto Hoffmann, October 29, 1973, in: UVW, Z 174, no. 577/1.

[40] Letter from Leiding to Hoffmann, quoted by Hoffmann in a speech to the Brazilian federal parliament October 10, 1973, in: Diario do Congresso Nacional, p. 7109.

[41] Letter from Leiding to Prof. Kurt Hansen (CEO of Bayer AG and chairman of the supervisory board of VW), April 25, 1973, in: UVW, Z 69, no. 286/1.

censorship and revoked the parliamentary mandates of several members of the only legal political opposition party, the MDB.

In 1969, also during Leiding's tenure in Brazil, VW do Brasil's in-house Works Security Department began to regularly exchange information with the Political Police (DEOPS).[42] Close personal links between the head of the Works Security Department and military institutions like the Policia Militar had certainly existed before. VW do Brasil recruited the heads of the Security Department from among officers of the armed forces who maintained their allegiance to the military elite. Up to 1969, VW do Brasil's head of security was an officer who had been appointed before the military coup of 1964, and he was promoted to the rank of reserve general. His successor Ademar Rudge was hired in 1969 when he held the rank of army major. During his career at VW do Brasil, which ended in 1991, Rudge was promoted to the rank of reserve colonel.

Ademar Rudge cooperated with the armed forces and the Political Police right from the start of his employment at VW do Brasil. In June 1969, the Air Force staff informed the DEOPS that subversive flyers had been discovered at the Volkswagen plant. The flow of information indicates that the Security Department must have informed the Air Force, which, in turn, notified the Political Police.[43] The first documented contact between the Security Department and the Political Police was established on December 11, 1969, through a formal notification that security guards had found the illegal leftist newspaper (*O Ferramenta*—"The Tool") in restrooms, changing rooms, and stairwells.[44] The Security Department did not limit its collaboration to this observation but started investigating on its own and passed the names of four suspects on to the Political Police. Since the records of DEOPS were cleansed by police officers right after the dissolution of the Political Police at the end of the military dictatorship, the surviving records do not contain information about whether the cooperation between DEOPS and the Volkswagen Security Department was based on a formal written agreement. DEOPS files indicate that the head of the Political Police for the São Bernardo do Campo

[42] On the collaboration between VW do Brasil and the Political Police, see also the Ph.D. thesis by Marcelo Almeida de Carvalho Silva, "As Práticas de Normalização da Violencia Operacionalizadas pela Volkswagen do Brasil na Ditadura Militar Brasileira (1964–1985)," Rio de Janeiro 2018 (Pontifica Universidade Catolica), pp. 225–256.

[43] São Paulo State Archive (AESP), DEOPS inventory, 50-D-007-1393.

[44] Report by Rudge to DEOPS, December 11, 1969, in: AESP, DEOPS inventory, 50-Z-030-0822.

region convened a meeting of corporate security department heads—among them VW, GM, and Chrysler—on November 11, 1969, to establish formal cooperation on security matters.[45]

There are several indications in the documentation that Ademar Rudge did not act on his own but rather with at least the tacit consent of the chief human relations officer and the executive board of VW do Brasil. During all of the 1970s, Rudge regularly sent security reports to the Human Relations Department about subversive political activities on the factory floor. Copies of these reports were passed to DEOPS. The distribution key of these mimeographed reports included DEOPS among the designated recipients. Since copies of Volkswagen security reports survived in the DEOPS files, there is documentary evidence of a formal collaboration. On important occasions, such as when communists were arrested in the Volkswagen factory, the list of recipients included the CEO and other board members.[46]

In 1970, Works Security guards discovered a newspaper from the illegal Communist Party of Brazil (PCB) on the factory grounds. The title ("Volkswagen from its workers' viewpoint")[47] and the content indicated that this paper had been written by Volkswagen employees. The well-informed criticism of the wage level and of unsafe working conditions, including the lack of safety gloves for welders and other kinds of essential accident prevention equipment, provided sufficient evidence that a communist resistance group had been established at VW do Brasil.[48] From the management's perspective, the content of this communist paper was at least unpleasant, if not embarrassing. The statement that five fatal work accidents had occurred during the preceding six months might have stirred unrest on the factory floor. The strategy of the clandestine communist resistance became apparent in July 1971 when the Air Force intelligence service intercepted a communist training document titled "How to establish the party in a big company."[49] This document revealed that a communist party cell had already been established in 1968. Since the unskilled and semiskilled workers had little political awareness and were more

[45] Jose Casado, "Repressão no patio do fabrica", *O Globo*, May 15, 2005.

[46] Report by Rudge to the Chief Human Relations Officer, September 9, 1974, in: AESP, DEOPS, 50-Z-341-1135 to 1138.

[47] Original title: ***Volkswagen vista por seus operarios.***

[48] AESP, DEOPS. 50-Z-341-0610.

[49] Information from the Air Force Ministry to the DEOPS, July 21, 1971, in: AESP, DEOPS, 50-D-7-1714.

concerned with a potential layoff in a recession period, the training document advised potential agitators to focus propaganda efforts on the better-educated and supposedly more class-conscious skilled workforce. Against conventional Leninist wisdom, the authors seemed to suppose that the so-called labor aristocracy was not corrupted by their employer and had the intellectual capacity to understand the concept of Marxist political economy.

The discovery of illegal flyers and newspapers by the Works Security Department helped the police agencies to pinpoint communist activities and to tighten the net in the search for suspects. At their request, the Works Security Department provided the Military Police (Policia Militar) with detailed information about two suspected communist activists among the Volkswagen workforce. Several months later, in late July and early August 1972, the Political Police started the roundup of the communist party cell at VW with the arrest of six employees—five men and one woman. The arrests took place on the premises of Volkswagen and in the presence of Works Security personnel. According to the detailed arrest report of toolmaker Lucio Bellentani from 2012, he was arrested during his night shift right at his work station.[50] The agents of the Political Police handcuffed him and took him to a Works Security room, where he was slapped and beaten in the presence of Volkswagen security men. During the following months, Bellentani and the other suspects were held in the São Paulo prison of the Political Police without any arrest warrants and suffered from the brutality of the prison guards and interrogators. Bellentani and his comrades were severely beaten and subjugated to harsh forms of physical torture and faked executions.

The VW Works Security Department did not limit its collaboration with the Political Police to providing information about suspicious activities and employees. VW's security guards turned a blind eye to police brutality at their own workplace and deliberately misinformed the spouses of the arrested workers about their whereabouts. In his regular report on political and economic developments in Brazil, Werner P. Schmidt, who was the CEO of VW do Brasil at that time, did not fail to inform his boss Rudolf Leiding in Wolfsburg about the arrest of the employees on account of alleged communist activities. But he omitted one important

[50] Transcript of Bellentani's testimony in: Commissão Nacional da Verdade "Vladimir Herzog", Relatorio Final, São Paulo 2013, 48–51.

detail—that Works Security personnel had been involved in the detection of the communist group and had actively supported the arrest.[51]

On several occasions, Leiding reacted to critical media coverage of political repression and torture in Brazil rather bluntly and did not show any compassion for those suffering as a result of human rights violations. Therefore, it seems safe to guess that Leiding would not have reprimanded his subordinate in Brazil for collaborating with the Political Police. The executive board of the Volkswagen AG did not ask discerning questions about the collaboration with the repressive institutions of the military regime before a major strike in the Brazilian car industry broke out in March 1979. Disapproving reports in the German media about the presence of the Policia Militar in the Volkswagen factory prompted Leiding's successor Toni Schmücker (1975–1982) to ask critical questions about why VW do Brasil, unlike other car manufacturers, was openly collaborating with the military regime.[52] The Volkswagen AG's human rights consciousness grew in response to the increasing sensitivity of German society and expanding media coverage of human rights matters in Latin America. Even the German government, which had largely remained silent about the human rights situation in Brazil up to 1979, reproached VW do Brasil for its heavy-handed and authoritarian management. After an official visit in Brazil and detailed talks with ministers, managers, and union leaders, Chancellor Helmut Schmidt publicly advised the managers of German corporations in Brazil to recognize trade unions as a legitimate part of a democratic society.[53]

In 1979, the most repressive stage of the military dictatorship in Brazil had already given way to the policy of relaxation (*distensão*) and the partial abolition of the emergency laws. In August 1978, the government removed the strike ban from the National Security Act. As a consequence, participation in strikes in nonessential economic sectors was no longer considered a criminal offense. The abolition of Emergency Decree No. 5 (Ato Instituçional No. 5) restored habeas corpus and protected strikers from unwarranted arrests. Since the Military Police lost their right to keep picketers in custody without legal arrest warrants, union activists' lives

[51] Letter from Werner P. Schmidt to Rudolf Leiding, September 26, 1972, in: UVW, Z 174, no. 575/1.

[52] Memo on the German TV broadcaster ZDF and its documentary "Auslandsjournal" on April 27, 1979, in: UVW, Z 174, no. 2116/2.

[53] "Große Luftblasen", *Der Spiegel* 16/1979, April 16, 1979.

were not seriously impacted by the still-frequent arrests of picketers and cooperation between the security guards of VW and the Political Police. But when VW do Brasil's Human Relations Department dismissed more than 100 strike activists, the reputation of Volkswagen in Germany was tainted. A critical report by the German TV magazine ***Monitor*** about blacklisted Brazilian workers and growing pressure from the German Metal Workers' Union (IG Metall) on the Volkswagen supervisory board forced Schmücker to act.[54] At this point, the unusually strong position of the unions at the VW AG in Germany was beneficial to the workforce of VW do Brasil. The representatives of the German Metal Workers' Union and the employee representatives (*Betriebsräte*) on VW's supervisory board used their powerful position to call for substantive change in industrial relations in Brazil. The IG Metall adopted VW do Brasil as a model case for international solidarity and demonstrated its resolve to extend corporate social responsibility beyond the borders of its home country.

In 1979 and 1980, the executive board of VW AG transformed itself from a passive bystander to an agent of change. In order to de-escalate the industrial dispute and to calm labor unrest, the board members of the parent company decided to gradually replace the authoritarian "master in his house" attitude of the management in the Brazilian affiliate by means of cooperative leadership. CEO Toni Schmücker decided not to attend the festivities marking the production of the fifth million Volkswagen in Brazil and sent Chief Human Relations Officer Karl-Heinz Briam on a fact-finding mission to São Bernardo do Campo. This was more than a merely symbolic statement of discontent. Briam, a former trade union activist, tried his best to convince VW do Brasil's executive board of the advantages of factory floor representation and dialogue with union representatives on wages and human relations.

Briam and Schmücker's patient and determined insistence yielded significant results at the end of the following year. After a second costly labor dispute in 1980, VW do Brasil became the first major industrial company in Brazil to allow representation of factory employees even though the labor code did not yet require it. Behind the scenes, Briam even organized a dialogue between VW do Brasil's management and the Catholic

[54]Briefing by Ekkehard Wesner (VW AG Public Relations Dept.) for Anton Konrad (Public Relations Dept.) and Karl-Heinz Briam (Human Relations) on the "Monitor" program on July 3, 1979, in: UVW, Z 174, no. 2716/2; letter from Eugen Loderer (Chairman of the Metalworkers' Union) to Schmücker, April 30, 1979, in: UVW, Z 1184, no. 355/2.

archbishop of São Paulo, a widely recognized supporter of workers' rights and a mediator between the managerial elite and the common people of Brazil. The change in management at VW do Brasil generated the first meaningful results in 1981.

Conclusion

Volkswagen established an assembly plant in Brazil as a consequence of country's rigid import policies. The decision to invest in a full-scale automobile plant was triggered by the government's ambitious plan to turn Brazil into an industrialized nation by means of an import substitution policy. VW's heavy financial commitment to the Brazilian government was sweetened by the positive outlook for development it had as a pioneering investor and the substantial financial benefits it reaped. After only a short time, Volkswagen gained abundant financial rewards in a dynamic market with restricted access for competitors and highly profitable conditions for manufacturers.

VW do Brasil and other foreign multinationals were not involved in the military coup of 1964. But there is sufficient evidence that foreign multinationals favored the coup so that the allegedly socialist policies of the democratically elected Goulart government could be rolled back. VW do Brasil benefited from the suppression of organized labor and the government control of depoliticized unions. Even during the impressive economic boom from 1968 to 1974, government wage controls prevented unions from claiming a fair share of productivity gains and profits for workers. Brazil's foreign trade and foreign currency agencies wielded sufficient power to impose restrictions on profit transfers. Foreign multinationals were not influential enough to keep the Brazilian government in a dependent position and had to accept its anti-liberal economic policy, but domestic protectionism and wage and price controls were important preconditions for companies' ability to earn high profits. Using financial incentives and deterrents as carrots and sticks, the government imposed an export-oriented sales strategy on foreign investors that obviously did not work against the financial interests of their parent companies.

Both the Volkswagen management in Brazil and the executive management of Volkswagen AG in Germany saw the military dictatorship in a very positive light and deliberately ignored growing concerns about human rights violations. The Brazilian and the German members of the executive board of VW do Brasil tacitly approved institutionalized cooperation between the Works Security Department and the highly repressive Political Police. This cooperation had severe repercussions for the six Brazilian staff members who were detected, arrested, and tortured in 1972. The Political Police might never have suspected them of engaging in subversive activities if the Works Security Department of VW do Brasil had not been ready to spy on employees and pass on their observations without regard for the consequences. Yet finally, in 1980, Volkwagen's management began to push for changes in labor relations and VW do Brasil once again took on a pioneering role, becoming the first major industrial company in Brazil to allow employee representation.

References

Archival Sources

Volkswagen Archive. Wolfsburg, Germany.
São Paulo State Archive. DEOPS inventory.

Bibliography

„Große Luftblasen", *Der Spiegel* 16/1979, April 16, 1979.

„Unser Kapitalismus kennt keine Scham", *Der Spiegel* 36/1972, September 18, 1972.

Baer, Werner. *The Brazilian Economy. Growth and Development.* Boulder: University of Colorado Press, 2008), 55–60.

Cardoso, Fernando Henrique, and Faletto, Enzo. *Abhängigkeit und Entwicklung in Lateinamerika.* Frankfurt: Suhrkamp, 1976.

Carvalho Silva, Marcelo Almeida de. "As Práticas de Normalização da Violencia Operacionalizadas pela Volkswagen do Brasil na Ditadura Militar Brasileira (1964–1985)." PhD thesis, Pontifica Universidade Catolica, Rio de Janeiro, 2018.

Casado, Jose. "Repressão no patio do fabrica", *O Globo*, May 15, 2005.

Cohen, Youssef. *The manipulation of consent. The state and working-class consciousness in Brazil.* Pittsburgh: University of Pittsburgh Press, 1989.

Comissão Nacional de Verdade. Relatório, 3 vols., Brasilia 2014.

Comissão Nacional da Verdade "Vladimir Herzog", Relatorio Final, São Paulo 2013.

Diario do Congresso Nacional. Letter from Leiding (Wolfsburg) to Hoffmann (Brasilia). October 10, 1973.

"Erfolg mit Fusca," *Der Spiegel* 39/1966.

Erickson, Kenneth P. *The Brazilian Corporative State and Working-Class Politics.* Berkeley and Los Angeles: University of California Press, 1977.

Institute of Brazilian Business & Management Issues. George Washington University, Washington D.C.

Moreira Alves, Maria Helena. *State and Opposition in Military Brazil.* Austin: Texas University Press, 1985.

Shapiro, Helen. *Engines of growth. The state and transnational auto companies in Brazil.* Cambridge: Cambridge University Press, 1994.

Vidal Luna, Francisco and Herbert S. Klein. *The Economic and Social History of Brazil since 1889.* Cambridge: Cambridge University Press, 2014.

Wellhöner, Volker. *"Wirtschaftswunder." In Weltmarkt, westdeutscher Fordismus.* Münster: Westfälisches Dampfboot, 1996.

Würtele, Werner. *Auf dem Weg zu einer authentischen Gewerkschaftsbewegung in Brasilien.* Heidelberg: Esprint, 1982.

CHAPTER 13

Securing the Expansion of Capitalism in Colombia: Canadair and the Military Regime of General Gustavo Rojas Pinilla (1953–1957)

Stefano Tijerina

Introduction

This chapter focuses on the administration of Gustavo Rojas Pinilla (1953–1957), the only military dictatorship in Colombia in the twentieth century. As a dictator, Rojas Pinilla ordered the bombing of "subversives" as a means to eradicate communism and set the stage for the acceleration of foreign direct investment into the country. The main aim of this chapter is to analyze the role played by American, Canadian, and European companies in this process. It will focus particularly on the relationship between the dictatorship and the Canadian subsidiary of the U.S. Company General Dynamics, Canadair, which saw in the initiatives of the military regime an

S. Tijerina (✉)
University of Maine, Orono, ME, USA
e-mail: stefano.tijerina@maine.edu

V. Basualdo et al. (eds.), *Big Business and Dictatorships in Latin America*, Palgrave Studies in Latin American Heterodox Economics, https://doi.org/10.1007/978-3-030-43925-5_13

opportunity to supply the dictatorship with jet fighters to eliminate the communists and establish the proper domestic conditions for international business to thrive. In this chapter, I first provide a brief introduction to the origins and main characteristics of this military dictatorship. Second, I analyze the main economic changes introduced during the period, as well as the role of foreign direct investment within it. Third, I study the re-escalation of violence from 1955 onward and the intensification of efforts to persecute the opposition. Fourth, I specifically examine the dictatorship's attempts to reestablish authority and the role of the sale of Canadian jet fighters to Colombia in 1956. The fifth section concludes the chapter.

The Rise of the Military Dictatorship in Colombia

For Rojas Pinilla to implement his foreign policy and modernization strategy successfully, he needed to be able to end the civil war that had erupted after the assassination of Liberal Party leader, Jorge Eliécer Gaitán, in 1948—a wave of violence that the conservatives and liberals had failed to contain.[1] This was precisely why liberal and conservative leaders, the business and working classes, and the international community had welcomed the rise of the military dictatorship.

The conservative administrations of Mariano Ospina Pérez (1946–1950) and Laureano Gómez (1950–1953) had failed to resolve the domestic conflict and instead further isolated the country's economy from the international market, escalating the risk of the nation to foreign investors. The Colombian military, "disgusted at being used to repress fellow citizens for partisan purposes," overthrew President Laureano Gómez and replaced him with their top leader, General Gustavo Rojas Pinilla, in June 1953.[2] The domestic and international communities welcomed the military regime because they perceived Rojas Pinilla as the only leader capable of bringing peace back to Colombia. Rojas Pinilla had already gained the respect of the United States and the admiration of the Colombian Conservative and Liberal leadership because of his role in the Korean

[1] For more on *El Bogotazo* and the civil war that followed the assassination of Gaitán, see Herbert Braun, *The Assassination of Gaitán: Public Life and Urban Violence in Colombia* (Madison: University of Wisconsin Press, 1985).

[2] Paul H. Lewis. *Authoritarian Regimes in Latin America: Dictators, Despots, and Tyrants* (New York: Rowman & Littlefield Publisher, 2006), 83.

War.[3] For the Colombian elite, the leader of the "heroes of the Korean War" was essential to the "restoration of domestic order and stability."[4]

General Rojas Pinilla was a reformist; he appealed to "the little man" by taxing the rich landowners and business class to "pay for public works, social welfare programs, and easy credit for small entrepreneurs and farmers."[5] His view resonated with many in the domestic business sector who were interested in the economy being stabilized and modernized. At the same time, Western powers supported his anti-communist stance and his views on economic development. Restoring social stability and strengthening capitalism in Colombia were good for international business interests, even if it meant supporting the regime with weapons in order to combat dissidence.

Trained as an engineer in the United States, he learned to view the world from the American perspective. He saw communism as a regional and global threat and was convinced that the economy could only be modernized by integrating the nation into the global economy. He was convinced that Western-style modernity and progress were the answer to Colombia's stagnant economy and that drastic sociopolitical and socio-economic changes needed to be implemented to achieve greater income equality and alter the course of the nation.

The dynamics that shaped the relationship between foreign multinational corporations and military regimes across Latin America and the Caribbean, which are analyzed in this volume, were not replicated in the case of Colombia. While countries such as Argentina and Brazil had already become important hosts of foreign investment by the time their military dictatorships surfaced, Colombia's internal political and social instability had prevented this from happening. Even though it was a major player in the world coffee industry and had significant foreign investment in oil, Colombia dwarfed behind other of its Latin American counterparts such as Argentina, Mexico, Brazil, or Venezuela.

It is therefore important to study the Rojas Pinilla dictatorship, because it enabled foreign business interests to finally secure access to the nation's resources and markets, and also contributed to consolidating the

[3] Colombia was the only Latin American nation to join the United Nations coalition in the Korean War. The infantry battalion and warship were led by General Rojas Pinilla. See Bradley Lynn Coleman, *Colombia and the United States: The Making of an Inter-American Alliance, 1939–1960* (Kent: The Kent State University Press, 2008).

[4] Coleman, *Colombia and the United States*, 136.

[5] Lewis, *Authoritarian Regimes in Latin America*, 83.

ideological, institutional, bureaucratic, and programmatic apparatus necessary for the World Bank to implement its economic development plan of 1950.[6] These social, political, and economic structural adjustments had been the point of contention between Colombia's left-leaning liberals and nationalist conservatives, since the Great Depression, ultimately impeding classical liberalism from flourishing within the cultural and economic context of Colombia. Moreover, the internal instability that resulted from the 1948 assassination of Jorge Eliécer Gaitán exacerbated the situation for foreigners interested in capitalizing on the vast natural resources and market potential that the World Bank had identified in its 1950 report.

The Rojas Pinilla dictatorship broke the elite's paternalistic social, political, and economic control over the nation's development that stagnated the nation's economic growth, allowing the country to experience rapid capitalist growth through the development of internal industrial growth, the acceleration of infrastructure development, and foreign direct investment. The case of Canadair highlighted in this chapter is just one example of how the Rojas Pinilla regime was able to attract foreign investment and services into the country.

The business and political history of Canadair's sale of jet fighters to Colombia contributes to the very limited historiography of the dictatorship period. Moreover, it illustrates how Rojas Pinilla fast-tracked foreign companies entering the Colombian market in an effort to make up for lost ground in the regional race for economic development. Likewise, foreign companies reacted quickly to the opportunity to enter the Colombian market under a military dictatorship, ultimately contradicting the Western claim that democratic stability was a necessary first step in implementing a successful market economy. In a Cold War world underpinned by the Western idea that democracy was the pillar for the structural development of capitalist economic growth, it was, paradoxically, a military dictatorship that finally laid the foundations for capitalist economic growth in Colombia.

[6] During the 1950s, the World Bank visited numerous nations across the Western Hemisphere with the intention of advancing the structural political, social, and economic adjustments necessary for the implementation of capitalist economic development. The World Bank tour made its stop in Colombia in 1950, but the structural changes were hard to sell in the context of the social and political instability that followed the assassination of Gaitán. See World Bank, *The Basis of a Development Program for Colombia*, ed. Lauchlin Currie (Washington, 1950).

The historical coalition of conservative and liberal political and economic elites that had shaped the nation's economic development pattern since independence for purposes of preserving their long-term power at the local, regional, and national levels ultimately collapsed with the rise of the military dictatorship.[7] Rojas Pinilla prioritized modernizing the nation and distancing it from the regionalist, protectionist, and isolationist economic development model advanced by conservative and liberal elites. Under the military dictatorship, industrial and service industries were modernized by means of the internal and foreign injection of capital, backed by the accelerated development of strategic infrastructure, including roads, highways, airports, and energy grids, among other strategic sectors. Accelerated coffee exports, together with aggressive foreign investment, ultimately served as key funding sources for the modernization initiative.

Economic Change and Foreign Direct Investment During the Rojas Pinilla Dictatorship

The American government and business sector welcomed Rojas Pinilla's pro-market reforms. After the 1948 incidents, the United States had distanced itself from the Colombian market, particularly during Laureano Gómez's administration, because of his nationalist and anti-American sentiment.[8] The rise of the Rojas Pinilla dictatorship represented an opportunity for the two nations to resume consolidating their partnership, which they had initially established by collaborating during the Korean War, focusing particularly on regional security.[9] This partnership eventually came to represent the door into Colombia for the United States and other Western investors; the security agenda enabled multinational corporations such as South American Gold and Platinum and Canadair to penetrate the market.

The military regime represented a move toward regional stability. Three days after the military coup, *The New York Times* described the transition

[7] Hésper Eduardo Pérez. *Proceso del Bipartidismo Colombiano y Frente Nacional* (Bogotá: Universidad Nacional de Colombia, 1989), 51–78.

[8] For more on the Gómez administration, see James D. Henderson. *Modernization in Colombia: The Laureano Gómez Years, 1889–1965* (Gainesville: University Press of Florida, 2001).

[9] Coleman, *Colombia and the United States*, 136.

of power from civilian to military control as "bloodless" and unanimously supported by the Colombian economic and political power structures.[10] Foreign media highlighted the new administration's commitment to "restoring peace" and eliminating "press censorship."[11] Five days after the military coup, the United States reestablished full diplomatic relations with the Rojas Pinilla administration, giving it its full support.[12]

The Canadian government also welcomed the military dictatorship. The *Winnipeg Free Press*, for example, pointed out the peaceful transition of power after the military coup, paying minimal attention to the violation of the democratic process in Colombia.[13] Six months after the military coup, the Alberta daily newspaper, *The Medicine Hat News*, presented a very favorable view of General Rojas Pinilla, describing him as the "leader" that brought "law and order" back to the country.[14] The West had given legitimacy to the military regime; Western nations believed in his nation-building project, and, more specifically, in his commitment to eradicating communism.

With the support of the national and international community, General Rojas Pinilla quickly moved forward with his nation-building program, which was rooted in strong Catholic values, Western-style modernity, and armistice. His civilian conciliation process rapidly decreased violence across the country as civil dissidents from both political factions turned their weapons over to the government in exchange for a pardon and the promise of being able to return to their land under the peace guaranteed by the military regime.[15]

The international market responded positively to Rojas Pinilla's peace process. In January 1954, just seven months into Rojas Pinilla's rule, President Eisenhower's administration, upon touring Latin America, concluded that Colombia's future looked optimistic now that General Rojas

[10] United Press, "New Bogota Leader Backed by Assembly," *New York Times*, June 16, 1953, 2.

[11] United Press, "Colombia Eases Control: Overthrown President Reported Coming to United States," *New York Times*, June 17, 1953, 18.

[12] Special to the *New York Times*, "Ties with Bogota Resumed by U.S.: Action by Washington Is 13th to Recognize New Regime Headed by Gen. Rojas," *The New York Times*, June 18, 1953.

[13] Associated Press, "New President Okayed," *Winnipeg Free Press*, June 20, 1953, 2.

[14] "Colombia Now Has Peace," *Medicine Hat News*, January 22, 1954, 2.

[15] Diana Henao Holguín, "Bandolerismo Rural en el Bajo Cauca, Magdalena Medio y el Nordeste Antioqueño (Colombia), 1953–1958," *Revista de Historia Regional y Local* 7, no. 14 (July–December, 2015): 298–303.

Pinilla "had ended the civil war" and the economy was "slowly returning to normal."[16] Rojas Pinilla, said the report, "had sent thousands of men from guerrilla warfare back to farming," paving the way for the continued dominance of the United States over trade in Colombia.[17]

In March 1954, a United Nations Council memorandum concluded that countries like Colombia had taken measures to "ease the flow of private investment capital."[18] The Rojas Pinilla regime implemented investment laws that facilitated "remittance of earnings and repatriation of capital" designed to attract private foreign investment, particularly in the field of manufacturing.[19] He quickly opened Colombia's market to international business interests.

In fact, the Rojas Pinilla administration implemented the structural recommendations set by the World Bank's first "general survey mission" back in 1950, which were designed to solve the shortage of capital and secure foreign funding for long-term national economic development.[20] Moreover, it swiftly implemented the peace process as a means to increase the flow of private foreign investment because it knew that, from the perspective of the World Bank, "stimulation of greater private financing" was "dependent on the securing of a more favorable business 'climate.'"[21]

The response from foreign investors was rapid and positive. Between 1953 and 1954 the military government established conversations with the International Petroleum Company, a Canadian subsidiary of Standard Oil of New Jersey, in order to develop refining capacity of by-products as well the construction of pipeline infrastructure for expanding local consumption.[22] British and American companies that controlled production in Colombia worked hand-in-hand with the government-owned Empresa Colombiana de Petróleos (later known as Ecopetrol) to further advance the industry during the Rojas Pinilla regime.[23] By 1954, cooperation

[16] Sam Pope Brewer, "South America Shows Advances in Economy," *The New York Times*, January 6, 1954, p. 47.

[17] Ibid.

[18] Special to *The New York Times*, "Investing Abroad Becoming Easier," *The New York Times*, March 6, 1954, p. 22.

[19] Ibid., p. 22.

[20] "Economic Growth Speeded: World Investments Flow Gains Ground," *Winnipeg Tribune*, May 31, 1954, p. 47.

[21] "Economic Growth Speeded," p. 47.

[22] "Colombia Expanding her Oil Industry," *The New York Times*, January 6, 1954, p. 51.

[23] Ibid.

between foreign companies and Ecopetrol had resulted in the construction of the Barrancabermeja refinery; the Cartagena refinery was completed two years later.

The president of South American Gold and Platinum Company, Lewis B. Harder, also set his sights on Colombia, attracted by Rojas Pinilla's initiatives. His objective was to diversify gold and platinum dredging operations. In the summer of 1954, he announced that his company was joining other foreign investors interested in financing the construction of a bottle and flat glass company, a consumer finance company tailored to the purchase of vehicles and farm machinery, and a company specializing in the construction of a petroleum pipeline for the expansion of the domestic market.[24] The representatives of the American company also indicated that they were considering investing in six other projects, including irrigation infrastructure and raising cattle.[25]

Aside from attracting foreign direct investment, the Rojas Pinilla regime was able to secure multilateral and bilateral technical assistance during the dictator's first year in office. The bilateral and multilateral foreign aid that flowed into Colombia during the military dictatorship "signified an unquestionable political endorsement of the authoritarian regime."[26] For example, during the 1953–1954 fiscal year, Colombia secured US $2.6 million in U.S. Official Development Assistance (ODA), making it the fifth-largest recipient after Brazil, Bolivia, Chile, and Peru.[27] Technical assistance projects funded by the United States and the United Nations included a pilot plant for the processing of iodized salt, as well as numerous programs for long-distance education, insect control, technical exchange, and industrial and agricultural fields like soil research, development of acclimated crop varieties, coffee research, irrigation, machinery

[24] "Financial and Business Sidelights of the Day," *The New York Times*, June 17, 1954, p. 43.

[25] "Financial and Business Sidelights of the Day," p. 43.

[26] According to Jon Kofas, aside from foreign direct investment, foreign assistance allowed donor nations to influence the policies and outcomes of the modernization and economic development processes of recipient nations like Colombia. This was evident during the military regime of Rojas Pinilla. See Jon V. Kofas. *Sword of Damocles: The IMF, the World Bank, and US Foreign Policy in and Chile, 1950–1970* (Westport: Greenwood Publishing Group, 2002), 18–87.

[27] "Sharing of Technical Knowledge is Transforming Retarded Sectors of the World," *The New York Times*, May 24, 1954, p. 8.

operation and maintenance, rubber development, cattle breeding, fish farming, and building materials.[28]

On the domestic front, the state put in place and directed economic development programs designed to jumpstart the light manufacturing sector. This import substitution industrialization (ISI) policy was funded by aggressive fiscal policies imposed on the local private sector and civil society. Together with a coffee boom in the 1953–1954 fiscal year, this ISI policy allowed the Rojas Pinilla administration to borrow and invest in modernizing the country. These domestic initiatives further incentivized foreign investors to inject capital into the Colombian economy.[29] The money was invested in a series of public works that were part of his modernization plan, which included the construction of roads, airports, bridges, ports, and other infrastructure projects.[30] These economic development projects funded by the Colombian government became another door through which international businesses were able to enter the country. The Magdalena River railway project, the construction of Bogotá's El Dorado Airport, Bogotá's 26th Avenue, the construction of the Paz del Río steel mill, the development of the National Television network, the oil refinery projects in Barrancabermeja and Cartagena, as well as the creation of the Corporación Autónoma Regional del Cauca (CVC) and the Anchicayá hydroelectric plant were all contracted out to foreign private interests.[31]

Such momentum generated greater incentives among foreign corporations to invest in Colombia as they placed their full support on the Rojas Pinilla regime and his peace process. The early strategy of securing ODA and increasing government spending on infrastructure and economic development was "used as leverage to facilitate direct foreign investment

[28] "Sharing of Technical Knowledge is Transforming Retarded Sectors of the World," p. 8.

[29] Government spending under the Rojas Pinilla administration increased 21 percent between 1953 and 1954 and 52 percent between 1954 and 1955; the following fiscal year saw a decline of 36 percent after the international price of coffee dropped. B.R. Mitchell, *International Historical Statistics: The Americas 1750–1993* (London: Macmillan Reference, 1998), 674.

[30] Alberto Valencia Gutiérrez. *La Invención de la Desmemoria: El Juicio Político contra el General Gustavo Rojas Pinilla en el Congreso de Colombia (1958–1959)* (Cali: Universidad del Valle, 2015), 82–83.

[31] Gutiérrez, *La Invención de la Desmemoria*, 83. The CVC was modeled on the American Tennessee Valley Authority, a broad-scale, long-term development designed to capitalize on the diverse natural resources of the region to generate industry and other engines of capital development.

and to secure trade privileges" with strategic countries such as the United States, Canada, Britain, and other European nations.[32] In return, multinational corporations and the international system extended loans and increased trade with the regime, rewarding it for its commitment to containing communism and its effort to further integrate Colombia into this very international system.[33]

As part of its 1955 Latin American strategy, the Kaiser Motors Corporation announced its interest in expanding its automobile manufacturing operations beyond Argentina, targeting Colombia and Brazil as additional sites.[34] That same year Fiat, Mercedes-Benz, and Austin also publicized their interest in establishing automobile manufacturing plants in Colombia, while the Italian Montecatini Company disclosed its plan to construct a US $12 million fertilizer plant.[35]

Foreign oil companies also responded positively to the pro-business environment of the Rojas Pinilla regime. The liberalization of petroleum legislation resulted in further foreign investment. In 1955, for example, Cities Service Company signed a contract "for joint exploration with the Colombian government of more than 2,000 acres of potential oil lands."[36]

United States Rubber Company also capitalized on the pro-business regime to expand its sales and production strategy overseas, diversifying its market beyond Venezuela. Its Colombian affiliate, Croydon del Pacífico, received a US $2.8 million injection of capital in 1956 to increase its production of tires and other rubber products.[37] The capital was invested in new power-generating equipment and curing facilities for making footwear, flooring, mechanical goods, and plastics.[38]

Foreign direct investment as well as multilateral and bilateral ODA had boosted the Colombian economy during the first few years of the Rojas Pinilla administration. These were signs that the international community

[32] Kofas. *Sword of Damocles*, 3.

[33] For more on the dynamics of foreign loans to authoritarian regimes, see Kofas, *Sword of Damocles*, 8–12.

[34] AP, "Kaiser Signs Pact With Argentina for 40,000-a-Year Auto Factory," *New York Times*, October 6, 1954, p. 37.

[35] "Colombian Economy Follows Coffee Price Ups and Downs," *The Hammond Times*, November 22, 1955, p. 5.

[36] "South Americans Are Encouraged by Recent Gains," *New York Times*, January 5, 1956, p. C49.

[37] Richard Butter, "Trouble Abroad? Opportunity Too: Amid Crises, U.S. Rubber Confidently Expands Its Operations Overseas," *New York Times*, September 24, 1956, p. 35.

[38] Ibid.

backed the military regime, even though violence had once again escalated by the end of 1954, as the peace process dwindled. Nevertheless, as an article in *The New York Times* indicated, although there was trouble in Latin America, there were opportunities, too.[39] Investment opportunities and profits had a greater value than Colombian citizens, at least from the perspective of the international system. It was important to continue doing business in Colombia; as an experienced U.S. diplomat told the press, the "relationship should be maintained ... but without appearing to endorse dictatorships."[40] International businesses wanted to protect their interests in emerging markets such as Colombia at any costs, even if it meant the return of the oppression of Colombians, as long as their brands and national governments were not connected to the human rights abuse.

Cracks in the Dictatorship and International Reactions

By 1955, violence had once again escalated in Colombia, threatening the positive response from the international investors and clearly signaling that Rojas Pinilla's peace process was failing. Peace and tranquility had not prevailed in rural areas, where violence returned to pre-Rojas Pinilla levels. In addition, the military government was incrementally persecuting the opposition, using the state propaganda system to blur the lines between the communist and the sociopolitical struggle in Colombia.[41]

By this point, General Rojas Pinilla had also shown signs that he did not intend to return political power to Conservatives or Liberals.[42] The use of force against civilians between 1954 and 1955 showed Colombians and the international community that his regime was willing to violate human

[39] Ibid.

[40] Tad Szulc, "Latin Nationalism Challenges Policy of U.S., Survey Indicates: Long-Range Plan Believed Lacking," *The New York Times*, April 13, 1956, p. 6.

[41] Rojas Pinilla hired the American public relations company, Hamilton Wright Organization, Inc. (HWO), to manage his international propaganda machine, the same company hired by Juan Domingo Perón in Argentina. The objective was to win the hearts and minds of Americans, Canadians, Europeans, Latin Americans, Caribbean governments, tourists, and private sector investors, encouraging them to invest in the new Colombia that he was constructing under his peace initiative. See Ana Lucía García-Villamarín, "La Imagen de Gustavo Rojas Pinilla en la Propaganda Política Durante la Dictadura Militar, Colombia 1953–1957," *Revista Colombiana de Ciencias Sociales* 8, no. 2 (2017): 311–333.

[42] James D. Henderson, *When Colombia Bled: A History of the Violencia in Tolima* (Tuscaloosa: University of Alabama Press, 1985), 13–15.

rights to rid society of those who were impeding his administration from moving forward with his nation-building plan. With the unquestionable approval of the United States and other Western nations, including Canada, Rojas Pinilla continued to escalate violence, and the political-legal environment, both locally and internationally, did not hold the military regime accountable in the slightest. In 1954, army and police bullets killed students in Bogotá, and in 1955, Colombian Air Force pilots bombed civilians in the Sumapaz region. These were clear signs that the military regime was becoming increasingly authoritarian. Moreover, national newspapers such as *El Espectador* and *El Tiempo*, as well as numerous other regional newspapers, were censored in 1955, further revealing the regime's violation of human and democratic rights.

The coverage of the 1955 assassination of 644 civilians during a three-month escalation of the conflict revealed the complicity between the Colombian state propaganda machine and the international media, which raised no questions about the human rights abuse and gave agency to the regime's intention of casting all of those who opposed it as "communists."[43] The government construed peaceful student protests against the escalation of violence as a communist plot organized by "political extremists bent on the dissolution of the country," an idea that was then advanced by American media.[44]

However, the assassination of students and the censorship of media in 1955 started to slowly turn the international media against the regime. Rojas Pinilla's propaganda machine and censorship policies covered up the bombings authorized in 1955 and 1956 to combat dissidents in the regions of Los Llanos and Tolima, but sectors of the international media disclosed the atrocities against civilian populations, making it very difficult for foreign governments to justify their support of the Rojas Pinilla regime.[45] This became particularly challenging for the United States government that was invested in a regime that was committed to fighting

[43] Ibid.

[44] United Press, "15 Die in Student-Army Strife in Bogota; Colombian Regime Puts Tight Curb on City," *The New York Times*, June 10, 1954, 12; Associated Press, *The Medicine Hat News*, July 21, 1955, 5.

[45] Jane M. Rausch, *Territorial Rule in Colombia and the Transformation of the Llanos Orientales* (Gainesville: University Press of Florida, 2013); Silvia Galvis and Alberto Donadio, *El Jefe Supremo: Rojas Pinilla, en la Violencia y el Poder* (Medellín: Nuevo Editores, 2002); and Germán Guzmán Campos, *La Violencia en Colombia: Parte Descriptiva* (Cali: Ediciones Progreso, 1968).

communism while at the same time reinforcing the foundations for capitalist economic development.

Using the U.S. Cold War pretext that "communism cleverly disguises itself," Rojas Pinilla ordered attacks on civilians, "bombing and strafing suspected enemy concentrations, which swelled the flood of refugees."[46] Many in Colombia, and throughout the international community, were critical of the administration's brutal display of violence, but the support of the U.S. government remained strong.[47]

Some sectors of the U.S. media stressed Rojas Pinilla's shift from peacemaker to "hard-fisted military dictator" after the 1955 incidents.[48] The international media also portrayed his "one-man regime" as undemocratic and totalitarian, yet there was no official pronouncement against his administration.[49] On the contrary, by 1956 the United States and Canada were willing to further arm the regime so that it could fight the so-called communists, providing opportunities for their private corporations to get directly or indirectly involved in the sale of arms and other military equipment and technology.

By 1956, reports of the return of guerrilla fighting in Colombia surfaced in the international media.[50] The regime utilized the American public relations company, Hamilton Wright Organization (HWO), to market the idea that what Colombia needed was greater foreign investment and ODA to help the administration bring peace back to the country.[51] Eduardo Zuleta Angel, Rojas Pinilla's ambassador to the United States, went so far as to remind the U.S. government that Colombia needed greater support for the regime, not a U.S. military intervention as

[46] Henderson, *When Colombia Bled*, 193.

[47] Ibid., 194.

[48] Sam Pope Brewer, "One-Man Regime Rules Colombia: People Say Rojas Pinilla Has Shifted from 'Peacemaker' into Military Dictator," *The New York Times*, September 16, 1955, 7. For more on international criticism of media censorship, see Sam Pope Brewer, "Colombia Regime Feuds with Press: Plans to Put Out Own Papers and Forces Radio Stations to Allow It Free Time," *The New York Times*, March 3, 1955, 7.

[49] Ibid.

[50] See Associated Press, "32 Die in Strife in Colombia Area," *The New York Times*, January 5, 1956, 6.

[51] Ana Lucía García-Villamarín, "La imagen de Gustavo Rojas Pinilla en la Propaganda Política Durante la Dictadura Militar, Colombia 1953–1957," *Revista Colombiana de Ciencias Sociales,* Vol. 8, No. 2: 311–333.

suggested by *The New York Times*.[52] Rojas Pinilla, said Ambassador Zuleta Angel, was a "loyal, sincere and faithful friend of the United States," a supporter of U.S. policy, and an ally in combating communism in the region.[53] What the dictatorship needed was more military aid and greater investment of foreign capital.

In a symbolic effort to support the last point, the United Nations organized the sixth conference of the United Nations Economic Commission for Latin America on behalf of the international system in September 1955. Three key points emerged from this meeting in Bogotá: Latin America needed to resolve its low labor productivity, its shortage of electric power, and the price fluctuations of its exports.[54] Based on these conclusions, the Rojas Pinilla regime argued that Colombia needed greater investment in technology and machinery to replace manpower with machines that could increase labor productivity; correspondingly, it also needed aggressive investments in the expansion of electrical power for industrial and mass consumption.[55] Without industrial capacity, there was "little hope of economic development."[56] The international community, he argued, needed to focus on the country's economic development and its internal efforts to establish a favorable climate for foreign investment.

As the domestic civil situation deteriorated, the Rojas Pinilla administration turned to military aid and modernizing the Colombian military as a means to secure civil control and continue to move forward with its foreign policy initiatives. The United States government, serving as an intermediary for its military industrial complex, moved diligently on this initiative as well.[57]

Rojas Pinilla took advantage of the U.S. desire to build a regional security partnership, purchasing military equipment from the United States and Canada as the international community watched his regime commit human rights abuses. Rojas Pinilla's desire to modernize the nation's military and the favorable response of international businesses eventually

[52] Eduardo Zuleta Angel, "Judging Colombia's Regime," *Letters to the Times: New York Times*, September 29, 1955, 32.

[53] Ibid.

[54] Sam Pope Brewer, "Troubles Sifted in Latin Economy," *New York Times*, September 5, 1955, p. 4.

[55] Paul Heffernan, "Americas Drawn Closer by Parley," *New York Times*, March 6, 1955, F1.

[56] Ibid.

[57] Coleman, *Colombia and the United States*.

opened a window of opportunity for General Dynamics to sell military equipment to Colombia via its Canadian subsidiary, Canadair, thus overcoming any pushback from American constituents and human rights advocates back in the United States.

The Dictatorship's Struggle to Survive and the Sale of Canadian Jet Fighters to Colombia

The 19 U.S.-manufactured B-26 bombers sold to the Colombian Air Force in 1954 were not effective in ending the guerrilla conflict. The British-made napalm dropped on civilians did not deter the "communists"; on the contrary, it revived political violence.[58] Officials back in the United States concluded "that better weapons, new equipment, and more training" were the only way to improve the performance of the Colombian armed forces.[59]

It was under these circumstances that the Canadian subsidiary of General Dynamics, Canadair, arrived in Colombia in 1956 to negotiate the sale of Canadian-manufactured F-86 Sabre jet fighters to the Colombian Air Force. As indicated by researchers in other chapters, local and foreign corporations had no problem overlooking the human rights violations perpetrated by military regimes across Latin America and the Caribbean as long as markets, resources, profits, and sales were secured in each market. The initiative of the Canadian government-business partnership in Colombia revealed that Canada's private sector was no exception.

A few months before the military coup of June 1953, a delegation of Canadian businesses had visited Colombia as part of a Latin American tour designed to survey business opportunities across the Western Hemisphere. The 1953 Goodwill Trade Mission, organized by the Minister of Trade and Commerce and Defense Production, C.D. Howe, had identified Colombia as a strategic market for Canadian business interests because of its relatively untapped resources and markets.[60] When the opportunity

[58] René de la Pedraja, *Wars of Latin America, 1948–1982: The Rise of the Guerrillas* (Jefferson: McFarland, 2006), 48.

[59] Ibid.

[60] Stefano Tijerina, "Canadian Official Development Aid to Latin America: The Struggle over the Humanitarian Agenda, 1963–1977," *Journal of Canadian Studies* 51, no. 1 (Winter 2017): 219.

emerged for Canadair to enter the Colombian market, this was seen as a door for future Canadian investments.[61]

The sale of six F-86s to the military government of General Rojas Pinilla in 1956 represented a new spatial dimension in the history of bilateral relations between Canada and Colombia. Moreover, it launched Canada's private sector into the global arms sales market and revealed the will of Western international businesses to support non-democratic regimes. Canadair provided Rojas Pinilla with the second generation of weapons he needed to escalate the bombing campaign against communist guerrilla fighters while, at the same time, aiding him in fulfilling his vision of modernity and progress. In the end, the US $3,000,000 deal was a waste of Colombian taxpayers' money; in 1970, the planes were grounded and replaced by the French Mirage 5.[62]

The Canadair F-86s were never used for civilian bombing missions, as initially intended, because the inhumane policy had ended together with the Rojas Pinilla regime in May 1957. But the modernization of the Colombian military forces was a step forward for Canadair's and the Canadian government-business partnership's long-term vision of business expansion into the Americas.

C.D. Howe, representing the Canadian defense industry, spearheaded the deal.[63] He intertwined the interests of General Dynamics together with U.S. military interests in the region and the military modernization objectives of the Rojas Pinilla administration to conclude a transaction that did not at first seem feasible.

Rojas Pinilla wanted to modernize Colombia's Air Force in order to effectively combat "communist" dissidents in the country, and Canadair had the right planes for the job. The general had seen the F-86 Sabre used to effectively combat the enemy in the Korean War, and he wanted to

[61] Similar doors had been opened by Canada's Royal Bank of Canada, Pato Gold Dredging, and the International Petroleum Corporation (a subsidiary of Standard Oil of New Jersey) before they were closed by American competition. On early Canadian business activity in Colombia, see Stefano Tijerina, "A 'Clearcut Line': Canada and Colombia, 1892–1979" (Ph.D. dissertation, University of Maine, 2011).

[62] Larry Milberry, *The Canadair Sabre* (Toronto: Canav Books, 2000), 324.

[63] Howe was instrumental in Canada's postwar industrial organization; it seemed that "he had almost run the country," touching "every major area of national development" including the design of the government-business partnership necessary for expanding Canada's markets overseas. Larry Milberry, *The Canadair Sabre*, 12–16.

replicate this effectiveness in Colombia.[64] General Dynamics also manufactured F-86 jet fighters but worried that selling them directly to the Rojas Pinilla regime could damage the delicate diplomatic fiber of the early Cold War. This was particularly the case after 1955 when the international press began to question the regime's human rights record. Howe came up with the idea that selling them through Canadair was the most viable strategy for both Colombians and the United States. Working as a proxy to U.S. interests was fine as long as the Canadian manufacturer had something to gain.

In a letter of intent issued in February 1956, the Colombian government agreed to purchase six F-86 jet fighters from Canadair.[65] The negotiations revealed how the company effectively built a government-business partnership with the Department of Trade and Commerce and Defense Production to close the transnational deal, and how the Rojas Pinilla administration secured international support by committing to the eradication of communism in Colombia. The sale of the F-86 jet fighters marked the first sale of Canadian jet aircraft to Latin America and the first time a deal of this sort took place "outside the Commonwealth and NATO."[66]

The Canadian subsidiary capitalized on Howe's 1953 Goodwill Trade Mission, which had laid the foundation for the advancement of bilateral relations between Canada and Colombia in the post-World War II era. It followed a series of other Canadian-Colombian projects that had been launched prior to the 1953 mission, including the contract for the construction of Colombia's merchant fleet, Flota Mercante Grancolombiana, and the development of the nation's first citizen identification card program.[67]

[64] For Colombia's role in the Korean War, see Juliana Saldaña, "Colombia's Legacy with Korea," *The City Paper*, April 2, 2013, accessed September 21, 2018, https://thecitypaperbogota.com/features/colombias-legacy-with-korea/2974

[65] L.B. Pearson, *Memorandum from Secretary of State for External Affairs to Cabinet: Proposed Export of F-86 Aircraft to Colombia*, ed. Department of External Affairs, Documents on Canadian External Relations (Ottawa, March 20, 1956), 1.

[66] Canada Department of Trade and Commerce, *Memorandum by Head, American Division: Export of Military Jet Aircraft to Countries in Latin America*, ed. Department of External Affairs, Documents on Canadian External Relations (Ottawa, October 19, 1956), 1.

[67] Canada Department of External Affairs, Information Division, *Canadian Goodwill Trade Mission to Latin America: Statement by the Minister of Trade and Commerce, Mr. C.D. Howe, Made in the House of Commons, February 26, 1953*, edited by Department of External Affairs, 1–11, Ottawa, 1953.

A few days thereafter, the Canadian government eagerly accepted the request and immediately asked the cabinet of Canadian Prime Minister Louis St. Laurent for a formal export permit.[68] Howe agreed to draft the "joint submission to Cabinet on behalf of Canadair."[69] He was convinced that the sale to Colombia would open the door for other Canadian businesses and "stimulate sales to other parts of the world."[70] The opportunity to expand sales of military equipment beyond NATO and the Commonwealth meant that Canada would be able to penetrate into the international arms sales market.[71] It also translated into a reduction of Canadair's overall costs, both for the production "of similar aircraft for the Royal Canadian Air Force" and for all production for Canadian government accounts.[72]

The cabinet's approval of the export permit, said Howe, was crucial to the expansion of "Canadian commercial relations with Colombia."[73] However, some cabinet members were not convinced that it was a good deal since it could irritate the "great powers," and particularly the United States, considering that it had traditionally had "the role of supplier of military equipment of this nature" within its jurisdiction.[74] It was also argued that other hemispheric actors might also take umbrage at the deal, since Canada was not included as a player in the norms for arms sales stipulated in the 1947 Rio Treaty.[75]

Several members of the Canadian cabinet were concerned that this sale could have a negative impact on Canada's reputation in the region and across the "free world," because it would be contributing to bolstering military equipment across the region, and particularly for a regime that

[68] Canada Department of Trade and Commerce, *Sale of F86s to Colombia*, ed. Department of External Affairs (Ottawa, February 27, 1956), 1. Louis St. Laurent was Canada's prime minister at the time, representing the Liberal Party.

[69] Ibid.

[70] Ibid.

[71] For more detail on Canada's role in NATO, see John Gellner, *Canada in NATO* (Toronto: Ryerson Press, 1970).

[72] Canada Department of Trade and Commerce, *Sale of F86s to Colombia*, ed. Department of External Affairs (Ottawa, February 27, 1956), 1.

[73] Ibid.

[74] Jules Leger, *Under-Secretary of State for External Affairs to Deputy Minister of Trade and Commerce: Possible Sale to Colombia of F-86 Aircraft*, ed. Department of External Affairs, Documents on Canadian External Relations (Ottawa, February 28, 1956), 1.

[75] Ibid.

was in clear violation of human rights and democracy.[76] The Canadian government believed that support for one of the many military dictatorships across the region would alienate the "liberal and progressive forces" Canada supported.[77] Secretary of State for External Affairs Lester B. Pearson indicated that the sale of jet fighters to Rojas Pinilla's military regime contradicted Canada's Colombo Plan in Southeast Asia, since it had previously denied arm sales to undemocratic regimes.[78]

Others who were concerned about attacks by communist propagandists concluded that the possible sale of military equipment to Colombia could turn Latin America's Left against Canada.[79] This was particularly relevant to Colombia, where communist guerrilla activity was escalating. Closing the deal with the Colombian government could endanger Canadian capital and business interests there, particularly in the areas of oil and gold mining.

Yet other members considered that after almost three years in power, the Rojas Pinilla administration had lost popular support and now "maintained itself in power only through the exercise of increasingly repressive measures backed solely by armed forces."[80] Canada's support for an "unpleasant type" of dictatorship was not good foreign policy.[81]

These cabinet considerations resulted in the Joint Intelligence Bureau submitting a request for further assessment and temporarily blocking the approval of Canadair's export permit. Howe, however, did not give up on his efforts to push the deal forward, quickly responding to the cabinet's concerns via his Associate Deputy Minister of Trade and Commerce, Mitchell Sharp.

On March 7, Sharp, who would head the 1968 Ministerial Mission to Latin America, explained that Canadair's deal involved more than just the sale of planes: it represented jobs for Canadians, revenues for the Canadian economy, and a greater opportunity for Canadian businesses to expand in Colombia and across the Western Hemisphere. He reported that in addition to the export of six jet fighters, Canadair had negotiated the establishment of "overhaul and service facilities for jet aircraft."[82] This included the

[76] Ibid.
[77] Ibid.
[78] Ibid.
[79] Ibid.
[80] Ibid.
[81] Ibid.
[82] Canada Department of Trade and Commerce, *Sale of F86s to Colombia*, 1.

training, supervision, and management of personnel, which would generate more than one hundred jobs for Canadians, as well as the need for "large quantities of Canadian equipment" required for servicing the Colombian operation.[83] The Department of Trade and Commerce and Defense Production also emphasized that if the deal was closed, there would "be a much larger flow of Canadian equipment into Colombia in the form of replacement parts," and that it would open the door for future purchases of other Canadian military equipment.[84] Moreover, it reminded cabinet members that the deal would greatly enhance commercial relations between Canada and Colombia:

> In addition to the forgoing ... Canadian firms may be given the opportunity to quote on radio beacon stations and telecommunications equipment which is urgently required in Colombia, not only for military aircraft purposes, but also for commercial aircraft needs. This in itself would constitute a substantial contract and by and large ... would bring Canada's name to the attention of the Colombian people in such a way that we could expect our commercial connections with Colombia to be considerably improved.[85]

The Department of Trade and Commerce and Defense Production also maintained that they saw no problem selling these planes to the Colombian Air Force, considering that the same planes had "been freely offered to Colombia by the United States" in the past.[86] It concluded by reminding the skeptic cabinet members that it was commonly agreed among cabinet members that Colombia "was a safe area in which to develop the type of business which is so important to our own developing aircraft industry."[87] A letter of intent lay on the desk of the offices of Canadair waiting for authorization from the Canadian government; according to Sharp, failure to approve the export permit would be a "real embarrassment."[88]

A week later, Secretary of State Pearson told skeptical cabinet members "that it would be difficult to refuse to sell to a country which wished to

[83] Ibid.

[84] Ibid.

[85] Ibid.

[86] Mitchell Sharp, *Associate Deputy Minister of Trade and Commerce to Under-Secretary of State for External Affairs: Possible Sale of F-86 Aircraft to Colombia*, ed. Department of External Affairs, Documents of Canadian External Relations (Ottawa, March 7, 1956), 1.

[87] Ibid.

[88] Ibid.

develop its legitimate defense and which was in an area of the world where there was no tension at the moment."[89] Furthermore, said Pearson, it was important to consider the negative implications this would have on the "maintenance of the Canadian aircraft industry."[90] Pearson had shifted his position on the issue and was now in favor of the deal. The pressure from pro-business sectors of the government had been effective. Big business prevailed in its effort to strengthen business relations with the military regime of Rojas Pinilla.

On March 20, Pearson sent a memorandum to cabinet members making a strong case for the sale of jet fighters to the Colombian Air Force. He reiterated Sharp's justifications, adding that Colombia would no doubt obtain the planes from another supplier if Canada did not release them.[91] He concluded by recommending the "approval ... for the issue of an export permit for the export by Canadair of six F-86 aircraft to Colombia."[92]

Shortly thereafter, the cabinet met again to discuss the urgent issue and concluded that the export permit should be issued. This would leave open the possibility of Canada selling jet fighters to other South American countries that might approach it since Ottawa would not be forced to issue the same refusal it had given to Colombia.[93] Pearson added that Colombia "was the best friend that Canada had in South America and it would be difficult to explain why the export of the aircraft could not be permitted."[94] The sale, said Pearson, would result in good business for Canada; it might stimulate sales in other countries and might open doors to other Canadian companies in Colombia, such as Canadian Aviation Electronics and the engine manufacturer A.V. Roe Canada.[95]

On March 22, 1956, the cabinet agreed "that an export permit be issued to authorize the transaction."[96] Early that summer, the six F-86 aircrafts were delivered to the Colombian Air Force.[97] This marked

[89] Canada Department of Trade and Commerce, *Extract from Cabinet Conclusions*, ed. Department of External Affairs, Documents on Canadian External Relations (Ottawa, March 15, 1956), 1.

[90] Ibid.

[91] Pearson, *Memorandum from Secretary of State for External Affairs*, 1.

[92] Ibid.

[93] Canada Department of Trade and Commerce, *Extract from Cabinet Conclusions*, 1.

[94] Ibid.

[95] Pearson, *Memorandum from Secretary of State for External Affairs*, 1.

[96] Canada Department of Trade and Commerce, *Extract from Cabinet conclusions*, 1.

[97] Canada Department of Trade and Commerce, *Memorandum by Head, American Division*, 1.

Canada's emergence "as a supplier of jet aircraft in Latin America."[98] Canada, the United States, and other European countries would dominate the sale of military aircrafts to Latin America throughout the Cold War. The Canadian government-business partnership had secured access to the Colombian market for Canadian companies.

In this instance, Canadair's interests had prevailed over domestic political concerns. The outcome had once again shown that if the Canadian government wanted to keep its aircraft industry alive and preserve its jobs, it needed to sell the equipment abroad because domestic demand was insufficient to keep the industry running. The sale of aircraft abroad "would make it far easier to maintain the industry as an up-to-date production facility" and allow the industry to transition from the production of a particular model to "the production of its successor."[99] The deal with Colombia demonstrated that Canadair could, in fact, reduce its inventory of what was considered obsolete by General Dynamics standards, selling to "less advanced countries" where the demand for substandard aircraft was high, while at the same time contributing to hemispheric security in the context of the Cold War.[100]

The sale contributed to the hemispheric containment efforts and revealed that Canada's industrial sector could also play a role in the U.S. hemispheric security strategy. As indicated by historian James D. Henderson, Americans believed that the threat of communism in Colombia was real, and that "Rojas and his military colleagues were not equipped to combat the communist element within the guerrilla movement."[101] Meanwhile, Canadair was convinced that the F-86s could be used to effectively "suppress revolt," even if they were not designed for guerrilla warfare.[102]

The jet fighters never saw the action Rojas Pinilla had envisioned. By the end of 1956, civil unrest had claimed the lives of 11,000 Colombians.[103] Rojas Pinilla's aggressive anti-communist stance fanned the flames of violence once again, ultimately pushing liberals, conservatives, the domestic

[98] Ibid.

[99] Ibid.

[100] Ibid.

[101] Henderson, *Modernization in Colombia*, 370.

[102] Canada Department of Trade and Commerce, *Memorandum by Head, American Division: Export of Military Jet Aircraft to Countries of Latin America*, ed. Department of External Affairs, Documents on Canadian External Relations (Ottawa, 1956), 1.

[103] Henderson, *Modernization in Colombia*, 374.

business sector, and the international community to turn against the regime.[104] In May 1957, the regime was overthrown by a rejuvenated conservative-liberal alliance known as the Frente Nacional (1958–1974). Just as the international community had welcomed Rojas Pinilla's military regime, it welcomed this undemocratic civilian regime without skipping a beat, rapidly shifting allegiance to the new power structures in Colombia.

The transition of power did not impact the dynamics of foreign businesses operating in the Colombian market. Canadair continued to provide technical support and equipment for the maintenance of the F-86s while other contractors such as A.V. Roe Canada continued to supply engines and parts until 1970, when the planes were grounded.[105] Global multinational corporations and investors remained committed to the Colombian market once Rojas Pinilla had established the social, economic, political, and structural changes necessary to secure foreign investment, and more so after the Frente Nacional assured them that the new status quo for businesses would be preserved.

Conclusion

The case of Canadair's sale of F-86 jet fighters to Colombia represented the modernization of Colombia's national security infrastructure. It also formed a part of the modernization of the aeronautical industry, which included the construction of airports, military bases, communications systems, as well as the expansion of the airline industry, allowing the market and the state to reach previously isolated and disenfranchised corners of the country, as in the case of the Caribbean island of San Andrés.

The international business community's positive response to the Rojas Pinilla regime, that this Canadair case study illustrates, makes it clear that foreign investors were tolerant of totalitarian regimes as long as they advanced their business interests. It also shows that secondary powers, such as Canada, were able to effectively use government-business partnerships to secure markets in Latin America, while serving the hemispheric security needs of the United States.

Canadair capitalized on the dictator's willingness to implement structural and institutional changes that favored foreign direct investors, potentially giving them access and influence over the nation's national security

[104] Ibid., 375.

[105] Larry Milberry, *The Canadair Sabre*, 324.

sector, as well as over the shape modernization of the aviation infrastructure would take. Similarly, numerous other multinational corporations were able to take advantage of the modernization initiatives to control and design other strategic markets, such as electricity, industrial food production, and manufacturing.[106]

Additionally, the close relationship that Rojas Pinilla built with foreign investors allowed him to access weaponry that was crucial to his efforts to repress opposition. This was not enough, however, to ensure his political survival when the traditional Colombian elite decided to end his regime.

The Rojas Pinilla regime, therefore, contained a historical temporal and spatial dimension that, for the most part, has been understudied. Canadair and all the other foreign companies that entered Colombia during this era exemplified a tendency among foreign corporations to establish operations under military regimes, as highlighted in other chapters of this book. Nevertheless, Canadair was unique in that it built its sales pitch around the idea of national security, selling weapons to a military dictatorship to help the undemocratic regime achieve peace in the Cold War context. Moreover, the Canadian company served as a bridge to other Canadian companies interested in conquering the Colombian market, using its subsidiary role to advance Canada's capitalist expansion.

As C.D. Howe had suggested it would, Canadair's deal with Colombia did help strengthen the trade relationship between Canada and Colombia and facilitated the entrance of other Canadian companies into the Colombian market. Such was the case of the Bank of London and Montreal and Kruger Inc.'s subsidiary, Papeles Nacionales S.A.[107]

[106] Marco Palacios, *Entre la legitimidad y la violencia* (Bogotá: Norma, 2003), 185–188.

[107] By 1963, the operations of the Bank of London and Montreal had expanded throughout the region, making Colombia its biggest South American market with a total of six branches. The new Canadian bank had joined the efforts of Royal Bank and other foreign banks that were eager to finance the modernization and other economic development initiatives of Colombia's undemocratic civilian regime. Daniel Jay Baum, *The Banks of Canada in the Commonwealth Caribbean: Economic Nationalism and Multinational Enterprises of a Medium Power* (New York: Praeger, 1974), 23. Gene C. Kruger, the son of Joseph Kruger I, a successful American paper merchant from New York who moved to Montreal in the early 1900s, built Kruger Inc. into a major producer of publication paper for the international market. In South America it specialized in the tissue business, and it presently controls large parts of the markets in Venezuela and Colombia. See Hugh O'Brien, "Kruger: A Long-Term Outlook for Steady Growth," *Perini Journal*, accessed March 1, 2011, http://perini.woland.it/index.php?option=com_frontpage&Itemid=97

Ultimately, Colombian business elites and the international community welcomed the regime for the sake of business; in the end, Rojas Pinilla's promise to end social conflicts in Colombia was good for all market stakeholders. Nevertheless, his inability to accomplish this goal and his opening of key strategic domestic markets to the international system eventually turned Colombia's business and political elite against him. The ensuing power shift did not alter the situation for foreign corporations and investors that remained active; in fact, many became perhaps even more active under the Frente Nacional regime, which also guaranteed and defended their business interests in Colombia.

References

Archival Sources

Canada Department of External Affairs, Information Division, *Canadian Goodwill Trade Mission to Latin America: Statement by the Minister of Trade and Commerce, Mr. C.D. Howe, Made in the House of Commons, February 26, 1953*, edited by Department of External Affairs. (Ottawa, 1953).

Canada Department of Trade and Commerce, *Extract from Cabinet Conclusions*, edited by Department of External Affairs, Documents on Canadian External Relations (Ottawa, March 15, 1956).

Canada Department of Trade and Commerce, Memorandum by Head, *American Division: Export of Military Jet Aircraft to Countries in Latin America*, edited by Department of External Affairs, Documents on Canadian External Relations (Ottawa, October 19, 1956).

Canada Department of Trade and Commerce, Sale of F86s to Colombia, edited by Department of External Affairs (Ottawa, February 27, 1956).

Leger, Jules. *Under-Secretary of State for External Affairs to Deputy Minister of Trade and Commerce: Possible Sale to Colombia of F-86 Aircraft*, edited by Department of External Affairs, Documents on Canadian External Relations (Ottawa, February 28, 1956).

Pearson, L. B. *Memorandum from Secretary of State for External Affairs to Cabinet: Proposed Export of F-86 Aircraft to Colombia*, ed. Department of External Affairs, Documents on Canadian External Relations (Ottawa, March 20, 1956).

Sharp, Mitchell. *Associate Deputy Minister of Trade and Commerce to Under-Secretary of State for External Affairs: Possible Sale of F-86 Aircraft to Colombia*, edited by Department of External Affairs, Documents of Canadian External Relations, (Ottawa, March 7, 1956).

Bibliography

Associated Press, "32 Die in Strife in Colombia Area," *New York Times*, January 5, 1956, 6.

Associated Press. "Kaiser Signs Pact With Argentina for 40,000-a-Year Auto Factory," *New York Times*, October 6, 1954, 37.

Associated Press, "New President Okayed," *Winnipeg Free Press*, June 20, 1953, 2.

Baum, Daniel Jay. *The Banks of Canada in the Commonwealth Caribbean: Economic Nationalism and Multinational Enterprises of a Medium Power*. New York: Praeger, 1974.

Braun, Herbert. *The Assassination of Gaitán: Public Life and Urban Violence in Colombia*. Madison: University of Wisconsin Press, 1985.

Brewer, Sam Pope, "South America Shows Advances in Economy," *New York Times*, January 6, 1954, 47.

Butter, Richard. "Trouble Abroad? Opportunity Too: Amid Crises, U.S. Rubber Confidently Expands Its Operations Overseas," *New York Times*, September 24, 1956, 35.

Coleman, Bradley Lynn. *Colombia and the United States: The Making of an Inter-American Alliance, 1939–1960*. Kent: The Kent State University Press, 2008.

"Colombian Economy Follows Coffee Price Ups and Downs," *The Hammond Times*, November 22, 1955, 5.

"Colombia Expanding her Oil Industry," *New York Times*, January 6, 1954, 51.

"Colombia Now Has Peace," *Medicine Hat News*, January 22, 1954, 2.

"Economic Growth Speeded: World Investments Flow Gains Ground," *Winnipeg Tribune*, May 31, 1954, 47.

"Financial and Business Sidelights of the Day," *New York Times*, June 17, 1954, 43.

Galvis, Silvia, and Alberto Donadio. *El Jefe Supremo: Rojas Pinilla, en la Violencia y el Poder*. Medellín: Nuevo Editores, 2002.

García-Villamarín, Ana Lucía. "La Imagen de Gustavo Rojas Pinilla en la Propaganda Política Durante la Dictadura Militar, Colombia 1953–1957." *Revista Colombiana de Ciencias Sociales* 8, no. 2 (2017): 311–333.

Gellner, John. *Canada in NATO*. Toronto: Ryerson Press, 1970.

Guzmán Campos, Germán. *La Violencia en Colombia: Parte Descriptiva*. Cali: Ediciones Progreso, 1968.

Heffernan, Paul. "Americas Drawn Closer by Parley." *New York Times*, March 6, 1955, F1.

Henao Holguín, Diana "Bandolerismo Rural en el Bajo Cauca, Magdalena Medio y el Nordeste Antioqueño (Colombia), 1953–1958." *Revista de Historia Regional y Local* 7, no. 14 (July–December, 2015): 298–303.

Henderson, James D. *Modernization in Colombia: The Laureano Gómez Years, 1889–1965*. Gainesville: University Press of Florida, 2001.

Henderson, James D. *When Colombia Bled: A History of the Violencia in Tolima*. Tuscaloosa: University of Alabama Press, 1985.
"Investing Abroad Becoming Easier," *New York Times*, March 6, 1954, 22.
Kofas, Jon V. *Sword of Damocles: The IMF, the World Bank, and US Foreign Policy in and Chile, 1950–1970*. Westport: Greenwood Publishing Group, 2002.
Lewis, Paul H. *Authoritarian Regimes in Latin America: Dictators, Despots, and Tyrants*. New York: Rowman & Littlefield Publisher, 2006.
Milberry, Larry. *The Canadair Sabre*. Toronto: Canav Books, 2000.
Mitchell, B.R. *International Historical Statistics: The Americas 1750–1993*. London: Macmillan Reference, 1998.
O'Brien, Hugh. "Kruger: A Long-Term Outlook for Steady Growth," *Perini Journal*, accessed March 1, 2011, http://perini.woland.it/index.php?option=com_frontpage&Itemid=97
Palacios, Marco. *Entre la legitimidad y la violencia*. Bogotá: Norma, 2003.
Pedraja, René de la. *Wars of Latin America, 1948–1982: The Rise of the Guerrillas*. Jefferson: McFarland, 2006.
Pérez, Hésper Eduardo. *Proceso del Bipartidismo Colombiano y Frente Nacional*. Bogotá: Universidad Nacional de Colombia, 1989.
Pope Brewer, Sam. "Colombia Regime Feuds with Press: Plans to Put Out Own Papers and Forces Radio Stations to Allow It Free Time," *New York Times*, March 3, 1955, 7.
Pope Brewer, Sam. "One-Man Regime Rules Colombia: People Say Rojas Pinilla Has Shifted from 'Peacemaker' into Military Dictator," *New York Times*, September 16, 1955, 7.
Pope Brewer, Sam. "Troubles Sifted in Latin Economy," *New York Times*, September 5, 1955, 4.
Rausch, Jane M. *Territorial Rule in Colombia and the Transformation of the Llanos Orientales*. Gainesville: University Press of Florida, 2013.
Saldaña, Juliana. "Colombia's Legacy with Korea," *The City Paper*, April 2, 2013, accessed September 21, 2018, https://thecitypaperbogota.com/features/colombias-legacy-with-korea/2974
"Sharing of Technical Knowledge is Transforming Retarded Sectors of the World," *New York Times*, May 24, 1954, 8.
"South Americans Are Encouraged by Recent Gains," *New York Times*, January 5, 1956, C49.
Szulc, Tad, "Latin Nationalism Challenges Policy of U.S., Survey Indicates: Long-Range Plan Believed Lacking," *New York Times*, April 13, 1956, 6.
"Ties with Bogota Resumed by U.S.: Action by Washington Is 13th to Recognize New Regime Headed by Gen. Rojas," *New York Times*, June 18, 1953.
Tijerina, Stefano. "Canadian Official Development Aid to Latin America: The Struggle over the Humanitarian Agenda, 1963–1977." *Journal of Canadian Studies* 51, no. 1 (Winter 2017): 219.

Tijerina, Stefano. "A 'Clearcut Line': Canada and Colombia, 1892–1979. Ph.D. dissertation, University of Maine, 2011.
United Press, "15 Die in Student-Army Strife in Bogota; Colombian Regime Puts Tight Curb on City," *New York Times*, June 10, 1954, 12.
United Press, "Colombia Eases Control: Overthrown President Reported Coming to United States," *New York Times*, June 17, 1953, 18.
United Press, "New Bogota Leader Backed by Assembly," *New York Times*, June 16, 1953, 2.
Valencia Gutiérrez, Alberto. *La Invención de la Desmemoria: El Juicio Político contra el General Gustavo Rojas Pinilla en el Congreso de Colombia (1958–1959)*. Cali: Universidad del Valle, 2015.
World Bank. *The Basis of a Development Program for Colombia*, edited by Lauchlin Currie. Washington, 1950.
Zuleta Angel, Eduardo. "Judging Colombia's Regime," *Letters to the Times: New York Times*, September 29, 1955, 32.

CHAPTER 14

Slippery Alliances in Central America: Multinationals, Dictators, and (Under) Development Policies

Marcelo Bucheli

Introduction

The Central American republics have long been considered the quintessential example of poor small countries ruled by a cartoonish dictator easily manipulated by foreign interests.[1] This reputation started in the 1910s,

[1] The Central American republics are usually grouped together with the Caribbean countries, which include the larger islands of Cuba, Santo Domingo (divided between the Dominican Republic and Haiti), and Jamaica, plus several small former British colonies and Dutch and French territories. In this chapter, I focus on the continental republics of Central America, but I am aware of the potential benefits for the goals of this volume of including Caribbean regimes such as that of the Duvaliers in Haiti or of Rafael Leonidas Trujillo in the Dominican Republic. The levels of poverty in these two countries have been historically higher than those found in Central America. See Victor Bulmer-Thomas, *An Economic History of Latin America Since 1820* (Cambridge: Cambridge University Press, 1993).

M. Bucheli (✉)
Gies College of Business, University of Illinois at Urbana-Champaign, Champaign, IL, USA
e-mail: mbucheli@illinois.edu

V. Basualdo et al. (eds.), *Big Business and Dictatorships in Latin America*, Palgrave Studies in Latin American Heterodox Economics, https://doi.org/10.1007/978-3-030-43925-5_14

driven by descriptions of the interaction between multinational American fruit corporations and the region's dictators. In fact, the American writer O. Henry coined the pejorative term "Banana Republic" in his novel *Cabbages and Kings* to describe the fictional country of Anchuria; he was inspired by what he saw in Honduras, which almost went to war with neighboring Guatemala due to the rivalries of two American corporations: Cuyamel Fruit Company and United Fruit Company.[2] With time, the term came to be used to describe any poor place ruled by a repressive regime that is at the mercy of foreign corporations and governments. Events that took place later on in the region did not help to improve this perception. Military coups were the norm throughout most of the twentieth century, and they gave birth to infamous authoritarian regimes such as those of the Somozas in Nicaragua and Efraín Ríos Montt in Guatemala. By the 1970s and 1980s, that small strip of land that did not produce any strategically important goods was at the center of the Cold War when most of those republics fell into bloody and highly destructive civil wars.[3] Despite the small size of these republics' economies and their high levels of poverty, the United States (particularly during the administration of Ronald Reagan) considered Central America a bulwark against the expansion of communism.[4] The alliance between these repressive regimes and the United States, in addition to their history of being dominated by foreign firms, only reinforced the general perception of these countries as stereotypical "banana republics."[5]

The Central American republics differ from the other countries analyzed in this volume in the sense that even though they were nominally sovereign states, their dependence on the United States was stronger than was the case for any other Latin American countries. The Panama Republic itself was a creation of American foreign policy when the United States supported a secessionist movement in what until then had been a Colombian province as a way to ensure American control over the strip of

[2] O. Henry, *Cabbages and Kings* (New York: Doubleday, 1904), 328.

[3] The only country that was spared from falling into a dictatorial regime or having a civil during the period covered in this chapter was Costa Rica.

[4] Ashley J. Tellis, "The Geopolitical Stakes in Central American Crisis," in *Central America and the Reagan Doctrine*, ed. Walter Hahn, 29–52 (Boston: University Press of America, 1987).

[5] The best-known example of this view can be found in Eduardo Galeano, *The Open Veins of Latin America* (New York: Monthly Review, 1997), 107–115.

land where the Panama Canal was eventually built. Before 1932, during times of an official non-interventionist foreign policy, the United States invaded Honduras five times, the Dominican Republic four times, Nicaragua four times, Panama four times, and Guatemala and El Salvador once each.[6] The strategic importance of the Panama Canal for the United States led the latter to keep a close eye on this territory for most of the twentieth century.[7] These reasons have led some scholars to classify the Central American republics as "American protectorates."[8] This particular status is of crucial importance in my analysis in order to understand the influence and power of American interests in those countries, the type of relationship sought by the regions' dictators, and the issues that led, in the 1970s, to the breakdown of the type of alliance built in the early twentieth century.

This chapter studies the relationship between the Central American dictatorial regimes and foreign investors. I cover a period ranging from the early twentieth century until the Cold War, with particular emphasis on the latter. I show that the alliance between foreign investors and the dictators was not the result of simple corruption, ideological affinities, or neo-imperial policies from the United States. Rather, I maintain that the dictators sought this alliance because the foreign investors provided them with economic and political stability (in the form of steady revenue resulting from exports and resources to keep the state apparatus functioning), together with the possibility of personal enrichment. As I show in this chapter, when those conditions were not met, the dictators broke their alliances with foreign investors. Conditions changed due to wider political and economic transformations that were beyond the dictators' control. While it lasted, the alliance guaranteed that regimes with little interest in

[6] For a detailed account of these "interventions," see Lester D. Langley, *The Banana Wars: United States Intervention in the Caribbean, 1898–1934* (New York: Rowman & Littlefield, 2001).

[7] For a complete account of the process of taking over the Canal Zone and the economic gains for the United States, see Noel Maurer and Carlos Yu, *The Big Ditch: How America Took, Built, Ran, and Ultimately Gave Away the Panama Canal* (Princeton: Princeton University Press, 2011). The United States eventually paid Colombia reparations for the loss of Panama under pressure from the lobby of American oil companies operating in Colombia, see Xavier Durán and Marcelo Bucheli, "Holding Up the Empire: Colombia, American Oil Interests, and the 1921 Urrutia-Thomson Treaty," *Journal of Economic History* 77, no.1 (2017):251–284.

[8] Victor Bulmer-Thomas, *Empire in Retreat: The Past, Present, and Future of the United States* (New Haven: Yale University Press, 2018), 60–71.

changing their countries' social structure would survive politically. This created a time bomb that went off in the 1980s, when most of Central America fell into bloody civil wars with global implications.

This chapter is divided into the following sections. The next (second) section contextualizes the chapter by providing a very broad description of the evolution of the Central American economies throughout the twentieth century. It shows how these republics continually failed to change their economic structure to achieve steady improvement in their citizens' welfare. The third section uses the case of the American corporation United Fruit Company (now Chiquita) to illustrate how the relationship between the dictators and foreign investors evolved throughout the twentieth century in Guatemala, Honduras, and Panama. United Fruit is considered the paradigmatic example of a corporation that "controlled" the Central American authoritarian regimes, so focusing on this particular firm provides a good general picture of how the relationship between foreign investors and dictators evolved. The fourth section studies the Somoza regime in Nicaragua. Few regimes in Latin America gained the level of global notoriety that the Somozas did. The case of this family shows how the alliance enabled rules not only to survive politically but also to increase their personal wealth. The alliance between the Somozas and the private sector collapsed when the family proved to be unable to control armed resistance and opposition from conservative segments of the society.

Central America: Coffee, Bananas, and Elusive Development

The foundations of the Central American republics' economic structure were established in the 1880s after a series of civil wars led pro-export-oriented Liberals to triumph over the inward-looking Conservatives. Once in power, the Liberal regimes started quickly organizing their economies around the exports of coffee and bananas, with the former dominated mostly by a domestic oligarchy, while the latter came to be controlled by foreign multinationals, mainly the Standard Fruit Company and the United Fruit Company (both based in the United States). As Victor Bulmer-Thomas shows, the Liberal policies inserted the Central American republics into the world economy, but this did not translate into political stability, a generally higher standard of living, a diversification of the economy, or solid public finances. This economic model, based on exports of primary goods with strong participation of foreign capital, consolidated in the 1920s and remained unchallenged during the 1930s (a period in which there were important calls from different politicians and intellectuals to abandon export-led growth for import substitution industrialization in the major Latin American economies).[9] Bulmer-Thomas also calls the 1930s Central America's "Dark Ages" because the global economic crisis led to a series of events through which the different countries in the region fell into authoritarian regimes with little opposition from the United States.[10] This acceptance turned into an open alliance during World War II, when the dictators helped to provide protection to the American interests in the Caribbean Basin (particularly in the areas close to the crucial Panama Canal).[11] The alliance with the United States during World War II also benefited the Central American regimes with the 1941 Inter-American Coffee Agreement, with which the United States committed to supporting coffee prices from Latin American producers through a series of subsidies and agreements.[12] Both the rulers of those countries and the American government benefited from the operations of the American multinationals in the region. The dictators obtained the obvious benefits of tax income and exports.[13] United Fruit contributed directly to the war effort by owning the main line of communication between Central America and the Panama Canal with the United States through its subsidiary, the Tropical Telegraph and Telephone Company. Additionally, while European markets were closed and German submarines threatened banana steamships, United Fruit focused its attention on the production of abaca, a raw material used for manufacturing cords used for the parachutes of the US Air Force.[14] By the end of the war, the structure of these countries remained unchanged.

[9] Victor Bulmer-Thomas, *The Political Economy of Central America Since 1920* (Cambridge: Cambridge University Press, 1987), 1–43.

[10] Bulmer-Thomas, *The Political Economy*, 68–69.

[11] Bulmer-Thomas, *The Political Economy*, 88–91.

[12] Alfredo Guerra-Borges, "El desarrollo económico," in *Historia General de Centroamerica*, vol. 5, ed. Héctor Perez Brignoli (Madrid:FLACSO, 1993), 17.

[13] Paul Dosal posits that in pre-World War II Guatemala, the more authoritarian the regime was, the more favorable the policies and regulations were for United Fruit. See Paul Dosal, *Doing Business with the Dictators: A Political History of United Fruit in Guatemala, 1899–1944* (New York: Rowman & Littlefield, 1995).

[14] Marcelo Bucheli and Ian Read, "Banana Boats and Baby Food: The Banana in US History," in *From Silver to Cocaine: Latin America Commodity Chains and the Building of the*

During the 1950s and 1960s, Central America went through profound changes in its economic structure. New export sectors emerged with the rise of cotton, sugar, and cattle. None of these sectors required large amounts of labor, so rural dwellers migrated en masse from the countryside to the cities, and rural poverty increased.[15] Unlike the banana industry, domestic capitalists controlled these sectors. The banana industry also witnessed important changes. During the 1950s, the banana market saw a gradual decrease in per capita consumption in the United States as Americans shifted their preference from fresh to processed fruit (e.g., canned and frozen food).[16] At the same time, Standard Fruit Company (United Fruit's main competitor) innovated with a new variety of banana that was more efficient, requiring less labor and more technology. Together with stronger criticisms from the labor movement, coffee elite, and emerging political groups about the privileges of the foreign fruit multinationals, these changes led the latter to decrease their land ownership in Central America.[17] Finally, the end of the war subsequently ended the Inter-American Coffee Agreement, prompting a fall in coffee prices. This was only stopped by a new International Coffee Agreement (1958), which brought new stability to this sector.[18] The confluence of all these factors motivated the rulers of these countries to start thinking seriously about industrializing their economies for the first time.

Industrialization in Central America faced four major bottlenecks. Markets were small, infrastructure was very underdeveloped, the education levels of the population were poor, and all the Central American countries were net oil importers. They tried to overcome the problem of market size by creating the Central American Common Market (CACM) in 1959, an initiative supported by the US government, which channeled funds through the Alliance for Progress created under the leadership of US President John F. Kennedy. In its early years, the CACM made the region dynamic by generating incentives for the creation of new

World Economy, 1500–2000, ed. Stephen Topik, Carlos Marichal, and Zephyr Frank (Durham: Duke University Press, 2006), 215.

[15] Guerra-Borges, "El desarrollo," 27–33.

[16] Marcelo Bucheli, ***Bananas and Business: The United Fruit Company in Colombia, 1899–2000*** (New York: New York University Press, 2005), 33–39.

[17] Marcelo Bucheli, "United Fruit in Latin America," in ***Banana Wars: Power, Production, and History in the Americas*** ed. Steve Striffler and Mark Moberg, 80–102 (Durham: Duke University press, 2003).

[18] Bulmer-Thomas, *The Political Economy*, 153.

industries. The signatories agreed on common external tariffs and the elimination of internal tariffs, which led to a 29 percent increase in intra-regional trade between 1960 and 1968.[19] The CACM also stimulated foreign investment. Before the CACM, Central America attracted around 30 percent of all the American direct investment in Latin America, but by 1965 this figure rose to 40 percent.[20] However, Bulmer-Thomas classifies this period as one of an "Illusion of a Golden Age" because the fruits of this economic growth were not evenly distributed and the countries did not end their dependence on agricultural exports.[21] Additionally, the Alliance for Progress money was notoriously misspent, with a significant part of it going to the economic sectors the elites were interested in advancing rather than to those that would promote long-term economic growth.[22] More importantly, one of the foundational goals of the Alliance for Progress was to finance agrarian reforms in the region, but the Central American governments never seriously developed such reforms due to strong resistance from the elites.[23]

Several big blows precipitated the eventual collapse of the CACM. The "football war" between Honduras and El Salvador propelled the former to withdraw from the organization, and Nicaragua took advantage of this situation to develop some protectionist measures.[24] A plan to integrate all Central American industries encountered the opposition of some elites in the region and lobbyists for the US manufacturing sector in the United States.[25] Finally, after President Kennedy was assassinated, the Lyndon B. Johnson administration significantly decreased support to the Alliance for Progress.[26]

[19] Guerra-Borges, "El desarrollo," 47–54.

[20] Walter LaFeber, *Inevitable Revolutions: The United States in Central America* (New York: Norton, 1993), 192.

[21] Bulmer-Thomas, *The Political Economy*, 175–176.

[22] John Coatsworth maintains that, despite its pro-democracy rhetoric, the Alliance for Progress ended up strengthening the dictatorships and the existing social structures. See John Coatsworth, *Central America and the United States: The Clients and the Colossus* (New York: Twayne, 1994), 90–121.

[23] LaFeber, *Inevitable*, 150–162.

[24] Vincent Cable, "The 'Football War' and the Central American Common Market," *International Affairs* 45, no. 4 (1969): 658–671.

[25] LaFeber, *Inevitable*, 192–193.

[26] William O. Walker III, "Mixing the Sweet with the Sour: Kennedy, Johnson, and Latin America," in *The Diplomacy of the Crucial Decade: American Foreign Relations During the 1960s*, ed. Diane B. Kunz (New York: Columbia University Press), 67–68.

During the 1970s, Central America faced new problems. The 1974 oil crisis made the weaknesses of the existing model apparent. As net importers of oil, the countries were hurt by the sudden rise of oil prices. Inflation in Western countries neutralized any potential benefits from the rise in the international prices of some of the commodities Central America exported. By that time, foreign debt was increasing rapidly, at a rate of 23 percent a year between 1973 and 1979 (from $1.932 billion to $6.874 billion). In El Salvador and Honduras, foreign debt grew at a rate of 32 percent a year for that period, while in Guatemala it grew at a 20 percent rate.[27] As the following sections show, this crisis spurred some of the authoritarian regimes in the region to recalibrate their political alliances in order to ensure their political survival. This recalibration included changes with respect to the way they related to foreign investors.

The Shifting Alliance of Foreign Capital and the Central American Dictators: The Case of United Fruit Company

This section uses the case of United Fruit Company, which is considered to be the quintessential example of a foreign corporation allied with right-wing dictators, to analyze how the alliances between foreign capital and authoritarian regimes evolved in accordance with wider changes in the world economy and domestic political and social changes. I provide an overview of this evolution from the beginning of the twentieth century but focus in the main analysis on the Cold War period.[28] I divide the periods of operation of this corporation in the following sections.

The Era of the "Banana Republics" and the American Hegemony in the Caribbean Basin, 1900–1945

This is a period in which the resistance to United Fruit's power and the nationalist initiatives came mostly from the labor movement, with the government responding by repressing the resistance and supporting United Fruit. Although some planters resented United Fruit's power,

[27] Guerra-Borges, "El desarrollo," 75.

[28] I adapted some of the information in this section from Marcelo Bucheli, "Multinational Corporations, Totalitarian Regimes, and Economic Nationalism: United Fruit Company in Central America, 1899–1975," *Business History* 50, no. 4 (2008): 433–454.

most of them feared communism more, so they allied with the government and United Fruit. Additionally, the overwhelming political power and military presence of the United States in the region gave the governments more strength in confronting the opposition.

Before World War II, the Central American and Caribbean economies depended highly on the United States. The percentage of exports to the United States over total exports was 49 for Costa Rica, 53 for the Dominican Republic, 27 for Guatemala, 87 for Honduras, and 94 for Panama. Similarly, Costa Rica bought 53 percent of its imports from the United States, the Dominican Republic 62 percent, Guatemala 50 percent, Honduras 67 percent, and Panama 55 percent. To make things worse, these countries' exports had a very low level of diversification. By 1913, 50 percent of Costa Rican exports were bananas and 35 percent coffee; Guatemalan exports were composed of 84 percent coffee and 6 percent bananas (which increased to 27 percent in the 1930s and was around 15 percent in the 1950s); Honduras exported 50 percent bananas and 25 percent precious metals; and Panama 65 percent bananas and 7 percent coconuts.[29]

The country that has been considered the quintessential example of the so-called Banana Republic is Honduras. In Honduras, the United Fruit Company and its competitor (and later acquired firm) Cuyamel Fruit Company participated directly in a series of military rebellions and coups in the 1900s and 1910s. Labor strikes against United Fruit that took place in the 1920s and 1930s were immediately repressed by the government. In 1932, General Tiburcio Carías won the presidential elections with a campaign financed by United Fruit and soon turned his government into a sixteen-year dictatorship.[30]

In Guatemala, United Fruit also counted on two very friendly authoritarian regimes. The first one was during the dictatorship of General Manuel Estrada Cabrera, who ruled between 1898 and 1921, and the second was that of General Jorge Ubico, whose regime lasted from 1931 and 1946. Estrada consolidated the generous concessions agreed upon between United Fruit and the Guatemalan government, which included

[29] Victor Bulmer-Thomas, *An Economic History of Latin America* (Cambridge: Cambridge University Press, 2003), 58, 74, 76; G. E. Britnell, "Factors in the Economic Development of Guatemala," *American Economic Review* 43, no. 2 (1953): 106.

[30] Mario Posas, "La plantación bananera en Centroamérica (1870–1929)," in *Historia General de Centroamérica*, Vol. 4, ed. Víctor Hugo Acuña Ortega (Madrid: FLACSO, 1993), 157.

not only land grants but also a 99-year-long concession over the construction and management of railway lines by United Fruit's subsidiary the International Railways of Central America (IRCA).[31]

Ubico's regime is one of the most infamous dictatorships in Latin American history. Ubico was a strong ally of the United States and welcomed foreign investors. When he came to power, IRCA presented this to its shareholders as a positive change.[32] In 1930, he signed a contract with United Fruit in which the company committed to building a port in exchange for land. However, by 1936 United Fruit dropped the port project so as not to compete with its affiliate IRCA. The port was never built, but Ubico permitted the company to keep its land and not pay any reparations.[33]

Ubico was a victim of the social changes going on in his country. A small but growing Guatemalan middle class composed of schoolteachers, government officials, and shopkeepers felt that a country controlled by a land-owning oligarchy left no room for them. In 1944, a group of young officials—led by Col. Jacobo Arbenz—supporting striking schoolteachers overthrew Ubico and organized elections for 1945.[34]

Reforms, Nationalism, and Rebellion in Honduras and Guatemala, 1945–1954

This is the period in which United Fruit faced government opposition to its operations for the first time. The election of Juan José Arévalo in 1945 and Jacobo Arbenz in 1951 as presidents of Guatemala created a brief era of government initiatives that sought to control United Fruit's power by increasing the revenues from banana exports. These policies created an alliance between the Guatemalan military, the local landowners, the US government, and the rulers of the other Central American countries against the Guatemalan government; Arbenz was overthrown in 1954.[35]

[31] Dosal, *Doing Business*, 37–51.

[32] International Railways of Central America (IRCA), *Annual Report 1931* (Boston, IRCA), 6.

[33] Gliejeses, *Shattered Hope: The Guatemalan Revolution and the United States, 1944–1954* (Princeton: Princeton University Press, 1992), 21.

[34] Dosal, *Doing Business*, 225–231.

[35] Marcelo Bucheli and Geoffrey Jones, *The Octopus and the Generals: The United Fruit Company in Guatemala*. Harvard Business School Case 805146 (2005).

In 1952, encouraged by some social reforms, the Honduran labor movement confronted United Fruit in a process that culminated in a strike threatening the very existence of the Honduran government in 1954. It all started in 1949, when Honduran President Tiburcio Carías Andino quit voluntarily on account of his age and named former United Fruit lawyer Manuel Gálvez as his successor. Carías might have been fooled by Gálvez's background. As soon as Gálvez took power, he freed political prisoners, permitted political exiles to return, created the country's first income tax, health insurance, social security, and an eight-hour workday. These actions encouraged labor unrest in the banana plantations led by communist organizations.[36]

In May 1954, the Honduran banana workers went on strike, demanding higher wages and better working conditions. This strike incited other strikes all over the country, particularly in the urban areas, and because of the peaceful nature of the strikes, the local media and government officials showed their support. United Fruit requested that Gálvez's government send the Army to end the strike, but the government declared itself neutral in this conflict, which was unprecedented in Honduran history.[37] In June 1954, the workers settled on an agreement with United Fruit, including a 21 percent wage increase (from the original 71 percent they had demanded) and health care for their families.[38] In fact, this strike is barely mentioned in the company's corporate reports to its stockholders.

Although communists and nationalists started the strike, a reformist attitude prevailed in the end. Gálvez himself was not a radical but a reformist and was always concerned about the communist influence among the strikers, which was never significant.[39]

Cold War, Alliance for Progress, and United Fruit's Retreat, 1954–1974

The 1950s and 1960s witnessed important changes in the banana market. First, banana consumption decreased in the United States because Americans were replacing fresh fruits with canned fruits.[40] Second, United

[36] Robert MacCameron, *Bananas, Labor, and Politics in Honduras, 1954–1963* (Syracuse: Syracuse University Press), 17–19.

[37] MacCameron, *Bananas*, 28–30.

[38] Ibid., 52–53.

[39] MacCameron, *Bananas*, 23–24.

[40] Bucheli and Read, "Banana Boats," 204–227.

Fruit was forced to comply with the anti-trust regulations by getting rid of some of its lands. And third, despite Arbenz's overthrow, the company remained suspicious and cautious of the political developments in this area.[41]

United Fruit faced its first permanent expropriations after the triumph of Fidel Castro in the Cuban Revolution in 1959. Although its investments in Cuba were not very important, the company feared that Castro's success could be used as an example by other countries. In that same year, Costa Rica passed new legislation that forced United Fruit to significantly increase its wages. These two events, in addition to the previous problems in Guatemala, prompted the financial analysts of Moody's Investors Services to classify United Fruit as a risky investment.[42]

In the late 1960s, the company publicly acknowledged that it had to adapt to the social and political changes going on in Latin America. In a retrospective analysis, Herbert Cornuelle, United Fruit's president, wrote: "No matter how successful we are in this process, we still will be perceived, however, I am sure, as a threat to national independence and sovereignty. The fact that we are domiciled in a foreign country and that we are big assures that."[43]

In 1970 United Fruit merged with AMK Corporation, creating a new company: United Brands. United Fruit then became part of a giant food conglomerate that included processed foods and meatpacking. In his first letter to the shareholders, Eli Black, the first president of the conglomerate, once again emphasized the political issues the company had to deal with:

> [While] these operations are in stable countries with enlightened governments, the fact is that all Latin American countries are being swept by strong winds of nationalist aspiration. [The company] knows that it must adjust to change in Latin America. It is adjusting. […] One of the most sensitive areas is that of land use policies. […] Since 1952 the Company has divested itself of 65 percent of its holdings in the four countries. Many thousand acres have been given to the governments for distribution; the remainder has been sold to individuals and firms. […] In several countries land has been given to unions to build low-cost housing financed by the company.[44]

[41] Bucheli, *Bananas and Business,* 33–38, 58–70.
[42] Bucheli, *Bananas and Business,* 58–64.
[43] United Fruit Company, *Annual Report 1968* (Boston: United Fruit, 1968).
[44] United Brands Company, *Annual Report 1970* (Boston: United Fruit, 1970).

Moody's analyses improved as long as the company sold its production assets in Central America. In this way, Moody's told potential investors that the risk of expropriation or destruction had decreased; this made the company less profitable but also less risky. By 1970, the company had divested most of its plantations in Central America and transferred them to local growers or governments.[45] Consequently, during this period United Fruit lost its lands not because of nationalism but because of the uncertainties of nationalism in the future.

The 1960s were also times in which the American government decided to follow a double-edged policy toward Latin America. Aware that poverty made communism attractive to lower classes, the US government encouraged and endorsed agrarian reform programs in the region through the recently created Alliance for Progress. The programs it supported benefited United Fruit, which sold its lands to governments that needed them for the reforms and had the monetary resources from the US government to buy that land. At the same time, the US government supported anti-insurgency policies and military coups among its allies.[46]

Aside from the nationalist initiatives in Cuba and Costa Rica, the period 1954–1972 did not witness major nationalist threats from the local governments. Costa Rica was the only democratic regime in Central America and Cuba the only socialist one, while pro-US military regimes still ruled in the rest of the isthmus.

The Oil Crisis and the Collapse of the Political Coalition

During the 1960s and early 1970s, most Latin American countries fell into the hands of military dictatorships. With the exception of Costa Rica, Colombia, Mexico, and Venezuela, military governments that were supported by the United States ruled the whole continent. Moreover, the Alliance for Progress did not survive the Kennedy administration, had a meager budget during the Johnson administration, and died under Ford after years of atrophy and neglect under both the Johnson and Richard Nixon administrations. The US military aid and other economic assistance continued in Central America during the Johnson administration as the US government considered the communist threat in that area to be higher

[45] Bucheli, *Bananas and Business*, 65–70.
[46] Coatsworth, *Central America and the United States*, 108–109.

than in the more solid South American dictatorships. However, this aid almost disappeared under the Nixon administration.[47]

The oil crisis that started in 1973 had a devastating effect on Central America. All the countries imported oil (whose price increased 400 percent in a few months), their economies were still highly dependent on banana and coffee exports (representing around 80 percent of the region's exports), and the area was still the poorest in Latin America. This crisis forced the local governments to realign their alliances and follow protectionist policies.[48]

The regimes of Colonel Omar Torrijos in Panama and General Oswaldo López Arellano in Honduras are clear examples of the shift in alliances during the crucial years of the early 1970s. Torrijos took power in 1969 after a military coup against the president, Colonel Boris Martinez, who had recently announced an aggressive agrarian reform and encouraged demonstrations against US control of the Panama Canal. Torrijos's coup and subsequent repression of some comrades who had participated in the coup were supported by the United States. Once in power, Torrijos made some changes to banking legislation that decreased regulation to a minimum, benefiting the Panamanian upper class.[49] United Fruit also supported Torrijos by giving him personal monetary donations. In 1970, Eli Black, the company's president, sent Torrijos a check for $25,000 with a note of support for the "cause you and your wife defend."[50]

General López Arellano had a background similar to Torrijos's. He came to power for the first time in 1963 via a military coup against President José Ramón Villeda, who had tried to create the first agrarian reform in Honduras under the opposition of the large landowners and the army. After the coup, López Arellano banned the National Peasant Federation, jailing peasant leaders and intellectuals. These initiatives did not stop the peasant movement, however, and the Honduran countryside experienced increasing turmoil despite government repression. In order to decrease tensions, López Arellano bought some lands for distribution among peasants in 1969, but this was stopped by his successor, Ramón Cruz, who took power in 1969. Cruz did not stay in power for long. In

[47] Coatsworth, *Central America and the United States*, 102–126.

[48] Bulmer-Thomas, *The Political Economy*, 204.

[49] Coatsworth, *Central America and the United States*, 128–129.

[50] Philippe Bourgois, *Banano, etnia y lucha social en Centro América* (San Jose: DEI, 1994), 116.

1971, there was another military coup that brought López Arellano back to power.

In United Brand's reports for 1972 and 1973, President Eli Black proudly showed how the company was changing its behavior in Central America toward a more progressive and egalitarian relationship with the region. Black presented the company's social programs saying, "[There] was a dramatic change in the image of our company. It is a reflection of many years of effort to improve the working and social conditions of our employees, especially in Latin America. Our changing image was exemplified in numerous articles in [the media] in which it was said of the company, 'It may well be the most socially conscious American company in the hemisphere.'"[51] In another section of the same report, the company quoted *The New York Times* in saying, "What emerges from talks with labor, management and government is a picture of a company that anticipated the changes that have swept Latin America and has quietly set about adjusting to them." As an example of how things had changed, the company gave a very detailed description of the economic and social aid it provided the Nicaraguans after the devastating earthquake it had experienced that year.[52] These changes, however, would not be enough for countries facing increasing problems in their balance of payments.

In September of 1974, pressured by the oil crisis, the governments of Costa Rica, Guatemala, Honduras, Panama, and Colombia signed an agreement creating a banana export cartel modeled on the Organization of Oil Exporting Countries (OPEC) called UPEB (Banana Export Countries Union, in its Spanish acronym). UPEB's main goals were (a) to increase taxation on bananas exported by the multinational corporations, (b) to control supply in order to control international banana prices, and (c) to modify the land and tax concessions granted to the multinational corporations by the local governments several decades before.[53] By this time, the banana-producing countries were not only dealing with the oil prices but also with the devastating effects of Hurricane Fifi, which had destroyed hundreds of Central American banana plantations.[54]

[51] United Brands, *Annual Report 1972* (New York: United Brands, 1972), 5.

[52] Ibid., 38–39.

[53] Hernán Vallejo, *Productos básicos, dependencia y subdesarrollo* (Bogota: Tercer Mundo, 1982), 83–88.

[54] See the dramatic Honduran government reports on the damages created by Fifi and the trade deficit in Banco Central de Honduras, *Informe Económico 1975* (Tegucigalpa: Banco Central de Honduras, 1975), iii, 32–43.

The founders of UPEB claimed that the producing countries were getting too small a share of the profits from banana exports. According to them, Central America was getting 11 percent of the income generated in the banana market, while the multinationals were receiving 37 percent and the retailers in the consuming countries were earning 19 percent.[55] In addition, the inflation the oil shock generated prompted local growers to pressure to increase the fixed price for purchasing bananas that they had agreed on with United Fruit decades before.[56] The new export taxes these countries wanted to impose under UPEB violated what had been originally agreed upon in the concessions given to the multinationals. These concessions had been granted for long periods of time (between 58 and 99 years, and sometimes indefinitely) and established an average tax of 2 cents per bunch, which is equivalent to 80 cents per ton. In order to increase the tax to US $55/ton, the governments of Costa Rica, Honduras, and Panama passed laws that nullified the previous contracts between the governments and the multinationals in 1974, 1975, and 1976, respectively. While a democratically elected government passed these measures in Costa Rica, the military governments of López Arellano and Torrijos in Honduras and Panama also did so. These laws not only increased taxes but also eliminated many of the generous concessions the foreign corporations had enjoyed up to then.[57]

The multinational corporations did not remain passive toward these changes. Both United Brands and Standard Fruit protested by interrupting their shipments and threatening the countries with export strikes and layoffs. Standard Fruit interrupted its exports from Honduras, and United Brands reduced its Costa Rican exports by 30 percent.[58] After this, the Central American governments began to use harsher language against the multinationals, with strong accusations ensuing on both sides. The situation reached a climax in June 1974 when two high-ranking Panamanian officials accused Standard Fruit and United Brands of conspiracy to

[55] Jose Roberto López, *Economía del banano en Centroamérica* (San Jose: DEI, 1986), 33–34.

[56] Bulmer-Thomas, *The Political Economy*, 203.

[57] United Nations Organization, Food Agriculture Organization, *La Economía Mundial del Banano* (Rome: United Nations, 1986), 79–80.

[58] Vallejo, *Productos básicos*, 284; Julian Presa, *Aportes para la historia de la UPEB* (Panama: UPEB, 1975), 11, 54–55; Frederick Clairmonte, "El imperio de la banana," *Revista Augura* 3, no. 1 (1980): 21–22.

murder Panama's Torrijos and of supporting military coups in the region.[59] In the meantime, the banana workers in Costa Rica went on several strikes supporting the creation of UPEB. Torrijos refused to give in to United Brands, saying that he would "take the war to its last consequences."[60] A diverse coalition of student groups, businesspeople, and labor unions mobilized to create a unified front against United Brands' attempts to sabotage the government initiative. By this time, the traditional coffee elite and those representing the new export sectors of cattle, sugar, and cotton were colluding with their governments in the struggle against United Brands. The firm had always had a conflict-laden relationship with the coffee elite, but the changes in the countries' economic structure, shifts in the United States policy toward United Brands, and strategies for political survival by the Central American rulers made the opposition even stronger. In spite of this, United Brands continued its boycott—destroying an estimated $1 million worth of its production and refusing to continue exporting. Torrijos promised to pay the 15,000 banana workers' wages as long as the conflict continued while Fidel Castro allied with Torrijos by offering to buy the Panamanian bananas.[61] These events helped Torrijos present his confrontation with United Brands as a war for national sovereignty to the people at home and abroad; this reinforced the popular national support he needed and helped him gain international popularity in the rest of Latin America. In the meantime, López Arellano decided to go forward with the most aggressive agrarian reform in Honduran history. He distributed lands he expropriated from Standard Fruit to 44,700 families and created 900 peasant cooperatives.[62]

The foreign companies did not get aid from the United States while they were fighting with the Central American governments. In fact, the producing countries even got loans for this program from the US-dominated multilateral institutions such as the Inter-American Development Bank (IDB) and the International Monetary Fund (IMF).[63]

[59] Vallejo, *Productos básicos*, 285.

[60] Vallejo, *Productos básicos*, 287.

[61] Ibid., 286–287.

[62] Guerra-Borges, "El desarrollo económico," 58–59.

[63] See the pleas by the Central American governors in Inter-American Development Bank (IDB), *Proceedings 1974* (Washington: IDB, 1974), 127–131; IDB, *Proceedings 1975*, 102–108; International Monetary Fund (IMF), *Summary Proceedings Annual Meeting 1975* (Washington: IMF, 1975), 102–108.

The conflict was finally settled in September 1974. With strong resistance from Torrijos and no help from the US government, United Brands accepted the new Panamanian policies, which also meant it accepted UPEB and the new political environment.

López Arellano did not end this conflict in an entirely upright manner. Investigations by the US Securities Exchange Commission (SEC) uncovered a corrupt scheme by the company to negotiate a reduction in the UPEB's export tax. The bribery case involved several high-ranking officials of the Honduran government, including López Arellano. United Brands admitted that it had paid $1.25 million in bribes to Honduran officials through the company's subsidiaries, whose books had been falsified to cover up these transactions.

The year the "Banana War" took place, 1974, was not a profitable one for United Brands. That year alone the company reported a net loss of $43,607,000, for which it blamed weather problems and the "Banana War."[64] The company informed the shareholders that the new agreements with the local governments were going to mean higher taxes and fees and less property in Central America, but added that the company "is proud of the long working relationships it has had with the nations of Latin America. We look forward to continued associations, which are mutually beneficial both to our company and to the peoples of the nations in which we work. We further have pledged to those nations our support as a responsible corporate citizen."[65]

As this section shows, the close relationship between the multinational corporation United Fruit Company and the Central American rulers was contingent on a series of factors that went beyond ideological affinity. As long as the firm provided the rulers with political and economic stability and the US government was part of the coalition, the alliance was strong. When conditions changed—which included external shocks, changes in the economic structure, and new priorities for the United States—the foundations of the alliance were undermined. In the next section, we show how the role of foreign investors in ensuring the political survival of a ruler also precipitated a kleptocratic regime, namely, that of the Somozas in Nicaragua.

[64] United Brands, *Annual Report 1975*, 1, 2, 4, 10.
[65] United Brands, *Annual Report 1975*, 3.

The Central American Sultans: The Somoza Dynasty and Foreign Investors

One of the most notorious regimes that ruled in a Central American country during the twentieth century was the one created by the Somoza family in Nicaragua. Three members of the family ruled Nicaragua in turn. Anastasio "Tacho" Somoza García (1936–1956) came first, then Luis Somoza (1957–1967), and, finally, Anastasio "Tachito" Somoza Debayle (1967–1979). "Tacho," the patriarch of the family, was a shrewd politician who started his career by playing a crucial role as an intermediator between the United States Marines, who invaded Nicaragua to end a conflict between Liberals and Conservatives, and the fighting factions. Somoza spoke perfect English after having lived and studied in the United States for several years, which helped him in his relationship with the United States over the years of his leadership. In a way, he can be considered the local official in charge of one of the American "protectorates" in Central America. The American occupying forces organized the Nicaraguan National Guard, a professional army intended to end the pattern of civil wars led by regional *caudillos*, which had dominated Nicaraguan politics for decades. The occupying forces also pressured President Juan B. Sacasa to appoint Somoza as the head of the National Guard.[66] This appointment proved to be crucial to the rise of the dynasty and its long-term survival, with the National Guard becoming a very effective force at keeping opposition under control for decades. Even before taking power, the National Guard (under Somoza's leadership) defeated and killed Augusto César Sandino, a legendary guerrilla leader who had fought against the American occupation forces.

"Tacho" Somoza was elected president for the Liberal Party in 1936 with virtually no opposition. The previous president had been a puppet Somoza had put in power with the help of the National Guard and was in office basically to prepare the ground for Somoza's eventual election. The coalition Somoza built to keep himself in power did not differ much from the ones created by other dictators in the region; it comprised the domestic and foreign private sectors, particularly in the export economy. However, something that made the Somoza family special was the way

[66] Javier Galván, *Latin American Dictators in the Twentieth Century: The Lives and Regimes of Fifteen Rulers* (Jefferson: McFarland, 2013), 108–109.

they used this coalition and their political power to increase their family fortune for three generations.

One of the first actions "Tacho" Somoza undertook in utilizing his alliance with the American interests to increase the family fortune happened during World War II. Somoza used Nicaragua's alliance with the United States to expropriate the coffee farms of German immigrants (who constituted a significant minority in the nation). The Germans' properties did not become state property, but Somoza's personal assets. He followed with other actions such as buying (while in office) the land where the Managua International Airport would be built and then writing a decree establishing that those lands were to be used for the airport and sold to the government. He did not stop there but continued expanding his business empire by owning 36 percent of the cement company hired by the government for public works. His greatest wealth, however, came from land ownership, which he acquired through a government credit system he controlled. Through land ownership he became a major cattle rancher in the country.[67]

Foreign investors were straightforward in the way they contributed to Somoza's wealth. As early as 1939, Somoza received generous gifts from the US Bragmans Bluff Lumber Company in the form of paid trips to the United States. Another mining company, Minas Matagalpa, paid Somoza US $0.10 per kilo of gold produced, which eventually represented a payment of US $175,000 a year. Another foreign investor, Alejandro Safie, who was interested in establishing a textile factory and a flour mill, had to negotiate with Somoza himself. Somoza proposed a partnership in which he would own 40 percent of the earnings (without any investment) in exchange for his "council and cooperation." After ten years Somoza would own 40 percent of all machinery.[68]

During his second presidential term, Somoza's investments became even more sophisticated. He was a major shareholder of the country's new airline (LANICA), the merchant marine company, a cargo port, plus several factories and textile mills. Despite how corrupt this seemed, the Conservative opposition rarely criticized the president for using the office to enrich himself, partially because he was careful not to touch the

[67] Knut Walter, *The Regime of Anastasio Somoza, 1936–1956* (Chapel Hill: University of North Carolina Press, 1993), 109–110.

[68] Walter, *Regime*, 109–110.

Conservatives' properties.[69] In the end, he was assassinated in 1956 (although his regime did not end) by a young, idealistic, university student of poetry. By the time of his death, his fortune was estimated in US $60 million, with personal holdings that included fifty-one cattle ranches, forty-six coffee plantations, and a variety of real estate (urban and rural) in Nicaragua, Costa Rica, and Mexico. By that time, he had become Nicaragua's largest landowner, possessing more than 10 percent of the arable land.[70]

After his death, "Tacho" was succeeded by his son Luis and later by Luis's brother Anastasio ("Tachito"). Although both Somozas modernized the economy in different ways, particularly by promoting the CACM, industrialization, and investments in infrastructure, they did not break their father's habit of using the office to enrich themselves. By the time "Tachito" took power, opposition was getting stronger. A new guerrilla movement known as the Sandinista National Liberation Front had been created and became a serious threat to the regime, eventually overthrowing Somoza in 1979. By that time, the Somozas had created a huge conglomerate that included the investments made by "Tacho" but also new ones. For example, "Tachito" functioned as Mercedes Benz's representative for Nicaragua, guaranteeing this firm contracts with the National Guard and city governments (for instance, Mercedes provided the National Guard with vehicles and even the municipal governments with garbage trucks). The Somozas also owned the firm that monopolized Nicaragua's cement industry, so that the family profited from infrastructure projects. Additionally, they owned the main cigarette factory and coffee plantations and cattle ranches all over the country.[71] The Somozas even used a tragic earthquake that shook Nicaragua in 1972 for their personal gain. With lots of foreign aid arriving in the country, they expected a construction boom after the earthquake, which would benefit their cement businesses. This dynasty mismanaged and openly appropriated the foreign debt, and also maneuvered to use the reconstruction for personal profit. Both the

[69] Ibid., 168–194.

[70] Galván, *Latin American*, 111.

[71] Dan LaBotz, *What Went Wrong? The Nicaraguan Revolution* (Leiden: Brill, 2016), 101. A good account of Somoza's fortune narrated by Somoza himself can be found in the documentary *Nicaragua Dictator* for the show "This Week" by Britain's Thames TV. In a candid interview conducted in 1978 (a year before being defeated by the Sandinistas), "Tachito" Somoza described all his investments in different sectors of the economy.

Sandinista and Conservative opposition used these examples of corruption to discredit the regime.[72]

Most Central American dictators were accused of corruption, but none exemplifies better how the relationship between the authoritarian regime and private businesses could personally benefit the dictator than the Somoza family. The section on United Fruit shows the factors that determine the alliance between the dictators and the private sector, while this section provides a specific example of how a family dictatorial regime used foreign investment not only for their political survival but also to increase the family's wealth. I find that the Somozas did not aim to break the alliance (as we saw in the cases of López Arellano or Torrijos with the foreign fruit companies) when global conditions changed because their personal income was at stake. The alliance, however, was cracking anyway. The Carter administration's approach to Central America ended the unconditional support for Central America that had prevailed up until then (Carter himself had decreased temporarily Central America's strategic importance by handing over the Panama Canal Zone to the Torrijos's government). The family's actions created resentment not only among the left-wing Sandinista opposition but also among Conservative businesspeople; these formed a coalition that managed to overthrow the Somoza regime, which had lost American support. Having created a kleptocratic regime, the Somozas did not have room to shift alliances when their political survival was at stake.

Conclusion

This chapter has presented the history of several relationships between foreign investors and authoritarian regimes in Central America. This strip of land has often been considered the quintessential example of a region with a firm alliance between American capital and dictators, and the republics they ruled have even been considered "protectorates" of the United States. The chapter showed that the main determinants for this alliance were foreign investors' capability of providing the dictators with resources to ensure their political survival and steady income from exports guaranteeing some economic stability. These conditions were reinforced by the convergence of the geopolitical agendas of the United States and the

[72] Mauricio Solaún, *US Intervention and Regime Change in Nicaragua* (Lincoln: University of Nebraska Press, 2005), 79.

dictatorships. I showed that the foreign firms supplied the dictators with these two benefits throughout most of the twentieth century. However, by the 1960s and 1970s, a series of changes broke the alliance: first, the Central American economies became less dependent on the operations of the fruit corporations. Second, the global banana market changed, decreasing the importance of Central American production. And, third, external shocks such as the oil crisis of 1974 forced governments to look for ways to improve the economy in order to avoid political crises. One way to improve the economy was to ally themselves with the labor force against American corporations that had lost their strategic importance for Washington. Other external shocks like the 1972 earthquake showed the weaknesses and darkest sides of those regimes, encouraging an emboldened opposition to get rid of them. By that time, the elements that had sustained or justified the alliance had disappeared. In sum, the alliances between the Central American dictators and American capital were not set in stone and were subject to shifts when wider economic and political conditions undermined the alliance's foundations.

References

Banco Central de Honduras. *Informe Económico 1975*. Tegucigalpa: Banco Central de Honduras, 1975.

Bourgois, Philippe. *Banano, etnia y lucha social en Centro América*. San Jose: DEI, 1994.

Britnell, G. E. "Factors in the Economic Development of Guatemala," *American Economic Review* 43, no. 2 (1953): 104–114.

Bucheli, Marcelo. *Bananas and Business: The United Fruit Company in Colombia, 1899–2000*. New York: New York University Press, 2005.

Bucheli, Marcelo. "Multinational Corporations, Totalitarian Regimes, and Economic Nationalism: United Fruit Company in Central America, 1899–1975." *Business History* 50, no. 4 (2008): 433–454.

Bucheli, Marcelo. "United Fruit in Latin America." In *Banana Wars: Power, Production, and History in the Americas* edited by Steve Striffler and Mark Moberg. Durham: Duke University Press, 2003.

Bucheli, Marcelo, and Geoffrey Jones. *The Octopus and the Generals: The United Fruit Company in Guatemala*. Harvard Business School Case 805146 (2005).

Bucheli, Marcelo, and Ian Read. "Banana Boats and Baby Food: The Banana in US History." In *From Silver to Cocaine: Latin America Commodity Chains and the Building of the World Economy, 1500–2000*, edited by Stephen Topik, Carlos Marichal, and Zephyr Frank. Durham: Duke University Press, 2006.

Bulmer-Thomas, Victor. *The Economic History of Latin America Since Independence.* Cambridge: Cambridge University Press, 2003.

Bulmer-Thomas, Victor. *Empire in Retreat: The Past, Present, and Future of the United States.* New Haven: Yale University Press, 2018.

Bulmer-Thomas, Victor. *The Political Economy of Central America Since 1920.* Cambridge: Cambridge University Press, 1987.

Cable, Vincent. "The 'Football War' and the Central American Common Market." *International Affairs* 45, no. 4 (1969): 658–671.

Clairmonte, Frederick. "El imperio de la banana." *Revista Augura* 3, no. 1 (1980): 21–22.

Coatsworth, John. *Central America and the United States: The Clients and the Colossus.* New York: Twayne, 1994.

Dosal, Paul. *Doing Business with the Dictators: A Political History of United Fruit in Guatemala, 1899–1944.* New York: Rowman & Littlefield, 1995.

Durán, Xavier, and Marcelo Bucheli. "Holding Up the Empire: Colombia, American Oil Interests, and the 1921 Urrutia-Thomson Treaty." *Journal of Economic History* 77, no.1 (2017): 251–284.

Galeano, Eduardo. *The Open Veins of Latin America.* New York: Monthly Review, 1997.

Galván, Javier. *Latin American Dictators in the Twentieth Century: The Lives and Regimes of Fifteen Rulers.* Jefferson: McFarland, 2013.

Gliejeses, *Shattered Hope: The Guatemalan Revolution and the United States, 1944–1954.* Princeton: Princeton University Press, 1992.

Guerra-Borges, Alfredo. "El desarrollo económico." In *Historia General de Centroamerica*, vol. 5, edited by Héctor Perez Brignoli. Madrid: FLACSO, 1993.

Henry, O. *Cabbages and Kings.* New York: Doubleday, 1904.

Inter-American Development Bank. *Proceedings 1974* (Washington: IDB, 1974).

Inter-American Development Bank. *Proceedings 1975*, (Washington: IDB, 1974).

International Monetary Fund, *Summary Proceedings Annual Meeting 1975.* (Washington: IMF, 1975).

International Railways of Central America, *Annual Report 1931* (Boston, IRCA).

LaBotz, Dan. *What Went Wrong? The Nicaraguan Revolution.* Leiden: Brill, 2016.

LaFeber, Walter. *Inevitable Revolutions: The United States in Central America.* New York: Norton, 1993.

Langley, Lester D. *The Banana Wars: United States Intervention in the Caribbean, 1898–1934.* New York: Rowman & Littlefield, 2001.

López, Jose Roberto. *Economía del banano en Centroamérica.* San Jose: DEI, 1986.

MacCameron, Robert. *Bananas, Labor, and Politics in Honduras, 1954–1963.* Syracuse: Syracuse University Press, 1983.

Maurer, Noel, and Carlos Yu. *The Big Ditch: How America Took, Built, Ran, and Ultimately Gave Away the Panama Canal.* Princeton: Princeton University Press, 2011.

Nicaragua Dictator. This Week, Thames TV, 1978.

Posas, Mario. "La plantación bananera en Centroamérica (1870–1929)." In *Historia General de Centroamérica*, vol. 4, edited by Víctor Hugo Acuña Ortega. Madrid: FLACSO, 1993.

Presa, Julian. *Aportes para la historia de la UPEB*. Panama: UPEB, 1975.

Solaún, Mauricio. *US Intervention and Regime Change in Nicaragua*. Lincoln: University of Nebraska Press, 2005.

Tellis, Ashley J. "The Geopolitical Stakes in Central American Crisis." In *Central America and the Reagan Doctrine*, edited by Walter Hahn. Boston: University Press of America, 1987.

United Brands, *Annual Report 1972*. New York: United Brands, 1972.

United Brands, *Annual Report 1975*. New York: United Brands, 1975.

United Fruit Company, *Annual Report 1968*. Boston: United Fruit, 1968.

United Fruit Company. *Annual Report 1970*. Boston: United Fruit, 1970.

United Nations Organization, Food Agriculture Organization. *La Economía Mundial del Banano*. Rome: United Nations, 1986.

Vallejo, Hernán. *Productos básicos, dependencia y subdesarrollo*. Bogota: Tercer Mundo, 1982.

Walter, Knut. *The Regime of Anastasio Somoza, 1936–1956*. Chapel Hill: University of North Carolina Press, 1993.

Walker III, William O. "Mixing the Sweet with the Sour: Kennedy, Johnson, and Latin America." In *The Diplomacy of the Crucial Decade: American Foreign Relations During the 1960s*, edited by Diane B. Kunz. New York: Columbia University Press.

Index

V. Basualdo et al. (eds.), *Big Business and Dictatorships in Latin America*, Palgrave Studies in Latin American Heterodox Economics, https://doi.org/10.1007/978-3-030-43925-5